P9-DGC-703

ALSO BY JENNA WEISSMAN JOSELIT

A Perfect Fit: Clothes, Character, and the Promise of America

Getting Comfortable in New York:
The American Jewish Home, 1880–1950

New York's Jewish Jews:
The Orthodox Community of the Interwar Years

Our Gang: Jewish Crime in New York, 1900–1940

THE WONDERS OF AMERICA

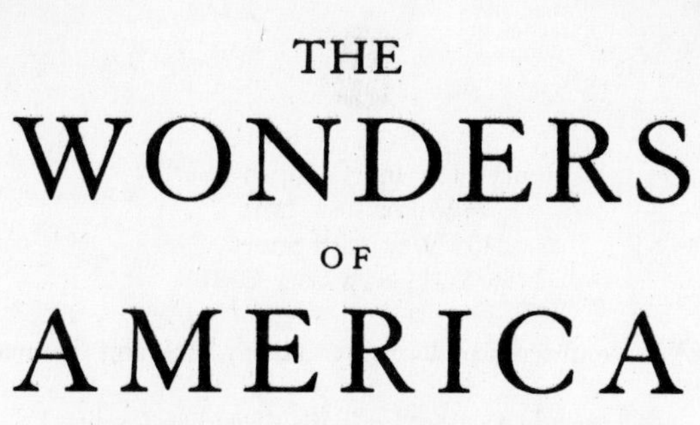

THE WONDERS OF AMERICA

REINVENTING JEWISH CULTURE 1880–1950

JENNA WEISSMAN JOSELIT

For Pennie—
With best wishes,
Jenna Weissman Joselit

AN OWL BOOK
Henry Holt and Company
New York

Henry Holt and Company, LLC
Publishers since 1866
115 West 18th Street
New York, New York 10011

Henry Holt® is a registered trademark of Henry Holt and Company, LLC.

Distributed in Canada by H. B. Fenn and Company Ltd.

Library of Congress Cataloging-in-Publication Data is available.
ISBN 0-8050-7002-8

Henry Holt books are available for special promotions and premiums.
For details contact: Director, Special Markets.

First published in hardcover in 1994 by Hill and Wang

First Owl Books Edition 2002

Designed by Fritz Metsch

Printed in the United States of America

1 3 5 7 9 10 8 6 4 2

TO THE MEMORY OF

JUDITH HOCHSTEIN JOSELIT

Acknowledgments

Writing at the turn of the century about the glories of a Friday night spent in the company of family and friends, Esther Jane Ruskay wondered what it was that made the occasion so gratifying. Was it the food? The wine? The sparkling conversation? The feeling of camaraderie? Even the most astute and sharp-eyed scientist, Ruskay concluded, would have a hard time pinpointing the event's elusive yet distinctive "quality."

Like Ruskay's Sabbath supper, this book has given me no end of pleasure. Five years in the making, it grew from a chance conversation in the corridors of the New York Public Library to an exhibition at New York's Jewish Museum and from an exhibition of several hundred objects into a volume of several hundred pages. Unlike Ruskay and her imaginary scientist, though, I have no difficulty conjuring up the source of my satisfaction: collegiality. At every stage in the complicated process of research and writing, I've been fortunate enough to encounter a steady stream of individuals—academicians, archivists, collectors, curators, designers, editors, librarians, and photographers—who have contributed materially and intellectually to the making of this book.

Heading the long list of people to whom I'm indebted are the archivists and librarians without whose custodianship of the past this book would have been much thinner. Their ranks include Aviva Astrinsky and Judith Leifer of the Center for Judaic Studies of the University of Pennsylvania; Kenneth Cobb of New York City's Municipal Archives; Norman Gechlik and Claire Dienstag of the Jewish Division of the New York Public Library; Julie Miller of the Jewish Theological Seminary's Ratner Center for the Study of Conservative Judaism; Peggy Pearlstein of the Library of Congress; Henry Sapoznik of Living Traditions, Inc.; Linda Schloff and Judith Shendar of the Minnesota Historical Society; Daniel Nevins of the Rabbinical Assembly of America; Shulamith Berger of the Yeshiva University Library; and Zachary Baker, Eve Sicular, and Marek Web of the YIVO Institute for Jewish Research. I'd also like to thank Karen Mittelman, Curator of Exhibitions, of the National Museum of American Jewish History, together with Susan Braunstein, Associate Curator of Judaica, and Barbara Treitel, Director of Visual Resources, of the Jewish Museum, for their steadfast assistance.

The onerous fiscal realities that attend the enterprise of research were eased considerably thanks to the financial support of the Lucius N. Littauer Foundation, the Memorial Foundation for Jewish Culture, and fellowships at the Annenberg Research Institute and the Center for the Study of American Religion at Princeton.

My colleagues at Princeton, where much of this book was written, not only listened patiently as I prattled on about material culture but, more to the point, sharpened my thinking. For this and other kindnesses, I'd like to thank Professors Robert Gibbs, Albert Raboteau, Jeffrey Stout, John Wilson, and Robert Wuthnow. With their singular sensitivity and sense of humor, Anita Kline of the Center for the Study of American Religion, Lynn Maselli, Harriet Stuart, and, above all, Lorraine Fuhrmann of the Religion Department made 1879 Hall a wonderfully hospitable and gracious environment in which to work—and roam. My students, in turn, kept me honest. To Kathleen Joyce and Diane Winston go my warmest thanks for reasons that I hope will become clear once they start to hold office hours.

Appropriately enough, some of the most stimulating exchanges I've had took place over a series of long lunches with two of my esteemed colleagues and friends, Barbara Kirshenblatt-Gimblett and Viviana Zelizer. Mentors in the best sense of the word, they have not only guided me through the shoals of academe but have profoundly shaped my understanding of the world as well.

When not at lunch, I've also benefited a great deal from the keen eye of Jeffrey Shandler and Daniel Soyer, each of whom, on numerous occasions, brought to my attention telling illustrations and articles. In this connection, I'd also like to acknowledge the contributions of Judy Zabar, Donna Forman, and Dr. Barr Forman. Peter Schweitzer's involvement with this project has been invaluable. With unflagging good humor and interest, he allowed me to draw liberally on his remarkable collection of Jewish Americana, numerous samples of which ornament the text. Much of this book's vitality and liveliness is due to him.

Whatever clarity this book displays is attributable exclusively to the editorial wizardry of Sara Bershtel. Thanks to her passion for excellence, love of language, and sensitivity to authorial ego, she has in me a friend for life. Ariel Kaminer's ministrations to body, soul, and text were most welcome, as was Ed Cohen's skillful copyediting.

Finally, my deepest thanks go to my husband, Joz, for his abiding interest in my work and unstinting patience with my work habits, and to my parents, Alice and Irving Weissman, for their pride in me. I'd like to think that my mother-in-law, Judith Hochstein Joselit, would have welcomed this book much as she welcomed me into her family. It's to the memory of her zest, ebullience, and generosity of spirit that I dedicate *The Wonders of America*.

Textual Note

WHEN IT COMES to rendering Hebrew and Yiddish words in English, multiple spellings abound. This book is no exception. Out of fidelity to the historical record, I've chosen to retain original spellings within quoted passages even when they differ from those used in the text.

Contents

"Imagine the wonders of America. To begin with, there's the land. It's flowing with milk and honey. People make heaps of money, they make fortunes, they literally scoop up gold! And business is so good, it makes you dizzy. You can do anything you want. If you want a factory, you set up a factory. If you feel like opening a little store, you open a little store. And the size of the cities! The width of the streets! The height of the buildings!"

"That's all very well . . . but tell me: Don't people die in America, just like here? Or do they live on and on?"

"Of course they die, but the *way* they die—that's what's wonderful."

—SHOLOM ALEICHEM,
from "Beryl Isaac and the Wonders of America"

THE WONDERS OF AMERICA

Introduction

UPON ARRIVING in the New World in 1904, folklorist Yehuda Leib Cahan could barely contain his enthusiasm for the vibrancy and color of local Jewish life. "Here folklore can be scooped up in handfuls," he exclaimed. The decades that followed Cahan's visit witnessed a continued efflorescence of Jewish cultural ingenuity and inventiveness that even he would have had difficulty imagining: by the 1950s, American Jewish culture could boast the likes of plastic dreidels, chocolate-covered matzohs, "yahrzeit memorandums," Chanukah bushes, tie clips in the shape of the Ten Commandments, floral Torah crowns, elaborate bar mitzvahs, kosher-style cuisine, and overwrought funerary monuments.

Often disdained, or, as Barbara Kirshenblatt-Gimblett has put it, "maligned for its vulgarity," American Jewry's cultural patrimony—then, as now—provoked a great deal of discussion. Throughout the interwar years and continuing well into the postwar era, as one generation gave way to another, Cahan's intellectual descendants began to chart, and reflect on, the broad cultural processes that gave rise to such unlikely artifacts as plastic dreidels and floral Torah crowns. Casting a broad net and speaking grandly of "transculturation, acculturation and deculturation," Jewish historians, sociologists, and folklorists looked closely at the everyday lives of their coreligionists. They studied the behavior of those who continued to believe in the "evil eye" and those who dismissed such notions as a retrogressive superstition; those who attended Friday-night services and those who played cards and mah-jongg instead; those who kept kosher "inside, but not out" and those who hung a mezuzah on their doorpost, where, according to Jewish law, it belonged, as well as those who kept one in a drawer, where it did not. Their "data" arrayed in neat, orderly columns, and illuminated with charts and graphs, latter-day students of American Jewish life proceeded to construct an "inventory of Jewishness," aligning identity, culture, and emotional attachment much like items on a grocer's shelf.

Despite intimations of rationality, these inventories revealed a culture that was anything but orderly, systematic, or consistent. Drawing on both the "freedom to observe" and the "freedom to neglect," American Jews, it turned out, were highly selective in their approach to ritual behavior and cultural identity. At different times and in different circumstances, they were given to ignoring, retaining, modifying, adapting, inventing, reappropriating, and reconstructing tradition. Time-honored and hallowed practices like the Jewish Sabbath (*shabbos*) and the Jewish dietary laws (kashruth) fell out of favor and into desuetude—a word much favored by Jewish theologians of the 1930s and forties. At the same time, though, brand-new ritual occasions, such as the bat mitzvah, came into being, and existing ones, like Chanukah, were expanded and augmented.

In choosing whether to observe the Sabbath, commemorate Chanukah, or celebrate a bat mitzvah, most American Jews followed their own counsel, trusting largely to personal discretion rather than the collective opinion of American Jewry's cultural arbiters. Well-intentioned, if largely unlettered, American Jews at the grass roots generated an independent sense of what was culturally meaningful and enduring, deriving it as much from American notions of consumerism, gender, privacy, and personal happiness as from Jewish notions of tradition, ritual, memory, and continuity. It's no wonder, then, that cultural consensus increasingly gave way to confusion (or *hefker*): as historian Abraham Duker lamented in 1949, "Every Jew carries his own *shulkan arukh*," a reference to the compendium of Jewish law and lore that had once ensured a common vocabulary and a shared sense of community.

Jewishness now varied across denominational lines and from household to household. For some Jews, geography superseded Torah. "The fact that we live in a Jewish neighborhood is enough

In its amber-hued depiction of a Passover seder, this popular advertisement for Fischer Russian Caravan tea highlighted the ties between the Jewish family, food, and religious ritual.

for our children to feel and know that they are Jews," one middle-class Jewish family informed sociologist I. Steinbaum. Others placed their faith in more worldly instruments. "Jewish education for girls is not essential," a second family admitted, insisting that "piano playing is more important." Still others cherished a vision of nominal Jewishness, arguing that "Jews should believe in the Ten Commandments and be true Americans. Nothing more."

Amid the welter of competing and multiple voices, one constant emerged: the centrality of family. Despite the divisiveness and fragmentation that characterized American Jewish life for much of the twentieth century, the community came together and coalesced around the ideal of a domesticated Jewishness in which the home and its inhabitants became the core of a modern Jewish identity. American Jews, divided by class, commitment, and ideology, might agree on few things, but they shared an abiding, deeply felt belief in the intimate connection between Jewishness and domesticity. "Sometimes the family was about all that was left of Jewishness; or, more accurately, all that we had left of

Jewishness had come to rest in the family," observed Irving Howe of his own kin, echoing a sentiment expressed prescriptively in the dozens of guidebooks and manuals on modern Jewish living that cropped up repeatedly throughout the interwar years. "The Jewish home," wrote Miriam Isaacs and Trude Weiss Rosmarin, authors of *What Every Jewish Woman Should Know*, one of the most popular of such texts, "constitutes the inexhaustible reservoir which replenishes the Jewish community and it is here that the foundations of the Jewish future are laid."

As the burden of cultural continuity shifted from the community to the family, Jewishness itself was redefined. Less a matter of faith or a regimen of distinctive ritual practices than an emotional predisposition or sensibility, it made few demands on its adherents, "flickering to life" at weekly Friday-night family gatherings and yearly Passover seders. Familial and familiar, this brand of domesticated identity also emerged radiantly and triumphantly at key moments in the life cycle. Birth, death, adolescence, and marriage called forth displays of Jewishness seemingly unrivaled and unprecedented in their mix of emotionality, consumerism, pragmatism, and pageantry. These exuberant yet short-lived bursts of Jewishness even gave rise to a down-to-earth sense of the divine. "The Jewish God," insisted one observer, "is a Household God."

In domesticating the divinity, exchanging gifts at Chanukah, using the Maxwell House Haggadah to conduct a Passover seder, and repairing to a local catering establishment like the Casa del Rey to celebrate a bar mitzvah, American Jews not only improvised on tradition but fashioned a singular culture. That culture, with a ceremonial rhythm all its own, is the subject of this book, which follows the efforts of three generations of American Jews as they proceeded with selective relish to map their cultural identity onto a calendar very much of their own making, first as immigrants, then as first-generation Americans, and finally as pioneers of a "new adventure in Jewishness," the suburban experience.

Along the way, American Jews accumulated a great many things, filling their armoires and attics with silver *shabbos* candlesticks, chromium Chanukah menorahs, colored-glass Passover dishes, and souvenirs of the Holy Land. Whether a priceless family heirloom brought over from the Old Country or a decorative trifle bought in the New—a *tshatshke*—objects inhabited and enlivened the lives of thousands of American Jewish families, rendering Jewishness tangible. They inhabit this narrative as well, attesting to the powerful ways in which the material world orders experience, affects memory, and sustains a sense of belonging.

When combined, the material and the expressive yielded a lively and volatile culture whose embrace of the immediate and the transcendant, the quirky and the hallowed, was virtually without parallel in modern Jewish history. That this culture took hold as it did, engaging American Jewry's collective imagination for nearly a century, is truly one of the wonders of America.

1
Kissing Business

"WHEN THE BRIDEGROOM places the wedding-ring upon the finger of the consenting bride, two persons consecrate themselves to the establishment of a *Jewish Home*," noted the wedded members of Boston's Temple Mishkan Tefila in 1922, firmly linking the private act of marriage to a lofty collective vision of community. The notion that marriage entailed a "covenant with posterity" was limited neither to Temple Mishkan Tefila nor to Boston but reverberated throughout the entire American Jewish community. Pinning their hopes for the future on the family, American Jews regarded marriage not as an end in itself but as a first step in the creation of a stable, loyal Jewish household. "Transmitting a civilization" and providing for "the continuity of a cultural inheritance as well as an ethnological one," the modern Jewish family bore the weight of generations.

To be sure, there was little new in the idea that the Jewish home was of considerable importance. A string of quotations to that

Fanciful, decorative motifs adorned many Jewish marriage contracts, or *ketubot*, of the pre–World War I era.

effect stretches as far back as antiquity. But, as the nineteenth century gave way to the twentieth, the home acquired new meaning, becoming the "nursery" of identity, religious expression, and culture. Long admired as a safe haven for its inhabitants in an often hostile world, the Jewish home was now placed at the core of modern Jewish identity, often becoming indistinguishable from Jewishness itself. "The primary and indispensable locus of Jewish life," Mordecai M. Kaplan stated unhesitatingly, "is undoubtedly the home."

This new perspective reflected modern America's estimation of domesticity as much as it did American Jewry's. Moving beyond an economic view of the household as the center of production, Americans of the mid-nineteenth century had recast the home in a new light: as an institution whose "chief functions" were "psychological and ideological." As the "custodian" of moral values, the home assumed responsibility for the emotional and ethical well-being of its members. When glossed with Judaism, the home assumed an even greater role. Likening it to a "domestic Temple" and members of the family to "ministering priests and helping Levites," American Jewry's cultural authorities championed the virtues of an unabashedly domestic and domesticated Judaism. They grounded Jewish identity in the family and localized its expression at home.

Yet even as family became more and more central, its stability became harder to ensure. Sermonizing about family matters was one thing; establishing a household composed of helping Levites was quite another, especially in America, where communal ideals were often no match for urban realities. Back in the Old World, a professional marriage broker, or *shadkhn*, arranged most unions, taking special care to find mates for all the young women of his community. "There are no Jewish old maids," noted one self-styled expert on Jewish matrimonial matters, "sooner or later *every* Jewish girl marries." But life in the New World added a whole new set of obstacles to what in the Old was often taken for granted. Here the prospect of romance, of free choice, stood in the way, subverting the very notion of an arranged marriage, confounding the *shadkhn*'s best intentions and complicating the search for a husband.

According to the *American Jewish Chronicle*, an English-language weekly that "cater[ed] to the intelligence of American Jewry," it was not uncommon to find "numbers of Jewesses" over the age of thirty-five who had never married and who never would. "Cultured and well informed, warm-hearted and sympathetic and thoroughly feminine," the unwed seemed no different from their married sisters. Why, then, hadn't they married? To find the answer, the magazine diligently consulted the records of marriage-license bureaus, supplementing them with interviews and anecdotal information. Happily, its findings revealed that the unmarried Jewess was an aberration, a momentary casualty of the immigrant experience. "The marriage standards of her old world parents were not her standards in the new world, with its modern influences and teachings," the paper explained. "The old world schadchen system does not appeal to the woman of fine sensibilities and high ideals, and therefore she does not resort to them. If fate sends her the man of her choice, she marries; otherwise, she does not." Although fate had been cruel to one generation of women, the *American Jewish Chronicle* optimistically reassured its readers that the situation was only a temporary one and that "fate will be more kind to the maidens of the present and the future. Romance will blossom and grow into marriage and the institution of the old maid will never become a Jewish one, as it never has been a Jewish one."

From the paper's perspective, the New World inverted the familiar order of things, giving rise to Jewish old maids on the one hand while minimizing the key role of the marriage broker on the other. The latter experienced more than his share of ups and downs in the United States as third-party, brokered marriages gave way to unions forged by two individuals in the heat of passion. Once the ideal of romantic love and its corollary, companionate marriage, had spread throughout the nation, arranged marriage, with its unsavory overtones of commercialization, fell into disfavor. In 1910, for example, the *American Hebrew*, another popular Anglo-Jewish weekly, noted that the marriage broker had fallen on hard times, unable to drum up business. "This might be welcomed as a sign that the young men in question are repudiating the undignified method of choosing a life partner represented by the shadchan," it harshly concluded. The *shadkhn*'s obituary, though, was premature. It wasn't that marriage brokers had become extinct by

1910. Rather, the appeal of romantic love, coupled with the cost of getting married and starting a family had, for the time being at any rate, deterred young men from falling into the arms of these "bearded cupids."

Eager for business, a few American *shadkhonim* made a concession or two to the modern era. Distributing heart-bedecked handbills that urged would-be customers to "Call and see the World Prominent Mr. Rubin," and proclaiming their services on the radio to strains of "O Promise Me," they acknowledged, and capitalized on, the romantic imperative. "Timid clients, especially the younger ones with fussy American ideas, sulk and get stubborn when they first put themselves into Rubin's hands," wrote Meyer Berger in a 1938 *New Yorker* portrait of Louis Rubin, the eponymous proprietor of Rubin's Prominent Matrimonial Bureau. "They insist on working a certain amount of romance into the thing, for which Rubin blames poets, songwriters, and the movies. Pin him down and he'll concede a pinch of romance is O.K."

Among Rubin's clients, love, courtship, and the prospect of nuptial bliss loomed large; even recently arrived immigrants seemed alive to its allure. Although in the Old World, the fiduciary considerations involved in selecting a life partner typically overshadowed emotional ones, immigrants took quickly to romantic notions. Love, courtship, passion, ardor—these were subjects of great interest and relevance. With much avidity, immigrants consumed feature articles about Lower East Side trysting spots, hoping to learn something about the social ecology of courtship. Delancey Street, they were told, was "the street of romance" along whose tree-lined boulevard young couples freely promenaded; the Williamsburg Bridge, known to some as the "headquarters of love," was also to be commended for the isolation of its elevated walkways and gentle river breezes. Urban parks, it was widely alleged, similarly facilitated the amatory spirit. As they strolled through the city's boulevards and verdant oases, many young couples no doubt drew on Alexander Harkavy's *American Letter Writer and Speller* as their own personal compass of courtship. With close to twenty pages of bilingual love letters, this text provided epistolary assistance to those unfamiliar with the "language of love," helping to inspire an entire generation of Yiddish lotharios. In one representative exchange, a suitor wonders what happened

פרייז 5 סענט.

Vol. I. No. 3. **The Jewish Ladies Home Journal** June, 1913.

די פרויען וועלט

א מאנאטשריפט געווידמעט די אינטערעסען פון דער אידישער פרוי און דער אידישער היים.

רעדאקטירט פון א. גרייזעל

קוקט איהר אמור (דעם מלאך פון ליעבע) מיט קאלטע, ריינע קוואלוואסער.

סובסקריפשאן פרייז: 50 ס. יעהרליך, 25 ס. האלב יעהרליך

THE HEBREW EDUCATIONAL PUBLISHING COMPANY, 65-67 SUFFOLK STREET, NEW YORK, N. Y.

Cupid and his amorous pursuits attracted a great deal of attention among Yiddish-speaking immigrant Jews.

to his request for a photograph of his beloved. "Do you remember about a month ago promising me that if I would give it the first place in my album, you would give me your photograph? I promised and have faithfully kept the page blank, but your picture does not come. Have you repented of your generosity?" In another entry, a young man yearns for word of his beloved Bessie. "Mail after mail finds me at the post-office to hear the same weary answer to my demand, 'No letters,' . . . or if I receive one, it is not the dainty envelope and clear pretty address for which I am ever watching so earnestly. . . . I long for some token of your affection." While the men in Harkavy's lexicon pined, the women scolded. "Why is there a cloud between us," Mathilda asks her beloved Henry. "Your manner is cold and constrained, you leave me early and no words of affection fall from your lips. . . . Tell me frankly what estranges you. If my love can comfort you in trouble, believe me it will not be wanting."

Other immigrant Jews turned to Yiddish newspaper columnists like Constance, a fixture of the *Froyen Zhurnal* (the Jewish Woman's Home Journal). "Dear Constance, To you, a stranger, I must come for advice which my own relatives refuse to give me," writes a young woman whose family was pressuring her to marry a moneyed young man whom she disdained. "It's bad enough struggling with a man you love. Imagine it with someone you dislike. Day and night I am tortured with his name. . . . Waking and sleeping I am tortured by the thoughts of this marriage. . . . Oh,

The etiquette of courtship was yet another subject of intense interest.

what shall I do?" Mothers too sought the anonymous counsel of the newspaper. "My children, who are somewhat modern, argue that religion and love are two different things, and that when one is truly in love, the man can be as free as he wants. . . . I would like to hear your opinion on this important matter," wrote an observant Jewish mother disheartened and confused by her children's newfangled approach to love. The columnist's response was strong and unequivocal: "The chances are ten to one that young Jewish women who have received a religious upbringing from their families will have a much happier life if they marry religious men." He continued sagely: "When all is said and done, everyone knows that the ardor, the steam of youth that we call 'love' is a thing that cools with time; during the first year after the wedding they kiss three times a day, during the second year the kissing-business diminishes, and after another year the family life of a couple reaches a healthy, normal state; the poetry goes away, and the prose—their ordinary life together—remains."

As the nuptially inclined looked increasingly to nature rather than the *shadkhn* for a mate, Yiddish guidebooks and etiquette manuals attempted to guide them carefully through the shoals of romantic distress. "Love is as difficult to describe as God himself," declared *Etikete*, a 1912 Yiddish compendium of manners and morals. Determined to bring order to the impetuousness and passion that characterized modern matters of the heart, this text and others like it held forth on the conventions of courtship, making sure readers knew how to distinguish between love at first sight and the truer, enduring kind. It discoursed on the proper age of marriage—twenty for girls, twenty-three to twenty-five for boys—and described at great length the "*mayles*," or qualities, a woman should look for in a man and a man should seek in a woman. Interestingly enough, the woman's prerequisites for an appropriate mate took up twice as many pages as those outlining the wifely virtues, an intimation perhaps that a proper husband was harder to find than a proper wife. Goodness, gentleness, and tenderness headed the list of a would-be husband's stellar qualities, as did industriousness and a strong sense of morality. Proper attire and manners were also not to be sneezed at. The ability to hold a spoon and fork correctly, to make pleasant conversation, and to accompany a lady, the guidebook explained, were critical aspects of a

A courting couple earlier in the century.

gentleman's makeup. Still, it was not manners nor appearance that counted most, it concluded, but rather the state of a man's soul.

When it came to selecting a wife, a different set of criteria were brought to bear: tidiness, efficiency, health, and common sense. While a beautiful wife was certainly to be desired, beauty alone was never enough to sustain a marriage, cautioned *Etikete*. Of greater importance was a woman's industriousness and housekeeping skills. Intelligence, like beauty, also fell into the category of laudable but not sufficient wifely qualities. "It's not necessary to have a philosopher for a wife," the manual advised, adding, "A little common sense is far better than a university education and modern theories." No less an authority than Louis Rubin himself confirmed *Etikete*'s advice. "Schoolteachers don't go as fast as stenographers, and career women generally are harder to pair off than the fluffy types," he told Meyer Berger. With men, though, the reverse was true. "College men, unless they're homely as all get-out, sell well in the marriage market even when they're not professional men. Doctors, lawyers, and dentists, however, rate highest with Jewish parents looking for sons-in-law."

These valuations of the suitable bride and groom not only reflected existing gender stereotypes but perpetuated them as well, giving rise to what historian Beth Bailey has called an "etiquette of masculinity and femininity." As a matter of course, Yiddish prescriptive literature maintained that women were weaker and more emotional than men, who, characteristically, were defined as stalwart and redoubtable breadwinners. Meanwhile, any behavior that deviated from this standard was branded as deficient, "not the true article." Take, for example, *Etikete*'s discussion of kindliness and gentleness, two qualities high on the list of a woman's prerequisites for a mate. While lauding them, the text strongly and explicitly encouraged young men to balance these attributes with more masculine ones lest they be regarded as an *alte bubbe*—an old woman or grandma. Women, in turn, were encouraged to downplay their intelligence and to polish their womanly skills as homemakers.

While earnestness characterized *Etikete*'s prescriptions on gender norms and courtship, the subject was treated elsewhere with biting humor. Articles such as "The Ten Commandments for Husband and Wife" poked fun at the seriousness with which immigrants regarded marriage and the prospect of falling in love. The matrimonial version of the Ten Commandments, published in *Froyen Velt* (the Jewish Ladies' Home Journal) in 1913, enumerated ten separate instances when it was permissible for husbands and wives to divorce one another. According to the sixth "commandment," "a husband may divorce his wife when she serves him food that she likes or that she thinks is healthy and doesn't care that he hates it." The ninth commandment enjoined the husband to divorce his wife "when she lectures him on how to behave and whom to see" while the tenth and final dictum gave the man license to leave his wife "when she throws up to him that her neighbor has nicer furniture or other things." The wife, in turn, had cause to divorce her husband when, in breach of the second commandment, "he immerses himself in a newspaper and doesn't say a word to her all evening." Telling his spouse how to dress or picking out her hats (the sixth and seventh commandments, respectively) also constituted grounds for divorce, as did the husband's habit of telling his wife "what a good cook his mother is." At once a reflection on and a critique of married life, "The Ten Commandments for Husband and Wife" drew on humor and satire to reinforce the importance of the companionate marriage of affection. "The Ten Rules for Young Women in Search of a Husband," which appeared on *Froyen Zhurnal*'s humor page in 1923, did much the same thing. Wryly, it laid bare the artifice and intrigue all too commonly associated with courting. Though broadly, even crudely rendered—"Don't waste money and effort on cosmetics, for in due course your husband will see you as you really are"—these ten little nuggets promoted sincerity and honesty in matters of the heart.

As romantic love continued to make inroads among courting couples, Jewish cultural authorities became increasingly alarmed —and vocal. When choosing a husband or a wife, romance and physical attraction, they insisted, were not enough. "Health, character, background, a high type of social and biological inheritance are required if the homes of the future are to be the soil upon which Judaism will flower and flourish," advised Rabbi Jacob Kohn in his influential 1932 guide, recommending that the "romantic spirit" be tempered by "considerations of physical heredity, cultural background and fine breeding." Kohn's comments, and the sense of urgency that informed them, echoed throughout the interwar Jewish community, inspiring many of its leaders to warn against a potential crisis "just as serious and significant as the crisis in religion, cultural relations, economic organization and the political order." Modernity, it seemed, wreaked havoc with the institution of matrimony. "If young men would look for character instead of judging how nimble she is with her feet and how well acquainted she is with the latest cabaret, they would have more to respect and divorces would be far less," declared Rabbi Israel Levinthal. Low standards, though, were only a part of the problem. "We prepare the young woman for fashions, dancing and interior decoration," wrote Rabbi Leo Jung. "Anxious mothers, sisters, friends want to make sure that she will know how to manage maids, arrange furniture, preside at a bridge party. But for the core of married life there is no preparation."

The apparent lack of preparation for marriage coupled with its seeming volatility engendered action as well as nail-biting, giving rise to the marriage educator and the marriage education movement. Drawn from the ranks of the academy and the ministry, the marriage educator sought to inform potential couples about the rigors of the nuptial state. "Young people," explained Rabbi Sidney Goldstein, one of the movement's leading Jewish lights, "never think seriously of preparation for husbandhood, wifehood or parenthood, the most difficult of all vocations and careers. Even intelligent and well-educated young men and women, graduates of colleges and universities, confess that they have done no more than read a few pamphlets or books." Leaving little to chance, Jewish marriage educators and their colleagues, including such academic luminaries as University of Chicago sociologist Ernest Burgess and the University of North Carolina's Ernest Groves, placed great stock in science, whose rigor and discipline they applied to the vagaries of emotion. "Now more than ever," they insisted, "there is urgent need for preparation, control and guidance." Or, as one popular magazine put it in 1937: "Chances for happiness in marriage may be raised to something approaching a sure bet if courtship and marriage are studied as a science."

The rationalization of love took many different forms, of which the most popular were accredited college courses on "Preparation for Marriage"; by 1949, students at over five hundred campuses throughout the nation, from Berkeley to the University of Utah, had the option of learning about the statistical probability of marital compatibility. Off-campus, lecture courses, study groups, and self-styled Institutes on Marriage and the Family offered by local synagogues, churches, and community centers also enjoyed considerable popularity. Thousands of prospective couples, newlyweds, and old-timers crammed auditoriums and lecture halls to hear experts expound on the "art and science of family living," their purview extending to such topics as "Biological Problems of Marriage," "Syphilis and Its Relation to Marriage and Family Life," "Psychological Problems in Marriage and Family Life," "Legal Problems in Marriage and Family Life," and "Intermarriage—A Problem in Adjustment." When not attending lectures, contemporary couples could also avail themselves of prenuptial conferences and ongoing consultation services, as well as a spate of booklets, pamphlets, and manuals to equip them with the knowledge "to cope more adequately with the problems that arise in marriage and family life."

A popular engagement gift, Rabbi Goldstein's tract *The Meaning of Marriage and the Foundations of the Family: A Jewish Interpretation* was among the most widely used by Jewish couples, Jewish marriage counselors, and clergy. Rabbi Samuel Glasner, preparing to speak in New Castle, Pennsylvania, on "Wedding-Bell or Wedding Knell?: The Problems of Marriage Today," drew on Goldstein's work, as did James H. S. Bossard of the Wharton School who assigned it specifically to the Jewish students enrolled in his course on the social problems of childhood. "Along with the Pope's Encyclical on Marriage, it should be a must for all students interested in family relations," the journal *Social Forces* stated admiringly; and Ernest Burgess, the dean of marriage educators, wrote Goldstein, "I congratulate you on having said so much that is important, and having said it so well, in so short a space." With chapters on truth, comradeship, fidelity, and the household budget, little distinguished this text from those either commonly drawn upon or penned by most marriage educators. What rendered it distinctive and appealing to Jewish couples, though, was its insistence on reconciling the "Jewish ideals of matrimony"—affection, trust, and mutual respect—with "studies now being made in the social-science laboratories." Quoting from Jewish history, law, and literature, Goldstein's text demonstrated that "the wisdom of centuries" was wholly compatible with contemporary thought.

In his search for the keys to Jewish marital happiness, Goldstein was joined by Leo Jung, an Orthodox rabbi determined to rescue the Jewish marriage laws from the obscurity and disregard into which modernity had cast them. More explicitly concerned about sexuality than most of his colleagues, Rabbi Jung equated the seemingly anachronistic, outmoded halakha, or system of Jewish laws, which regulated sexual congress, with modern-day notions of happiness, self-respect, and personal freedom. Rarely using the word *sex* (he preferred to speak of love, passion, and emotion), the Manhattan rabbi argued for its centrality in marriage, especially when channeled and controlled and consensual. "Love must not become a vulgar thing of *routine*, dictated by whim or caprice, stimulated by food or drink or exceeding masculine desire," he wrote in a 1930 pamphlet *The Jewish Way to Married Happiness*, urging men to display consideration and sensitivity. Happily, Judaism provided a structure by which the sexual urge could be domesticated. "Judaism develops the proper attitude through a system of marriage laws which serve, not as a restriction, but as a safeguard, of freedom, growth, beauty in marriage," the rabbi explained, alluding in his typically veiled way to the fact that during her menstrual period and for a few days thereafter, the married Jewish woman abstained from sexual relations with her husband. "Jewish Law to a marvelous extent takes care of woman's constitutionally physiological difficulties, decreeing times of solitude in accord with the laws of nature and in divine comprehension of her mental and emotional needs." By Jung's reckoning, the family purity laws were hardly the retrogressive or oppressive institution their critics made them out to be; on the contrary, they enhanced woman's worth, dignity, and sense of self. Citing authorities as diverse as Dr. Mary Stopes, the British champion of reproductive freedom, and Dr. I. Macht, whose article "Phyto-Pharmacological Study of Menstrual Toxin" underscored the hygienic and eugenic bases of *taharah* (ritual purity), Rabbi Jung offered a protofeminist interpretation of these ancient prescriptions. "When you hear the word which some whisper and others hardly dare breathe, please realize that it is a sacred word, that it has built happiness in the past and has retained happiness for the present."

To those newlyweds burdened with cultural and emotional illiteracy, Jung's advice and Goldstein's manual offered a wealth of insight into modern as well as traditional Jewish concepts of marital responsibility. Reassuring and comforting, their words demonstrated that in everyday matters of love and sex, Judaism had all the answers.

MUCH LIKE ROMANCE, America's bridal culture was hard to resist. Quickly and wholeheartedly, immigrant Jews and their children embraced every one of its tangible manifestations: from the purchase of costly engagement rings and the distribution of expensive invitations—"printed in as luxurious a black and gold as ever came out of an Essex Street hand press"—to the mounting of elaborate June weddings. As early as 1898, the magazine *American Jewess*, intrigued by the goings-on within the "New York ghetto," sent a reporter to cover a "genuine Jewish ceremony," hoping to provide the monthly's well-heeled readers with glimpses into an exotic, seemingly timeless culture where weddings made up in emotional excess what they lacked in physical amenities. Much to its surprise, the paper discovered that weddings on the Lower East Side resembled those in Cincinnati down to the fancy invitations, catered suppers, and elegant attire. What's more, traffic in nuptial novelties was booming. "With its pomp and display which indicates Oriental origin, [the wedding business] is one of the industries which always flourishes in the New York Ghetto, and is affected by none of the mercantile or political disturbances which frequently influence ordinary business," the magazine stated categorically.

A steady and enduring enterprise, satisfying the community's nuptial needs was not only a big business but a conspicuous and irresistible form of consumption. Fiction as well as memoir literature is replete with poignant O. Henry-like stories of struggling newcomers determined to have themselves a grand American wedding. "When I had a few dollars saved up I had a wedding on Essex Street. Fancy it wasn't, but still we had it in a hall. We had music," a onetime immigrant told Irving Howe. Another remembered, a bit more ruefully, "I was married in Clinton Street. It was a big hall. The nicest wedding you could have. I had about twenty carriages standing by the door and my husband kept paying but he didn't have enough so he had to ask my uncle to lend him fifty dollars. He had to pay the cook, pay this one and that one. To stop all this paying we had to leave the wedding early." Abraham Cahan's "A Ghetto Wedding," published in 1898, is perhaps the most detailed and moving of such cautionary tales. It tells the story of Goldy and Nathan, two immigrants who (barely) scrape together enough money to have a "respectable wedding." That phrase, Cahan writes, "played in [Goldy's] vocabulary the part of something like a well-established scientific term, with a meaning as clearly defined as that of 'centrifugal force' or 'geometrical progression.' " Anything short of a white satin gown and matching shoes, two carriages, a five-piece band, and a crowded, dazzling reception constituted a "slipshod wedding" and was to be eschewed at all costs.

The happy couple, alone in the world, send out one hundred embossed invitations to family, friends, acquaintances, and fellow workers but receive few responses and fewer gifts. They had hoped for a Brussels carpet, a bedroom set, and a pier glass with which to outfit their new home, yet all they receive is a rickety end table,

With its exuberant detail, this 1911 Jewish marriage contract celebrated as well as recorded the union of Anna Brenner and Frank Zimring.

an inexpensive alarm clock, and an icebox. "That was all." Undaunted, Goldy and her groom go ahead with their plans, only to find no more than twenty guests at the wedding reception, where one hundred and fifty place settings had been laid. "Goldy looked at the rows of plates, spoons, forks, knives and they weighed her down with the cold dazzle of their solemn, pompous array." To add insult to injury, the newlyweds are unable to afford the cost of the carriage they had hired for the evening and are forced to walk home in their wedding finery. Harassed by a group of drunks, they all but succumb to despair when, magically, salvation comes with the realization that they have each other. Love triumphs over materialism.

Perhaps had Goldy and Nathan—and who knows how many real-life counterparts—heeded the advice proffered by Yiddish etiquette manuals they would not have found themselves in such a fix. *Etikete*, for instance, firmly and repeatedly exhorted its readers to stay within their means and not submit to the temptation to purchase a diamond ring or host a lavish reception they could ill afford. Don't be silly and wasteful, it implored, urging brides not to equate their fiancé's love with the size of the ring they might receive. No fan of diamond rings but mindful of their popularity, the manual suggested that young couples choose a less expensive token of mutual affection, even though, it conceded reluctantly, "a *minhag* is a *minhag* [a custom endures]." Mindful, too, of the emphasis placed on gift-giving, Yiddish etiquette manuals gently pointed out how wedding consumerism was fraught with missteps and thwarted expectations. Those who regard an elaborate wedding reception as an "investment" whose costs would be more than offset by bridal presents are, at the very least, sure to be disappointed, and at worst are guilty of "foolish schnorring," it declared. If $500 is spent on the wedding and the couple expects to recoup $1,000 or $2,000 in wedding gifts, they are sadly mistaken. It never turns out that way. The guests feel unappreciated, welcome only because of the gifts they bear; and the couple, inevitably, are disappointed by the paltry presents they receive. "No one is satisfied."

For all the ink spilled on the subject, the folk of the Lower East Side and other Jewish immigrant communities went their own way. They flocked to catering halls, spent lavishly on wedding attire by purchasing "white, shimmering and cloud-like" wedding

Despite limited resources, many Jewish immigrants aspired to an expensive, "respectable" wedding.

gowns, dreamed of expensive gifts and hired elaborate carriages to transport them to the wedding reception when they could have just as easily walked. "Mr. Hirsch lived even closer to Pythagoras Hall than we did," recalled a veteran wedding-watcher, "but when he married off his eldest daughter, the wedding party went in five open carriages from the Hirsch residence on East Broadway through Rutgers Street, turned left at Henry Street, turned left again at Jefferson Street into East Broadway, and drew up, as if after a long journey, at Pythagoras Hall." Competition among catering establishments such as Pythagoras Hall—"a vision of opulence"—was fierce as dozens of facilities touted the merits of their modern and appealing amenities. The Victoria Hall boasted of its "electric *khupe*," whose dazzling array of lightbulbs, then the height of novelty, replaced the more traditional Jewish *chupah*, or wedding canopy, fashioned out of velvet or needlepoint; others, like Clinton Hall, whose ballroom could easily accommodate as many as four hundred guests or as few as twenty-five, boasted, naturally, of their flexibility. Still other establishments placed a premium on food whose lavishness exceeded the imagination of even the most rapacious of eaters. "I had known chicken exclusively in its austere boiled state, garnished with whole, waterlogged onions or accompanied by masses of noodles," recollected a dazzled guest at a typical Lower East Side wedding banquet. "But chicken *fricassee* was so special a form as to make it seem improbable that it can ever be served in any home, however pretentious. It was known by reputation to most of the children of the neighborhood, but only a few had ever come face to face with it. I could now testify that it deserved its fame."

A new showcase of affluence and *yikhes* (status), the "respectable wedding" spread quickly within immigrant Jewish circles, generating its own etiquette. Reports the *Hebrew Standard* in 1910: "An East-side family, having come up in the world, arranged a fashionable wedding in one of the large halls of which there are so many in this section. They were very anxious to have everything *comme-il-faut.* They concluded that a down-town rabbi would never tone with the other accessories. They called in therefore one of the fashionable uptown rabbis—the best in the market." Unfortunately, things didn't work out well between the two parties; unlike fairy-tale weddings, this one didn't have a happy ending. The uptown rabbi took noisy exception to the ten-dollar check slipped surreptitiously into his palm by the bridegroom. "Oh no, that'll never do," he insisted. "If you wanted to pay only $10 you might have called in a down-town rabbi. For an uptown rabbi, you must pay more!" Tensions between uptown rabbis and downtown grooms ran so high that on at least one occasion, in December 1916, the two parties ended up in municipal court. The groom claimed that the "job" performed by the rabbi wasn't worth more than three dollars and refused to pay a penny above that price. The rabbi countered by arguing that inasmuch as he had not only performed the wedding but had also offered the postprandial Seven Blessings, or *sheva brakhos*, he deserved twenty-five dollars. Unswayed by this claim, the groom insisted that the rabbi's decision to attend the wedding banquet had more to do with his stomach than religious propriety. After listening carefully, trying to grasp the intricacies of Jewish nuptial practice, the judge decided that the two parties should compromise. Surely the holy task of legally uniting two loving hearts is worth ten dollars, he "*paskened*," or adjudicated.

As immigrant Jews moved to "bigger and better neighborhoods," the setting for the ideal wedding moved along with them. Couples no longer exchanged wedding vows standing underneath the electric canopy of a downtown catering hall. "Wedding temples" presided over by enterprising reverends like Rev. S., master of the beautiful and "concise" ceremony, or such self-styled "professors" as "Prof. Irving Goldberg, the well known Master of Ceremonies," enjoyed considerable vogue, especially among the "unsynagogued." Fancy midtown hotels adorned with friezes of cavorting nymphs and refined social clubs decorated with Art Deco's restrained geometry also drew a substantial clientele. In New York, the "palatial" Concourse Plaza Hotel at 161st Street and the Grand Concourse attracted families beguiled by the "richness and comfort assured . . . in these lavish surroundings"; in Boston, the Copley was a popular and preferred site. "The club and the hotel have usurped the proper function of the synagogue," reported the Central Conference of American Rabbis, a Reform organization, in 1910, noting that in the North as well as in the South, "synagogal weddings are few."

Jews of all denominations participated in this trend. When, in 1914, Sadie Fischel, the daughter of Harry Fischel, a leading Orthodox Jewish philanthropist known as the "Russian Jacob Schiff," married David Kass, her wedding was held at the Hotel Astor, one of New York's toniest marriage venues. A photograph of the occasion shows hundreds of well-dressed couples, the men in tails (an occasional yarmulke among them) and the women in beaded gowns and feathers, celebrating amid the alabaster nymphs and gargoyles of the Astor's main ballroom. In honor of the event, and in keeping with the family's dietary proclivities, the hotel purchased all new equipment. "This occasion," Mrs. Kass related years later, "gave the impetus to the present day kosher hotel arrangements for large public functions." The Fischel-Kass nuptials had the further distinction of being one of the first weddings at which a pocket-sized *bencher*, or grace-after-meals booklet, bearing the couple's name and the date of the wedding, was distributed as a commemorative, if potentially useful, wedding token. Subtle and tasteful, it contained the entire Hebrew (and English) text of the prayer as well as the lyrics to "Hatikvah," the Jewish national anthem.

Not all weddings were as tasteful as the Kass-Fischel nuptials. Held in the ballroom of a large restaurant in the Times Square area of Manhattan, one "affair," as catered celebrations came to be known, featured fountains spraying chilled wine and liqueurs. "All one had to do," reported a besotted guest, "was to hold a glass under one of them and select the desired beverage." Equally dazzling were the antics of the photographer, who "outdid himself in an effort to let no move pass unrecorded." According to one eyewitness, the picture-taker "snapped [the bride and groom] marching to the Hupah; he photographed them as the groom placed the ring on the bride's finger. But when they finally kissed at the conclusion of the ceremony, he really hit a peak and directed them to protract their kiss longer so that he might have an opportunity to immortalize it for generations to come."

Choreographed by the photographer and directed by impresarios like Professor Goldberg, weddings increasingly lost much of their sacrality, becoming more of a party and less of a religious occasion. Jewish caterers played a significant role in the festivities. In addition to preparing the wedding banquet, they provided "everything that goes with the ceremony," including the *chupah*, yarmulkes, and, if need be, even the rabbi and cantor; they also arranged for the flowers, music, menu cards, cigars, cigarettes, coat check, and the *mashgiach* (the kashruth supervisor). "Professional help in these important matters is certainly the easiest and always the proper way to provide for your wedding guests; and you will find that professional knowledge and extra services rendered in a 'complete package' often hold down your expenses," prospective brides and grooms were told.

Anxious couples, grateful for the advice, eagerly took their cue from professionals of all kinds. "Parents used to ask the rabbi for specific information," related a Minneapolis rabbi in the 1940s. "Today the rabbi will discover, much to his surprise, that either the bride or her mother is carrying a copy of Emily Post's rules of etiquette in much the same manner as if it were a Bible." Guidebooks such as Ruth Jacobs's *The Jewish Wedding: An Explanation of Its Ancient Rituals and Modern-Day Etiquette with Suggestions for Proper Dress, Procedure, and Arrangements* also came in handy. Written in both Yiddish and English, and published by the Calvert Distillers Company, whose blended whiskey went into "the most preferred drinks at all Jewish weddings," this publication succinctly addressed and resolved such uncertainties as how to set a

Scenes from a New Jersey wedding of the 1940s.

wedding date, what to wear, and what to do under the wedding canopy. For starters, Ruth Jacobs ("In New York she is the leading Jewish television star and receives top billing on Jewish radio") suggested that the prospective bride and groom consult their local rabbi, cantor, caterer, or hotel banquet director as to "date availabilities." She then waxed eloquent on the various sartorial challenges that a wedding presented. Separating weddings into four general categories—"informal daytime," "formal daytime," "informal evening," and "formal evening"—Jacobs dispensed detailed clothing tips for each occasion. For a "formal evening," it was de rigueur for the bride to wear a white or pastel wedding gown with a long train and veil, elbow-length gloves, and a formal floral bouquet; her attendants were encouraged to wear a long formal dress with "covered shoulders" and a "tiny, dressy hat." Men were expected to don full evening attire, including opera hat, white kid gloves, and a boutonniere, while formal evening clothes, a hair ornament or hat, and a corsage constituted a "mother's" appropriate accoutrements.

Jacobs imparted religious wisdom too. Lucidly and concisely, she described the religious ceremony, the seven marriage benedictions, and the breaking of the glass that concluded the religious portion of the proceedings. Explaining that the glass-breaking commemorated the destruction of the Temple in Jerusalem, Jacobs went on to offer a newer, more contemporary interpretation of the practice. "There is another, more spiritual meaning," she wrote. "The bride and groom should remember that life is transitory, and that it is furthermore beset by all sorts of problems and difficulties. And, just as the fragile glass can be broken by a hard blow, so can connubial bliss be disrupted by lack of harmony, lack of sympathy with each other, lack of tolerance."

As guests gathered to toast the newlyweds, photographers, floral designers, and caterers magically transformed the traditional wedding meal, or *seudah*, into an extravaganza. To the amusement of some and the consternation of others, the lavish Jewish wedding made its way from the (sur)reality of the catering hall into the world of fiction, as contemporary novelists like Herman Wouk turned their critical energies and literary talents to its depiction. Like Cahan before them, they focused on the Jewish wedding as a metaphor for the dazzling, bewildering possibilities inherent in the encounter between Jewish tradition and the American milieu. In the penultimate chapter of Wouk's best-selling 1955 novel *Marjorie Morningstar*, the eponymous heroine weds lawyer Milton Schwartz in the Gold Room of the Hotel Pierre, a scene described with mathematical precision: five hundred guests, a seven-piece orchestra, a ten-course dinner, and two photographers, one for still shots and the other for movies. A profusion of flowers, a captivating mise-en-scène—a staircase strewn with roses from which the bride made her grand entrance—and dancing till the wee hours of the morning stamped the event as "the Lowenstein Catering Company's number-one wedding, the best there was, the best money could buy." As Marjorie grandly parades down the aisle, she is momentarily assailed by doubts. "She saw a tawdry mockery of sacred things, a bourgeois riot of expense, with a special touch of vulgar Jewish sentimentality." But, as the bride

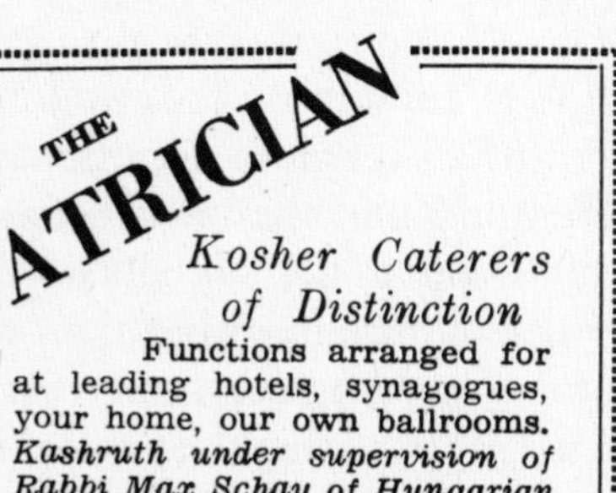

Dignified and Exclusive Service for all Social Functions at Moderate Rates CALL
Half Moon Kosher Caterers
For Catering at Our Beautiful Ballrooms and Other Hotels, Temples or your Home.
HALF MOON HOTEL
On the Boardwalk Brooklyn, N. Y.
Tel.: Esplanade 2-6666

IRVING BRAND
Kosher Caterer
Beautiful Ballrooms for Weddings, Confirmations, Banquets
Dietary Laws Strictly Observed
Accommodations 10 to 1000 Persons
CONCOURSE PLAZA HOTEL
161st Street & Grand Concourse
Located Suite 220 JErome 7-0117

New York's Most Exclusive Kosher Caterers
at all hotels, synagogues, homes and our own ballrooms
PARAMOUNT CATERERS
Main Office: 183rd St. & St. Nicholas Ave., Wash Hts. 7-3780-1
WEINSTOCK & ZISKIN—HOSTS

Kosher caterers boasted of their sophistication and elegance.

takes in the faces of her family, beaming with pride and delight, these doubts fade away. "She was what she was, Marjorie Morgenstern of West End Avenue, marrying the man she wanted in the way she wanted to be married."

Though Marjorie (and thousands of would-be Marjories) welcomed the glittering Jewish wedding, far less appreciative were the clergy, and a number of guests as well, blinded by the camera's flash or crushed at the smorgasbord table; for them, the dazzle and hubbub detracted from the wedding's solemnity. "Jewish weddings are often approached as events, or at best, as ceremonies, and the idea that they represent values that should last a lifetime seems to elude the otherwise preoccupied celebrants," explained one disgruntled guest. "Their overattention to the demonstrative displays of the occasion diverts them, and they often miss the private spiritual purposes of their very public enterprise." Is this what has become of our "cultural heritage"? So lamented Bezalel Kantor in a 1949 article entitled "Simchas in America." American Jews, observed another contemporary, "tend to theatricalize and, at times, even 'vulgarize' the religious ceremony and wedding banquet in a way that deprives them of all religious significance. Kleig lights distract during the ceremony and the broken flashbulbs are more in evidence than the broken glass," an allusion to the newfangled practice of shattering a lightbulb rather than the traditional glass at the conclusion of the wedding ceremony. Rabbis should protest, the article suggested, even raising the possibility that they refuse to officiate at such dos.

Most clergymen, though, sought less controversial ways of restoring the wedding's sanctity. Hoping to eliminate or at least minimize the commercially induced excess, rabbis in places as different as Dallas, Minneapolis, and Brooklyn urged their congregants to show restraint. "It isn't proper when the grandmother walks up [the aisle], to sing or to play the Barcarolle, or . . . to have 'Sweetheart' or 'One Enchanted Evening' sung," explained one member of a panel discussion on "Marriage and the Family." "It is wrong to have the photographers ask the Rabbi to wait a second because 'we have got to have another kiss from the bride and groom.' You can have the bridesmaids dressed as you like; that is not our business. You can have any kind of floral decorations; that is your affair. But we would like you to feel that this is the day—whether you have a small wedding or a big wedding, a beautiful magnificent wedding or just an intimate family wedding—that everybody connected with the family is going to be part of that ceremonial. . . . We want to come back to the old type of wedding."

For many, a return to the "old type of wedding" entailed a shift in venue: back to the synagogue. "Marriages may be wrought in Heaven," declared one clergyman, "but they ought to be solemnized in the synagogue." Toward that end, an increasing number of synagogues during the interwar years constructed their very own "splendid accommodations" for weddings and other jubilant occasions. Urging June brides to consult the synagogue's catering department, which purportedly provided "Excellent Service and Ideal Surroundings," the American synagogue sought to return the "marriage rite and the celebration [to] where they rightfully belong." Synagogue administrators joined with the clergy in promoting "affairs." Eager to cultivate new sources of income for the synagogue, they sent out letters to the parents of prospective brides, encouraging them to make a "definite appointment" with the caterer's representatives, who were available every Sunday morning, when "many inquiries are made re: weddings and catering." Admittedly, not only did the synagogue face stiff competition from hotels and halls, but, when soliciting business, had to conduct itself on a higher plane. "The synagogue must be careful to keep itself in a highly dignified position and not resort to the cheap unethical advertising and publicity that is produced by the ordinary catering establishment," advised the executive director of the Ocean Parkway Jewish Center. Still, it was worth the effort. "From the spiritual viewpoint the wedding certainly belongs in the synagogue. Certainly, from the executive viewpoint, it must be brought to the synagogue."

Despite claims to tradition, however, the synagogue wedding represented a fairly recent innovation in American Jewish practice. The way rabbis and executive directors spoke, one might easily assume that their advocacy of the synagogue wedding represented a long-standing and deeply rooted Jewish tradition. But that was simply not so. For centuries, the synagogue's sanctuary had been off-limits to wedding celebrations lest displays of merriment and frivolity mar its sanctity. In the mid-nineteenth century, German

Jewish reformers overturned that age-old proscription. Motivated as much by politics as by aesthetics, they hoped to demonstrate that Jewish marriage was no mere economic transaction, as non-Jewish authorities commonly believed, but an event of the highest moral probity and sanctity, equivalent to divine worship. East European Jews were slower to change. Typically, their weddings were held either at home or in the courtyard, rather than the sanctuary, of the local synagogue; with affluence, a growing number of urban Jews began to repair to a catering facility as well. Later, in the New World, the enduring presence of *minhag* (custom) coupled with an absence of space—most synagogues, no matter how grand their sanctuaries, lacked adequate recreational facilities—inspired immigrants to seek out a catering hall when having a *simcha*.

American Jewry's affinity for the catering hall was hard to overcome. "I realize," wrote Rabbi Israel Levinthal, whose synagogue boasted one of New York's premier kosher catering facilities, "that customs and habits are not changed overnight." Still, he and many others persisted, acting on the deep-seated belief that, given the remodeled and newly outfitted synagogue, there was "no excuse for having the marriage removed from the sacred surroundings." Firm in his convictions, Levinthal was inclined to overlook instances of raucous and inappropriate behavior in the synagogue sanctuary. Some of his colleagues, though, were not nearly as tolerant. "Please remember that you are in a House of God, a Holy Place," guests at one synagogue were informed as ushers handed them a ten-point list of "behavior rules" designed to refresh their knowledge of appropriate synagogue etiquette. "Avoid loud laughter or discussion in the Temple," read the list. "Do not powder your nose or paint your lips. Applaud only at the conclusion of the Ceremony after the breaking of the glass—not before."

Shifting the wedding from the courtyard—or its functional, latter-day equivalent, the catering hall—to the sanctuary was by no means the only change to have affected the modern-day ceremony. Even as the merits of a synagogue wedding were proclaimed and touted, American Jews and their representatives tinkered with virtually every aspect of the service, leaving little unaltered. Some communities dispensed with the *chupah* altogether

RULES AND REGULATIONS WHILE WAITING IN THE TEMPLE FOR THE WEDDING CEREMONY

1. Please remember that you are in a House of God, a Holy Place.
2. Cover your head in the vestibule before entering the Sanctuary.
3. Avoid loud laughter or discussion in the Temple.
4. Do not powder your nose or paint your lips in front of the Holy Ark.
5. Do not permit children to run up and down the aisles or on the pulpit.
6. Do not smoke in the Temple.
7. It is not proper to chew gum in the Temple.
8. You may applaud only at the conclusion of the Ceremony after the breaking of the glass—not before.
9. Please remain standing at the conclusion of the Ceremony until after the wedding procession has returned to the vestibule.
10. Light no cigarettes until you are in the vestibule.

Wedding guests were expected to abide by the strict conventions of synagogue etiquette.

or substituted a bower of flowers and ferns; others eschewed the *ketubah*, the Jewish marriage contract. "The changes which have taken place in Jewish life and law have divested the document of its ancient meaning and importance," explained the Reform-oriented Central Conference of American Rabbis of its decision to eliminate the *ketubah* entirely from the marriage ceremony. Instead, its members relied solely on the standard American matrimonial formula. Still others adapted the *ketubah*'s traditional "quaint" provisions to reflect a more modern view of marital responsibility. In the 1950s, the Conservative movement, for example, added a special prenuptial provision to the Aramaic text. Designed to protect the wife in the event her husband refused to grant her a divorce, the new *ketubah* gave the wife the right to institute divorce proceedings, a prerogative traditionally held only by the husband. This act, boasted a movement spokesman, is a "landmark," likely to place Conservative Judaism "not only on the map of the world, but also on the map of history."

While some augmented the Jewish wedding, others subtracted, and still others improvised. Reform Jews, for example, did away altogether with the breaking of the glass, arguing that "the crude dramatic performance tends to distract rather than to inspire, to mar rather than to enhance the impressiveness of the occasion." Even the ring itself, traditionally a modest, unembellished, simple gold band, assumed a new, more elaborate, form. "Do you permit the use of a ring with precious stones?" Conservative rabbis were asked in a 1930s survey concerning ritual behavior, the very question suggesting the extent to which that practice had already taken hold even within Conservative circles. Sixty rabbis answered yes; two replied they would do so "only in the case of an emergency"; and one lone clergyman, acting in the spirit of Solomon, requested that "a plain band . . . be used for the ceremony with permission to put the other band on later." One hundred rabbis, though, indicated a preference for the traditional plain ring.

The double-ring ceremony was yet another contested issue, one whose roots—like so much else associated with the modernized Jewish wedding—date back to late-nineteenth-century Germany. At the time, a growing number of well-educated, cultured, and affluent German Jewish brides began to ask permission of their rabbis to present a ring to their bridegrooms, even though that practice was not a Jewish one. "These ladies stated that they did not wish to be completely passive at the marriage altar, as if they were objects, and as though the marriage ceremony could be performed without their equal participation," wrote Rabbi Joseph Aub, who was sympathetic to their cause. Their request put the Reform movement in something of a double bind. Although unwilling on the one hand to integrate a foreign, non-Jewish practice into the fabric of Jewish law and lore, Reformers were equally committed to gender equality and didn't want to contradict their own principles by summarily dismissing the ladies' entreaties. After much discussion and heated debate at the Augsburg Synod of 1871, it was resolved that the matter be one of personal choice and preference. "We do not wish to introduce [the double-ring ceremony]," the conferees decided, "but freedom of conscience should prevail everywhere." And so it did—both in Germany and in the New World, where "modern rabbis" welcomed the double-ring ceremony as an expression "of the full equality of woman with man in the conjugal relation and in moral life."

* * *

A labor of love, this elaborately decorated cake was made by Diana Forman in celebration of her daughter's nuptials.

IN A COMMUNITY so committed to domestic felicity and marital stability, divorce provoked feelings of consternation and shame. "Divorce is an evil inasmuch as it manifests unrest in domestic conditions," explained the Reverend Dr. J. Leonard Levy of Pittsburgh's Temple Rodef Shalom. "It is an evil because of the wrongs inflicted, in some many cases, upon innocent childhood. It is an evil because it indicates, in a constantly increasing ratio, restiveness under moral restraint. It is an evil because it disrupts domestic life." Reminiscences confirm the disruptiveness of divorce. "My aunt was divorced," recalled a woman who had grown up in Brooklyn during the 1930s; "the family kept her hidden." Offering a similar perspective, a Jewish resident of Boston noted how "in that time and circumstance, divorce was out of the question—a notion entertained only in mad dreams. You stuck it out . . . no matter what, for better or for worse."

But not everyone did. Within the immigrant Jewish community of the pre–World War I years, many men, mistaking "liberty for license," abandoned their wives in what was widely known as a "poor man's divorce." My wife "has been here for five years and I have wanted to leave her ten times," explained one bounder. "She is a very undesirable woman. She often insults me in the presence of strangers." After seventeen years of marriage, another man ran out on his wife, claiming she was a "poor manager, a

א גאלעריע פון פערשוואונדענע מענער.

The *Jewish Daily Forward*, one of America's leading Yiddish newspapers, prominently displayed the names and faces of men who had deserted their wives.

coffee addict, neglectful of the children." She, in turn, accused him of being "brutal in sex matters." Whatever its origins, desertion affected thousands of immigrant Jewish families. In New York and Chicago, Detroit and Boston, authorities estimated that anywhere from 10 to 15 percent of Jewish women on relief had been abandoned. Family desertion, noted one concerned social worker in 1905, "has continued to grow so serious that attempts to diminish it are no longer confined to philanthropists and professional charity workers. The agitation has become general."

The *Jewish Daily Forward*, reflecting the community's alarm, maintained a "Gallery of Missing Husbands." Much like the photographic "rogues' gallery" used by the police, this domestic Yiddish version contained the faces as well as brief biographies of a quorum of errant husbands so that alert readers could report their whereabouts to the authorities. Hats perched uneasily on their heads, a stilted smile on their young faces, these "rogues," ironically enough, were often pictured in their wedding finery. The National Desertion Bureau, a Jewish organization established in 1911 to coordinate legal, financial, and philanthropic efforts on behalf of the deserted, went even further by taking systematic steps to apprehend "recreant husbands" and return them to their families. Working in concert with the courts and local government, it sought to compel the deserter to support his family; failing that, he was encouraged to grant his wife a legal divorce. Between 1912 and 1922, over twelve thousand cases, many of them repeat offenders, came to its attention.

In the years that followed, instances of desertion waned; legally obtained divorces took their place. Once heralded for its distinctive "domestic virtues," the American Jewish community began to approximate that of other Americans in the frequency of shattered marriages. "Divorce has an increasing incidence among Jews, almost equal to the rapidly rising rate of the rest of the population," glumly observed Rabbi Leon Lang in 1945. Fifty years earlier, when the ratio of marriages to divorces in the "general community" was 9.4 to 1, the ratio of Jewish marriages to divorces was more on the order of 24 to 1. By the 1940s, however, that divide had narrowed. The Jewish community now celebrated 4.9 marriages for every one divorce, as compared with 3.3 marriages for every divorce within American society at large. Jewish leaders like

Lang accounted for this about-face in a number of ways. Some blamed the speed and tempo of modern urban life, others the relaxation of religious practice. Still others pointed a finger at feminism. "Never before have wives and mothers insisted with such emphasis upon their right to freedom, even from the bonds of family routine," wrote marriage authority Rabbi Sidney Goldstein, noting the "widening revolt of women against the domination of the husband in marriage and family affairs." But, he conceded, men were equally at fault, especially those who demonstrated "increasing restlessness." This quality, he asserted, "may be only an expression of the restless spirit of the age. It is more likely, however, that it is an expression of the spirit of adventure innate in the heart of every man and an indication of the resentment men feel against what is regarded as the regimentation of family life."

Still, Jews who fled from the confines of marriage were not ostracized. Unlike Catholicism, Judaism neither prohibited divorce nor stood in the way of couples seeking to obtain one. "Judaism has the same view propounded by sociologists today," explained one Jewish matrimonial expert. It "takes the stand that blunders are possible in marriages as well as in all other human affairs." And yet, despite its legitimacy, divorce—or, as the community delicately termed it, "marital mishaps"—occasioned so much internal discomfort that the subject rarely made itself felt. Where thoughts of Jewish families involuntarily torn asunder by war or migration inspired an outpouring of reminiscence, fiction, and filmmaking, the garden-variety, voluntary breakup of a Jewish family did not.

Although the social and human cost of divorce was downplayed, if not ignored, Jewish newspapers and rabbinical proceedings were full of detailed, and often heated, exchanges on its legal ramifications, particularly those that related to the Jewish bill of divorce—the *get*. Ignorant of American divorce law, immigrant Jews mistakenly believed that a rabbinical divorce was a valid legal document, as it had been in the Old World, and therefore dissolved their marriages simply on the strength of its ecclesiastical authority, an innocent act that frequently landed them in jail on charges of bigamy. In Chicago, Philadelphia, Baltimore, Pittsburgh, and New York, the press was full of sad stories of immigrants like

Rabbi S. D. Posner
235 5th Street
Tel. Montgomery 2437 W

שלמה דוד פאזנער
ראב״ד דק״ק דזשוירזי סיטי

Jersey City, N. J., ... 191.....

Written in Aramaic, the *get*, or Jewish bill of divorce, legally dissolved an unhappy marriage, freeing the wife to remarry.

Mr. Mullershvick, who married Rosie Fink after having granted his first wife, Dora Reiss, a Jewish divorce—for which, he told the judge, he had paid ten dollars. Unmoved by this claim, Judge McMahon sentenced the hapless husband to a four-month prison term. "The only way for anyone to get a divorce," the judge declared, "is to get it at the proper tribunal and in a legal manner."

Legal-aid societies sought energetically to educate immigrants in the ways of American nuptial law. The Educational Alliance Legal Aid Society, for example, published broadsides and circulars that explained the distinction between "ecclesiastical divorce in Russia and here," hoping to make clear that in America a Jewish couple could not be considered legally divorced unless they first obtained a civil divorce. When that strategy failed, legal-aid lawyers would appear alongside those indicted for bigamy, pleading their innocence before the bar or, alternately, attempting to mitigate the severity of their sentence. Rabbinical associations, fearful lest the specter of Jews in jail for bigamy become a "menace to the reputation of the Jewish people," also participated in the "campaign of education." The interdenominational New York Board of Jewish Ministers, for example, issued a proclamation in November 1910 that upheld the supremacy of civil law.

> Be it resolved, that while we deplore the hardships that may sometimes arise through the difficulty of fulfilling both the obligation of the religious divorce . . . and of the civil divorce demanded by the law of the State,
>
> Nevertheless, we, the New York Board of Jewish Ministers, unanimously declare that in no circumstances is any Rabbi to give a religious divorce (Get), unless he have documentary evidence that the civil marriage has been annulled or a divorce has been given by a competent court of any State of the Union.

In the years that followed, the "unregulated giving of *get*" ceased to be a problem. Most Jewish couples intent on splitting up did away with the *get* entirely, arguing that rabbinical divorces "are in every respect unnecessary and in this age and land, opposed to the spirit of American institutions." Those of a more traditional cast, however, felt differently about the *get*'s ongoing importance. Orthodox and Conservative clergy would no sooner dispense with that religious document than they would sanction the consumption of unkosher meat or the violation of the Sabbath. Disregard of Jewish marital law, they felt, threatened to upset the Jewish social structure with its legally rooted notions of personal status; worse still, it threatened to break irrevocably with centuries of tradition. Remarrying without a *get* "not only undermines the traditional laws of marriage and divorce but it tends to generate disrespect for tradition in general," insisted Rabbi David Aronson. "It creates the most sinful situation in Jewish life."

Despite the strength of rabbinic convictions, the legality or illegality of an ecclesiastical divorce became increasingly irrelevant to the lives of second- and third-generation American Jews, a steadily growing number of whom no longer bothered to obtain one before tying the knot for a second time. Where earlier generations could little imagine remarrying without having the religious document in hand, their grandchildren and great-grandchildren felt it had as much relevance to their lives "as knee breeches and powdered wigs." American Jews had little ken, and even less appreciation, of the legal construction of divorce, Jewish-style. "I venture to say that over 90% of our divorcées in America . . . will not hesitate to remarry without one," observed one disheartened clergyman in 1940, referring to the *get*'s waning influence. Divorced from an established tradition whose meaning eluded them, the folk went one way and the elite another.

WHERE DIVORCE threatened to rock the domestic foundations of American Jewish life, exogamy, or intermarriage, seemed certain to demolish them altogether. The ultimate romantic escapade, exogamy pitted the rights of the individual against those of the community, the claims of personal freedom and individual happiness against those of cultural loyalty and patrimony. "I wanted a new thing—happiness," explained the heroine of Leah Morton's acclaimed 1926 novel *I Am a Woman—And a Jew* as she prepared to marry a non-Jew. "I was not a girl representing a race. I was not a Jewish maiden responsible to a race. . . . I was no Biblical Rebecca sorrowfully pleading for her race. I was an American, now, just as he was."

As Morton's account makes clear, the decision to intermarry entailed choosing between two competing ideals. In the opening years of the century, though, few American Jews had to make that choice: intermarriages seldom happened. "As yet, marriages between Jews and Christians are of rare occurrence," observed popular essayist Esther Jane Ruskay in 1902, "and when they do take place, there is raised such a storm of criticism and disapproval for all parties concerned that any tendencies in this direction are kept in healthful check." Inhibited by social convention, the rate of intermarriages seemed unlikely to accelerate. "A few anthropologists may believe the day will come when Americans will be as little opposed to mixed marriage as were medieval Bagdad and Toledo under the Saracens," editorialized the *Jewish Times* years later, in 1930. "But in the main there is little peril that Americans will take the slogan of the Melting Pot too literally. Historic, long-established integers will be preserved with little impairment, and America will be unified through means other than racial fusion."

If anything, "intermarriage" took the form of unions between Reform and Orthodox Jews, or *yekkes* (German Jews), with *Ostjuden* (East European Jews), a development that aroused alarm in some and skepticism in others. "The fact is that to intermarry with the German reform Jew has become a sort of *yichus* [mark of status] with the Russian orthodox Jew, who will never think of taking his rabbis into his confidence in questions of matrimony," the *American Jewish Chronicle* peevishly related in 1916. Commenting on a recent resolution of the Union of Orthodox Rabbis of America that had condemned such interdenominational unions, the newspaper sounded a note of resignation: "Nature, and social conditions, will forever remain the final arbiter in determining all questions of love and marriage." True enough, but did such marriages work out? "Are certain types of American Jews so far apart socially and spiritually that marriage between them means unavoidable unhappiness?" *Der Tog*, a popular Yiddish daily, wondered in a 1928 feature article, "Is There a 'Jewish Intermarriage'?" "Lack of spiritual harmony," the article explained, might result when one partner was "sincerely religious" and the other sincerely nonreligious. "How will Lily L. feel when she sees her husband keeping a cap always on his head, when she is accustomed to feel that no gentleman remains covered in the presence of a lady? . . . When he objects to her pushing the electric-light button on or off on the Sabbath, when he watches her piling milk-dishes together with meat-dishes in the sink? . . . Is there any solution?"

Perhaps love did not conquer all, but it certainly made the news, especially when Jews and non-Jews exchanged wedding vows. Such marriages occurred so infrequently in the years prior to World War I that on the rare occasions when they did take place, they created quite a stir. In 1902, for example, the marriage of German-Jewish grandee Edward Lauterbach's daughter to the scion of an aristocratic Fifth Avenue family merited an entire editorial in the Socialist *Jewish Daily Forward*, which, characteristically, used the opportunity to fume about the perils of social climbing among the members of the German-Jewish establishment. Several years later, the union of Rose Harriet Pastor, a Lower East Side tenement dweller and former factory worker, and millionaire James Graham Phelps Stokes, a resident worker at the University Settlement, also generated reams of gossip and, as one contemporary put it, held the "imagination of New York in a strange captivity." The *New York Times*, for one, considered the engagement front-page news. "J. G. PHELPS STOKES TO WED YOUNG JEWESS," the paper proclaimed in April 1905 as it detailed the history of their courtship. Not above instigating a few rumors of its own, the article broadly hinted that the Stokes family deeply disapproved of Graham's choice, a charge that the bridegroom felt publicly compelled to disavow by denying the existence of "serious opposition" on the part of his family. "That is entirely false. There is nothing but the utmost cordiality and delight," he was quoted as saying. The *Times* also carried details of the couple's Episcopalian wedding ceremony, which was held at The Point, the Stokeses' Connecticut residence. "East Side settlement workers of the same social standing as the Stokes family crowded into the stages and carriages with the friends of the bride and bridegroom who work in the shops and live in the tenements of the lower east side," the paper noted, its social antennae vibrating at the idea. "There was no thought of class distinction among them and they laughed and chatted together in the most familiar way, as they rode up the hill to the church." While the guests might have (temporarily) abjured class distinctions, the *Times* kept piling them on. "The only difference between the men from the east side and their fashionable brothers," it crowed, "was that those from the tenements had braved the weather in frock coats and high hats, while their wealthy brethren had, as a rule, thought Summer clothing appropriate to a morning wedding."

Mrs. J. G. Phelps Stokes At Home
By Lillian Baynes Griffin

The unlikely union between foreign-born Rose Pastor and patrician J.G.P. Stokes tickled the fancy of the American public.

The Anglo-Jewish press, even more concerned than the *Times* with the affair's broader implications, worried lest the match between the millionaire and the so-called Flower of the Ghetto (a "newspaper misnomer," sniffed the *American Hebrew*) affect the way young Jewish New Yorkers thought about intermarriage, heightening its "practicability." Jewish women, they feared, couching their analysis in gendered terms, seemed the most likely to emulate Rose Pastor's example, given their emotional vulnerability and their propensity toward envy and daydreams. "Let Jewish girls beware, and not permit themselves to be dazzled," warned the *Hebrew Standard*, cautioning them against succumbing to the "will o wisp of universal brotherhood." "It is but an empty dream . . . differences of temperament, of training and of surroundings, are more powerful than the arrows with which Cupid has pierced the hearts of men and women." More than a decade later, some within the American Jewish community continued to link a "growing tendency" toward intermarriage to the precedent set by Rose Pastor. Writing in 1916, in one of the earliest and most systematic inquiries into exogamy, Celia Silbert insisted that of the twenty-five intermarriages recorded recently in the Marriage License Bureau, a goodly number were inspired by Stokes's conduct and that of another Jewish social worker, Rose Walling, who had also married a non-Jew. "Perhaps the greatest impetus to intermarriage in general on the East Side, was given some years ago when several intermarriages occurred between certain social workers of a non-Jewish social centre on the East Side. The examples set by these leaders were observed and imitated by their young charges and several intermarriages among them resulted."

Rose Pastor Stokes inspired literature as well as marital behavior. In what was soon to emerge as a literary trend, her good fortune and Cinderella-like destiny figured as the subject of much popular American Jewish fiction of the interwar years. Anzia Yezierska, for example, drew on Rose's real-life romance in her novel *Salome of the Tenements*, an improbably entitled tale that recounts the stirring love affair between "John Manning the millionaire," an elegant gentleman who devotes himself to bettering the lives of the less fortunate, and Sonya, the endearing tenement girl, "a vivid exotic—a miraculous priestess of romance," whom he magically plucks from obscurity and a life of grinding poverty. In Yezierska's telling, no kinder fate could befall an immigrant woman, "a nobody from nowhere," than to marry one of America's noblemen. Farfetched and generally unattainable, intermarriage symbolized for her and countless others the romance of America and the fantasy of possibility—or, as she put it, "the oriental and the Anglo-Saxon trying to find a common language."

Yezierska was by no means the only American-Jewish writer to equate intermarriage with freedom, personal liberation, and the invention of the American self, nor, for that matter, was she alone in finding the topic particularly compelling. Throughout the 1920s and 1930s, dozens of potboilers, many them authored by Jewish women, offered readers tantalizing, juicy insights into the drama of intermarriage. From Marion Spitzer's *Who Would Be Free*, a ringing endorsement of mixed marriage, to Fannie Hurst's *Apassionata*, "the story of the girl who preferred the love of religion" to that of a non-Jewish man, the make-believe of fiction enabled American Jews to contemplate what was simultaneously too painful and too fantastical to confront in real life.

American Jews also learned about intermarriage from the stage. For much of the 1920s, Broadway resounded with hosannas for *Abie's Irish Rose*, one of the most popular plays of all time. "As much of an American institution as the circus," the production ran for over five and a half years, generated nineteen different touring companies, and earned its creator, Anne Nichols, herself a party to a mixed marriage, over five million dollars. "America's third largest industry" (to quote H. L. Mencken) owed its success to its playful, humorous approach to the dilemmas of intermarriage. By combining the conventions of a drawing-room comedy with the elements of vaudeville, the play made light of what many considered to be a vexing moral, cultural, religious, and social issue. The plot hinges on the various subterfuges to which Abie Levy must resort to keep secret his recent marriage to Rosemarie Murphy, an Irish Catholic nurse. After much travail and duplicity reminiscent of a Feydeau farce, Abie's religious parents eventually come to terms with their new daughter-in-law; tolerance and love triumph over religious prejudice. A big hit with the "subway public," which warmed to the spectacle of Catholics and Jews hurling insults at one another only to reconcile in the end, *Abie's Irish Rose* validated the notion of intermarriage. On stage and off, it dramatized the promise of America.

To American Jewry's cultural authorities, though, intermarriage was no laughing matter. Mixed marriage, community leaders warned, was "bound to prove Judaism's undoing." Employing the best funerary imagery, they spoke grimly of the ways in which "intermarriage furnishes a nail to the coffin of the Jewish race," and "sounds the death knell" of American Judaism. Intermarriage, like death, threatened the community with the prospect of "loss," dissolution, and disintegration by irrevocably loosening the ties that bound the American Jew to his or her community. "The opposition of the Jew to intermarriage is . . . not based on any pride of blood or sense of superiority, but merely the instinct for self-preservation," explained Rabbi Stephen S. Wise, adding tersely that it is a matter of "race continuity." Wise's colleague Rabbi David de Sola Pool put it this way: "Every religious group is zealous for its own interests. But we Jews have an added reason. . . . The Jewish people and Judaism, at all times fighting for survival, have the right to claim the loyalty and self-sacrifice of every individual Jew."

Even as Stephen Wise and his associates waxed eloquent over the prior claims of history, a growing number of social scientists began to turn their attention to the etiology of exogamy and the politics of identity. The first empirical study of intermarriage, Julius Drachsler's *Democracy and Assimilation: The Blending of Immigrant Heritages in America* (1920), carefully sifted through and presented data culled from over 100,000 marriage licenses. Drachsler's work contained several findings of considerable moment. For one thing, he found that American Jews staunchly maintained an unusually high degree of endogamy. Among whites, Jews were the least likely to marry outside the faith. Taking both the first and second generations into account, the sociologist found that only 1.17 percent of American Jews had intermarried in the years 1908 through 1912, as compared with 16.73 percent of Italian Americans and one third of all German Americans. More striking still was Drachsler's finding that, American Jews notwithstanding, the general rate of intermarriage over time had steadily increased, from approximately 11 percent among first-generation immigrants to about 32 percent among their second-generation descendants. This revelation, rendered in neutral, careful language, confirmed that the much-touted melting pot was no mere rhetorical flourish.

In the wake of *Democracy and Assimilation*'s publication, the sociological study of intermarriage moved away from probability and statistics and toward the "social psychology of Jews who intermarry." Highlighting the personal factors that led to intermarriage, a number of influential studies constructed a typology of Jewish exogamy. Jews who married out of the faith seemed unerringly to fall into such categories as the reluctant, the rebellious, the marginal, and the emancipated. These categories, faintly reminiscent of the Four Sons of the Passover Haggadah, were meant to cover the entire span of human behavior and to explain the contingencies of love in ways that mere statistics could not. Those classified as "the reluctant," for example, married outside of the fold in an attempt "to solve a neurotic conflict regarding heterosexual relations," while the "emancipated" reportedly sought release from "infantile family ties."

While critics at the time complained that these categories were so nebulous that "they may be used in classifying almost any individual, whether he inmarries or intermarries," the process of typologizing profoundly affected the way most American Jews thought of intermarriage: in pathological terms. The net effect, if unintended consequence, of these classifying schemes was to brand the intermarried as deviant and the act of intermarriage as an aberrant phenomenon. Admittedly, American Jews had always been inclined to think in such terms, to draw on the rhetoric of dysfunction when discussing intermarriage. As far back as 1916, when the rate of exogamy was at an all-time low, one American Jewish writer put it this way: "*What's the matter* with the Jewish girls and boys of the East Side? What is it that makes them break Judea's holiest and most sacred ties and unite with strangers in marriage? Are they losing faith in each other? Do they no longer attract each other . . . or is it that the Jewish marriage institution is becoming passé and, like old fashion, must be discarded and new modes adopted?" Science now provided the answer, one reassuring in its absoluteness and absolution. That a statistically insignificant number of its sons and daughters had gone astray by marrying out of the faith had nothing to do with Judaism but with deficiencies in their personal makeup. There was nothing "wrong" with Judaism, or with its encounter with modernity; the problem, such as it was, rested with those on the margins—literally and figuratively—of American Jewish life. According to this line of reasoning, whose internal logic was both compelling and comforting, intermarriage didn't affect "us"; it happened to "them."

In addition to the community's determination to marginalize intermarriage and the intermarried, a number of vigilant American Jewish leaders sought actively to thwart the possibility that the pace of intermarriage would quicken in the future among the more balanced, healthy members of Jewish society. Drawing on the insights of sociology, they fashioned various strategies of resistance, basing them "not on the ground of tradition but on a good sociological basis." One of the most popular and enduring "sociological" arguments against mixed marriages was the frequency with which they seemed to fail. If it's happiness you're after, cautioned writers on the subject, you're not going to find it with someone of another faith. "While some intermarriages have resulted in happy unions, the majority have resulted otherwise," Celia Silbert insisted in her 1916 essay "Intermarriage on the East Side." "Hardly, if ever, are they contracted with the full consent or knowledge of the parents. Usually the newly-weds begin their wedded life with strong opposition on the part of their families, and under unfavorable auspices. They lead a checkered existence, frequently followed by an aftermath of regret, heartache and tragedy."

Statistical evidence supported Silbert's assertion. Studies conducted by anthropologist Maurice Fishberg and sociologist Arthur Ruppin revealed that mixed marriages were three to four times more likely to "dissolve" than endogamous ones, a statistic that was repeated so often and by so many different sources that it took on a life of its own. Equally chilling, it seems, was the adverse effect of intermarriage on fertility. "If reliance is to be placed in statistics, we must conclude that nature herself stamps her mark of disapproval upon intermarriage," explained St. Louis rabbi Mendel Silber in 1908, citing a study of the comparative fertility of Protestants, Catholics, and Jews. Where 430 children were born to parents who were both Protestants, 520 to parents who were both Roman Catholics, and 441 to parents who were both Jewish, 165 were born to Christian fathers and Jewish mothers, and only 131 to Jewish fathers and Christian mothers.

Marriage education experts also threw their weight behind endogamy. Highly esteemed authorities like Judson Landis, author of *Building a Successful Marriage*, one of the most successful guides to modern marriage ever published, disapproved of mixed marriages, claiming they posed "serious hazards to success." Devoting an entire thirty-one-page chapter to the topic, he insisted that exogamous couples had more marital woes than endogamous ones. "All couples have some problems after they marry; in the mixed marriage the number of problems is increased and some problems which would normally exist are intensified." To drive

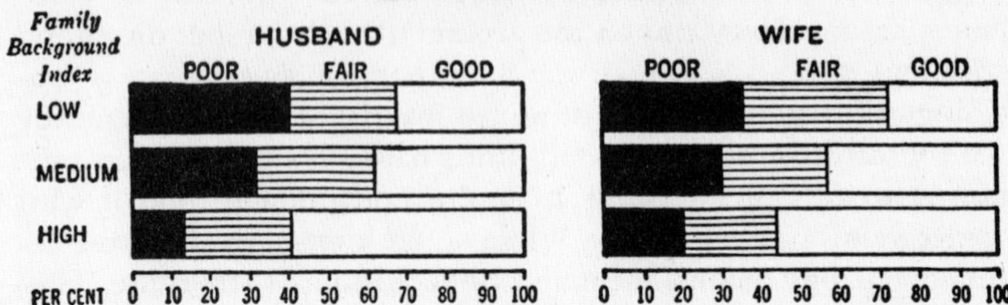

The "Index of Similarity in Family Background and Adjustment in Marriage" purported to measure marital compatibility.

home his point, Landis reproduced the "Index of Similarity in Family Background and Adjustment in Marriage," a chart compiled by Ernest Burgess, the dean of marriage educators, that predicted marital success or failure based on degree of social, economic, and cultural compatibility. The caption that accompanied the boldly illustrated chart declared authoritatively: "Young people who come from similar backgrounds have fewer handicaps to happiness in marriage."

Together with Landis, the Jewish community grounded its contemporary opposition to exogamy in terms of cultural and religious compatibility, or what the *Jewish Daily Forward* catalogued as "different household customs, different kinds of food, different intimate manners." "The weight of my whole background was against it," a young woman who had considered intermarriage told sociologist James Slotkin in 1938. "A *goy* was a *goy* and I was a Jew and that's all there was to it—like east and west, you know." Another respondent, a man who had married a non-Jewish woman, ruefully spoke of the astonishment with which his wife's friends initially greeted him. "They'd never known a Jew before and were quite astonished that my interests were the same as theirs: that I liked games, hunting and swimming; that I could hold my liquor without getting noisy. They'd been taught that Jews were extremely different." When all was well, such differences were of little moment, argued the community's representatives; but should conflict and tension arise, the "heredity of civilization" would surface and wreak havoc. "Why, even in cases where one mate is an Orthodox Jew and the other a Reform Jew, it is bad enough," a Jewish social worker from the South noted. "Yet, how much worse it would be where the difference would be as great as another religion."

Despite the popularity this avowedly modern argument enjoyed, not everyone agreed with its premises. Rabbi Jacob Kohn, for example, felt it simply did not go far enough in explaining the Jewish opposition to exogamy. "We dare not rest the whole weight of our case on so frail a foundation," he insisted. "Husbands and wives may diverge in their esthetic tastes, in their politics, in their philosophic views and yet somehow maintain a happy home life." The family expert offered, instead, what he believed to be a far more "cogent" argument: the fate of the children. Astutely, he shifted the terms of the discussion away from considerations of individual, personal happiness toward the "gravitational pull" of the future generation and the burdens of cultural continuity. "Intermarriage does not present an even chance of the next generation's being of Jewish . . . descent. On the contrary, it denies the Jewish people any chance at all of perpetuating itself or its genius or its cultural inheritance." Those who contemplate intermarriage, he warned, "are not playing fair with Judaism. They are helping to give a death blow to the Jewish people and its spiritual heritage." By linking endogamy to children and child-centeredness, two of his generation's most popular concerns, Kohn succeeded in providing an altruistic and singularly modern rationale for its observance and one that seemed to ring true. In fact, of all the reasons invoked against intermarriage, this one has become the explanation to which most postwar American Jewish authorities resort in their campaign against exogamy.

Kohn's views underscored the extent to which marriage was not something American Jews entered into lightly. Often, it entailed choosing between competing agendas. "There are two tendencies in regard to marriage," explained Emily Solis-Cohen when she appeared before the Women's League Convention in 1925 to talk about "The Jewish Girl's Thoughts on Jewish Life." "The one is to consider marriage a personal matter only. The other is to think in terms of posterity, to insure the physical and mental heritage of the child. Jews are asked to think for posterity one step further, and to regard marriage as one of the means of perpetuating Judaism." In the majority of instances, American Jews of marriageable age succeeded in negotiating between posterity and the personal by marrying one another and laying the foundations for a Jewish household. It was not until the 1960s, after all, that the Jewish intermarriage rate began its dramatic and steady ascent. As late as 1953, exogamy was "reliably estimated" at between 5 and 10 percent. In other cases, the conflict between posterity and the personal resulted either in the "shackling of Cupid," as one newspaper delicately labeled romantic distress, or intermarriage.

No matter where Cupid's arrows might land, the American Jewish community succeeded in defining love and the pursuit of matrimonial harmony in collective terms. Rejecting the notion that love was a private, consensual matter between two individuals, the overwhelming majority of American Jews refused, well into the 1960s, to accept that an American Jewish woman or man would willingly, knowingly, and happily marry outside of the faith; those who did were anathemized. American Jews also rejected the notion that an individual's makeup was defined only in terms of his or her present-day actions. "In each of us is stored up thousands of years of traditions and inheritances. . . . Oh, how quickly they come to the surface. How often I have seen it in my ministry," sermonized Israel Levinthal in a 1932 address, "What Intermarriage Means to the Jew." "We are not selfish beings," he added. "We belong to a race, and a people and an historic faith. We do have parents and family and have to think of what this step means to them." As American Jews contemplated marriage, they were reminded repeatedly that their personal actions had consequences that extended beyond their immediate household into the community at large. "In true and happy marriage there must be a community of love, a community of respect and reverence, and a community of sentiment." True marital happiness, it seemed, could be found only in the "sanctuary of love" provided by the Jewish family.

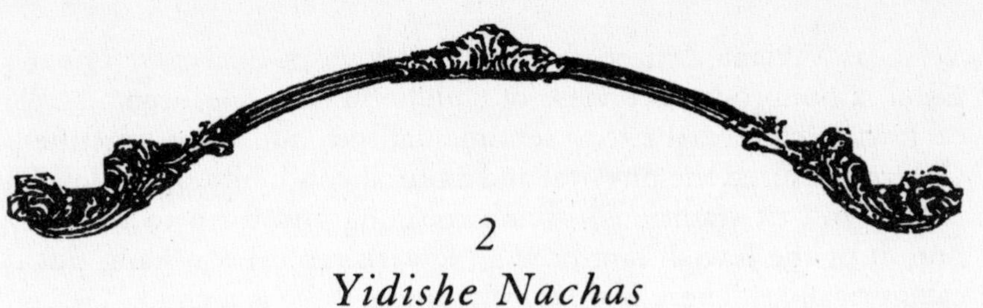

2
Yidishe Nachas

❦

In 1928, the Jewish community of Brownsville proudly took to the streets to celebrate its Golden Jubilee. A "bewildering display of colored lights, flags and immense wooden spears from which hung long shields announcing the joyous birthday" decorated Pitkin Avenue, the neighborhood's mercantile and social center. A constellation of marching bands with beating drums and blaring trumpets gaily made its way along the thoroughfare while five cantors entertained passersby with a medley of Jewish tunes. The high point of the celebration, though, was neither the peripatetic musicians nor the performing cantors but a baby contest featuring twelve hundred contestants. Eagerly, parents offered up their babies for inspection by a specially chosen team of doctors from the Brownsville and East New York Hospital. After much ado, the medical men selected fifteen "100 percent specimens" as contest winners, hailing them as "a mark of distinction for Brownsville" and rewarding their proud parents with prizes. Afterward, as the parade of twelve hundred baby carriages proceeded grandly down Pitkin Avenue, one sponsor of the Golden Jubilee was heard to remark that as far as he was concerned "one baby was as good as another."

While the notion of babies competing for cash prizes was no doubt foreign to the East European imagination of many of Brownsville's Jewish residents, the sentiment it reflected—the preciousness of children—surely was not. Children were traditionally valued within Jewish culture not for their material contributions to the family economy but for the emotional satisfaction—the *yidishe nachas*—they provided. A fairly new conception in the

West, as Viviana Zelizer observes in her work *Pricing the Priceless Child*, a nonproductive view of childhood had long been a staple of Jewish culture. Prized, sentimentalized, and even sanctified, children ensured the physical and cultural continuity of the Jewish people and its traditions, giving meaning and form to the very notion of the Jewish family. As Newark rabbi Leon Lang put it categorically, "There is no family unless there is a child."

It's no wonder, then, that Jewish culture throughout the ages focused much of its energy on its children. "Traditionally, the Jewish family is child-centered, with a hopeful orientation toward the future," observed anthropologist Nathalie F. Joffe in her 1954 study *The American Jewish Family*. It is the next generation—the young—who are the central concern of each family." Anthropologists like Joffe were not alone in highlighting the Jewish child's salience. As early as 1917, medical practitioners such as Dr. W. M. Feldman in his tome *The Jewish Child: Its History, Folklore, Biology and Sociology* enlisted a dazzling array of talmudic, midrashic, and rabbinic sources to establish the child's centrality within Jewish culture. Diligently chronicling the history of Jewish childhood, Feldman sought to demonstrate the intrinsic modernity of Jewish attitudes toward its offspring, or, as one perceptive critic put it, "to make clear that Hillel was the forerunner of Montessori." Whether in the time of Moses or that of classical Greece, the world of the Talmud or that of contemporary Britain, the Jewish child had always been the object of considerable affection and attention, Feldman proudly pointed out. Throughout history, Jewish parents had taken great pains to monitor their children's health and well-being, "fly[ing] to the doctor for almost every trifling infantile ailment." They also placed a premium on education. "Even from the very cradle it is the ambition of Jewish parents to see their sons grow up learned men," the doctor asserted, "and no sacrifice is too great for them to make in order to realize that ambition."

Reared in an environment of sacrifice and dedication, Jewish children had every reason to be content. "Happy the children who . . . live in the simple, practical atmosphere of the Jewish Home," commented Esther Jane Ruskay, making sure to salute the Jewish mother for her part in creating such a salubrious milieu. Thanks to the mother's ministrations and displays of "unobtrusive

The Levine family at the turn of the century.

charity and religious well-doing," her young, Ruskay noted approvingly, enjoyed a "temperate and well-ordered life, with none of the evils and none of the fears" of contemporary life "to puzzle or to threaten" them. In the years that followed, others joined with Ruskay in celebrating the mother as the "presiding genius" of the Jewish home. "The ideal Jewess," proclaimed the *United Synagogue Recorder* in 1925, "is a homemaker," a notion echoed years later by a California Jewish homemaker. "The greatest part the Jewish woman can play in the future of a healthy Judaism," asserted Rose Goldstein, "is through the conduct of her own household." Some within the Jewish community even went so far as to place the Jewish mother on a real-life pedestal. In 1919, a group of artistically inclined Jewish women commissioned sculptor Boris Schatz to fashion a statue of Yocheved, Moses' mother. This monument to motherhood, they hoped, "would in a measure offset the popular conception of ideal Motherhood as depicted by Christian artists in the representation of Mary" by suggesting the "depth of maternal love which is characteristic of the Jewish woman."

In its emphasis on motherhood as a "higher calling," the Jewish community was not simply harking back to an age-old, static idea but was in fact reflecting a modern view, one that "ascribed world-historical importance to woman's maternal role." In the "Age of Mother-Power," as one magazine dubbed the pre–World War I era, society "deeded" mothers all of the responsibility for the physical, emotional, and moral well-being of their offspring, heightening and enlarging their sphere of influence while restricting the father's realm to that of "money-getter" and "bill-payer." Nutritionist, nurturer, and moral steward, modern American mothers were called upon to produce healthy, well-balanced children who exemplified kindness, "moral stamina," and "innumerable other traits."

Anything but spontaneous and intuitive, modern motherhood, or "mothercraft," as it was called, required discipline, control, and scientific expertise. "That motherhood now is regarded as much more serious and complicated an affair than it was formerly, is an established fact," noted one observer in 1916. "This can be proved by the number of books, magazines and newspaper articles devoted to all phases of preparation for and responsibilities of motherhood. Almost daily we read of new methods, new plans, new ideas for the better development of our young." Women had only to pick up a copy of *Good Housekeeping* or the *Woman's Home Companion* to learn that motherhood had evolved from a "sacred duty" into a "scientific study." No longer could mothers trust to instinct or even to family traditions when raising their children; instead, they had to be educated in the "meaning of motherhood," whose purview encompassed bacteriology just as much as babies.

Baby Week, a national educational movement spearheaded by the United States Children's Bureau and aimed at rationalizing infant health care and reducing infant mortality, epitomized the scientific approach to maternity and its hold on the American public. Launched first in Chicago in April 1914 and in New York two months later—before becoming a biennial event—the movement quickly spread across the country, enlisting the support of such national organizations as the General Federation of Women's Clubs, the International Pure Milk and Food League, and the newly established federal Children's Bureau, in addition to local school groups, settlement houses, and philanthropies. In New York, where death claimed 98 out of every 1,000 newborns, Baby Week enjoyed the wholehearted cooperation of the city administration, which organized an interethnic and interreligious steering committee to chart and implement the week-long festivities.

Residents were encouraged to don "Baby Week Colors—baby pink and baby blue," while thousands of billboards and subway posters blanketed the five boroughs, bearing the slogan "Better Parents! Better Babies! Better City!" Synagogues and churches set aside a Saturday and a Sunday, respectively, for a "Baby Sabbath" and a "Baby Sunday" during which clergy sermonized on the importance of proper health care; local movie houses showed films on infant hygiene while public schools mounted special exhibitions on nutrition and health care. The city's educational institutions, eager to reinforce traditional gender roles, also established "Little Mothers Aid Associations" where young girls between the ages of ten and twelve were taught how to care for their younger siblings. These young girls, reported one eyewitness, "know now that babies can be just as much fun as dolls."

Outside the precincts of the public school, much of Baby Week's efforts focused on milk. Despite the "conceded fact" of breast

Public School 76, Manhattan
921 Lexington Avenue.

Honorable John Purroy Mitchel
Dear Mayor Mitchel
The Little Mothers' League requests the honor of your presence at the Exercises to be held in the school building on Monday morning, June 22, "Babies' Day," at half after ten o'clock, or at any other hour during the school day that will suit your convenience.

Respectfully yours,
Mary A. Magovern
Principal.

"Babies' Day" loomed large on the school calendar.

milk's superior nutritional value, the architects of Baby Week sought to promote pasteurized cow's milk, then a novelty, as a healthy and affordable alternative. "MILK HAS ITS DAY IN BABIES' BIG WEEK," trumpeted the *Times* as mothers were invited to visit and inspect any one of fifty-five milk stations, where they could purchase the product at cost. Whether city-owned and -operated or privately funded, like the formidably named Nathan Straus Pasteurized Laboratories, milk stations provided the beverage at a subsidized rate and educated consumers in its proper use and storage. Keep milk "clean, covered and cold," cautioned "Milk Don'ts for Mothers," a chart listing no fewer than twenty related health tips. "Don't buy milk unless you are sure that it is clean; Don't blow the milk to cool it." On-site nurses, who charted the growth of newborns and infants and chatted with their mothers, furthered the association between milk and health.

In the days that followed "Milk Station Day," Baby Week participants took part in an intensely competitive "Better Baby" contest in which "model babies," nourished on commercially produced milk, demonstrated tangibly its health-giving properties and, as the mother of one prize-winning baby related, "testified to the value of the milk stations." Winners, among them Olga Cohen, a nine-month-old, twenty-one-pound Lower East Side baby, took home cash prizes ranging as high as twenty-five dollars and were invited to march up Fifth Avenue in the week's culminating event: a festive parade. Drawing thousands of spectators brandishing pink and blue balloons, the parade featured a motorcade of mothers and babies. Floats filled with children of different nationalities added to the excitement, providing proof that "motherhood unified the various peoples come to our shore." Imaginatively conceived and executed, Baby Week publicized the critical importance of combating infant mortality by familiarizing residents with the "facts" about diet, health care, and child-rearing. "If there is anything that any New Yorker didn't know about babies by the end of the week," proclaimed one city official, obviously wearied by the goings-on, "it will not be the fault of the Mayor's Baby Week Committee."

From Nathan Straus, the distinguished philanthropist, whose largesse established the city's very first milk stations, to the prize-winning Olga Cohen, New York's Jewish citizenry participated actively in the week-long celebration. Still, Jewish mothers needed little inducement to visit a municipal milk depot, several of which had dotted the Lower East Side for more than two decades. As early as 1904, well before Baby Week highlighted the importance of pasteurized milk, Jewish women of the Lower East Side, observed medical anthropologist Maurice Fishberg, "had taken advantage of Mr. Straus's philanthropy, and when unable to nurse their babies at the breast feed them on 'Straus milk.' " Eager to familiarize themselves with American notions and norms of child care, Jewish immigrant women throughout the country took time out of their busy schedules to attend classes, meetings, and clubs run by New York's Educational Alliance and Cleveland's Kitchen Garden and Trade School. "The women are not obliged to dress up. They come without their hats. And above all, they waste no time in getting back to their homes and duties," recalled one eyewitness. At these casual gatherings, mothers heard speakers hold forth, often in fractured Yiddish, on "The Moral Education of Children at Home" and "The Importance of a Fresh and Clean Food Supply," or viewed films like *Cheating the Garbage Pail*, a graphic illustration of the efficient use of leftovers. Some topics proved more popular than others. "A series of health talks in Yiddish, by a physician or a nurse, illustrated if possible, will always bring a ready response from the mothers," one charity worker observed in 1919.

Even as they attended classes, immigrant Jewish women learned as much, if not more, about *muttershaft* (Yiddish for "mothercraft") from Yiddish periodicals and prescriptive literature. "The printed page," noted social reformer Oscar Leonard, "has a certain influence which the spoken word hardly possesses." Jewish women's magazines like *Froyen Velt* and *Froyen Zhurnal* barraged their readers with a steady flow of *eytses* (advice) on American child-rearing conventions. Hardly an issue went by without some kind of discussion regarding "the role of the modern mother" or "the young American Jewish mother." Pamphlets such as Jacob Mayerson's *Mutter und Kind*, a 1911 publication much admired for its concise and practical synthesis of scientific information, also took the mystery out of mothering. Clear and straightforward, it provided a wealth of information on pregnancy, childbirth, infant care, hygiene, childhood diseases, and proper diet. Its illustrations and

36 טאבעלע: ווי פיעל, ווי אפט און ווי שטארק צו געבען די מילך.

פאר א קינד אין דעם עלטער פון	ויפיעל באטעלס אין 24 שטונדען	וויפיעל אונצען אין יעדן באטל	ווי אפט געבען דאס באטעל	וויפיעל % פראטעין	וויפיעל % פעטס	וויפיעל % צוקער
די 2טע וואך ביז 1 מאנאט	10	פון 2 ביז 2½	אלע 2 שטונדען 3 מאל ביינאכט	פון ½ ביז ¾%	פון 1 ביז 1½%	5%
פון 4 וואכען ביז 2 מאנאט	10	פון 2½ ביז 3	אלע 2 שטונדען 3 מאל ביינאכט	1%	2%	6%
פון 2 ביז 3 מאנאט	8	פון 3½ ביז 4	אלע 2½ שטונ. 2 מאל ביינאכט	1¼%	2%	6%
פון 3 ביז 4 מאנאט	8	פון 4 ביז 4½	אלע 2½ שטונ. 2 מאל ביינאכט	1½%	2½%	6%
פון 4 ביז 6 מאנאט	7	פון 5 ביז 6½	אלע 3 שטונדען 2 מאל ביינאכט	1¾%	2½%	6%
פון 6 ביז 9 מאנאט	6	פון 6½ ביז 7½	אלע 3 שטונדען 1 מאל ביינאכט	2%	3%	7%
פון 9 מאנאט ביז 1 יאהר	6	פון 7½ ביז 8	אלע 3 שטונדען 1 מאל ביינאכט	2½%	3½%	7%
פון 1 יאהר ביז 1½ יאהר	5	9	אלע 3½ שטונ. 1 מאל ביינאכט	3½%	3½%	7%

When it came to feeding their infants, immigrant mothers took their cue from scientific manuals like *Mutter und Kind*.

tables, such as one on the frequency of feeding, further systematized the natural processes of mothering for the Yiddish-speaking mother-to-be. "This little book," wrote one grateful reader, "is worth its weight in gold, because of the potential good within its covers."

Information on the taboo topic of birth control was also readily available, thanks to Max Maisel's Grand Street Press of Literature and Knowledge, a publishing company known for its progressive politics. Maisel issued, among many other works, Yiddish translations of Margaret Sanger's *What Every Mother Should Know*, and its companion, *What Every Girl Should Know*. Dubbed by one detractor, *"What No Girl Should Know,"* this controversial text contained seventy-one pages of information on sexuality and "voluntary motherhood." *Unser Gezund*, "a Jewish monthly for enlightenment in health questions" published by Ben Zion Liber, another radical social and health reformer, also carried news of the birth-control movement and of Sanger's tribulations with the law. "Forget not, dear friends, that Sanger's cause is our cause," he exhorted, urging his readers to reject "*die alte minhagim*," the old ways, in favor of contraceptive freedom. In addition, Liber published *The Truth About Sexuality*, an illustrated pamphlet that dealt with "sexual problems from an individual and Socialist perspective."

Strange as it may seem, resourceful citizens intent on learning more about contraception could also obtain information by attending the Yiddish theater, always a reliable barometer of contemporary issues. In July 1916, shortly before Sanger was imprisoned on charges of violating the Comstock Act, Harry Kalmanowitz's play *Birth Control or Race Suicide*, premiered at New York's National Roof Garden Theater. A melodrama in four acts, it featured music by Friedsell, a popular composer of the period, and dramatized the politics of birth control within an immediately recognizable Jewish domestic context. (Children under sixteen were not admitted.) Months later and miles away, S. Grossman's play *A Woman's Duty in Birth Control*, another four-act production on the popular issue, made its debut at a Yiddish theater in Chicago.

Whether watching a play about birth control, attending health-care lectures, or consulting Mayerson's *Mutter und Kind*, Jewish immigrant women displayed much openness to modern notions and norms of child care, childbirth, and birth control. As a group, they demonstrated a collective willingness to adopt new forms of reproductive behavior, rejecting a "tangled jungle of popular superstitions, old wives' remedies and horse-block advice" in favor of alternative sources of authority: physicians and girlfriends. "I found my doctors through a neighbor," recalled one Jewish woman whose two children were born in the 1920s. "I was friends with her, I was a young woman, she was a young woman . . . we always talked about these things."

Changes in birthing practices reflect this adaptability. At the turn of the century, most births took place at home, where midwives like Bobba Hannah presided. With her bonnet, knitted capelet, and spotless apron, the Lithuanian-born midwife was a familiar figure among Pittsburgh's small immigrant Jewish population, for whom she delivered over 3,500 registered births. "All the children called her 'Bobba,' " reminisced one longtime friend.

"They knew that she had 'brought' them." On the Lower East Side, midwives were also much in demand: according to the *Jewish Daily Forward*, which in 1902 profiled their activities, they were "busier than doctors." That midwives usually charged far less for their services enhanced their appeal. In 1902, for instance, a midwife's fee ran between five and ten dollars, while a doctor's rarely fell below fifteen. Social taboos rooted in gender as well as economic considerations shaped this preference. The female presence of Bobba Hannah and other midwives reassured and comforted birthing mothers who were often embarrassed to be seen and touched by an outsider—especially a man. Immigrant women customarily relied on midwives rather than physicians, explained social reformer Grace Abbott in her 1915 study of "the midwife problem" in Chicago, "not only because she is cheaper than a doctor, but because the woman prefers a midwife to a doctor who is a man."

Equally mistrustful of hospitals as of doctors, Jewish women at first hesitated to make use of them. When, in 1906, the Jewish Maternity Hospital at 270 East Broadway first opened its doors, it encountered formidable resistance from women inclined to associate public medical facilities with death and dying. "Never before had Jewish mothers resorted to hospitals to usher their newborn babies into the world," the *American Hebrew* explained. "No decent woman goes to a hospital to give birth" was the condemnatory slogan of the East Side. Instead, they preferred to give birth at home, where amulets and printed sheets of cabbalistic inscriptions known as *Shir ha-Ma'alot* decorated the walls of the maternity room and family and close friends hovered reassuringly nearby. But within a few years, as both the quality of hospital care improved and public confidence deepened, the overwhelming majority of Jewish women elected to have their babies in a facility like the Jewish Maternity Hospital. When Jewish birthing practices are compared with those of Italian, German, and Slavic immigrant women in America, for instance, Jewish women had dramatically more hospital than traditional home births. As early as 1908, 86 percent of registered Italian births, 68 percent of German, and 74 percent of Slavic ones were home births; among "Russians," a commonly used code for Jews, the figure was only 25 percent. "Expectant mothers from all over greater New York clamor for admission," noted a proud supporter of the Jewish Maternity Hospital as it prepared in 1926 to break ground for an even larger facility on upper Fifth Avenue. "Today there is hardly an expectant mother on the East Side or in Harlem who does not apply for admission."

That many maternity facilities were modern, up-to-date, and operated under Jewish communal auspices surely added to their appeal. The birthing mother "will not be obliged to break the Dietary Laws . . . and will be treated as though she were surrounded by her own kith and kin," explained the 1892 Annual Report of the Jewish Maternity Hospital of Philadelphia, one of the nation's oldest. "She is brought into an atmosphere of cleanliness, of refinement, of quiet, calm and peace, such as her life has never perhaps known before." Ensuring tranquillity as well as a healthy birth, Jewish maternity hospitals also labored to instruct the new mother in all sorts of extranatal matters. "From the day they register," Dr. Nathan Ratnoff observed of the hospital's clientele, "they become our protegées. At the hospital they are given instruction as to how to take care of themselves. . . . After confinement they are still our wards. Their wants are still supplied.

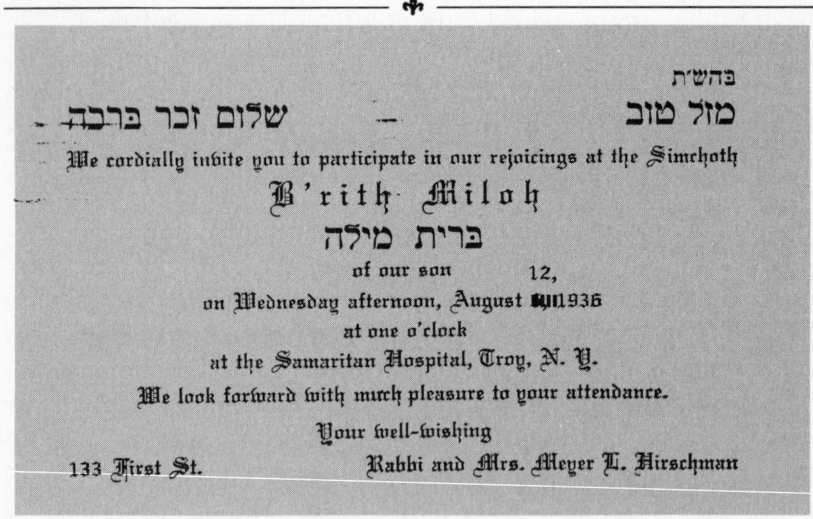

בהש"ת

מזל טוב — שלום זכר בּרבה

We cordially invite you to participate in our rejoicings at the Simchoth

B'rith Miloh

בּרית מילה

of our son 12,

on Wednesday afternoon, August [illegible]1936

at one o'clock

at the Samaritan Hospital, Troy, N. Y.

We look forward with much pleasure to your attendance.

Your well-wishing

133 First St. Rabbi and Mrs. Meyer L. Hirschman

A growing number of American Jews celebrated the circumcision of their newborn sons in the hospital rather than at home or in the synagogue.

The Albert family, ca. 1909.

They get clothes for the new babies. They get clothes for themselves." When not receiving clothes, mothers also received advice—often in Yiddish—on infant hygiene, fresh air, diet, exercise, and "mental occupation."

Jewish immigrant women and their daughters also took to American notions of the smaller family, reducing, often by half, the number of children they bore: where in the Old World, families commonly included six to eight children, in the New World the acceptable norm was four. "Family limitation is so acutely desired by many that dangerous expedients have been employed," observed social worker Harry Lurie of Chicago's Jewish population. "Women at home will do most anything," confirmed a dismayed reporter. "They will jump from chairs; they will exert themselves, to a great extent. They will take quinine pills; they will take hot applications, hot mustard baths, and what not." Alternative and less strenuous methods of controlling conception soon displaced jumping from chairs. In 1916, Jewish immigrant women lined Brownsville's Amboy Street to await the opening of Margaret Sanger's birth-control clinic. "Everywhere we were received in the friendliest spirit and with surprised expressions of gratefulness and joy," recalled a member of the clinic's staff. "Not once were we rebuffed or our motives misunderstood." A decade later in Chicago, the Jewish Social Service Bureau established coeducational classes in "sex instruction" that drew a substantial audience of husbands and wives. According to a bureau spokesman, those who attended not only learned about contraception but also invigorated their marriages. "The removal of the fear of pregnancy," he related, "has had a therapeutic value in the marital relationship of many of our families."

CONTROLLING FAMILY SIZE was one thing; controlling emotion was quite another. Immigrant Jewish women seemed to enjoy mothering—perhaps too much. They had "a superb store of admonishments, curses, imprecations, explanations, songs and folksayings," explained one student of American Jewish maternal behavior, adding that their "vocabulary of endearments alone could fill a modest sized paperback." To keep the world at bay and away from their children, mothers called on the evil eye, spit three times and placed a red ribbon in the baby's carriage. When not muttering imprecations or warding off evil, many Jewish mothers expressed maternal zeal by running to the doctor at the sound of a child's cough or the sight of a sniffle. "The malnutrition, marasmus and rickets so common among tenement infants is comparatively infrequent among the Jews," Maurice Fishberg pointed out in a study of immigrants and health. "Physicians have attributed this condition to the fact that Jewish mothers take more care of their children. . . . Being always sober (I have never seen a Jewish woman intoxicated) they are in a position constantly to exercise their maternal function with a painstaking diligence and assiduity not common among the poor of other races." Statistics confirm the tangible effects of maternal diligence. As early as the 1890s, Jewish children experienced a remarkably low mortality rate, especially when compared to that of their neighbors: 28.7 deaths per 1,000 live births, as opposed to 76.4 among the Italians and 82.6 among the Bohemians.

Not everyone, though, gave the Jewish mother high marks for her "assiduity" and "passionate assertions" of affection. Eschew "blind and unreasoning love," *Froyen Zhurnal* counseled its readers, calling upon them to discipline their emotions. Don't bring up your children to think that "the entire universe is at their disposal." Stop worrying, cautioned health professionals, criticizing Jewish mothers for displaying a disproportionate degree of anxiety over what their children wore and ate. "The Jewish mother," observed a writer in the *Medical Woman's Journal*, "betray[s] an unusual amount of concern about the problem of feeding her children. . . . She insists that she cannot jeopardize their well being by giving inexpensive cuts of meat, grade B eggs, less than a quart of milk each day or canned vegetables even when the fresh they prefer

Pitching their products to young moms, food manufacturers affirmed the centrality of motherhood.

are out of season and costly. In her mind, there is a relationship between food and health which is not calculated on the basis of scientific findings, but on her association of 'best foods' with expensive foods."

Cultural anthropologists joined with health professionals in voicing grave concern. Injecting culture, biology, and a hint of pathology into the discussion, such authorities as Mark Zborowski and Martha Wolfenstein, members of Margaret Mead's influential Research into Contemporary Cultures project, questioned the Jewish mother's aptitude for child-rearing. Her much-remarked-upon protectiveness, they argued, was not only culturally distinctive but dysfunctional and neurotic, the result of centuries of persecution and tension. In bold strokes, the two anthropologists portrayed the Jewish mother as a woman "known for nagging, quarreling, worrying and hypochondria," a woman given over to drama and emotional martyrdom. "Suffering is the major theme of Mrs. S's life," wrote Wolfenstein of one Jewish immigrant mother. "Every encounter, fraught as it is with intense emotion, assumes a dramatic quality."

Landmarks in the field of cultural anthropology, these intriguing and malleable "hypotheses" soon took on a life of their own. Extrapolating from Mrs. S's idiosyncrasies to immigrant Jewish mothers as a whole, and drawing almost exclusively on the selectivities of memory, Zborowski and Wolfenstein mistook a specific cultural moment for a millennial tradition. In so doing, they defined the emotionally extravagant and overprotective Jewish mother as a timeless cultural *type*, enshrining her within the American popular imagination.

A STEADY SOURCE of affection as well as expertise, the modern American mother was also responsible for elevating the moral and educational tone of her family. Scheduling music lessons and arranging occasional trips to museums and weekly visits to church, she cultivated in her children an appreciation for life's nobler, more transcendant values. Jewish women went a step further, insisting that a "Jewish mother's *prime* function is to safeguard her home and to make it Jewish." In fact, by the 1920s, as the physical demands of acculturation lessened, the prescribed Jewish version of the good mother had more to do with tradition than with good health. Mother's classes, that staple of maternal training, now instructed the Jewish woman on how to transform her home, that erstwhile laboratory, into a "classroom in Judaism," thus enabling her to assume the "great and noble responsibility" for her family's ritual attentiveness and Jewish cultural identity. In his Newark home, Philip Roth recalls, it was his mother "who was the repository of our family past, the historian of our childhood and growing up and, as I now realized, it was she around whose quietly efficient presence the family had continued to adhere." Much the same could be said of thousands of Jewish households throughout the country. "The Jewish mother," explained a Minnesotan Jewish parent, "has a double responsibility. . . . She must not only raise good American children but also good and loyal Jewish children. . . . Her tasks naturally are more arduous and difficult than the ordinary mother's."

Belief in the Jewish mother's "double responsibility" presumed that it was up to her, and her alone, to transmit and inculcate Jewish values (however variously defined) in her children. "Modern Judaism in remodeling the synagogue, the school and the home," explained Rabbi Kaufmann Kohler, "placed new obligations, duties and responsibilities upon the Jewish daughter, mother and wife." Elaborating further, Kohler's colleague Rabbi Israel Levinthal allowed as how "we need woman to do the work of female and male. She alone can save Judaism." Increasingly, acts of cultural transmission were linked to and conceived of as a maternal matter in which fathers played a secondary and largely ceremonial role. "The religious training of my children," one male parent openly acknowledged, "is entirely in the hands

Modern American Jewish society expected mothers to tend to the Jewish education of their sons and daughters.

of my wife." Jeannette Miriam Goldberg of Jefferson, Texas, couldn't have agreed more. "Woman is the aboriginal God-appointed educator, and it is her responsibility and moral duty to rear her children in a religious atmosphere."

In preparation for assuming this expanded cultural role, Jewish mothers sought advice from experts. Eschewing "folk-fancies and superstitions," they turned to the authors of manuals and guidebooks in search of information on the "ABC of Jewishness." Explicitly didactic, and eager to make literate Jews of its female readers, American Jewish advice literature defined and interpreted Jewish customs in a sophisticated, twentieth-century idiom. "Our men are so driven by the struggle for existence that the duty of leading the children in the proper path falls to woman's share," observed Rabbi Abraham E. Hirschowitz. The rabbi went on to wonder whether "the Jewish daughters of today [are] ready to undertake this task." To smooth the way, he published *The Religious Duties of the Daughters of Israel*. Hirschowitz's slender volume contained a wealth of practical information, including the procedure for koshering meat, prayers for one's wedding day, and a "short form" of the grace after meals. Deborah M. Melamed's *The Three Pillars*, a book for the "training, practice and teaching of the Jewish woman," filled a similar need. With its lucid expositions of Jewish lore and law, this "brief but warm-hearted" text enjoyed considerable vogue throughout the late 1920s and 1930s as a popular engagement and wedding gift; some circles even touted the book as an appropriate Chanukah present for young girls thanks to its ability to explain in lively detail "what a Jewish woman ought to know." Miriam Isaacs and Trude Weiss Rosmarin's *What Every Jewish Woman Should Know* (1941) brought an unabashedly highbrow approach to the field. Geared explicitly toward the "intelligent Jewish woman," a phrase that appears on nearly every one of its ninety-six pages, this text applied contemporary notions of discipline, decor, cuisine, and women's culture to American Jewish life. "The position of responsible leadership the Jewish woman occupies in the Jewish community *makes it imperative* for her to be well prepared for her task," the authors state time and again, urging their readers to apply themselves diligently to the systematic study of Jewish culture and tradition.

Jewish women also sought advice from one another. The Iowa,

Nebraska, Kansas, and Missouri branches of the National Federation of Temple Sisterhoods, for example, sponsored a "symposium" on "The Needs of the Jewish Child" and "The Obligations of the Parent"; and the female members of Philadelphia's Har Zion Temple "prepared themselves for understanding what their children study in [Hebrew] school" by forming a "Mother's Class." In New York, an interdenominational group of Jewish women—the *American Hebrew* called them "feminine Paul Reveres"—banded together in 1926 to form Ivriah, an organization dedicated to disseminating Jewish education. Insisting that "the way to make the home Jewish is to make the mother Jewish," Ivriah's 1,500 members met regularly in small groups in one another's homes to study and discuss the Bible and Jewish history and literature. Jewish women's study groups even took to the airwaves with local radio broadcasts on such topics as "The Relation of the Jewish Mother upon the Spiritual Life of Her Young Child" and "The Modern Means of Preserving the Jewish Atmosphere for the Child."

ONCE A YEAR, Jewish mothers and their families, like Americans everywhere, took time out from their everyday routine to celebrate motherhood. Despite repeated claims that "we need no Mother's Day to remind us of the place of Jewish women; we Jews have Mother's Day every day," American Jewry found the American analogue hard to resist. First conceived in 1908 by Anna Jarvis, a Methodist schoolteacher, as a church-based memorial to her recently deceased mother, Mother's Day spread quickly throughout America. Within a few short years, it had become a national holiday, a secularized and civic celebration of maternal love and sacrifice. By 1919, thanks to the participation of America's burgeoning flower industry, the occasion had blossomed into America's leading "floral holiday." Attentive to the rhythms of the secular calendar and eager to demonstrate the consonance between Jewish and American notions of maternity, American Jews also marked the day. They held special prayer services in the synagogue on the Sunday of Mother's Day, sponsored "mother-daughter collations" and mounted "mass celebrations" in Jewish community centers.

The Jewish Welfare Board published a thirty-page booklet on ways to commemorate the special day, noting that "our members should find in this holiday a special significance because of the part the Jewish mother plays in Jewish home life and which she has played in Jewish history." Its suggestions ranged from reading portions of Grace Aguilar's "The Martyr Mother" and singing "Mother O' Mine" or the Yiddish "A Brivele der Mamen," to festooning both the lectern and the assembled guests with white carnations. "It is the floral emblem of mother love embodying

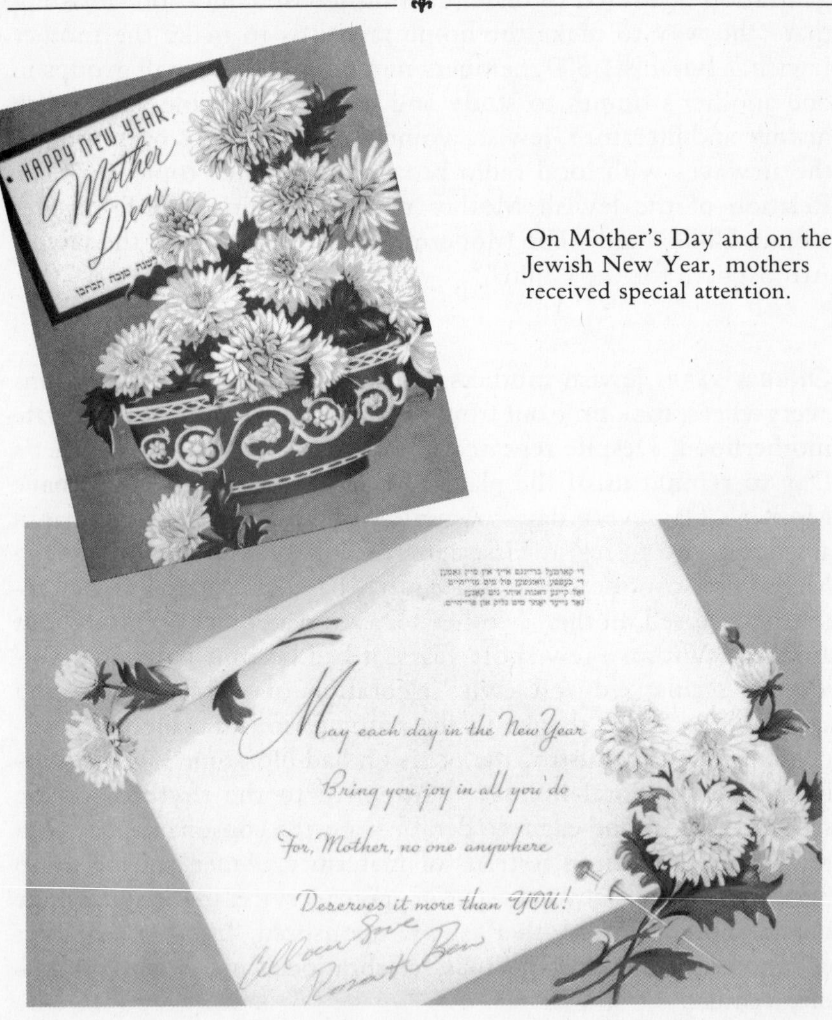

On Mother's Day and on the Jewish New Year, mothers received special attention.

sweetness, purity and endurance," the Welfare Board explained. In Sioux City, Congregation Shaare Zion invented its own salute to motherhood by creating an annual "Mother's Night Service," which was held on the Friday night preceding Mother's Day. As the choir intoned *Ayshet chayil* ("Women of Valor," a traditional paean to Jewish womanhood), the daughter of one of the congregation's mothers ascended the podium to deliver an emotional speech. "I speak on behalf of all daughters in appreciation of all Mothers," stated Lucille Mushkin in her 1937 address. "I tremble at the enormity of the task. . . . Tonight we loudly yell, 'Mother, we love you, as ever, Mother you are a darling.' " Other synagogues, like Temple of Aaron in St. Paul, Minnesota, created a Sunday-morning service noteworthy for its ceremonial presentation of a flower to each mother.

Froyen Zhurnal went even a step further in its embrace of Mother's Day. In a remarkable instance of cultural synthesis, one that highlights the affinity between received wisdom and modern canons of behavior, the Yiddish women's magazine proposed that the Jewish festival of Shavuoth be redefined as the Jewish mother's festival par excellence. By wedding an invented tradition, that of Mother's Day, to an established one that harked back to the Bible, the paper suggested that Jewish women could transform the ancient festival, which commemorated not only the giving of the Ten Commandments but, more to the point, the story of Ruth and Naomi, into a celebration of maternity and womanhood. But that was not all. *Froyen Zhurnal* went even further in its embrace of syncretism by claiming Mother's Day as a Jewish invention. It is fine to celebrate the American Mother's Day, the monthly affirmed, but wouldn't it be more appropriate to celebrate the Jewish version? "Bring flowers into the synagogue, for Shavuoth is Mother's Day . . . the very *first Mother's Day ever proclaimed!*"

MUCH LIKE THEIR MOTHERS, Jewish children, too, found themselves the objects of intense public scrutiny and the beneficiaries of a steadily increasing array of publications, playthings, and programs designed to assist them "to become better boys and girls but also better Jews and Jewesses." *Helpful Thoughts*, an illustrated magazine for the Jewish family and school, was among the earliest examples of an American Jewish juvenile literature. The creation of Julia Richman and Rebekah Kohut, among others, it debuted in 1896 "in order that Jewish children can have a little paper all their own." Through lighthearted games, songs, puzzles, capsule biographies of "Great American Jews and Jewesses," polite chatter, and moralizing short stories and fables such as "Why Doggies Have Cold Noses," a story of Noah and his Ark, the monthly advanced the "sacred cause of Judaism" among the young. Living up to its name, *Helpful Thoughts* also featured an advice-wielding grandmother who, in a monthly column, "Foundation Stones of Judaism," urged her youthful readers to augment their lives with various theologically oriented activities. Before going off to sleep, "why not try an experiment and say goodnight to God," she gently suggested in one characteristic entry. "Say whatever is in your heart. Try this for a few nights and then write to me again to tell me whether the night seems so dark." Grandmother's advice seemed to win her a loyal readership for, within a few short months of the magazine's debut, she proudly boasted that "today my grandchildren number nearly three thousand." That potential subscribers also received such journalistic inducements as a bicycle, a dictionary, and "a splendid Kodak" no doubt enhanced the magazine's popularity as well, swelling the number of its readers.

Although *Helpful Thoughts* lasted for only a decade, it spawned several literary descendants, among them *The Jewish Child*, a biweekly publication of the Jewish Education Commission of Chicago. Equally determined "to make Jewishness attractive and to hold our young within the tradition," it too featured games, drawings, puzzles, songs, and inspirational articles on current events and noted Jewish personalities. Unlike *Helpful Thoughts*, though, whose language and orientation reflected an exclusively youthful clientele, *The Jewish Child*, despite its name, pitched much of its material to an adult audience: Jewish mothers. Urging them to see to it that their children received a Jewish education and that mirthful holidays like Purim were enthusiastically celebrated, the magazine editorialized: "We know that all about us there is a non-Jewish environment. . . . We know that even against the preaching and teaching of our Rabbis and teachers the child will be sent to violin school and the dancing lesson on Saturday. We know—and you know—that all this is done. And yet no one will ever doubt

Page Twelve WOMEN'S LEAGUE OUTLOOK

A NEW BOOK FOR A JEWISH CHILD

BRING THE HOLIDAYS AND FESTIVALS TO YOUR CHILDREN IN AN ATTRACTIVE WAY

THE ADVENTURES OF K'TONTON

A Little Jewish Tom Thumb
BY SADIE ROSE WEILERSTEIN
With Illustrations by Jeanette Berkowitz

When you were very young didn't you imagine yourself playing with a Jewish Christopher Robin? Well here he is ready to step out and become your child's closest playmate book friend.

HERE ARE SOME OF THE ADVENTURES:

HOW K'TONTON TOOK A RIDE ON A CHOPPING KNIFE AND WISHED HE HAD'NT.

HOW K'TONTON PLANNED A PALACE FOR THE SABBATH QUEEN.

HOW K'TONTON TOOK A RIDE ON A RUNAWAY TRENDEI.

WHAT HAPPENED TO K'TONTON ON HIS LAG B'OMER PICNIC.

HOW K'TONTON MASQUERADED ON PURIM.

K'tonton with Flag

"How K'Tonton Masqueraded on Purim"

He skipped over the big brass mortar and stood on tip toe to see over the top. But the mortar was too high.

"I'll have to climb the hill," said K'tonton. He ran up the side of a sack of flour that was lying close by. Now he could see deep down in the mortar. He could see the poppy see at the bottom and the powder leaning ainst the side.

"That's a good slide," d K'tonton. He loved sliding down thi "I'll slide down and take a taste of th poppy seed —Mother wouldn't mind just a little taste."

He reached out and swung his legs over the top of the pestle. A thought popped into his head. "I must stop before I reach the bottom. I might get stuck." But he couldn't stop. He was going too fast. Blimp! He was in poppy seed up to his waist . . .

K'tonton Climbing into Mortar

Price $1.65

As the edition will soon be exhausted we advise you to send your order now, accompanied by check, in advance of publication

to

The Women's League of the United Synagogue of America
N. E. Corner 122nd Street and Broadway
New York City

K'tonton on the Chopping Knife

One of the most popular Jewish children's books of the interwar years, *The Adventures of K'tonton* thrilled young Jewish readers.

that in the innermost soul of every Jewish mother there is that yearning to forge another link in the chain of Jewish continuity."

Jewish children's books constituted yet another link in that chain. From Emily Solis-Cohen's delicately ornamented English translation of Judah Steinberg's Hebrew tales, *The Breakfast of the Birds* (1917), and Gerald Friedlander's *The Jewish Fairy Book* (1920), to the spirited mishaps of K'tonton, "a little Jewish Tom Thumb," created in 1930 by Rochester author Sadie Rose Weilerstein, an American Jewish children's literature gradually took root. Playful, lighthearted, and adventuresome, it reinforced the ties between domesticity and Jewish identity in an entertaining and "attractive way." Where K'tonton, much like his American counterpart, was forever getting into trouble, tumbling into a giant-sized mortar or being carried off by a runaway dreidel, the American Jewish boys and girls featured in *What Danny Did* and *Good Shabbos* and *Happy Chanuko* inhabited far more ordinary surroundings. Through simple text and bold illustrations, these popular books showed recognizably American, familiar faces setting the *shabbos* table or playing dreidel, thus once again normalizing Jewish ritual expression. "It is the sort of book about which children will say, 'Why that's me!' " observed the *United Synagogue Recorder* in 1929, referring to *What Danny Did*. "Nothing interests them more than to find themselves talked about in a book. Mothers in reading

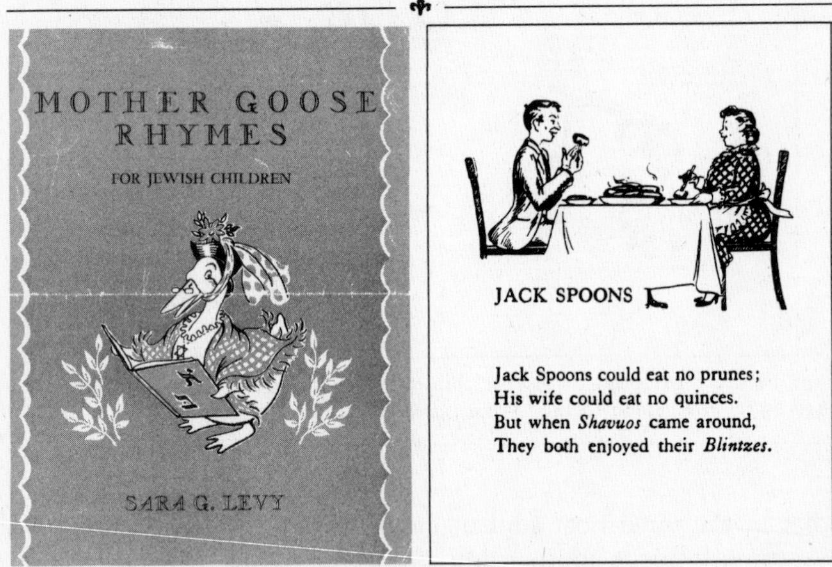

Mother Goose Rhymes for Jewish Children set the familiar nursery rhymes to a distinctly Jewish rhythm.

Brightly illustrated primers like Y. Kaminestski's *In der Haym und in der Shuel* (At Home and at School) introduced American Jewish children to the Yiddish language.

these stories to their children need only substitute their own child's name for Danny's and the illusion will be complete." Concomitantly, a sprightly Yiddish children's literature flourished, especially in the form of primers. Teaching the mechanics of Yiddish literacy, texts such as *Der Yidisher Lehrer* (1915) and *Mayn Alef-beys* (1937) drew on bold graphics and nursery rhymes to enable American-born youngsters to identify Yiddish words and such basic linguistic concepts as reading from right to left. "Like their English counterparts, American Yiddish primers make playful use of language," writes Jeffrey Shandler, an authority on the genre, pointing out that, for all its playfulness, "ideology pervades the Yiddish primer." Through its combination of pictures, words, and contexts, which often situated fathers in a sweatshop or families at a protest march, the primer introduced children to both the linguistic and the cultural meanings of *yidishkayt*.

Those interested in playing at being Jewish, not just reading about it, also had much to draw on as more traditionally minded parents took to heart communal exhortations to make holiday and

Sabbath celebrations lively and entertaining. K'tonton's creator, Sadie Rose Weilerstein, for example, invented a "special Shabbos box" housing toys to be used only on the Jewish Sabbath. "There's always something fresh to interest the child," she wrote, "and you ward off that deadening, all too familiar complaint, 'You can't *do* anything on Shabbos.' " Another parent, Mrs. S. J. Winer, hosted a party every Saturday afternoon for her children and their friends. "Every child loves a party. Let the Sabbath be connected in the child's mind with joy and happiness."

Toy manufacturers supplemented parental efforts by producing a line of Jewish-oriented novelties that ran the gamut from pinwheels and board games—including a Judaized version of Monopoly in which exotic Holy Land sites replaced Boardwalk and Park Place—to cookie cutters shaped like a Jewish star and oversized dreidels like the four-foot-tall "Maccabee." A creation of the Dra-Dell Corporation of Bergen, New Jersey, this object "expresses a true holiday spirit in the home. . . . It becomes a center for holiday gift-giving. It decorates and illuminates the

The "Maccabee" was designed as an alternative to the Christmas tree.

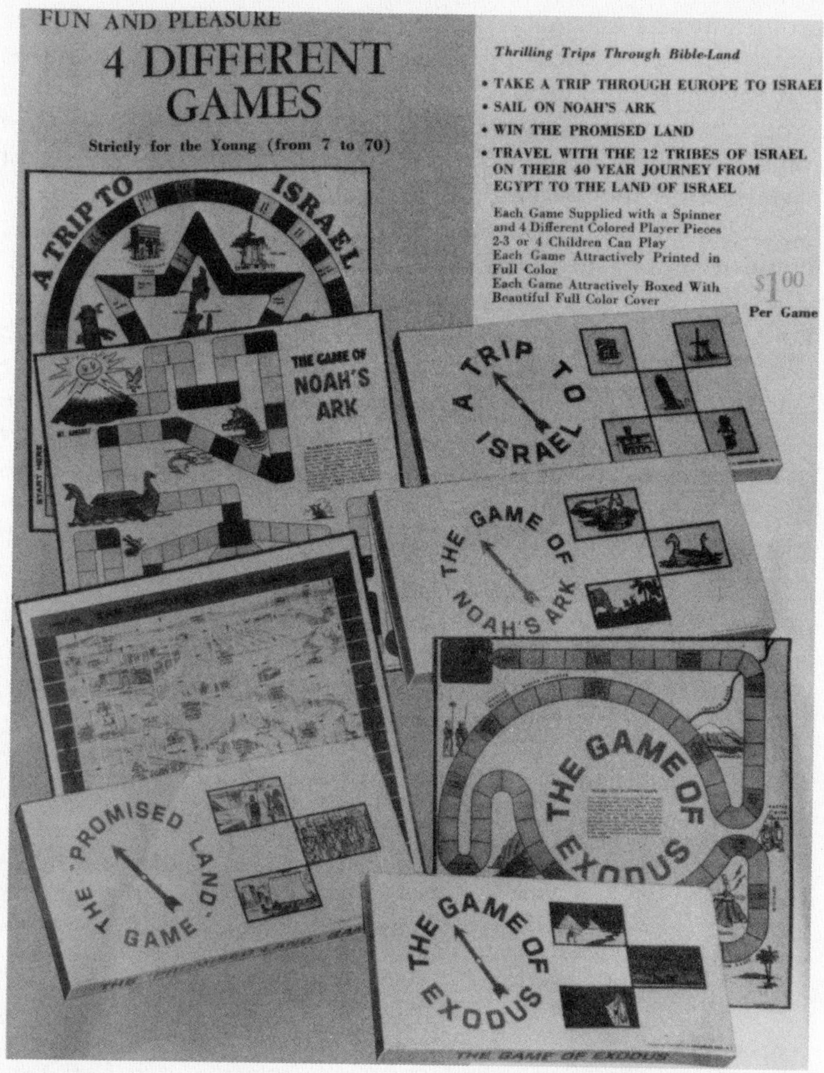

Board games with Jewish themes vied with Candy Land and Monopoly for the affections—and consumer loyalty—of American Jewish youngsters.

season of proud tradition [and] joy . . . and is a fine addition to the Chanukah atmosphere.'' Playful, lighthearted, and ephemeral, these objects reflected the needs of a new community of Jewish consumers: children. "A year ago, it was impossible to secure a fitting gift as a Chanukah present for a Jewish child," noted one mother in 1937. "Now fortunately, there are new books, games and Palestinian products."

At Chanukah, and throughout the year, youthful consumers could also have their pick of over a hundred different varieties of Bible Dolls, "the doll with a purpose." Sheathed in "authentic" Biblical garb and eleven inches tall, the Sarah, Rebekah, and, for those more ecumenically inclined, the Mary Magdalene doll, presented latter-day audiences with the opportunity to learn more about the Bible and the origins of Judaism; the Hadassah Lady doll or the K'tonton version, in turn, appealed to a more contemporary-minded audience. "People spend a lot of money on buying Teddy Bears, Golliwogs and Donald Ducks but they never think of buying a doll that can do more than just amuse children for a short period," remarked the Bible Doll's creator, Diana Forman, who in the 1940s formed the Philadelphia-based Bible Doll

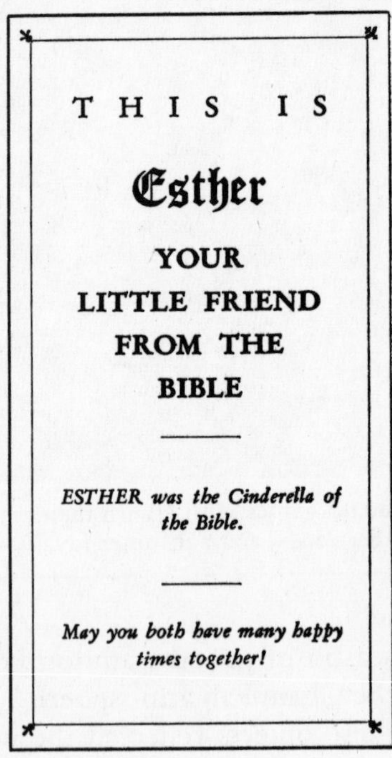
THIS IS

Esther

YOUR
LITTLE FRIEND
FROM THE
BIBLE

ESTHER was the Cinderella of the Bible.

May you both have many happy times together!

Though dressed in the costumes of the ancient Near East, the Bible Dolls were intended to have a more universal appeal.

Diana Forman, the "Bible Doll Lady," and a few of her Bible Dolls.

Company of America. "A Bible Doll is not just a religious doll —it tells a story and at the same time teaches the child to be good." Under Mrs. Forman's watchful eye, the company grew steadily. Gimbels and Wanamaker's carried its products while RKO Films profiled "The Bible Doll Lady." "The Doll creates happy experiences and memories which are associated with the Bible," Mrs. Forman explained in one of her many public appearances, insisting that "the first contacts of the child with The Book must be happy ones." True to her intentions, Forman went to great lengths to dress her dolls in historically accurate costumes, claiming to have read over four thousand books on the ancient Near East and to have visited dozens of archaeological sites. "Seeing the doll . . . holding it, undressing and dressing it, the child learns through other senses besides that of hearing. . . . The world of the Bible becomes the child's own."

More than just a (well-dressed) doll, each play figure came packaged with a small vial of Holy Land soil, some "shining, twinkling ornaments," and its own didactic fable, or "storyette." "Be Proud of your Bible Doll," read the accompanying label copy. "It is the only one of its kind in the world! It is the Original, World-Famous Creation of the Bible Doll Lady, Mrs. Max L. Forman. . . . It is the great character-doll of our generation—the outstanding doll on the market today." So outstanding was its commercial appeal that in the mid-1950s the Madame Alexander Doll Company, one of America's leading doll manufacturers, purchased the Bible Doll Company outright. It then transformed one of its own popular products—the eight-inch, fully jointed "Wendy" doll—into the very model of a Biblical matriarch.

PLAYING WITH DOLLS or musical instruments, the Jewish child was a busy child. "You ought to hear her play the violin and count up to a hundred in Hebrew," suggested Julia's mother to a reporter for the *American Jewish Chronicle*. "She is a little pale, just now, but she is a very clever little girl." What with public school in the morning and Hebrew school or Yiddish *shule* in the afternoon, piano and violin lessons, dance class and basketball practice, the Jewish child's day was fragmented into seemingly unintegrated components, or what one expert called "subjective disharmony."

The heavily Americanized names typically borne by the children of immigrant parentage tellingly reflected this disharmony. In formulations so popular they characterized an entire generation, Judith became Julia, Bezalel became Burton, Isaac became Irving, and Rebecca turned into Riviana. "Matching" the Hebrew or Yiddish name of an ancestor with its latter-day linguistic equivalent, some parents, like those of the improbably named Delmore Schwartz, sought onomastic inspiration in the amenities of modern urban life. According to his biographer, the poet enjoyed speculating about the origins of his name. "Sometimes he would insist he had been named after a delicatessen across the street from the house where he was born, sometimes that his mother had been fond of an actor who was named Frank Delmore. In still other versions, the name was taken from a Tammany Hall club, a Pullman railroad car, or a Riverside Drive apartment house."

Julia's and Burton's parents, mindful of the risks of acculturation on the one hand and the attendant costs of alienation on the other, were eager for guidance. How to balance and "adjust" their child's life, given the absence of a "one hundred percent Jewish environment"? How to raise American-born children to feel a "life-long attachment" to the Jewish people and its culture? In search of answers, parents (or, more precisely, mothers) turned to the local Jewish community center and the synagogue, where they took classes in "Jewish Music and Games for the Child" and "Jewish Arts and Crafts for the Child," or heard such major cultural personalities as Rabbi Mordecai M. Kaplan lecture on "What to Aim at in the Upbringing of the Jewish Child."

Many also sought direction in the discipline of child study, which by the 1920s had come into its own. Under the direction of specially trained "parent educators," they gathered together to review what one such expert called "the principles of child psychology based on specific Jewish problems." A further extension of the scientific approach to maternity, child study appealed largely to women who enthusiastically consumed and acted upon the advice of outsiders. "They flocked to child study classes because they satisfied a felt want," observed Rabbi A. H. Fedder. "The women in my congregation learned more about Jewish History and Jewish values through a course in child psychology than through the Pulpit or cultural meetings."

Child-study sessions confirmed what many Jewish mothers and fathers had suspected: that American Jewish childhood constituted an inherently problematic phenomenon, and a seemingly novel one at that. "In fact, our time has not only brought the emancipation of the woman but the emancipation of the child as well," observed one concerned Jewish parent in 1932. "Never before has there been such a cleavage between the life of the last generation and what seems to be in store for the new." Well into the 1940s, a loosely bound coalition of clergy, psychologists, child-study experts, and parents sounded the same refrain: the seemingly unprecedented dilemma of rearing a fully integrated, or, as the lingo would have it, a "fully adjusted," American Jewish child.

At its most basic, this concern reflected the modern American notion that childhood constituted, in and of itself, a special phase with a singular psychological dynamic. At the same time, though, it reflected a particularly Jewish set of anxieties. "Now you might ask what is the difference in the Jewish child from any other child. Why has a Jewish child a *distinct psychological problem*?" psychologist Israel Strauss observed in a speech before an audience of anxious Jewish parents. As he saw it, the Jewish child was highly susceptible to neuroses, a condition for which the elders were to blame. Asserting that "the fault is not with the child but with the parents," Strauss cautioned his listeners not to subject their young charges to undue pressure by complaining about low marks or demanding excellence in all things lest, as a group, Jewish children fall prey to psychological disorders. "Jewish parents are very anxious to have their child excel," he went on to explain. "They frequently carry their desires to excess in having the child exhibit his powers—whether he can play the Rachmaninoff Prelude at ten; whether she can dance as Isadora Duncan at eleven. . . . They little realize that in this tendency to exhibitionism they are creating in that child an overstimulation which can have deleterious and injurious effects later on."

Others, like Rabbi Jacob Kohn, the author of *Modern Problems of Jewish Parents*, laid the problems of the American Jewish child squarely at the feet of his or her father. Heavily influenced by the "new fatherhood" of the interwar years in which men were encouraged to find meaning at home and within the domestic rituals of child-rearing, the spiritual leader roundly criticized the Jewish father for his inattentiveness. By Kohn's lights, the decision to leave matters of faith and ritual entirely in the hands of one's wife was sure to have a chilling effect on the next generation, especially in the case of boys. "If the concerns of Judaism and Jewish life are of little moment to the father, if the synagogue is only the goal of the mother's pilgrimage and the father regularly keeps his distance, the son will draw the conclusion that religion in general and Judaism in particular are feminine accomplishments and Jewish life a feminine indulgence." Fathers, faced with the prospect of an entirely feminized Judaism, were exhorted to assume their rightful place in the pews of the synagogue and at the Sabbath dinner table. Only their active participation, it seemed, could secure the future of Judaism and with it, the cultural loyalty of all of its children. "If the man does not live as to illustrate the fact that Judaism and Jewish morality have a virile strength and make peculiar appeal to the manhood of the Jewish people, not even the women of Israel will long be interested in it."

Getting the father to attend synagogue was one problem; attracting the child was yet another. "Of all the problems that beset the American Rabbi of today," admitted Rabbi Israel Goldfarb in 1927, "none is more complex and more difficult to solve than that of how to bring the child closer to the Synagogue, how to arouse his interest in things Jewish and how to secure his permanent attachment to the ideals of our faith and people." Clubs, junior congregations, and choirs—or what one rabbi called "laboratories of character-building and soul-molding"—were urgently needed to counter and offset the amount of time the Jewish child spent in a non-Jewish atmosphere and to shore up his or her relationship to the Jewish body politic.

Of all the "special devices" recommended by the rabbi, none, however, figured as prominently and promisingly as bar mitzvah and confirmation. Happily, these twin rites of passage coincided with the "apex of the child's impressionable period," providing an unparalleled opportunity for communal bonding and religious expression. "Wise parents," urged one authority on Jewish parenting, "will make of the Bar Mitzvah or Confirmation a lever with which to raise the whole moral and spiritual level of the child's life. No other occasion is so important or so auspicious." Or quite so much fun, either, as American Jews were quick to discover.

3
Red-Letter Days

"THE YEAR OF THE BAR MITZVAHS—then we were alive! . . . I remember the whole time as a continued bazaar of parties and celebrations. Every other week, one after the other, I saw my friends rise up and declare their manhood while the rest of us sat in the back rows, apart from the relatives, giggling, throwing spitballs, with our *yamelkas* slanted on the side of our heads at a sharp angle. So then, we were admitted."

Within the American Jewish community, bar mitzvah and other Jewish ceremonies marking admission to adulthood not only stirred profound emotion but also enjoyed unprecedented popularity. Twentieth-century American Jews, otherwise lax, and relaxed, when it came to ritual, wholeheartedly celebrated this particular rite of passage, endowing it with greater cultural and religious significance than it had ever possessed before. "The bar mitzvah has become the most important milestone in a Jew's life in America," noted one student of American Jewish mores in 1949. "Never in our millennial history was so much importance attached to this ceremony." Added another, "No ceremony is more universally observed than the Bar Mitzvah ceremony, or more eagerly looked forward to by the child." Coming-of-age rituals like bar mitzvah, confirmation, and bat mitzvah reflected as well as shaped a tangle of relationships between tradition and invention, gender and the marketplace, religious authority and grassroots behavior. As much about Jewish notions of adolescence as about Torah, the popularity of these ritual events also points to the revitalizing effects of consumption on religious behavior. Mirth-filled celebrations, they attest to the inventiveness of the folk and the vitality of invented traditions.

By far the oldest of the three practices, "with the advantage of antiquity," bar mitzvah dates back to the thirteenth century and marks the moment when a young man, at age thirteen, is called to the Torah for the first time; in many communities, it was also customary to call upon the youthful celebrant to display his erudition by making a speech. Traditionally more of a "punctuation mark" than a watershed, the Old World bar mitzvah publicly marked a change in status, the attainment of religious maturity, and the assumption of additional religious responsibilities, such as the daily donning of tallis and tefillin—prayer shawl and phylacteries. But as far as transitional moments go, the bar mitzvah was rather a quiet, humble one, bereft of fanfare. Accompanied by a modest repast, the event, as a Jew from Rumania recalled, "was no ceremony at all. . . . There was a little herring, some *kichel*, and a few drops of *schnapps*, for the immediate family, and *that was that.*"

In the process of transplantation from the Old World to the New, this rite of passage assumed a brand-new centrality and immediacy. Taking a meaningful, if restrained, religious event and transforming it into something larger than (and quite different from) the sum of its parts, immigrant Jews invented the "fancified" bar mitzvah. The newfound American success of the bar mitzvah, one of the few Jewish ritual practices to grow rather than diminish in popularity, caught the attention of contemporary observers. Not all of them, though, were buoyed by its transformation. Moses Weinberger, for one, was actually displeased, rather than heartened, by the attention his coreligionists lavished on it. Writing in 1887, he fiercely criticized the way the bar mitzvah had developed into "the greatest of holidays among our Jewish brethren." Long on show and short on religiosity, the American bar mitzvah, by Weinberger's standards, epitomized American Jewry's wrongheadedness and spiritual vacuity. "As for phylacteries, there isn't much business in them in America," he noted by way of explanation. "I see, dear reader, that you look upon me with amazement. A question forms on your lips: Don't boys by the hundred celebrate every year their *bnei mitsvah*, amid enormous splendor and great show? Yet you say there isn't much business in phylac-

Jewish greeting cards often depicted the bar mitzvah boy donning a new pair of phylacteries as his father happily looked on.

teries. . . . Let me implore you, my friend, to leave me alone. Don't press me to reveal everything at once. Go away!"

Weinberger's comments had little effect (except on historians). They failed to cool the American Jewish public's exuberant, if short-lived, embrace of ritual. If anything, bar mitzvah celebrations gained in liveliness. In the years prior to World War I, dozens, if not hundreds, of Jewish preparatory schools dedicated to teaching a curriculum of "aleph-bais to bar mitzvah" dotted Jewish immigrant neighborhoods, reflecting a kind of collective pre–bar mitzvah frenzy. At these "bar mitzvah factories" where the instruction consisted of little more than the basics of Jewish history, the *aleph-bays*, and the "procedure of public prayers," the bar mitzvah boy speedily learned all he needed to know so that he could dispatch his ritual obligations with a minimum of discomfort and embarrassment. It was the rare student who took away anything more than a set of memorized *pesukim*, or Biblical passages, a fleeting familiarity with Hebrew, and a few ancient tunes. From a pedagogical perspective, as Weinberger and others were wont to point out, these schools failed miserably in furthering cultural literacy or fostering a deep and abiding appreciation for *yidishkayt*. But then, that wasn't their objective. Rather, their task was to facilitate ritual performance. Very much a folk creation, the "bar mitzvah factory" was designed, and successfully served, as a democratic and highly accessible purveyor of ritual know-how and etiquette, especially for an otherwise indifferent audience. "The American Jew observes zealously the custom of celebrating Bar Mitzvah," explained an instructor of bar mitzvah boys. "Even those who are not greatly concerned that their children shall receive a good Jewish education, *are very particular* in the matter of Bar Mitzvah."

In tending to these particularities, many instructors relied heavily on published compilations of ready-to-declaim "bar mitzvah drashas," of which there was a great and growing number. With five hundred and seventeen "choice speeches, toasts and sermons in Yiddish, English and Ancient Hebrew," Professor G. Selikovitsch's *The Jewish-American Orator*, a 1908 publication, headed the list. Diligent students could also consult Solomon Uselaner's much-touted *Jewish Laws and Customs or Bar-Mitzvah Guide*, Rabbi Simon Glazer's *The Bar Mitzvah Pulpit: Sermonettes for Bar-Mitzvah Boys and Others*, Jacob Katz's *Attaining Jewish Manhood*, and Reuben Kaufman's tantalizing *Bar Mitzvah Manual: The Piano Method*. Compilations like these filled the vacuum left by the clergy but, more to the point, they also helped to codify and standardize many of the folk practices associated with bar mitzvah, the most prominent—and nerve-racking—of which was the "bar mitzvah speech." Welcomed by instructors, bar mitzvah boys, and parents alike, bar mitzvah manuals reduced the strain of adolescent speech-making to a series of easily memorized formulas. Speeches typically opened with a greeting to one's parents, teachers, and honored guests and closed with the tendering of "heartfelt thanks" to the president of the *shul* and other luminaries. In between, the texts ranged from such concepts as "This is the most important day of my life. For Today I am admitted into the Brotherhood of Israel," to the more succinct "Today I am a man," to "From today on I am a perfect Jew. . . . With this holy baggage I stand now in this holy place as the happiest candidate in the beginning of my career as a Jew." A handwritten version of one such bar mitzvah text, now reposing in the archives of the YIVO Institute for Jewish Research, reflects the degree of parental anticipation and involvement in a son's "red-letter day." At the bottom of the four dense Yiddish paragraphs that constitute the speech, the bar mitzvah boy's mother appended the following message: "Dear Rabbi. I didn't correct anything. I just copied the speech but wrote some words the way we express ourselves; instead of *u* we say *i; o*, we say *u*. It is very hard for Sidney to pronounce the Jewish words. We talk to him Jewish but he answers in English. Do you think he could pronounce it right?" Responds the rabbi reassuringly: "He will be alright."

American bar mitzvah protocol, which also placed much stock in looking right, inspired the creation of the "bar mitzvah suit." A secular counterpart of the tallis and tefillin the bar mitzvah boy was ritually enjoined to wear, this garment represented the first full-length, grown-up piece of modern clothing he ever owned. Much like the family furniture, it was intended to last forever, and for many former bar mitzvah boys it actually did, or at least until they got married. Men's furnishings stores like Joe & Paul's, "the aristocrats of clothing" on New York's Lower East Side, and the Stanton Street Clothiers Association routinely catered to the bar mitzvah trade, furthering the association between secular norms of dressing up and public piety. In print and on the radio, they advertised the virtues of their wide selection of somber serge and gabardine suits. "Never has such outstanding clothing been offered for men and young men who are only satisfied with the best. . . . Never have they been so beautiful, so tasteful. . . . And remember: we aren't dragging you by your sleeve. You get what you want, you buy what you want and you are always handled properly and royally on Stanton Street."

An abundance of studio photographs depicting bar mitzvah boys in manly attire and full ritual regalia communicates something of the importance Jewish families attached to the sartorial imperatives of the day. Clad in his new suit, a man-sized fedora (or oversized yarmulke) perched awkwardly on his head, the bar mitzvah boy was brought to the neighborhood photography studio to have his picture taken in what had rapidly become yet another new convention. Some studios situated their hapless subject within a garden of tropical foliage where he gazed raptly out into the distance. Others favored a more rugged approach and posed the celebrant with one hand resting on his chest and the other holding a Bible aloft. Images abound: boys with hats, boys with yarmulkes, chunky boys, gawky boys, boys that looked more like the members of Spanky's gang than new recruits to the "household of Israel." Studies in awkwardness and yearning, these photographs highlight both the singularity of the occasion and that of the bar mitzvah boy himself, who, when all was said and done, "revel[ed] in the feeling of importance derived from being the central figure of a public celebration."

In addition to adorning the mantelpiece or hugging the wall, photographs of the bar mitzvah boy often decorated the invitation, yet another increasingly popular manifestation of the ritual's fancification. Like bar mitzvah boys themselves, invitations came in all sorts of shapes and sizes. Some tended to be rather earnest and straightforward, with a minimum of ornamental detail. Taking their cue from Alexander Harkavy's *American Letter Writer and Speller* (1902), they dutifully recited the relevant facts. "We request the pleasure of your company at a dinner given in honor of the bar mitzvah of our son, on Saturday, September 7, at 11 a.m., at our residence." Others, especially those dating from the 1920s onward, tended toward the fanciful. These versions featured the face of the bar mitzvah boy flanked by the American flag or, more inventively, were designed in the manner of a Torah scroll, complete with wooden rollers. When unfurled, one panel contained the text of the invitation, another the guest list, and the third a menu. Invitations shaped like Jewish stars or dyed blue and white, the colors of the Jewish flag, also enjoyed wide appeal.

Initially, "at homes" were the most favored and socially acceptable form of reception. Following the Sabbath morning service (and a modest collation), guests would make their way to the celebrant's house for an intimate luncheon. In some circles, it was also customary to hold a private reception on the Sunday afternoon following the bar mitzvah service. In the years prior to World

Treasured mementos, bar mitzvah photographs documented the transition from childhood to manhood.

War I, the *American Hebrew*, and other Anglo-Jewish newspapers like the *Jewish Times* ("the only representative Jewish paper in Maryland and the District of Columbia"), published news of these occasions on their social page, which also featured the relevant details of recent betrothals, marriages, and births. Under the heading "Bar Mitzvahs," the interested reader could learn that Mr. and Mrs. Seamon Danzieger of Fifty-first Street, Borough Park, would be at home from three in the afternoon on December 4, 1910, to celebrate Jerome's bar mitzvah, or that Mr. and Mrs. Herzog of 117th Street would be receiving guests from seven to ten on January 1, 1911, to mark Myron's coming of age.

Beginning in the second decade of this century, or possibly even before, as "stepping out" acquired a newfound respectability among the middle class, catering establishments such as the DeLuxe Palace and Pythagoras Hall, and swell urban hotels like the Schenley and the Warwick, supplanted the home as the venue of choice for the "better class bar mitzvah." More a function of social class and pocketbook than of denomination, the elaborate public party appealed to all segments of the American Jewish population. Eager to demonstrate their newly acquired affluence and sophisticated ease, many American Jews expended considerable effort and money hosting a party, or "affair"—an elastic term that embraced bar mitzvah as well as wedding celebrations. "The main event," recalls Rabbi Stuart Rosenberg, who had come of age in Flatbush during the early 1930s, was not the synagogue service but the party that followed later that evening. His was held at the fashionable Casa del Rey, a Coney Island establishment, replete with a band, lots of guests, much food, and many gifts. "That was part of the new style of American Judaism." Synagogues, too, were quick to capitalize on the emerging popularity of this new style by expanding to make room for handsomely appointed ballrooms, reception areas, lavish lounges, professional kitchens, and their very own caterer. "We will conduct the catering services with dignity and decorum, in keeping with the nature of your institution and in conformity with the rules and regulations of your Board of Trustees and your Building Committee," pledged Kotimsky & Tuchman, New York caterers, to Congregation B'nai Jeshurun, adding that they would also "comply and conform with all dietary laws and rituals" in exchange for the "exclusive catering privilege."

The "bar mitzvah party reception," as one Philadelphia family called it, was a lively occasion filled with festively attired friends and family. Equal parts family reunion and ritual celebration, the party served as a locus for domestic exchange and conviviality, an association which the Yiddish stage and screen furthered. From *Semele's Bar Mitzvah*, a theatrical production of the 1930s, to *Bar Mitzvah*, an operetta composed by Boris Thomashefsky and P. Laskowsky that later became a popular Yiddish film, the event was identified with scenes of nail-biting, teary-eyed family drama, and reconciliation. Although intended (and dramatized) as a family affair, the bar mitzvah's guest list often contained more business associates than intimates; it was not uncommon to find that "the child was utterly unacquainted with nine-tenths of the invited guests." Regardless of status, invited guests were treated to the

American Jews transformed the bar mitzvah of their sons into one of the centerpieces of modern Jewish life.

sight of platoons of waiters scurrying between elaborately bedecked tables and intimidating headwaiters barking orders; in the background a "murmuring orchestra" played the latest American hit tunes as couples danced the lindy, the fox-trot, and, in the years following World War II, the cha-cha and the rumba as well. Known to musicians on the East Coast as "club dates" and on the West as "casuals," bar mitzvahs, along with weddings and other parties, developed into a steady source of income for members of the Jack Lewis or Max Kletter Orchestra—the preferred term for "anything larger than a trio." Novelties such as colored yarmulkes, calligraphed place cards, and party favors were also on hand to dazzle the guests, as were eye-catching ice sculptures of graceful swans and gawky bar mitzvah boys.

Food, not the bar mitzvah boy, generally took center stage. Five- or six-course dinners, much like that served at Leon Alexander's 1928 bash, suggest something of the lengths to which aspiring parents would go to make their son's fête an unforgettable occasion. Guests at this Philadelphia gathering were treated to a seemingly unending array of dishes, from "fruit cup naturelle" and "baked halibut with potatoe parisienne" to "fancy assorted cakes and sherbits" and "caffe noir." In the absence of a ritually prescribed repertoire of bar mitzvah foods, celebrants like Leon Alexander's parents had a wide range of culinary options from which to choose. Restrained only by kashruth (and then not always), the menu reflected a pronounced bias in favor of haute cuisine, or, more to the point, its lexicon of fancy-food words. Typically, bar mitzvah menus offered up hefty portions of such elegant French dishes as "roast young poulet," "salad de fruit," and "Petit-four la Sylvan," a confection named after the bar mitzvah boy himself. Stuffed derma, "dainty knishes," noodle pudding, seltzer and Cel-Ray Tonic, staples of the American Jewish diet or what one caterer called "Jewish niceties," shared pride of place with stuffed squab, asparagus tips, and other delicacies new to the Jewish palate. Elaborate desserts, from "ices fantasie" to cherries jubilee and crêpes suzette, brought the meal to a rousing finish. As one bemused guest noted: "Caterers, restaurants, great angle they got. . . . Anything they can set fire to they charge ten times as much. Set fire to a twenty-cent flapjack, crêpes suzette for two dollars."

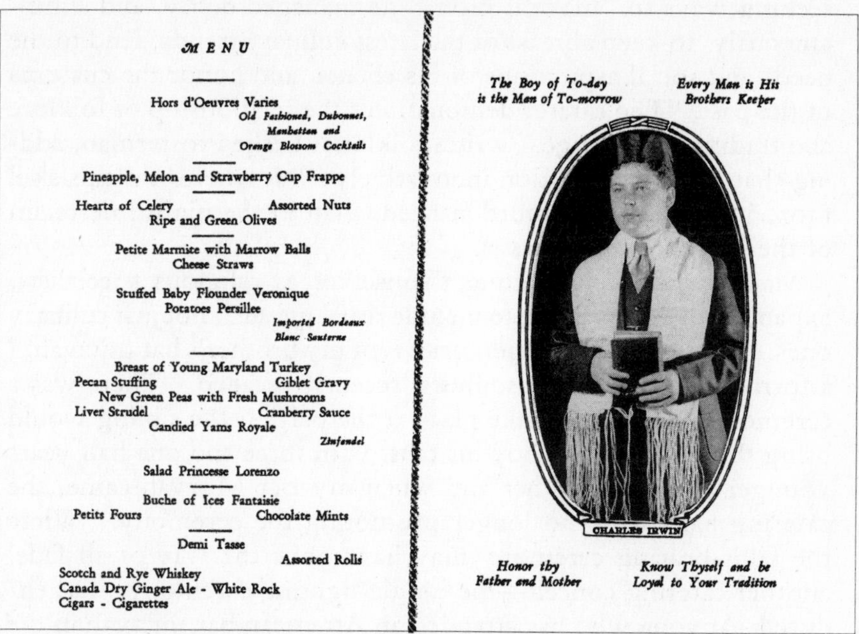

MENU

Hors d'Oeuvres Varies
Old Fashioned, Dubonnet, Manhattan and Orange Blossom Cocktails

Pineapple, Melon and Strawberry Cup Frappe

Hearts of Celery — Assorted Nuts
Ripe and Green Olives

Petite Marmite with Marrow Balls
Cheese Straws

Stuffed Baby Flounder Veronique
Potatoes Persillee
Imported Bordeaux Blanc Sauterne

Breast of Young Maryland Turkey
Pecan Stuffing — Giblet Gravy
New Green Peas with Fresh Mushrooms
Liver Strudel — Cranberry Sauce
Candied Yams Royale
Zinfandel

Salad Princesse Lorenzo

Buche of Ices Fantaisie
Petits Fours — Chocolate Mints

Demi Tasse
Assorted Rolls

Scotch and Rye Whiskey
Canada Dry Ginger Ale - White Rock
Cigars - Cigarettes

The Boy of To-day is the Man of To-morrow

Every Man is His Brothers Keeper

CHARLES IRWIN

Honor thy Father and Mother

Know Thyself and be Loyal to Your Tradition

An abundance of food characterized the American bar mitzvah party.

Behind the scenes, setting fruit aflame and wielding considerable power, lurked the caterer, "Supreme in the Art of Cuisine and Complete Arrangements." With the increasing commercialization of food services and the attendant popularity of dining out, the caterer and restaurateur of the interwar years stepped out of the kitchen and into the limelight. Social choreographer, *chef de maison*, and cultural authority, especially when it came to kashruth, Jewish caterers such as Patrician, Kotimsky & Tuchman, Alexander Brothers, Kaplan's, Knapp Mansions, and Elsie Marvel (the "ultra-fashionable in food and service"), acquired a newfound prominence within the American Jewish community. "The caterers had given the old folkway modern form and variety," observed Herman Wouk in *Marjorie Morningstar*, referring to the traditional practice of a kiddush, or ceremonial repast. "There was a five-hundred-dollar kiddush, a thousand-dollar one and so forth." As the caterer expanded upon time-honored tradition, seeking ways to "make it nicer," he managed deftly, and simultaneously, to keep abreast of the latest culinary trends, tend to the needs and social aspirations of his clients, and honor the customs of the past. "The caterer demonstrates the relationship of folklore and tradition to change," writes folklorist Leslie Prosterman, adding that he "uses tradition innovatively." Nowhere was this skill more in evidence, or more in need, than in the nighttime realm of the bar mitzvah affair.

Many caterers, presenting themselves as religious specialists, expanded their repertoire to include ritual matters, not just culinary ones. "One of my vivid memories is of my brother's bar mitzvah," a former resident of Bensonhurst recently recalled. "There was a ceremony that used to take place at the parties, the sibling would bring the Bar Mitzvah boy his talis. I am three and one half years younger than my brother and when my Bar Mitzvah came, the catering halls were no longer promoting the ceremony." While the tallis-bearing ceremony may have gone the way of all fads, another catering conceit—the candle-lighting ceremony—has endured. Anyone who has attended an American bar mitzvah in the past fifty years is certain to have encountered it. The high point of the evening, this established folk (or catering) ritual rivaled the traditional synagogue service in meaningfulness and emotional intensity. "There is the march, the bringing in of the *Bar Mitzvah* cake, the lighting of the thirteen candles, or of fourteen—one for luck. . . . So much importance is now being attached to this commercial hall ceremonial, that we have heard of cases where it has replaced the synagogue ritual completely," one eyewitness recalled. Invented from whole cloth (or cake), this affecting ritual transformed a widely performed activity—cutting a birthday cake—into a quasi-sacred event. To the strains of some faintly reminiscent Jewish melody (oftentimes the only demonstrably ethnic sound of the evening), the bar mitzvah boy, flanked by his parents, called upon various relatives, one by one, to step forward and light a candle. As the wax from dozens of illuminated tapers dripped down upon the cake, which itself was decorated to resemble a torah scroll or a giant set of tefillin, the names of deceased ancestors were evoked and their lives memorialized.

More enduring and tangible memories came in the form of gifts. In Sam Levenson's classic comic sketch, "The Story of a Bar

No bar mitzvah party was complete without the candle-lighting ritual, an American invention.

Mitzvah Boy," an otherwise indifferent candidate is goaded into preparing his lessons with the constant refrain, "You'll get presents, you'll get presents." That phrase, repeated constantly over a four-month period, sinks deep into the hapless celebrant's unconscious, with the result that he begins his bar mitzvah *drasha* (speech) with the immortal words, "Today I am a fountain pen." Then at the height of fashion as bar mitzvah gifts, fountain pens enjoyed great appeal, as did watches, wallets, cuff links, stocks and bonds, and matching book sets like the *Encyclopaedia Britannica*. "For *This* Bar Mitzvah present," rhapsodized an advertisement for the solidly bound volumes, "your boy will bless you all the years of his life!" While secular items predominated, "gifts of Jewish significance," such as gold-plated plaques of the Ten Commandments, gold-stamped editions of H. P. Mendes's text, *Bar Mitzvah for Boyhood, Youth and Manhood*, and simulated-parchment bar mitzvah certificates designed to resemble diplomas also made "the ideal gift to the Bar mitzvah." Meanwhile, manufacturers and distributors of Judaica invented the novel concept of a "bar mitzvah set" in which tallis and tefillin were sold together as an attractive, conveniently priced package.

Enormously popular with the laity, not to mention the bar mitzvah boy himself, the commercialized bar mitzvah engendered fierce and unrelenting clerical criticism (much of which continues even today). "Some of these parties are unbelievably fantastic and would appeal to our sense of humor by their incongruity, did they not display a tragic spiritual ineptitude," observed Rabbi Jacob Kohn in 1932. From his vantage point, the "fantastic" reception not only overshadowed the sanctity of the bar mitzvah per se but overwhelmed it entirely, a view widely shared by such colleagues as Mordecai M. Kaplan. The Reconstructionist leader, confiding in his diary, went so far as to attribute the "disintegration of Jewish life" to the cocktail parties and "ribald vaudeville acts" so common at bar mitzvahs. Other observers, among them *Commentary*'s Norman Podhoretz, also objected to the "vulgarities and accidental accretions of American Jewish life" like those depicted by Herman Wouk in *Marjorie Morningstar*. "Does the survival of Judaism in America depend on Lowenstein?" he asked, referring to the Morgenstern family's star caterer.

As a cultural metaphor, the fictional Lowenstein effectively em-

Something for Your Bar Mitzvah
To
From
Now that you have reached the goal
Of your Bar Mitzvah Day,
May these wishes
and "remembrance"
Bring some extra joy
your way!

Bar mitzvah gifts, from fountain pens to checks, contributed greatly to the spirit of the occasion.

bodies the bar mitzvah's, and with it, American Jewry's, irrevocable decline, a permanent lowering of standards and sanctity. And yet, where the community's cultural custodians saw only "deterioration," the folk, by contrast, saw color, liveliness, fun, and good-natured sentimentality. Where the elite believed consumption and religious ritual to be two competing and adversarial cultural systems, the folk joined them together, demonstrating in the process that consumerism did not so much destroy religious ritual as revitalize it.

A few rabbis occupied the middle ground. Sympathetic to the allures of consumerism and the aspirations of their congregants, they attempted to channel the sensibility of the folk by diverting it toward more overt forms of Jewish expression. While not opposed to merrymaking or gift-giving, which they believed to be "quite in keeping with child psychology and not out of harmony with the importance of the event in the child's life," they sought to situate these practices within a Jewish context. "If parents

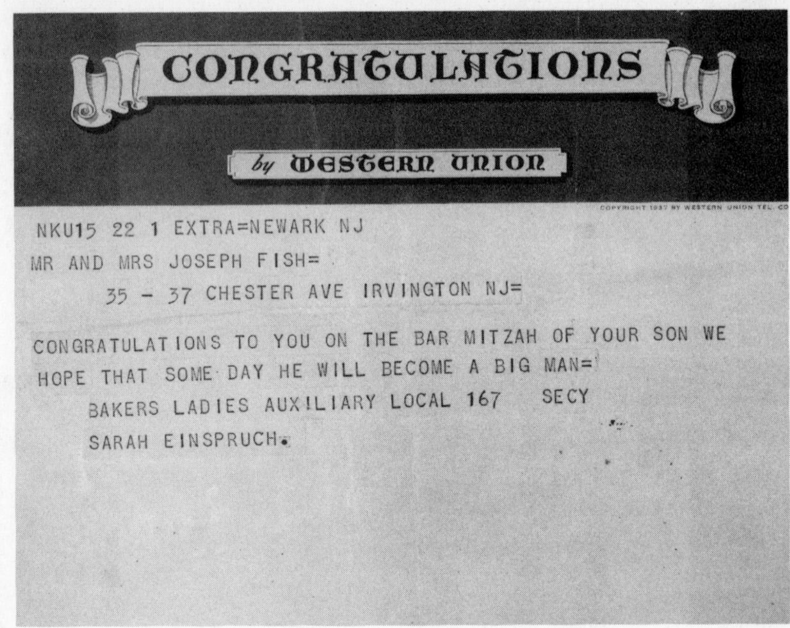

CONGRATULATIONS

by WESTERN UNION

COPYRIGHT 1937 BY WESTERN UNION TEL. CO

NKU15 22 1 EXTRA=NEWARK NJ

MR AND MRS JOSEPH FISH=

35 - 37 CHESTER AVE IRVINGTON NJ=

CONGRATULATIONS TO YOU ON THE BAR MITZAH OF YOUR SON WE HOPE THAT SOME DAY HE WILL BECOME A BIG MAN=

BAKERS LADIES AUXILIARY LOCAL 167 SECY

SARAH EINSPRUCH.

Friends and business associates often turned to Western Union to express their good wishes.

permit themselves to be guided by good taste, a number of these gifts will have Jewish significance," one of their number asserted, recommending Jewish art objects and subscriptions to Jewish magazines rather than fountain pens, wristwatches, or money. The clergy also hoped to influence parents regarding "the proper uses of a party," by which they meant "bringing out the *Jewishness* of such an affair" through the recitation of the appropriate food blessings, singing Jewish songs, and dancing Jewish folk dances. The United Synagogue, for its part, published a series of guidelines relating to receptions held on the premises of the synagogue, urging celebrants to see to it that nothing disrupted the sanctity of the Sabbath or violated the tenets of kashruth. "Every effort should be made to insure that all functions of the Synagogue should be essentially spiritual in quality and purpose. Accordingly entertainment or music which tends to mar the sanctity of the Sabbath Day shall be considered improper. Instrumental music for social dancing shall not be employed on the Sabbath."

In each instance, whether upholding the sanctity of the Sabbath or the legitimacy of an overtly Jewish gift, delicately balancing the aesthetic, ritual, and cultural concerns of the bar mitzvah took priority over the vernacular aspirations of the folk. After all, cautioned Jacob Kohn, "these celebrations should not be too elaborate lest the child forget that the important thing is Judaism and not his own immature self."

MUCH TO THE DISMAY of many Reform clergy, bar mitzvah's popularity gradually made inroads within their own circles as well, threatening to displace the hegemony of confirmation, a nineteenth-century creation of the "founding fathers" of Reform Judaism. "Let it be said unequivocally," stated Reverend Roland B. Gittelsohn in 1946, "that in the United States today Bar Mitzvo is definitely an accepted part of the pattern of Reform Judaism." By the time Gittelsohn published "Bar Mitzvo Practice in Liberal Jewish Congregations," confirmation had itself become a longstanding Reform tradition, but that was not always the case. An invention of the early 1800s intended to replace bar mitzvah, which Reformers considered to be outdated and unduly "oriental," confirmation made its way to the United States in the 1840s, making its debut at New York's Anshe Chesed. By that time, amid growing interest in women's issues, confirmation came to symbolize a neutral, nongendered vision of religious equality and performance. As the *Rabbi's Manual*, the official handbook of the Central Conference of American Rabbis, explained years later, in 1928, Reform Judaism substituted confirmation for bar mitzvah "seeking to equalize woman with man in all religious obligations."

Like first communion, with which it was often compared, confirmation marked the religious maturity of fourteen-to-sixteen-year-old girls and boys by means of a dignified, stately public ceremony. Designed to coincide with the flexible springtime festival of Shavuoth, the occasion featured "troops" of girls clad in white dresses and boys in dark suits fervently proclaiming their allegiance to Judaism, America, and their parents. As the choir sang assorted hymns, confirmants (or confirmands—the terms were interchangeable) marched dramatically down the sanctuary's center aisle and up the steps to the pulpit, where they stopped to

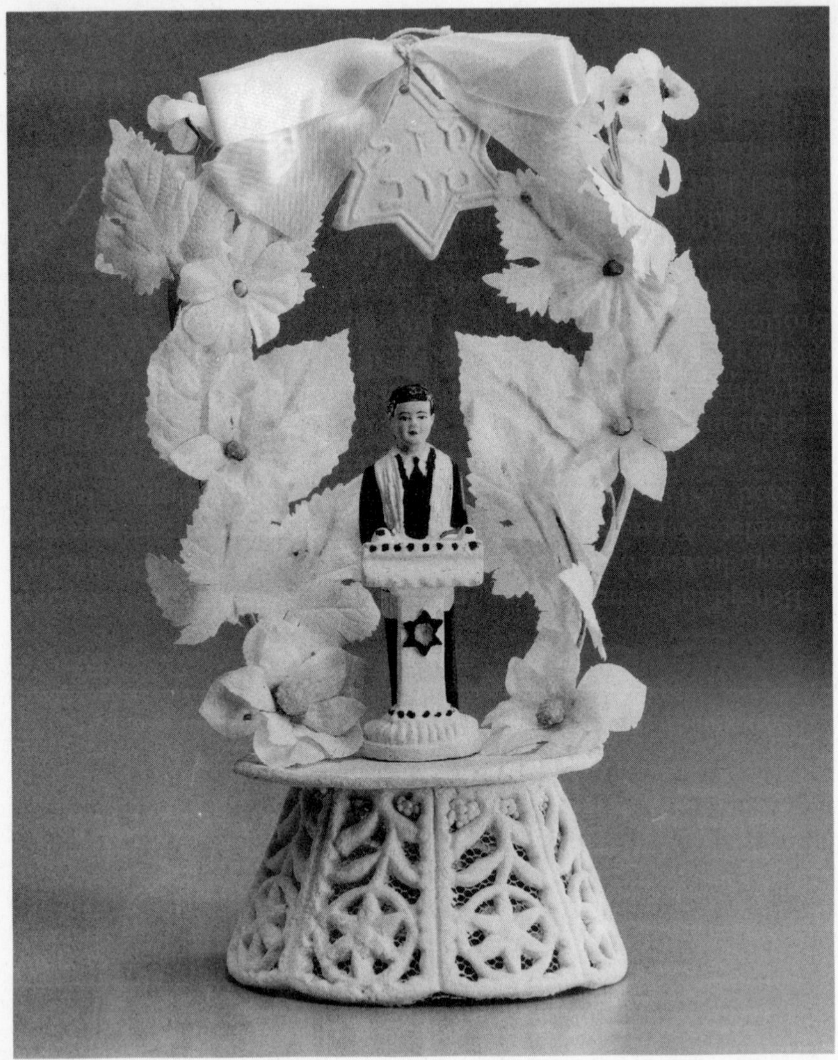

Commercially manufactured bar mitzvah cake decorations provided the finishing touch.

lay individual "floral offerings" before taking their seats. An integral aspect of the confirmation ritual, these horticultural displays reflected the high seriousness with which late-nineteenth-century culture regarded its flora. Esteemed as much for their expressiveness as their ornamentality, flowers carried numerous meanings: daisies stood for honor and pansies for wisdom, while "variegated roses" symbolized reverence. In drawing on the so-called language of flowers, confirmation imaginatively extended its meaning to include religiosity as well.

Once on the stage banked with daisies and pansies and perfumed with the aroma of roses, confirmants were given the opportunity "to shine in public" either by reading a poetic passage or by holding forth on such profundities as "The Meaning of Prayer." Similar in some respects to a high school graduation, the Jewish ceremony marked the completion of a period of study during which Jewish teenagers deepened their understanding of and commitment to Jewish tradition. "From the day of my Confirmation," explained Louis Rosenberg of Texas, a first-prize winner in the *American Hebrew*'s Annual Confirmation Essay Contest, "my Judaism is not

Confirmation's popularity spread throughout the nation, even as far as South Dakota, where, in 1925, a small group of confirmants and their rabbi proudly posed for this portrait.

merely a faith of my fathers; a belief handed down to me from my parents. From the day of my Confirmation, my Judaism is my choice from among all faiths. . . . After eight years of this instruction, Shavuoth, our Spring festival, has harvested this flower—my Judaism."

Slow to take hold, confirmation gradually developed into a permanent feature of the Reform Jewish calendar. "The confirmation has become in recent years a much more general ceremony than it formerly was," observed Moses Cohen at a 1902 gathering of the Council of Jewish Women. "For many years it was rather an exceptional thing. . . . It is now becoming the goal almost of all those who start, at least, to attend Jewish School." Little more than a decade later, the *American Hebrew* observed that confirmation had "grown to be one of the most popular ceremonials of Jewish life in America." Once entrenched, the rite of passage generated its own commercial momentum. "All over the land jewelers and florists and booksellers and dressmakers and tailors are preparing for their annual harvest; Confirmation Day is at hand." Confirmants and their parents engaged in a flurry of ritually inspired activity: taking elocution lessons, selecting a dress, reckoning with the caterer, exchanging gifts. "For weeks in advance, the girls are excitedly busy shopping for the pretty white dresses; the parents of the boys and girls are kept busy 'hearing' their speeches or recitations until every member of the family can repeat it verbatim; and the sisterhood is busy planning the floral decorations for the pulpit, which on that day becomes a veritable bower of peonies, dogwood and palms." A popular topic of discussion on the street and in the stores, confirmation also made its way into print as the subject of Marion Spitzer's controversial 1924 novel *Who Would Be Free*, a fictional portrait of the American Jewish bourgeoisie. "Dr. Hirschberg wanted the girls to pick fresh daisies," noted the book's protagonist, Eleanor Hoffman, as she prepared for her confirmation. "But the girls rebelled. They had too much to do the day before confirmation to waste time going down to the country. There were last minute fittings and hair curlings and manicures to be attended to. And arrangements for parties, and dozens of other unavoidable things."

In life, as in literature, the drama of confirmation threatened to overwhelm its solemnity. "Time to Cry 'Halt,' " cried Rabbi Horace

J. Wolf, a young Reform rabbi from Rochester, New York, in 1915, insisting that confirmation "exchange its acquired character of a spectacle for its natural character of an impressive religious rite." For starters, he suggested abolishing or, at the very least, muting the excessive formalism of the ceremony, in which the rabbi plays "the dual role of drill-master and elocutionist; he is teaching the Confirmants how to march and countermarch, when to advance and when to retreat, how to keep step and at what angle to hold the head." Calling for simplicity, the Rochester cleric urged his colleagues to do away with the performance aspects of the ceremony and "free the day from its parade and artificiality." Apart from the service's studied formality, what most upset the young rabbi was the competitive spirit it unleashed. Competition over dresses, gifts, and fancy parties sullied the event's sanctity, resulting in snobbery, ill-will, and heavy hearts; material things transformed the observance into little more than an excuse for "loot-gathering" and "trophy-gathering excursions." "Would it be possible to limit the amount of money which the girls of the Class should spend on their Confirmation dresses," Rabbi Wolf wondered, pointing to a number of high schools that had recently instituted a similar policy with regard to graduation attire. "This year, in my judgment, offers a splendid opportunity to remove the monetary frills and the financial outlay usually attending Confirmation."

Wolf was by no means the first to sound the alarm over what another colleague called the "shams, the pomp, the luxuries, the extravagancies" of confirmation, nor was he the first to suggest initiating sumptuary laws. For years, his fellow clergy had gone over much the same territory, urging parents to cultivate modesty, sobriety, and fiscal restraint. "It is wrong when children and mamas and papas too, think so much about the clothes. The girls wear white dresses because it means they are pure and innocent," admonished Reverend Edward N. Calisch as early as 1898, adding, "It is only a sign and we must not think so much of the sign that we forget that for which it stands." Gift-giving also gave rise to criticism, some of it rather subtle and aimed at children. Throughout the 1890s, Jewish juvenile literature contained numerous stories gently condemning the commercial excesses of confirmation and hinting broadly that would-be confirmants curb their appetite for material bounty. Julia Richman's "Ada's Confirmation Presents" typified the genre. Her tale unfolds against the background of a group of young girls eagerly discussing their hoped-for gifts. "I don't know what I'll get, but when my sister was confirmed two years ago, she got seventy-six presents, and I'll have more than that," says one young girl, as others gleefully describe the diamond ring and piano they hope to receive. But Ada, the story's heroine, resists the temptations to which her friends fall prey and forgoes a promised trip to Europe so that she can help a poorer classmate celebrate her confirmation. Richman and her colleagues felt so strongly about the appeal of this fable that reprised, barely reworked versions, with or without Ada, appeared time and again.

On other occasions, critics came down harder and more directly on the "promiscuous giving of presents" by seeking either to channel the practice in a more appropriate direction or to curb it entirely. If you must give a gift, why not make it a prayerbook or a Bible, suggested the National Federation of Temple Sisterhoods, having in mind perhaps the "flexible white leatherette" confirmation Bible produced by Bloch Publishers. With gilt edges, lightweight paper, and a special page for inscriptions, this volume constituted "an appropriate gift for Confirmation, Bar Mitzvah, Birth-Day etc." Better still, they implored, why not refrain from giving gifts altogether and instead make a charitable contribution to the local synagogue, the American Jewish Relief Fund, the United Way, or the Hebrew Union College Scholarship Fund? Similarly minded individuals throughout the country sought to eliminate not just gift-giving but elaborate private receptions as well, praying that a more modest public gathering tended by the Temple would take root. For over two years, Rabbi Hyman Enelow lobbied for a public reception at his Louisville, Kentucky, congregation but to no avail; his congregants balked at the idea. Also unavailing were efforts to require participants to wear "simple dresses." "I don't know of a Rabbi who has failed to urge it; the Rabbis will have to continue to urge it every year," admitted one chastened partisan, momentarily conceding defeat. In the absence of legal authority, America's clergy could only persuade, cajole, coax, and exhort their coreligionists to mend their ways; with no formal backing, attempts to enforce sumptuary laws ran aground.

It would take at least another generation before these recom-

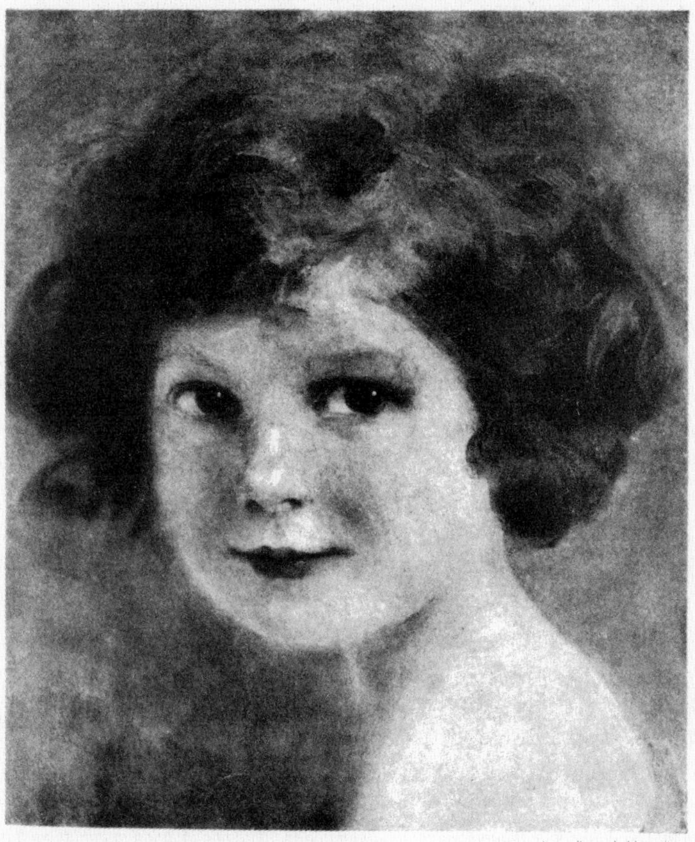

Once a year, this popular Jewish weekly devoted an entire issue to confirmation events nationwide.

mendations took hold. Surveying confirmation practices in 1931, Rabbi Louis I. Egelson of Ohio happily reported that efforts to encourage "simplicity in dress" and a public reception had borne fruit. With the exception of ten rabbis who still encountered congregational resistance, the "balance seemed to have succeeded . . . in keeping Confirmation on a high plane." In lieu of fancy dresses, many celebrants now wore ceremonial robes, white for the girls and black for the boys, and participated in a public reception. Efforts to discourage gift-giving, though, didn't fare quite as well: seventeen rabbis admitted they "make a great effort but with little success." Undeterred, Egelson concluded that "the externals of dress, of receptions, of gifts are not too greatly accentuated as to make them insuperable obstacles detracting from the sanctity or sincerity of the ceremony."

In the interim, Wolf and his colleagues persisted in decrying the "abuses of Confirmation," which they catalogued at length in the pages of the *American Hebrew*. For nearly a month in the spring of 1915, the paper carried a lively discussion of contemporary confirmation practices, revealing in the process considerable divergence of opinion within the ranks of the Reform clergy. While many were inclined to agree with Wolf, a surprisingly large number did not and instead seemed to tolerate their congregants' foibles. Rabbi Joseph Silverman, a senior member of the Reform establishment, for instance, suggested that the zealous young rabbi was guilty of throwing out the baby along with the bathwater. The "evils" Wolf complains about are no more a part of confirmation than they are of bar mitzvah or marriage, Silverman related. "The evils are the result of an unrefined taste. . . . The mistake that Rabbi Wolf makes is to berate Confirmation instead of the people who are untutored and ill-bred." Others, like Rabbi Enelow, saw nothing wrong with exchanging presents. "I don't believe in robbing life of its little joys in the name of an all-compelling and all-saving sociology. Gifts have their right and place in life."

After three weeks, the debate ran its course. Although the participants were unable to reach a consensus on the fine points of either performance or presentation, most agreed in the end that excessive competitiveness and showmanship were not in keeping with the spirit of the day. Indeed they were opposed not only to

"Jewish conceptions but to fundamental principles of American democracy." The clergy then called on the parents to initiate the "needed reforms" and to remain vigilant lest commercialism continue to run amok. Such vigilance was critical not just to the success of confirmation but to that of American Jewish life as a whole. As the *American Hebrew* put it in an elaborately worded editorial: "If 'All Israel are brethren,' as the noble motto runs, the little Israelite cousins should not show in any way their divergencies of social position. Every effort should be made to keep the canker of social display, which is the ruin of modern life, out of the religious sphere. Jews were never, hitherto, snobs, and it would be lamentable that the unfortunate tendencies toward snobbery in modern life should penetrate within the walls of the temple."

Throughout the entire exchange, no one questioned whether confirmation had actually lived up to its stated purposes. Did it equalize gender roles within the community? Enlarge the parameters of women's participation? Retain the interest and further the loyalty of the young to Judaism? None of these questions was ever posed, not by participants in the debate nor, for that matter, by those participating in subsequent rabbinical conferences. Take, for instance, the fuss over appropriate "confirmation costume." No one stopped to consider the ways in which that discussion, with its exclusive references to dresses and jewelry, reinforced existing stereotypes of the frivolous female or, worse still, mocked the highminded rhetoric about "the equality of girls." The irony of the situation entirely escaped collective attention.

Instead, it took a female confirmant, none other than Henrietta Szold, the future founder of Hadassah, to raise the possibility that, when it came to equality, confirmation had fallen short of its stated goals. Although her views on confirmation were fueled more by general concern over the Jewish education of girls than by the specific "evils" of confirmation, they cast some light on how an informed female laity might have viewed Reform Judaism in general and confirmation in particular in the years prior to World War I. "Jewish reform never presented so attractive an aspect as when it put the Jewish education of women upon its banner," Szold wrote. Unfortunately, though, it failed to realize its promise. "The confirmation service for girls, in which the principle embodied itself, and which was to be the flower of female education, fell far short of fulfilling the hopes it had aroused. . . . It was sterile, ineffectual. It failed to stimulate the Jewish development of women, because it was an assertion of the principle of Jewish education in theory only. In practice it put up with a minimum of superficial knowledge and an apology for Jewish training."

Whatever one makes of Szold's scathing assessment of Reform Judaism, she touched on a fundamental truth: the increasingly gendered one-sidedness of confirmation. For all the talk about "raising woman to man's level," confirmation had the opposite effect: it segregated them. Just as religion in general tended to be widely derided as a "feminine indulgence," confirmation came to be seen as "girls' business," drawing first a plurality, then the overwhelming majority, of its celebrants from among the fairer sex. Gender lines hardened in the years following the Great War, when a growing number of Reform congregations—some 92 percent, according to one study—reintroduced the male bar mitzvah ceremony.

Back by popular demand, bar mitzvah spoke to, and apparently satisfied, a somewhat inchoate search for identity and connectedness among Reform Jews of the interwar years, an increasing number of whom had East European antecedents. Unlike confirmation, an elite formulation that had been imposed on Reform Jews from on high, bar mitzvah enjoyed what was perceived to be an unimpeachable authenticity and historicity. Stretching back centuries and deeply rooted in history, bar mitzvah constituted an enduring link with the past; moreover, it seemed to provide an organically Jewish opportunity for sentimental expression and ritual celebration. Modern-day Jews also found attractive bar mitzvah's emphasis on the individual rather than the group, and applauded the way it provided "a psychological and emotional experience such as the group Confirmation ceremony cannot equal."

The laity's expressed affection for bar mitzvah confounded many within the Reform movement who, believing the ritual to be a dead letter, found it hard to fathom how modern-day Jews could prefer it to a self-consciously modern rite like confirmation. How to explain its resurgence? Its hold on Reform parents? Bar mitzvah's surprising vitality threw them into a quandary. Though reluctant to displease their congregants, who, in a radical departure from the norm, seemed to favor more, not less, ceremonial involvement, Reform's ideologues were equally reluctant to dispense with confirmation, one of their most cherished traditions. That confirmation was designed initially to supersede and nullify bar mitzvah complicated matters still further. Could the movement accommodate both rituals without compromising confirmation's historical and ceremonial integrity or reducing it to an "inglorious anticlimax"?

These and other questions generated a whirlwind of data-gathering and editorializing. Within the space of ten years, between the 1930s and the 1940s, the denomination commissioned a number of different inquiries into such topics as "Confirmation Practices" and "Bar Mitzvo in the Metropolitan Area" to ascertain the strength of bar mitzvah and the corresponding weakness of confirmation. Well into the 1950s, interest in the issue ran high as rabbis continued, with unusual intensity, to exchange views in the pages of professional rabbinical publications like the *CCAR Journal* (the official organ of the Central Conference of American Rabbis). What makes the debate so interesting is the way in which it reveals the complex interplay between tradition and innovation, elite and folk culture. At stake was not simply the perceived superiority of one rite over another but rather the religious authority of the rabbinate, the inviolability of denominational tradition and its time-honored commitment to equality between the sexes—in a word: Reform's soul.

If the statistics compiled by the Committee on Confirmation Practices are correct, a majority of Reform rabbis either tolerated or enthusiastically promoted the reinstatement of bar mitzvah. Some instituted the practice because it seemed to betoken a desire for increased ceremonial life among their congregants, surely a welcome development; others were heartened by the way bar mitzvah brought people into the synagogue on a Saturday morning, filling pews that would otherwise remain empty and contributing to a lively Sabbath spirit; as the rabbi of one Brooklyn congregation put it, bar mitzvah "has rescued the Saturday morning service from disappearing altogether." Then there were those who felt that inasmuch as the whole ceremony "takes less than ten minutes," there was simply no reason not to institute it.

Not all Reform clergy, though, were moved by the imperatives of tradition or brevity; a goodly and articulate number adamantly refused to suspend their traditional animus. Instead, they questioned the warm welcome extended by their colleagues, intimating that religious opportunism, or "salesmanship," lay behind it. They also questioned the motivations of the folk, whose interest in bar mitzvah seemed to them to be mawkish, sappy, inappropriate—a "nostalgic indulgence." Some even hinted that class differences within the movement accounted for its popularity. "Bar Mitzvah in a Reform synagogue is, at best, little more than a concession to the sentimentality of parents who may have joined a liberal-progressive congregation, but who still are maudlin about this medieval puberty rite," asserted Albert Goldstein, referring not too subtly to the increasingly heterogeneous character of the Reform laity. Others frowned on bar mitzvah because of the frivolity it engendered, a critique, one supporter of bar mitzvah quickly pointed out, that "might be levelled with at least equal strength against Confirmation."

Diehard traditionalists remained particularly disturbed by the prospect that reinstating bar mitzvah would upset the gender norms on which Reform prided itself and which distinguished it from the other denominations. Retaining bar mitzvah in addition to confirmation, they feared, would be "an atavistic restoration of religious discrimination between the sexes" that could only result in contemporary forms of religious inequality, including but not restricted to the feminization of confirmation. After all, were bar mitzvah to take root, boys could choose from among several new options: they could mark their bar mitzvah and then, if they or their parents were so inclined, continue with confirmation; alternatively, they could conclude their Jewish education at age thirteen. In any case, the religious experience of Reform girls would move along a different track. Unlike the boys, the girls had no ritual alternatives: either they completed a course of study culminating in confirmation or they were left with nothing. Bat mitzvah, then in its infancy, was little known and less understood and though, in time, it took hold within Reform circles, it never posed as serious a threat as its male counterpart. (After all, there was little reason for Reform Jews to import bat mitzvah, an emergent ritual for girls that was popular in Conservative circles, when in confirmation they had their own, well-established equivalent.

Much to the consternation of the American rabbinate, confirmation increasingly attracted more young women than young men.

As Rabbi Israel Bettan put it years later when comparing the bat mitzvah with its male counterpart, "two figments do not make one fact.")

Granting parity to bar mitzvah, on the other hand, posed a tremendous threat to the denomination's integrity and identity because it threatened to make of Reform Judaism an exercise in religious imbalance. This time, though, the gender equality being sought was not that of womankind but of mankind. Although the rhetoric remained the same, the agenda was entirely new: in pleading against bar mitzvah, Reform clergy attempted to stave off what appeared to them as the incipient feminization of Reform Judaism. Having compared notes with colleagues in other denominations, they knew all too well that many young men would simply terminate their Jewish education upon becoming a bar mitzvah, leaving confirmation, and, in turn, the entire realm of ritual matters, to the women. "In the liberal temple, women are the Jewishly informed half of the congregation," one clergyman observed, recommending that those in search of proof had only to compare the sisterhood with the brotherhood. "The trend toward gynarchy in the churches is neither an excuse for the Synagogue nor even an example we must necessarily follow." Accordingly, there was no choice but "to bar bar mitzvah."

EVEN AS REFORM JEWS hotly debated the merits of bar mitzvah, their Conservative counterparts, turning the tables, debated those of confirmation. By the mid-thirties, that practice enjoyed "strong popular appeal" and was marked by over 65 percent of Conservative congregations; a decade later, according to one authoritative survey of synagogue ritual, "the ceremony of Confirmation for both girls and boys has taken root in virtually all Conservative congregations." Much like the Reform adoption of bar mitzvah, Conservative Judaism's embrace of confirmation was a lay initiative, prompted by the parents of Jewish adolescents, who thrilled to its pageantry, theatricality, and seeming indispensability. As one eyewitness related, Jewish parents have "come to view confirmation as the *necessary*, formal induction of the youth into the Jewish faith."

Given confirmation's unmistakably distinctive origins, many Conservative rabbis failed at first to share their congregants' affinity for this foreign import. "When it comes to taking over a church ceremony, we should be wary," insisted Cincinnati rabbi Louis Feinberg in 1922, referring to confirmation's roots as a Judaized version of a Christian rite. "Besides, Jewish life is so filled with ceremonies . . . that it is unwise to add any new custom unless it can be proved that the innovation is a positive spiritual gain. Is confirmation such a gain? I maintain it is not." For about a decade, Feinberg's colleagues seemed to side with him. By the early 1930s, though, the tide had turned in favor of confirmation for reasons that Leon Lang, author of the 1936 study "What Have We Done with Confirmation," a survey of confirmation practices among Conservative Jews, made clear, on both the personal and institutional levels. Initially, the Newark rabbi confessed, he too was inclined to disapprove of confirmation; like Feinberg, he harbored doubts about its legitimacy and efficacy. But sustained encounter with the service and its positive impact on American

Jewish life led him (together with dozens of colleagues) to change his mind: the more he thought about the modern Jewish experience, the more he believed confirmation filled a void by lending "warmth and a rich emotional color to our Jewish life." Still, as Lang and his colleagues went about making room for confirmation within the Conservative movement, they sought to endow it with a new name: consecration. Interestingly enough, though, that designation failed to take hold. Parents and children, observed one Conservative rabbi in 1936, simply prefer to call it confirmation. "We find that 'Confirmation' is the more popular term, and in one community where the rabbi is particularly emphatic about calling his exercises 'Consecration,' the parents and children generally refer nevertheless to 'Confirmation.' "

By whatever name, the ceremony's color, warmth, and emotionality doubtless played a role in its diffusion; more to the point, though, was its perceived value as a strategy. Ever since Moses Weinberger penned his original critique back in the 1880s, American Jewry's cultural authorities likened the American bar mitzvah to what sociologist Stuart Schoenfeld has recently called a "ritual

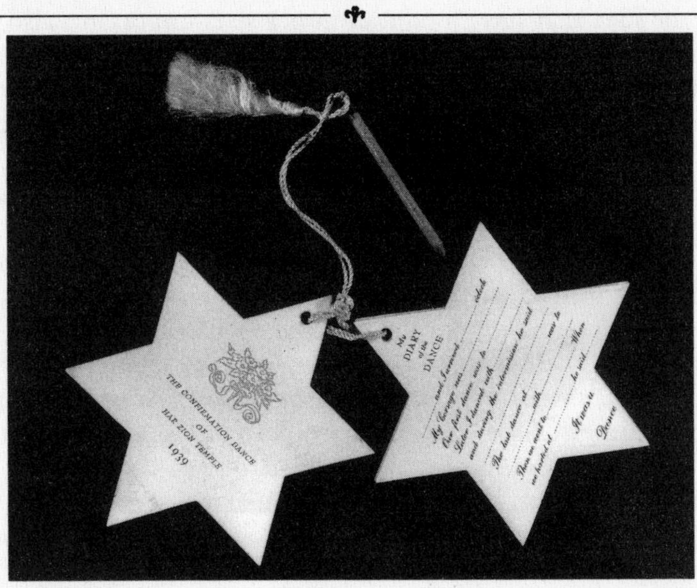

Philadelphia's Har Zion Temple celebrated confirmation with a dance as well as a sacred service.

of discontinuity." No sooner did the bar mitzvah boy's parents pay the bill, it seemed, than the bar mitzvah boy dropped from sight, rarely setting foot in a synagogue again, let alone continuing his Jewish education. "There are enough Jews in New York who have not entered a synagogue since they were bar mitzvah, excepting perhaps to recite kaddish, to form several hundred congregations," one observer noted dolefully in 1933. "Upon becoming a bar mitzvah," explained another, the boy "feels that he is now, by virtue of a ritual act, a 'complete' Jew."

Disturbed and puzzled by this turn of events, which they often labeled as "mortality," American Jewry's cultural elite struggled to find ways to retain both the bodies and the minds of their former charges. Some turned to the classroom, others to the clubhouse, and still others to confirmation. In a memo to Rabbi Simon Greenberg of Har Zion Temple in Philadelphia, the synagogue's educational director, Samuel Sussman, lamented what he called "bar-mitzvah drops," pointing to a precipitous decrease in the number of post–bar mitzvah Hebrew school students. "Undoubtedly," Sussman wrote, showing a rare touch of optimism, "the situation can be bettered if the Jewish educators can teach the parents—sell them the idea that Jewish education per se is important; also that bar-mitzvah is not an outstanding Jewish event. The entire idea of bar-mitzvah must be toned down. . . . The boy must be made to feel that bar-mitzvah *is just a birthday* that has nothing to do with the question of more or less Jewish education."

In efforts to "tone down" the bar mitzvah, educators like Sussman sought not only to reduce the temptation of theatricality and self-display but to elevate bar mitzvah's underlying educational standards as well. Those occupying the pulpit or running the Hebrew schools could do little about the social side of things, but they could do something about setting an appropriate tone in the sanctuary. At the Brooklyn Jewish Center, for example, prospective bar mitzvah "lads" were urged to meet regularly with the rabbi or cantor before their scheduled debut. They were also coached in the proper way to deliver their prayers: "slowly and in a spirit of reverence. The boy should remember that he is not addressing the Congregation, but he is speaking to God."

Instilling an awareness of God was only a part of the agenda. Equally critical was setting up "criteria" designed to stiffen the educational requirements the bar mitzvah boy had to fulfill before assuming his manly obligations. In that way, synagogue officials hoped to make clear that the course of study culminating in bar mitzvah was not an end in itself—"Finis to the book"—but an ongoing commitment. Parents and children have got to understand, insisted Rabbi Israel Goldstein, that the bar mitzvah ceremony "is something earned, a something for which the child has worked, a privilege which he has earned, and not an empty ceremony contingent upon a parrot-like recitation of a few Hebrew passages." Toward that end, synagogue ritual committees designed all sorts of procedures to invigorate and at the same time to standardize the educational process. "No boy shall be Bar Mitzvah at the Saturday morning services unless he shall have at least one year's attendance at a regular (three-day-a-week) Hebrew School or its equivalent," insisted the members of one Brooklyn synagogue, while other congregations insisted on a minimum of two, three, and even four years of study; still others compelled would-be bar mitzvah boys to take a speed test to demonstrate their proficiency in reading a certain number of words per minute from the siddur, or prayerbook. In communities as diverse as Akron, Miami, and Atlanta, local boards of Jewish education instituted a set of minimum requirements that a bar mitzvah boy would have to satisfy before he could ascend the pulpit. In that spirit, one lone Jewish educator even suggested that rabbis refuse to participate in a bar mitzvah ceremony in which the celebrant had made it clear that he was not going to continue with his Jewish education. "The rub, of course, is in trying to get a new attitude to Bar Mitzvah officially adopted," admitted Abraham Segal in the pages of *The Reconstructionist.* "No hard-headed synagogue official will accept probable and permanent future benefits to Judaism as compensation for immediate financial loss through antagonizing the family of the Bar Mitzvah."

In pursuit of enthusiasm, not antagonism, Jewish educators and rabbis sought to keep bar mitzvah boys close to the synagogue by appealing directly to their adolescent social needs. "The adolescent craves fun. He wants his interests hitched to action, and therefore he demands a full and rounded program," explained Congregation Ahavath Israel's rabbi of his decision to form a Tefillin Club for post–bar mitzvah graduates in his Philadelphia synagogue. Through father-son breakfasts, basketball games, fishing trips, an occasional dance, and a regularly scheduled Sunday-morning prayer service, the Tefillin Club attempted "to capitalize on a few adolescent tendencies." Hundreds of synagogues across the country, drawing on the latest trends in adolescent psychology, or what one pundit called "boyology," followed suit by establishing "post–Bar Mitzvah Clubs" and in some instances "junior congregations" composed entirely of male adolescents. The synagogue club maintained many of the same conventions as its more secularly inclined cousin, from strict membership requirements and initiation rites to probation; membership, though, was not subject to a demonstration of athletic prowess but one of religiosity. "In my own Congregation I have organized a post–Bar Mitzvah club known as B'nai Israel, which, because of its splendid success, is an answer to the problem," noted Rabbi Israel Goldfarb in 1927. In this elite institution, membership was open only to those who demonstrated an "ability to read Hebrew, observance of the Sabbath, regular attendance at Synagogue, laying of T'fillin and wearing of Tsitsis."

A club of a different sort, confirmation furthered both the educational and the social needs of the post–bar mitzvah set. It began, observed Rabbi Simon Greenberg in 1925, "as a sort of revolt against the Bar mitzvah idea of hothouse preparation" and went on to become a way of developing the "Jewish personalities" of American-born male adolescents over the age of thirteen. Students in the confirmation class met once or twice a week during the school year to study Jewish history, Bible, ethics, current events, and "community civics," a vast and unwieldy curriculum designed more to "cultivate attitudes" and foster communal spirit, or "*kehillah*-mindedness," than to transmit information; in many instances, would-be confirmants were also expected to attend synagogue services regularly. Through knowledge and practice, or what Rabbi David Aaronson preferred to call "equipment," confirmation attempted to deepen the adolescent's ties to the Jewish community, preparing him for his role as a responsible Jewish adult.

Although the Conservative movement's embrace of confirmation was intended primarily as a response to those who might otherwise be exclusively "bar mitzvah minded," it was not inattentive to the needs of adolescent Jewish girls either. At a time when bat mitzvah had not yet become a widely accepted practice, a few particularly perspicacious rabbis, such as Harry Halpern of New York's East Midwood Jewish Center, proposed that confirmation serve exclusively as a female ritual. Writing in 1927, he suggested the ceremony be "a matter for girls only . . . given to the girls in lieu of Bar Mitzvah for boys," an idea that Rabbi Abraham Neuman of Philadelphia's Congregation Mikveh Israel, among others, took to heart. In 1930, the Conservative clergyman inaugurated a "Consecration Service" designed "to give the girls the equivalent of the Bar Mitzvah ceremony." Closer in practice to confirmation than to bar mitzvah, Neuman's consecration ceremony consisted of a fourteen-part Sunday morning service in which "consecrants," sometimes individually and at other times collectively, read a series of Hebrew and English prayers, including two blessings over the Torah, chanted a brief portion from the Bible, recited the Ten Commandments, and were blessed by the rabbi. "There was no active opposition to the service on the part of the conservative element," wrote Neuman to his colleague Israel H. Levinthal, who had expressed keen interest in the new ritual. "Much of the innate dislike of change was turned to great enthusiasm after the service was actually held."

For his part, Levinthal, rabbi of the Brooklyn Jewish Center, was also intrigued by the notion of creating a service that would initiate girls into Jewish religious life "with the same dignity and potency with which boys mark their Bar Mitzvah period." After eliciting the advice of colleagues like Neuman, he broached the idea of a consecration service for girls to his congregants in a Sabbath sermon in 1935. A year later, on the first day of Shavuoth, the "new experiment" made its debut following the conclusion of the regularly scheduled prayer service. "Precisely at eleven, the members of the Consecration Class will start the procession to the pulpit," noted the *Brooklyn Jewish Center Review*, inviting members of the congregation to join in the festivities, which consisted, characteristically, of musical selections, benedictions, Torah blessings, and individual speeches on the numerous contributions of Jewish womanhood to Jewish life, the synagogue, and the home. (The number of variations on the theme would expand or contract depending on the number of celebrants.) Despite a certain

A proud confirmant of the 1930s, resplendent in her white gown.

amount of communal apprehension, the event went off without a hitch. "What most impressed the congregation," the *Brooklyn Jewish Center Review* reported a month later, "was the dignity as well as the sacred simplicity of the service. Everyone felt that it was an innovation worthwhile, that it would strengthen the Jewish loyalties of the girls in our community and would create within their hearts a closer bond uniting them with their faith and their people."

Rhetorically and symbolically equivalent to bar mitzvah, confirmation and consecration integrated girls both educationally and ceremonially into the life of the community by providing them with a course of study, and with a formal ceremony to mark its conclusion. "There was a want in the Synagogue for some ceremony by which the adolescent girl could be made to feel that she, too, has a share, a privilege, and a responsibility in the religious life of Israel," acknowledged Buffalo rabbi M. M. Eichler. Confirmation "is a formal recognition of this fact—that woman has attained equality in sharing the burdens and responsibilities of Jewish religious and communal life." But as Eichler himself realized, confirmation's recognition of Jewish womanhood was more symbolic than real: it publicly celebrated and acknowledged the Jewish woman's role but did little to further or even redefine it. Much like the Mothers' Courses, lectures, and prescriptive literature to which it was inextricably bound, confirmation was intended to foster cultural literacy and identity among future Jewish mothers. "The Jewish girls of today, who will be the mothers and home-makers of tomorrow, must be prepared for the Jewish educational responsibilities they will have to shoulder in later life. Girls and boys should therefore receive the same intensive and purposeful Jewish training. Under no circumstances should Jewish girls be deprived of a Jewish education," insisted Trude Weiss Rosmarin, herself a graduate of the Frankfurt Lehrhaus and a Ph.D. in Semitics. Even those with less formidable credentials than Weiss Rosmarin's favored augmenting and deepening the Jewish education of young girls. Writing in the pages of the *Jewish Forum* on "the problem of the young girl," Beatrice S. Genn, a young journalist, lamented the dearth of educational opportunities available for American Jewish women of her age. "Less thought has been given by Jewish educators to the religious training of the young girl than to any other phase of Jewish life. It has been taken for granted since time immemorial that the girl will do as her parents tell her and will absorb whatever she may need from her environment." But times have changed, she insisted. Young women attend high school and college, hold down jobs, and are exposed daily to the challenges of modern America. "Being alert and intelligent, they ask questions, they want to know the reasons for the observances, they demand explanations of truths based on faith."

Confirmation sought to meet that demand by providing young Jewish women like Beatrice Genn with a deeper sense of Jewish history and culture than that typically supplied by a weekly Bible class, Sunday school, or a grandmother's superstitions. Still, mastery of Jewish texts was not the objective of the confirmation class, nor, for that matter, was an enhanced religious life. However modern it may have seemed at the time, classroom instruction was a conservative strategy, the means to an avowedly traditional end: binding the modern Jewish girl to her tradition much as her mother and her grandmother before her had been bound to theirs. Providing the Jewish female adolescent with a new set of ritual tools or possibly even a novel way of thinking about women's spirituality was never a consideration; rather, the objective throughout was to inculcate a traditional affective sensibility toward Jewishness and Judaism. "In this way," explained Levinthal, referring to his synagogue's consecration service, "we are helping to train a generation of young Jewish women who will understand their place in Jewish life and their duty to the Jewish people."

It's in this sense, then, that comparing confirmation for girls with bar mitzvah for boys was a lot like comparing apples and oranges, an observation made by few clergy at the time. Often conflating the two, many Conservative rabbis ended up making such murky statements as "the Bar-mitzvah is the Confirmation ceremony of the boy, and the Confirmation is the Bath Mitzvah ceremony of the girl," thoroughly confusing the issues, miring them in semantics. They were not the same. "The cry that confirmation raises woman to man's level is a specious argument," argued Louis Feinberg in 1922, pointing out the substantive differences between the two rites of passage. "In Temples where men too are exempt from practically all Mitzvos the inconsistency is less evident. But in our synagogues where men are expected to observe, the individual Bar Mitzvah celebration, hallowed with age, is of greater value; while for girls a ceremony corresponding to Bar Mitzvah but without the concomitant obligations would be a hollow thing. Are we ready to make them responsible for Tzitzis, Tephillin and all the other Mitzvos? If not, the discussion is irrelevant."

The relationship of confirmation to gendered notions of ritual obligation and performance remained a lively issue throughout the 1930s and forties and into the postwar era as well; its existence was complicated further by the simultaneous emergence of a new womanly ritual, the bat mitzvah. Credit for the first American bat mitzvah is generally attributed to Mordecai Kaplan, whose twelve-year-old daughter, Judith, was called to the Torah on a Friday night in March 1922 at the newly established Society for the Advancement of Judaism, in New York. As she recalled many years later, "I was excited and I knew it was the right thing and I wanted it with all my heart. Yet I was a little chagrined at being different, not like all the other girls." At the time, word of this seemingly radical innovation traveled quickly, moving from traditional religious circles to more liberal ones. "It is very interesting to note," the proceedings of the Central Conference of American Rabbis related later that year, referring in a rather roundabout way to Mordecai Kaplan, "that in the city of New York a professor in the Seminary, the rabbi of an orthodox congregation had a Bar Mitzva of girls. This is very interesting and shows that the other wing of Judaism is also making progress."

The innovation itself spread as quickly as gossip, from Westchester's Emanu-El Synagogue, which in 1924 maintained a bat mitzvah class, and Chicago's Humboldt Boulevard Temple, where young girls read a portion of the haftorah in English on a Friday night, to Cejwin Camps, where in the summer of 1935 the entire camp participated in a Saturday-morning bat mitzvah, an event so memorable in the life of the camp that it figured subsequently in a commemorative souvenir album. Surveys tabulating and identifying denominational forms of religious expression also reflect bat mitzvah's steady progression from a once aberrant to an increasingly normative phenomenon, particularly within the context of the Conservative movement, with which it was increasingly

By the 1950s, bat mitzvah celebrations were on their way to becoming accepted practice.

identified. In the early 1930s, only a handful of Conservative congregations had institutionalized the practice. Of 110 Conservative synagogues surveyed in 1931, for instance, only six had implemented a bat mitzvah ceremony; three planned on introducing it in the near future, and two hoped to integrate it into the Friday-evening service. One unnamed rabbi, pressed to account for his decision *not* to conduct a bat mitzvah, replied, "The Bar Mitzvah ceremony is enough of a farce." The historical record does not reveal whether or not this individual cleric overcame his objections, but a steadily increasing proportion of his colleagues apparently overcame theirs: by the late 1940s, reported another study, over a third of Conservative congregations had instituted the ceremony, while "the number of those planning to institute this new ritual is growing constantly."

Bat mitzvah was slower to take hold outside the parameters of the Conservative movement, but eventually it did. In 1944, for instance, the *Orthodox Union*, which, as its name implied, reflected the views of America's Orthodox Jewish community, featured an article entitled "The Bas Mitzvah Comes to Our Synagogue," which described an apparently successful attempt by Jerome Tov Feinstein, the rabbi of a traditional Brooklyn congregation, to implement a bat mitzvah ceremony "without infringing upon the Shulchan Aruch [the compendium of Jewish law]." As in so many other instances, the impetus for the service came from one of his congregants, a "mother," who reportedly said to the rabbi one Sabbath morning in the spring, "Rabbi, I liked the Bar Mitzvah ceremony very much. But, tell me, Rabbi, why don't you do something for the girls?" As Feinstein tells the story, he agreed with the mother's assessment of the situation. A bat mitzvah, he explained, was necessary on two accounts: it enabled the Jewish girl to realize her "responsibilities in a religious sense," and it eliminated the feeling that "in the Orthodox synagogues the girls do not count." In short order, the rabbi brought the matter before the congregation and the sisterhood, from whom he received "unanimous assurance that they would aid me in every way in carrying out the program." Even the most traditional element of the congregation—"the men who come to daily services as well as . . . our daily Shulchan Aruch class"—supported the rabbi's objective. By the fall, the congregation had organized a bat mitzvah class; after a few months of work, studying such texts as *What Every Jewish Woman Should Know* and *The Jewish Home Beautiful*, one girl was "ready." An inordinately large group, attracted by curiosity and "a bit of publicity," attended the congregation's "Late Friday Evening Oneg Shabbat" to witness the debut of the first bat mitzvah girl in its history. She chanted the kiddush, the blessing over the wine; she made a speech "along the lines of a Bar Mitzvah"; and, after successfully answering a series of questions based on her course readings, she was installed as a member of the Junior Sisterhood. A *succès d'estime*, the bat mitzvah won hearty raves, especially from the congregation's women, who, related the rabbi, "began to feel that they were given a 'square deal.' " For all their optimism, though, it would take at least another generation before bat mitzvah became as established and widespread a practice within Orthodox circles as it was within Conservative circles.

Like the Orthodox, Reform Jewry was also slow to welcome the bat mitzvah. By the 1950s, though, the practice had begun to take root. According to a 1953 "laymen's survey" of Reform practices, an estimated 35 percent of congregations had introduced some kind of bat mitzvah service, which they viewed as a "logical consequence" of bar mitzvah. Much like the male service, which itself had given rise to controversy some years earlier, bat mitzvah's popularity troubled a few Reform rabbis. "Frankly, I am puzzled," wrote one anonymous clergyman, seeking rabbinic guidance. "I understand the classical Reform position on bar mitzvah but what of bas mitzvah, with which the old-line rabbis were thoroughly unfamiliar. Has Reform Judaism changed its course or is it just drifting into another port?" A 1954 responsum published in the *CCAR Journal* answered the query by coming out against the female service, whose worth and value it questioned. "When a new religious practice is urged upon us, of whose value our fathers had no estimate and we have had no convincing demonstration, it is not enough to point to some by-product of possible utility, as we attempt to do in the case of the Bar Mitzvah ceremony." Accordingly, concluded the ruling, "Bas mitzvah has no place in Reform Jewish practice."

THOUGH CLEARLY A LIABILITY in some quarters, bat mitzvah's novelty lent itself more generally to improvisation and innovation, providing both clergy and laity with the unprecedented opportunity to make things up as they went along, refining some features, adding or eliminating others. The bat mitzvah, acknowledged Josiah Derby, a Conservative educator, "is a *briah hadasah* [a new being] of our creation, without precedents and prejudices." By the early 1950s, bat mitzvah had assumed all of the trappings of a set piece, thanks to the Committee on Rituals and Ceremonies, which distributed its own list of "suggested ceremonies" to the members of the Conservative rabbinate. Earlier, though, practices varied markedly from congregation to congregation. At Chicago's Temple Anshe Emet, the bat mitzvah service, like the bar mitzvah itself, was held on a Sabbath morning, except that it celebrated the coming of age of a group of girls. Other synagogues, focusing on one girl at a time, set aside an *erev shabbat*, or Friday evening, because it offered "wider latitude for variety and experimentation" than the traditional Sabbath service. Also, holding bat mitzvah ceremonies at the Friday-evening service was not without "practical virtue" for it avoided potential scheduling conflicts with the Saturday-morning bar mitzvah. But even then, diversity rather than uniformity prevailed. At some institutions, lighting the Sabbath candles signaled the start of the celebration, at others the bat mitzvah girl led the congregation in evening prayers; at some synagogues, much of the service was conducted in Hebrew, at others, English predominated. Some bat mitzvah girls chanted the entire haftorah with the traditional blessings while others recited the traditional Jewish paean to womanhood, *Ayshet chayil* ("Women of Valor") instead.

Regardless of its various manifestations, the bat mitzvah remained preeminently a sacred rite enacted solely within the context of the synagogue and its sanctuary. Although parents were encouraged "to place the Bat Mitzvah ceremony on an equal footing with Bar Mitzvah," fanciful invitations, elaborate partying, and excessive gift-giving rarely, if ever, overshadowed the proceedings; at most, a lovely collation or "fellowship hour" followed immediately upon the conclusion of the service, and the bestowal of presents was kept to a minimum. No fountain pens or stock certificates awaited the bat mitzvah girl, although pioneer Judith Kaplan Eisenstein remembers having received a tennis racquet and a Kodak camera, the first in the family. An exercise in modesty, the bat mitzvah may have become de rigueur but seldom de trop. "How many parents will celebrate a daughter's Bat Mitzvah with the same lavish extravagance they throw away on the Bar Mitzvah?" asked one clergyman, knowing full well that in this case the overwhelming majority of Jewish parents opted for understatement.

This show of celebratory restraint aptly reflects how contemporaries understood and related to bat mitzvah. Where the male puberty rite, an established tradition of long standing, needed a jolt of consumerism, some "Hollywood ballyhoo," to render it attractive and meaningful to American Jews of the interwar years, its female analogue satisfied on its own modest terms. Mediating between the needs of the folk, the mandate of the clergy, the plasticity of Jewish ritual, and the rigidity of gender, the new female puberty rite fit perfectly with the tenor of the times. It went far enough in addressing and correcting the "girl problem," of which cultural custodians so frequently spoke, without fundamentally challenging the status quo or disturbing such essentialist notions as "femininity self-concept," a term used as late as 1955 by Rabbi Sanders A. Tofield to describe what he perceived as fundamental differences in the ritual orientations of men and women. At Tofield's congregation, the Hebrew school graduation took place on the eve of Simchas Torah, a festival during which it was customary to dance publicly with the Torah. "Girls decline the honor," he noted. "They seem to regard handling the Torah a masculine prerogative; it disturbs their femininity self-concept."

Bat mitzvah did no such thing. Pleasingly neutral and unthreatening, this new womanly ritual entailed no radical redefinition of gender roles, nor did it enlarge or in any way alter the synagogue's cultural geography. Instead, it symbolically affirmed, and confirmed, the construction of a religious identity grounded in gender, status, and age. Basically, bat mitzvah represented a coming to terms with modern notions of adolescence, a concept so ingrained in the American collective imagination that, as Professor Adele Bildersee complained in a 1937 address before the Young People's League of the United Synagogue of America, "most of us are wearied by [its] very sound." Adolescence became the basis for ordering experience, classifying personality, defining behavior, and, increasingly, shaping ethnic, cultural, and religious identity. In their attentiveness to adolescence and its consequences, Americans demonstrated a heightened sense of what historian Howard Chudacoff calls "age consciousness." "The cultural emphasis on precise age and on social organization by age induced Americans not only to assess themselves through comparison with their peers but also to attach greater significance to age-defined milestones in their lives," he writes, offering the enhanced prominence of birthday celebrations as a case in point. Over the years, birthdays had evolved into elaborately staged and emotionally charged occasions. Don't ignore such moments, warned the American etiquette writers of the 1900s, hailing them as "garlanded milestones in the road of life."

Much like the secular birthday, bar mitzvah, confirmation, and bat mitzvah also represented a "garlanded milestone," a highly ritualized and sacralized occasion that served both as a chronological marker of time's passage and as a statement of the Jewish self and its relationship to the community at large. When seen from this perspective, American Jewry's concern with adolescent "red-letter days" falls into place. Both the elite and the folk, each in their own way, sought to reconcile the demands of tradition with the possibilities of modernity by providing a Judaic gloss on adolescence and age consciousness. They didn't always succeed; at times, the community's cultural authorities promoted too elitist and high-minded a vision, while the folk, dazzled by America's consumerist aesthetic, promoted one that was much too quotidian. The elite pursued order, rationality, and coherence; the folk, a good time, a socially justifiable occasion for sentiment, camaraderie, and high spirits. Ultimately, both offered a singularly American vision of modern Jewish identity. Most of his friends, wrote Stuart Rosenberg, "needed at least one day in their lives to prove that they were still Jewish. More accurately, their parents required it, as a kind of coming-out party for public display and conspicuous consumption. Their reasons had nothing to do with Judaism." This may be. And yet, whatever Rosenberg's bar mitzvah and those of his generation may have lacked in Judaism, they more than made up for in Jewishness, or what sociologist Herbert Gans has called "symbolic Judaism," an inchoate and at times ineptly rendered but consistently heartfelt and deeply intentioned emotional and cultural sensibility.

Admittedly, the Jewishness proclaimed by Rosenberg's parents and exemplified by the bar and bat mitzvah was selective, a cultural hodgepodge of traditional practices and ideals that fit comfortably within the American context. Together with food and holidays, the bar mitzvah represented a variant of Jewish popular culture that, as Gans explained, "salvage[s] from Jewish tradition only those themes, objects, and experiences which bring pleasure and at the same time never conflict with or disrupt the basically American way of life." Fashioned in the people's image of what it meant to be Jewish in modern America, glittering occasions and red-letter rituals like bar mitzvah, bat mitzvah, and confirmation brought pleasure to thousands of grandmas and grandpas, mothers and fathers, sons and daughters eager to dramatize their Jewishness.

4
Home Sweet Haym

"As soon as one steps across the threshold of a Jewish home, one should see and feel that this is a Jewish house," young couples were instructed. Make sure to fasten a mezuzah on the doorpost "so that the spirit of Judaism may warm and inspire the members of [your] household." Despite such lofty sentiments, it was by no means clear what actually made a home tangibly Jewish. Apart from a mezuzah, was a Jewish home marked by a particular style of home furnishings? An abundance of publicly displayed Jewish ritual objects? Paintings of the Holy Land? Such questions engaged the collective American Jewish imagination for much of the twentieth century. For Diana Forman, the Philadelphia artist and dollmaker active in the 1940s and fifties, the answer was by no means simple. Her idea of the quintessential Jewish home encompassed no fewer than sixty-five distinct objects. Every room within Forman's spacious, idealized Jewish house, including the bathroom, was liberally festooned with Jewish imagery, *objets*, and iconography. Judaica was "scattered about" everywhere: the living room contained biblical and "Palestinian" paintings, the library housed approximately 2,500 volumes of "Hebraica and Judaica," and in the bathroom a series of towels monogrammed in Hebrew adorned the towel rack. Lampshades illustrated with Tissot Bible scenes and a cluster of papier-mâché Bible dolls, which she herself designed, decorated the children's rooms. While few Jewish women were as vigilant, or as fanciful, as Forman in tending to the Jewish appearance of their homes, many American Jewish communal leaders joined her in prescribing a Jewish visual idiom. Much like the family that in-

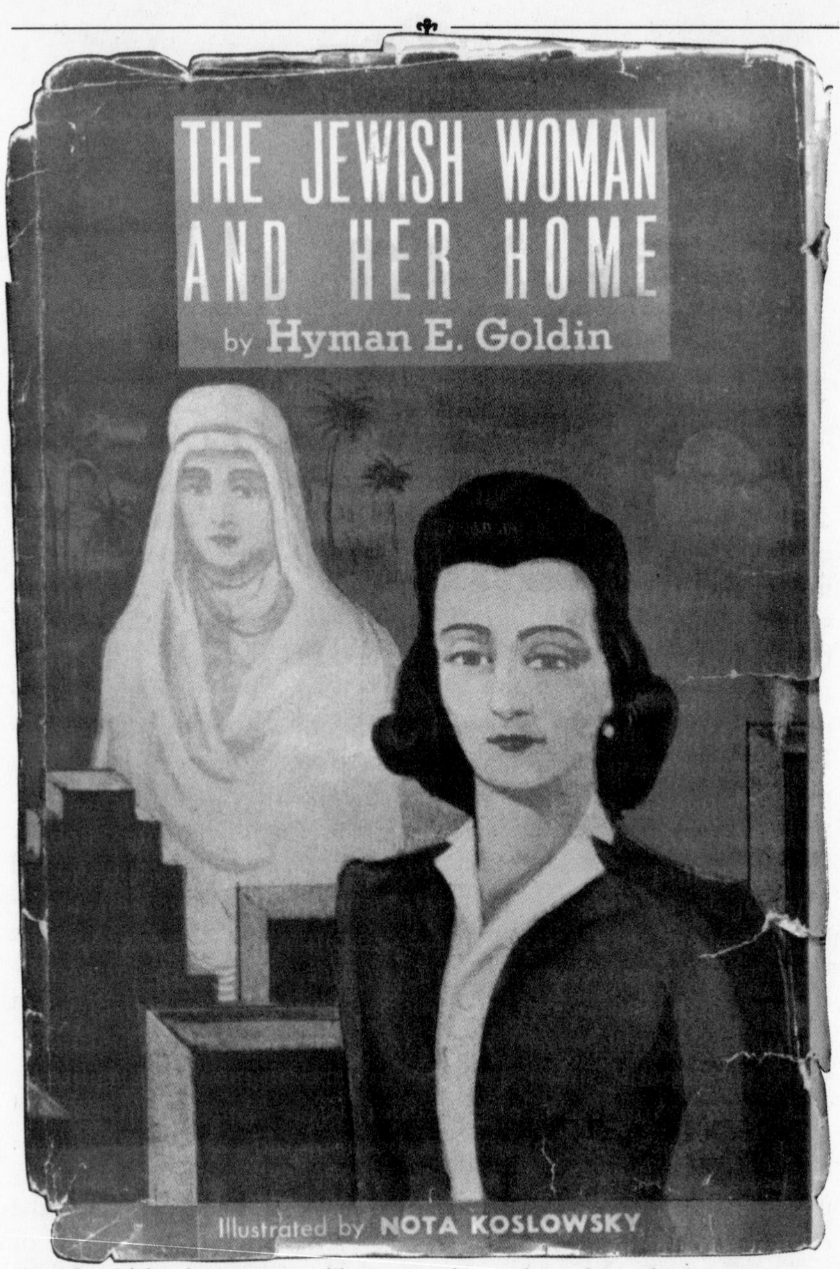

Ritual guidebooks grew steadily in popularity throughout the interwar years, satisfying a profound need for practical information.

habited it, the interior of the model Jewish home emerged as a subject of intense communal concern well into the 1950s.

At first, that concern was fueled by the engine of Americanization. Beginning in the 1880s, America's established German Jewish community embarked on a systematic campaign to refashion the newly arrived East European immigrant, whose style, appearance, and personal hygiene differed markedly from its own. Teams of social reformers, settlement-house workers, and home economists enthusiastically joined together to promote an "architecture of visible health." This aesthetic placed a premium on order and neatness, seeking through its control over dirt to establish the physical parameters of an American domesticity. Insisting that "in fitness and cleanliness lies beauty," the advocates of decor reform established a firm set of guidelines for tenement interiors, a "Gospel of Simplicity" that advocated the "good, honest straight lines" of Mission furniture, simple, unadorned muslin curtains, rugless wood floors, white walls, and a modicum of decorative objects.

The "Gospel of Simplicity" was propagated in a number of ways. For one thing, it formed the basis of the curriculum at Jewish settlement houses and vocational schools, such as New York's Educational Alliance and Cleveland's Kitchen Garden and Trade School for Girls, where young unmarried women and their mothers were instructed in the "wholesome and orderly" decoration and maintenance of their homes. Under the guidance of well-meaning and well-heeled instructors, students pored over detailed syllabi, model budgets, and itemized lists of "suitable furnishings"—like those found in Mabel Hyde Kittredge's 1911 bible of tenement decor, *Housekeeping Notes: How to Furnish and Keep Home in a Tenement Flat.* At Lillian Wald's Henry Street Settlement, a model apartment allowed the "people of the tenements" to see for themselves how best to furnish and maintain a healthy home. Established in 1904, the "Flat" or "Housekeeping Center," as it was officially known, became so popular that an Association of Practical Housekeeping Centers was formed to disseminate its methods throughout the nation.

The whitewashed and spartanly furnished rooms of the "Flat" offered a domestic vision that was as much ideological as it was physical. Manifestly concerned with space, its conventions actually

WHAT MAKES A HOME JEWISH?

(The Home of Rabbi and Mrs. Max L. Forman)

A. Porch

1. Israeli Mezuzoth in Every Doorway in House
2. Rug with Hebrew Monogram
3. Curtains Embroidered with Hebrew Alphabet
4. Magen David Mirror
5. Two Bookcases
    a. World-famous Handmade Bible Dolls
    b. Ceramics, Leather, Wood Objects with Jewish Motifs
    c. Models of Seminary, Synagogue etc.
    d. Replicas of Bible Objects: altars etc.
6. Two Wallcases
    a. Bible Dolls in various media
    b. Doll Personifications: Rabbis, Bar Mitzvahs, Confirmands, Hadassah nurses, K'tonton etc.
    c. Holiday Centerpieces
    d. Souvenirs, Place Cards

B. Living Room

1. Sculptured Placques of Children, with Biblical Verses in Hebrew
2. Three Lamps made of Biblical Figures and Scenes
3. Painting of David and Goliath - Carlo Dolci
4. Painting of Judith and Holofernes - Italian School
5. Painting of Jews Crossing Red Sea
6. Painting of Palestinian Scene
7. Shadow Boxes of Bible Dolls
8. Statuary of Moses
9. Articles from Israel - Ash Trays, Chess Box, etc.
10. Antique German Sabbath Lamp
11. Bible Stand
12. Footstool Upholstered with Rachel's Tomb Scene
13. Afghan and Headrest with Hebrew Monograms

C. Dining Room

1. Mirror with Talmudic Quotation on Wall
2. Mirror with Bible Quotation for Table Centerpiece
3. Placque of Jael and Sisera
4. Chest with Dolls used for Centerpieces for Holidays etc.
5. Bureau with Hebrew Monogrammed Silver, Glassware, Napkin Rings, Holiday Ceremonial Objects
6. Chest with Hebrew Religious, Secular, Israeli, and Children's Records and Games
7. Painting on Marble of Crossing of Red Sea
8. Illuminated Page of Medieval Manuscript of Hymnal
9. Mounted Silver Seder Dish
10. Stereopticon with Palestine Pictures
11. Mounted Medieval Chanukah Menorah
12. Havdalah Spice Boxes, Elijah's Cup, Wine Goblets, etc.
13. Seder Towel Rack with Hebrew Monogrammed Towel

Diana Forman, the "Bible Doll Lady," brought imagination and verve to the task of furnishing a real-life Jewish home.

had more to do with the cultural ramifications of dirt and the social implications of housekeeping, or what the Council of Jewish Women called "housewifely wisdom," than with aesthetics. This vision, at once corrective and assimilationist, attempted to eliminate the "Three D's—Dirt, Discomfort, and Disease" of the immigrant experience and to replace them with middle-class American notions of decoration, sanitation, and public hygiene. Essentially a civic exercise in cleanliness, it drew on the idiom of home decor to make its point. In our housekeeping course, explained the *Settlement Journal* in 1904, we teach our students "how to arrange the rooms comfortably, tastefully and prettily, and with all due regard to hygienic principles. Housekeeping, under these circumstances, is elevated very much and becomes not only an art but a science, and thereby does away completely with the stigma of drudgery." Other reformers sought to prettify Jewish immigrant neighborhoods by bringing "flowers to the slums." "The Jews seem to care less of any people in New York for growing things," Miss Ada Fairfield of the Plant, Fruit, and Flower Guild told a *New York Sun* reporter in 1905, hoping to change the locals' minds about the importance of flower boxes and gardens. A decade later, the Council of Jewish Women opened a "Home-making Center and Model Flat" in the heart of Brownsville. Within six months, over 1,500 Brooklyn women and young girls had visited the Center, attending its lectures on interior decor and sanitation and absorbing American "domestic methods." The average immigrant girl, the Council allowed, explaining its decision to establish the facility, knows little about the care of a home or a family, "nor does knowledge gained on the other side enable her to cope with the exigencies of domestic life in our large cities."

Jewish social reformers consistently downplayed the "knowledge gained on the other side," dismissing traditional notions of sanitation as wholly inadequate while branding as "debris" the East European preference for bright colors and overtufted furniture. When it came to taste and cleanliness, immigrant women, social settlement workers believed, were utterly "deficient," and hence in need of instruction in "the laws of health and hygiene," whose precepts they defined in unequivocally American terms. Almost formulaic in their precision, these laws upheld the middle-class ideal of the home as a private retreat in which each room, from the kitchen to the parlor, retained a specific function. As the "hub of the home," the kitchen received special attention. Little in that room escaped scrutiny, from the shape and design of the cupboard to the uses of the colander, whisk broom, and Dover eggbeater, whose efficient combination of form and function endeared it to domestic reformers. Sensitive to the expense inherent in properly equipping a kitchen, they devised imaginative alternatives to commercial products. "Neatly labeled" glass jars, suggested Mabel Hyde Kittredge, could be profitably used in lieu of expensive canisters; pickle barrels could serve handily as laundry receptacles; a soapbox could do double duty as an "extra bureau"; and an "improvised refrigerator" could be made by boring holes into a grocery box and fitting it to the outside of a kitchen window. In each instance, prescriptions for the kitchen's outfitting and upkeep assumed a neatly ordered workspace given over exclusively to preparing and consuming food.

Immigrants tended to accept this wisdom only in part. Much to the disappointment and frustration of the settlement-house community, many persisted in using and decorating their homes according to their own, more deeply felt, imperatives. The austere lines of Mission furniture so cherished by followers of the "Gospel of Simplicity" were simply not for them. Sonia Kochman, a domestic expert from Cleveland, gave voice to some of these frustrations in her record of a trying encounter with one immigrant woman. "Mrs. A.," she wrote, following a visit to her home in 1916, was "difficult to impress. Among other things she told us that she is too busy to be bothered with the new ideas or improvements and that she had been married for twenty-five years and has never tried anything new since. . . . Mrs. A. was evidently determined to stop progress and so it was useless to argue with her."

As this exchange suggests, disjunctions between the ideals of the model flat and the realities of the tenement experience were probably more common than instances of agreement. Time and again, extant photographs of tenement interiors reveal a style of decor clearly at odds with that of the model flat. Replete with colored wallpaper, brightly patterned linoleum, and yards of lace and fabric trimmings, the typical tenement interior was hardly subdued. Lavishly illustrated merchant calendars and popularly

Cluttered and colorful, tenement interiors conflicted with the stylistic conventions of domestic reformers.

priced chromolithographs hung everywhere, their popularity as much a function of necessity as of taste. "We pasted down the floppy wallpaper," a tenement dweller explained, "and on the worst part of the wall, where the plaster was cracked and full of holes, we hung up calendars and pictures from the Sunday newspapers." Photographs of relatives left behind in the Old World, vividly colored paper *yorzeit* (memorial) plaques, and an array of kiddush cups, Sabbath candlesticks, and other ritual items added to the domestic disarray.

In Jewish immigrant homes, "good taste" frequently gave way to urgent social need. "Our small apartment, housing eight persons, offered few opportunities for privacy," recalled a former tenement inhabitant. "My parents occupied the only bed in the house. . . . I [slept] on four chairs set up each night in the kitchen. In the morning, the chairs would be pulled from under me, one by one, as they were required for breakfast." Even the much-vaunted parlor was pressed into service. During the day a doily-filled venue for entertaining guests and showcasing prized possessions, by late evening it contained rows of cots on which family members and boarders slept. "Packed with furniture," most tenement kitchens also defied the American canon. A far cry from the laboratory-like environment advocated by domestic reformers, the kitchen was a multipurpose room whose daily activities included cooking, socializing, schoolwork, the manufacture of commercial products like cigarettes and shirtwaists, and, of course, sleeping.

The characteristic clutter of the Jewish tenement reflected not just stylistic preferences or shortage of space but also the availability of consumer goods. In the New World, immigrants encountered a culture of abundance unlike anything they had known before. "The number and variety of pencil boxes alone took one's breath away," one young immigrant consumer recalled. "There seemed to be no limit to the complexity of pencil boxes." There also seemed to be no limit to the number of goods available, either at the city's department stores, those self-styled "cathedrals of commerce," or, closer to home, on the "market streets" of the immigrant enclave whose rickety pushcarts laden with fruit, vegetables, teas and coffees, bolts of fabric, clothing, dry goods, pots, dishes, and bolts of fabrics—everything short of a piano—made America's bounty tangible and accessible. Beguiled by this abundance, immigrant Jews took to shopping with an avidity that transcended the mere acquisition of consumer goods; it's perhaps no exaggeration to say that, for many, shopping became a tangible instrument of integration and Americanization. "More than simply commodities, things were evocative aspects of American culture," writes historian Andrew Heinze. "Easier to comprehend than the English language or the vote, they served as the most accessible tools with which Jewish newcomers could forge an American Jewish identity." Acquiring a piano, a matched parlor set, or an assortment of bibelots made the immigrant feel literally *at home* in America.

Managers of the domestic budget, immigrant Jewish women purchased virtually all of these items, often juggling the weekly gas bill with the butcher's monthly charges. Inventive and resourceful in their use of money, they developed a series of fiscal strategies that enabled them to reconcile their limited economic resources with their consumer needs. "My mother was very adroit at explaining to [my father] the sudden presence of things around

Consumer goods like Community Silver were widely advertised in the Yiddish press.

the house," recalled Samuel Chotzinoff, describing how she relied heavily on the popular installment system—"buying on time"—to purchase a chair or a flowered silk tablecloth. With its obliging terms, installment buying enabled many consumers to purchase items they could otherwise ill afford. Hundreds of retailers like Kramer and Wagner, a Brownsville emporium, tantalized housewives by offering "furniture worth $100 available at $1 a week," an opportunity that was surely hard to pass up. In other instances, women turned to the Hebrew Free Loan Society of New York or the East Boston Ladies Free Loan Association for interest-free loans with which to stabilize, and sustain, their private economies. The records of the Hebrew Free Loan Society of New York indicate that in 1912 "housewives" seeking to make good on a store deposit or to pay the rent constituted a substantial 14 percent of its clientele.

These strategies facilitated the acquisition of things whose appeal, clearly, was not lost on the immigrant consumer. The world of appearance mattered a great deal. Neither economic restraints nor even political affiliation dulled the aesthetic sensibility of immigrant Jewish women, whose vision accommodated both sartorial matters and socialism. Thanks to their fiscal skill and the apparent pleasure they took in consumer goods, Jewish women—of all classes—enjoyed a reputation as conscientious consumers. When, in 1895, the *American Jewess*, a new magazine catering to middle-class Jewish women, sought to interest prospective advertisers in the fledging publication, it unhesitatingly made the following observation cum sales pitch: "More than 80% of all the articles used every day of our lives, are bought by women—wives, mothers, sisters. Advertise, therefore, in the *American Jewess*, the only paper devoted to Jewish women—the best buyers in America." Though their funds were far more limited than those of the *American Jewess*'s well-heeled subscribers, immigrant women's interest in consumer goods was just as pronounced. "The fact that women constitute a large and intelligent class of readers of the *Forward* is reflected in the volume of advertising directed at them through the pages of this paper," the Yiddish daily proclaimed. "Local stores, including department stores in particular, who are keen buyers of space are well aware of this fact."

Where the *Jewish Daily Forward* delighted in the Jewish consumer impulse, others, it's worth noting, frowned upon it. Israel Levinthal, for one, turned his considerable homiletical skills to denunciations of female consumerism. In sermons variously entitled "Flapperism in Civilization and Religion," and "Style," a Friday-evening address whose "effect," he wrote, was "excellent," the popular Brooklyn rabbi lambasted the Jewish woman's preoccupation with shopping and her "blind adherence to fashion." Insisting that he was no Puritan—"I too can see the beauty of a well-ordered garment"—Levinthal urged his female congregants to cultivate their intellects with the same ardor and interest they reserved for shopping. Jewish women "should know that there is something else in the world worthwhile than fashion and dress, that they should realize the value and priceless blessing of intellectual interests."

Advertisements for fashion, dress, and other consumer goods whetted the immigrant's appetite as much as they shaped it. The Yiddish press sparkled with advertisements, some of which exclusively engaged women shoppers and others a broader clientele. "No one is more interested in having a beautiful home than women," claimed B. V. Cantor, distributors of "beautiful furniture," in a 1913 advertisement in *Froyen Velt*, hoping to appeal to the female consumer with coordinated bedroom and parlor sets. Cantor's competitors, meanwhile, emphasized economy over beauty by championing the virtues of "Grand Rapids Furniture—At the Cheapest Prices," and music stores like Saul Birns's played on the popular bourgeois notion "What Is a Home Without a Piano?" in pitching their musical wares. Readers of the Yiddish press were equally familiar with a galaxy of brand-name products whose ranks included Uneeda Biscuit (with its In-Er-Seal), Gulden's Mustard, Rid All Bug Liquid, Grand American Ice Cream, Colgate's Dental Cream, Eagle Brand Condensed Milk, Community Silverplate, Coca-Cola, Chevrolet, Dutch Master Cigars, Bayer Aspirin, Lifebuoy Soap, and Doan's Kidney Pills (a nostrum for stomach distress). The nation's leading Jewish Socialist paper, ironically enough, actively encouraged consumerism by publicly touting the purchasing power of its readership. "The Jewish field," the *Forward* insisted, "is a quality-market par excellence." In a well-designed and -conceived attempt to convince manufacturers and advertisers that it paid to advertise in the *Forward*, the daily published a hefty-sized illustrated pamphlet, *The Fourth American City—The Jewish Community of New York*, which portrayed the American Jewish community as the quintessential consumer writ large. "Of all immigrant peoples, the Jews maintain the highest standard of living," this document explained. "Their annual expenditures for food, clothing, furniture and furnishings, fuel and light, and miscellaneous commodities reflect a collective purchasing power that is truly staggering. Over $373,000,000 is spent annually by the Jewish community for living, or at the rate of more than $1,000,000 per day!" The brochure, which drew on an elaborate set of charts, graphs, and illustrations to document its findings, emphasized American Jewry's economic potential. "There is nothing strange, mysterious or secret about the Jewish field. It is just like any other portion of the great American market of which it is an integral part. Good merchandising principles are just as sound when applied on the East Side or the Bronx as in Portland or Sacramento," it asserted, offering the resources of its very own Merchandising Service to familiarize manufacturers with the "Jewish field."

Cultivating stylishness as well as cleanliness, the immigrant press assisted Yiddish-speaking consumers unaccustomed to the complexities of decorating a home; after all, recalled one former immigrant, "homes in Valusi, [Rumania,] were not furnished with parlor sets of velvet." Such feature articles as "Practical and Contemporary Kitchens," or "How to Beautify Your Home," extolled the virtues of cretonne drapes, venetian blinds, doilies, and white tiles while "Our Furniture Page," *Froyen Zhurnal*'s full-sized, sharply illustrated layout of coordinated bedroom sets, mirrors, and rococo highboys provided a visual object lesson in home decor. In addition, a regularly featured "Home Decorations" column served as a kind of crash course in the decorative arts by intro-

OUR FURNITURE PAGE

THE LATEST FURNITURE DESIGNS WILL BE SHOWN ON THIS PAGE EVERY MONTH

Edited by HENRY NERGE, Manager of the Metropolitan Furniture Merchants Association

Froyen Zhurnal, a Yiddish women's magazine of the early 1920s, carried numerous articles on interior decor.

ducing readers to the concept of a decorator, whom the magazine likened to a "doctor of home decor," and training them to distinguish between Sheraton and Chippendale styles of furniture. Much of the discussion centered on ways to save the consumer from making ill-advised purchases. "Many years ago, people had little need of bedroom sets or parlor sets," the monthly related;

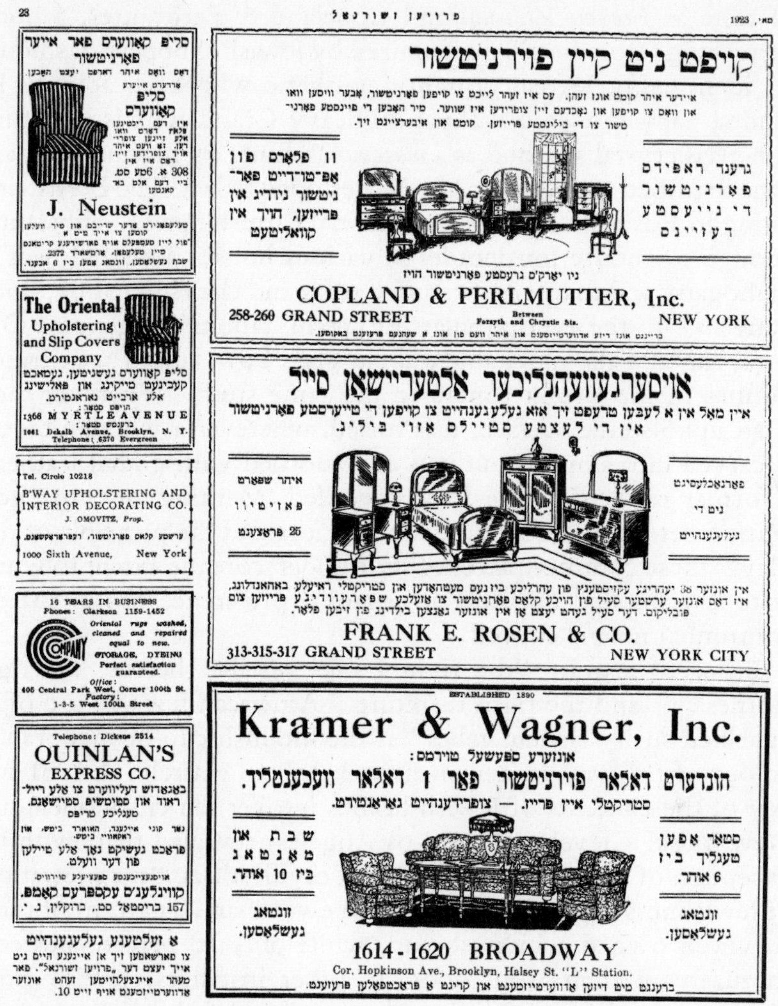

Jewish neighborhoods abounded in local furniture stores like Copland & Perlmutter.

"they didn't know the difference between a gilded table or a Windsor chair. Today, however, when considerable emphasis is placed on the appearance of one's home and on owning period furniture, make sure you know what you're buying! When it comes to matters of style and design, one must be a *maven*."

In their effort to make *mavens* of Jewish consumers, such arbiters of taste as *Froyen Zhurnal* and Copeland & Perlmutter, a home furnishings store heavily patronized by Jewish shoppers, fashioned an identifiably Jewish domestic aesthetic whose vocabulary included gaily flowered wallpaper, heavy Grand Rapids furniture, cut-glass crystal as stolid as a *masevah* (a funerary monument), and "the dignified concept of a 'set,' " designed to last. The Bernsteins, living in Boston, acquired "substantial furnishings . . . substantial enough to endure for decades in various houses: outsized beds of mahogany and maple, overstuffed sofas and chairs in nappy, florid patterns . . . the ever popular 'Egyptian' tapestry, a genuine Oriental rug and the inevitable red cut glass bowl full of wax fruit." Homes in the Bronx contained the same stuff. "Wherever there is an upholstered surface, it is tufted; wherever a wooden one, it is carved into sinuous outlines and adorned with gilded leather," a former resident of the Bronx recalled. Marking an entire generation determined to "cultivate interiors and the principle of display," these commonplaces of style underscore the extent to which taste is grounded not only in personal preference but in shared, communal norms as well.

Eager to acquire "the right books on the shelves, the right clothes . . . and the right furniture," American Jews all too often banished such "ancient relics" as the kiddush cup or menorah to an out-of-the way corner or discarded them entirely. A 1931 survey of the contents of Jewish homes in over ten cities (including New York, Cleveland, and Los Angeles) revealed that, with the exception of a menorah and a pair of candlesticks, "manifestations of Jewishness" were barely visible. Fewer than 20 percent of those surveyed owned a kiddush cup, while only 40 percent posted a mezuzah on their front door. In other instances, Jewish ritual objects were dismissed as "curiosities." Old-fashioned or poorly designed, "Jewish markers" clashed harshly with the conventions of modern home decor and the cultural aspirations of its residents. The son of upwardly mobile parents recalls that a gilt-framed picture of his *zayda* (grandfather) hung prominently in their home for many years until the family concluded that it "didn't look 'nice' with the new furniture, and so Zayda was relegated to the bedroom. A Van Gogh print was put in his place." Where stylishness was not the issue, function was: in many homes, lack of use rendered Jewish items of little visual or cultural value; instead, they simply collected dust. "In general, it may be said that more of our homes have these ceremonial objects than use them for ceremonial purposes," reported the 1931 Jewish-household survey. "Chances are only fifty-fifty," observed yet another contemporary student of Jewish domestic interiors, "that there are *any* books of Jewish content on the average American Jew's bookshelf. As to whether he even reads these books, we have no information."

Occasionally, Jewish objects would be recycled, adapted for some other use. Grandmother's formerly cherished candlesticks now decorated a bookshelf, kiddush cups were transformed into cigarette holders, and a much-used gefilte-fish pot became "an emblem of the past, an ornament in [the] living room." Even when utilized appropriately, most extant American Judaica possessed little aesthetic appeal; fashioned out of cheap materials like tin and inexpensive fabrics like "sleazy" white satin, American Judaica simply didn't lend itself to being proudly displayed. "The average form of the familiar *mezuzah* is almost an insult to Jewish 'beauty of holiness,' " lamented one clergyman; another witheringly compared the willingness of Christian Americans to spend lavishly on Christmas tree decorations while "the average Jew . . . contents himself with the fifteen-cent tin Menorah."

Not everyone, however, was content with the apparent triumph of this neutral idiom of home decor. On the eve of World War I, a chorus of disapproving voices began to make itself heard. "Pause on the threshold of your own doorway. Are you at all conscious of the fact that you are entering a Jewish home? Is there any Jewish character in the furnishings? Or is it a nondescript home with the Regency period stressed or perhaps Louis the 14th or 15th? . . . Has it everything *but* a feeling of being a Jewish home in which a Jewish family lives?" Seeking to make as much room for King David as for Louis Quatorze, Jewish public figures like Mathilde Schechter, a founder of the Women's League for Conservative Judaism, and writers like Trude Weiss Rosmarin championed a new cultural understanding of style, one that moved beyond Americanization to celebrate the physical "charm and beauty" of Jewish material culture. "Go to at least as much trouble to create a beautiful Jewish environment as you would, say, to make a success of a bazaar or bridge [game]," they exhorted, as their public crusade for an aesthetically pleasing visual Jewishness began to take hold across the country. Throughout the interwar years, guidebooks devoted entire chapters to the subject of Jewish home furnishings while women's organizations constructed and displayed miniature model Jewish homes at annual conventions. The Jewish Home Institute, meanwhile, encouraged American Jews to write to its Department of Information for practical advice on how "to make your home Jewish," even as Mordecai M. Kaplan, not generally known for his interest in the material side of Jewish life, suggested that American Jews design furniture and bric-a-brac "that would reflect Jewish individuality. There is no reason why it should not be a rule in Jewish life that the home of a Jew ought to have something in its furnishings, pictures, ornaments and library that would give the unmistakable impression of it being a Jewish home."

The Jewish "ethics of home decoration" defined the home

When furnishing their homes, many middle-class American Jews preferred a neutral style of decoration.

as a sacred space, "teem[ing] with aesthetic, ethical and religious-inspirational possibilities." Often likened to a stage set designed to inspire its residents with the plenitude of Jewish culture, a Jewish home worthy of the name contained, at the very least, a pair of Sabbath candlesticks, a menorah, several mezuzahs, and Jewish artwork, periodicals, and books. Literature occupied the "place of honor." The *sine qua non* of every Jewish home, books attested to the enduring ties between the so-called People of the Book and the love of learning. "No matter how small or poor a Jewish home may be, it should not be without a *Jewish Book Shelf,*" Trude Weiss Rosmarin stated categorically, urging Jewish women, especially the newly married, "to make the Jewish book again a living force and an inspiring reality in the family." One of her contemporaries felt equally strongly about the presence of the little blue tin Jewish National Fund receptacle, insisting that "every Jewish home ought to have a JNF Box." Jewish appointments were intended to convey a moral statement that went far beyond the physical: manifestations of group identity, they served as constant reminders of Jewish ideals and practices.

"Beautify the Jewish home," charged the architects of visible Jewishness, underscoring its aesthetic dimension. "Get a pretty mezuzah for your doorpost. Don't be content with the cheap and tawdry." In these and other clarion calls, Schechter and her adepts claimed beauty and prettiness as intrinsically Jewish concepts, redefining the very nature of Judaica in the process. Fusing high style with Jewish style, they not only emphasized the inherent compatibility between the two but reconstituted Judaica as a bona fide form of artistic expression. Its value no longer inhered in its cultic, ritual function but in its decorativeness. "The arrangement of the various cult objects necessary for performing the Jewish home-observances provide the Jewish woman with a singular opportunity for beautifying her home."

Mathilde Schechter's own home, an amply appointed apartment on New York's Morningside Heights, exemplified her commitment to visual Jewishness. In the living room, a space filled to overflowing with abundant drapery, richly textured carpets (including an animal skin rug), and flowing plants, Jewish objects were carefully positioned and smartly displayed: a brass *shabbos* lamp dangled gracefully near the marble mantelpiece while an illuminated *ketubah*, rich in floral imagery, was set among the plants. The private sanctum of her husband, the legendary scholar Solomon Schechter, also bore witness to Mathilde's determination to infuse contemporary notions of stylishness and taste with a soupçon of Jewishness. From the book-lined walls, two Old World portraits of Schechter's parents—one of his mother wearing an old-style kerchief and the other of his bearded and yarmulked father—bore down fiercely on the room's handsome masculine clutter.

An enthusiastic, energetic hostess whose home was always filled with guests, Mathilde Schechter was known to some as the "queen of the drawing room" and to others as the quintessential Jewish homemaker, or *baleboste*. At her funeral in 1920, Henrietta Szold, a longtime family friend, delivered a eulogy entitled "The Lineaments of Mathilde Schechter," in which she highlighted both aspects of Schechter's personality. Lovingly, the Zionist leader portrayed the German-born Mathilde as a woman whose pursuit of Jewish culture was an avocation as well as a vocation. "For she with her aestheticism and her sympathy was above all a homemaker. Even when she went beyond her four walls and made her way into the arena of public life . . . she still remained the homemaker. Mathilde Schechter possessed the love of beauty and the power of expressing it within the frame of the Jewish ceremonial." Almost forty years after Schechter's death, Adele Ginzberg recalled fondly how she had taken her and the other young faculty wives under her wing, initiating them into the "American way."

For Schechter and her artistically inclined descendants, the display of a visibly Jewish interior did not run counter to the "American way" but, rather, presumed and actualized it. "The American-Jewish woman," wrote one of their number, "need therefore not be afraid that, by beautifying her home with Jewish symbols and by infusing it with the Jewish spirit, she is acting disloyally toward her country or engendering in her children a divided spirit of conflicting loyalties. On the contrary, by fostering her Jewish religious and cultural heritage, the Jewish woman enriches the American scene with beautiful and significant values." The Jewish woman, she ringingly concluded, "should therefore proudly display the marks of Jewishness in her home. There is no reason for her to hide her Jewishness."

A portrait of Solomon Schechter's mother graced the study of his Morningside Heights apartment.

Once Jewish home decor became a matter of upholding values and transmitting a cultural message, it could no longer be entrusted to individual whim and fancy. Far from frivolous or incidental, its implications were far-reaching and affected the Jewish domestic enterprise as a whole. Jacob Kohn's attitude toward Jewish home furnishings is another case in point. In a concise cultural analysis of style, the guidebook author highlighted the powerful interrelationship between decor and identity. "In the homes of cultivated people, if the pictures on the wall never depict Jewish life, if the art objects represent only an interior decorator's whim and never include objects of Jewish art, especially Jewish ceremonial art objects, our young people begin to feel that the world of most immediate interest and the world of the highest culture is, even in the view of their parents, something quite distinct from the Judaism, which in theory they hold so precious," he incisively pointed out. "If in the home the Oriental rug must be the very best which the family can afford, but the Chanukah Menorah, or the service of the Seder table, or the kiddush cup and the candlesticks for the Sabbath, are the cheapest and the tawdriest of objects and to be conveniently hidden away in some dark cupboard when not in use, we should not be astonished if our sons and daughters draw devastating conclusions from this very simple and evident evaluation of the factors of Jewish living."

BY THE LATE 1920s and early thirties, a growing number of American manufacturers began to develop a range of consumer goods designed to appeal expressly to a middle-class Jewish clientele. At first, there wasn't much of a market for American-made menorahs like the one created in 1919 by H. Luria & Sons and advertised in the December issue of *Der Tog*. "The first and only Hanukkah menorah made of true silverplate in America," it stood thirteen inches tall, without candles. Luria's "lovely artistic design," however, failed to catch on. *Der Tog*'s immigrant readers had brought Jewish objects with them from the Old World and had no reason to buy new ones, no matter how pleasing their design. Their children, in turn, made do with inherited Judaica or with the "makeshift" stuff their own offspring brought home at holiday time from afternoon Hebrew school or *shule*; an increasing number of American Jews simply did without.

This situation began to change as a small but steady flow of fine-art reproductions and artifacts produced or sponsored by nonprofit Jewish women's organizations such as the National Federation of Temple Sisterhoods, a Reform organization, and the

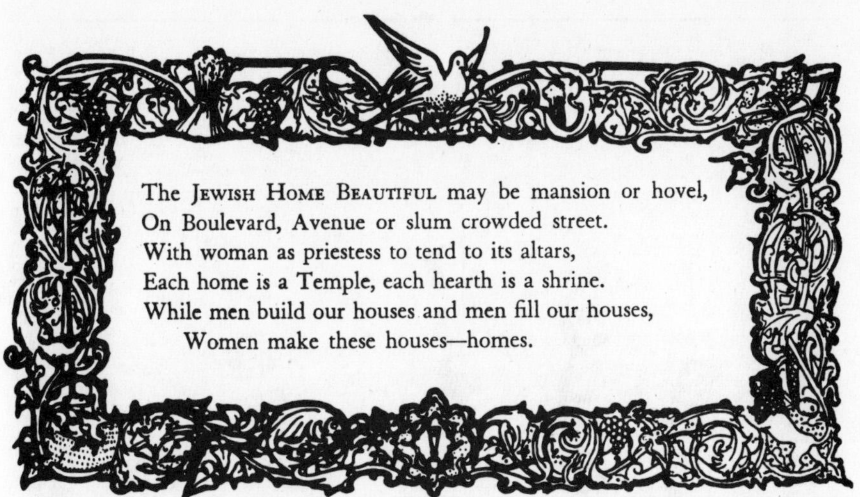

The JEWISH HOME BEAUTIFUL may be mansion or hovel,
On Boulevard, Avenue or slum crowded street.
With woman as priestess to tend to its altars,
Each home is a Temple, each hearth is a shrine.
While men build our houses and men fill our houses,
Women make these houses—homes.

Many Jewish women of the 1940s took this credo very much to heart.

Women's League for Conservative Judaism made its way into the marketplace. These two national alliances of local synagogue sisterhoods, established in 1913 and 1918 respectively, provided thousands of American Jewish women throughout the country with the opportunity to hone their aesthetic sense even as they tended to charitable matters. Holding a "ceremonial object day," attending monthly lectures on Jewish art, and mounting public exhibitions, both within and without the synagogue, sisterhood women proved eager to nurture "a sentiment" for Jewish ritual artifacts. Toward that end, the National Federation of Temple Sisterhoods produced an annual "Art Calendar," which featured the works of artists such as Josef Israels, Boris Schatz, Hermann Struck, Moritz Oppenheim, and Rembrandt. "An artistic reminder of things Jewish," the calendar quickly developed into one of the Federation's most successful ventures. The 17,000 copies of the Rembrandt edition sold out almost immediately, prompting one of its admirers to note that "it was the opinion of many that the Rembrandt Calendar for 5686 was the most artistic of any distributed so far." Combining artistry with practicality, the conveniently sized calendar discharged a number of functions simultaneously: it familiarized the rank and file of American Jewish women with (mostly) Jewish artists while also providing easy

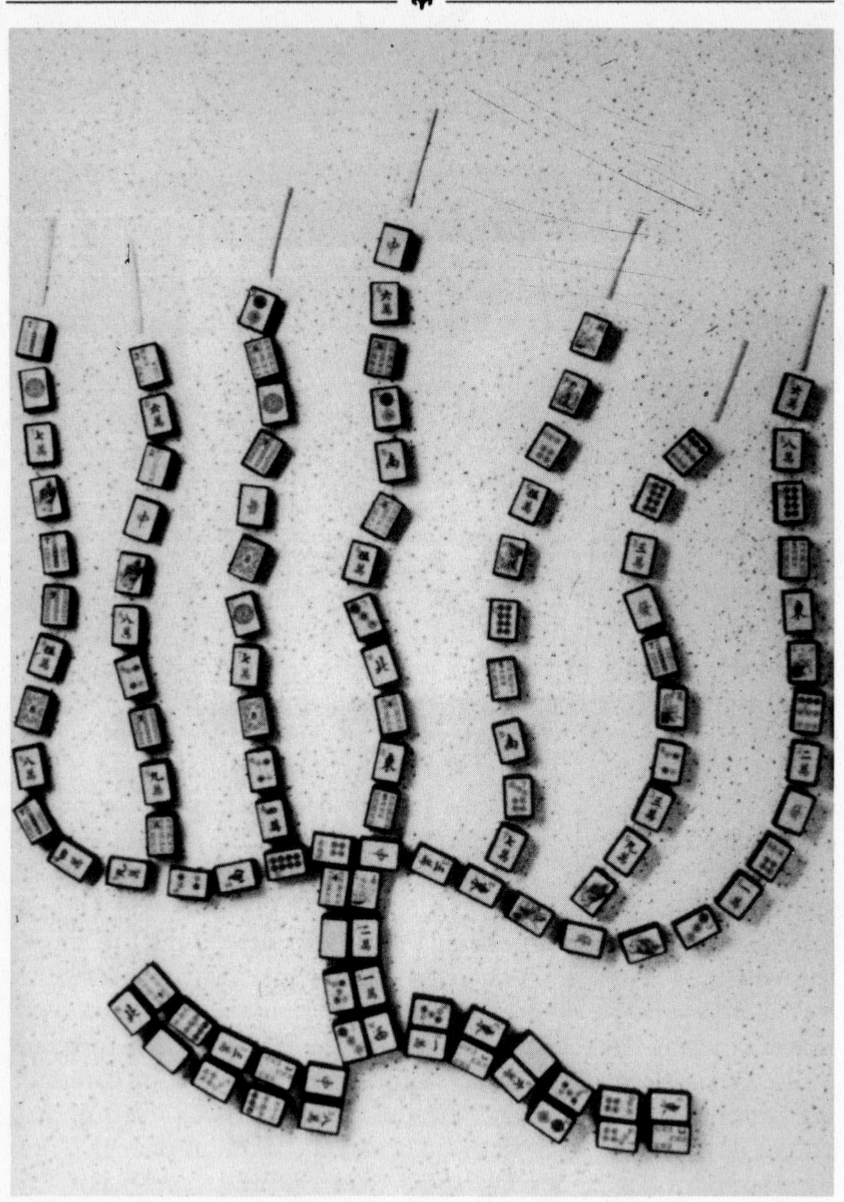

Fashioned from mah-jongg tiles, this menorah reflects a singularly novel approach to Jewish ritual art.

access, in English, to the dates of Jewish holidays at a time when few American calendars did so. A steady source of institutional income, the art calendar, commented Mrs. Abraham Simon, the Federation's president, "proved to me not merely that the aesthetic is desired by our people, but rather that it is possible to educate our people up to an insistence upon art's ability to satisfy modern Jewish needs."

Inspired no doubt by the Federation's success, the Central Conference of American Rabbis, in conjunction with the Union of American Hebrew Congregations, also tried its hand at producing Judaica. Following its success at commissioning a "Chanuko lamp" for synagogue use, the Reform rabbinical association considered manufacturing a smaller version for domestic use. According to the 1948 report of the Joint Committee on Ceremonies, only the high cost of labor precluded making a menorah "that will sell at a moderate enough price to make feasible its introduction on a large scale." In the meantime, the CCAR's production of an illustrated marriage certificate, hailed as an "exquisite work of art," succeeded where the "Chanuko lamp" did not. An initial printing of more than three thousand copies quickly sold out. This proven artistic success inspired the CCAR to prepare a complete set of artistically rendered certificates to mark such major moments in Jewish life as circumcision, the naming of a baby girl, bar mitzvah, confirmation, high school graduation, and burial.

The purchase of Jewish objects, whether special-edition or mass-produced, was limited and occasional. Endowed with the heightened quality of a gift, these items were inextricably associated with special Jewish occasions—bar mitzvahs, confirmations, weddings, and holidays. By 1910 or so, the giving of presents at selected ritual and life-cycle moments had developed into an extremely popular American Jewish social practice, paralleling a similar development within middle-class American society at large. Taking advantage of the increasing availability of affordable decorative trifles, Americans of the pre–World War I era transformed social events into culturally sanctioned exercises in gift-giving. This newly fashioned social norm took hold so speedily and completely that by the first decade of the twentieth century, no wedding, birth, engagement, Christmas celebration, or dinner party was complete without the tendering of presents. What's more, concern with the "philosophy of presents" and the etiquette of gift-giving—what to give, when, and to whom—animated the popular literature of the period. *Harper's Weekly, Woman's Home Companion*, and dozens of other popular periodicals frequently contained lively discussions regarding Christmas gifts, wedding gifts, engagement gifts, hostess gifts, useful gifts, homemade gifts, and floral gifts, as well as gift suggestions for men, babies, invalids, travelers, girls, and women, all attesting to a collective fascination with the availability and diversity of gift items and gift-giving occasions.

The popular demand for gift items soon attracted the attention of American Jewry's earnest cultural custodians, who, characteristically, encouraged the purchase of Jewish items for confirmations, bar mitzvahs, and weddings, as well as Chanukah. "Symbols count—the members of the Women's League need hardly be reminded of that," editorialized *Outlook* in September 1930. "This season of the year, when there is a general exchange of gifts, is your opportunity to make somebody's home more Jewish." Much like the decor of the Jewish household, gifts, too, were expected to possess an avowedly Jewish flavor: "For Jewish occasions let there be Jewish gifts!" In no uncertain terms, synagogue bulletins, guidebooks, and women's magazines encouraged the commodification of Jewish culture by advising their readers to substitute Jewish books, etchings, bookends, and ritual objects for the footballs, baseballs, detective books, fountain pens, and frivolous bibelots they would otherwise purchase. "Readers and friends who are puzzled by the problem of what wedding gift to send to a young couple would act wisely if, instead of buying one more of the knick-knacks which will uselessly crowd the shelves of the bride, they would give the couple some of the beautiful and meaningful Jewish things," suggested *What Every Jewish Woman Should Know*. With the growing popularity of elaborate bar mitzvah (and, in the 1950s, bat mitzvah) receptions, the need for relevant Jewish items accelerated. "A silver talis clip, a kiddush cup, ten commandments or mizrach plaques are unusual gifts for boys," recommended the sisterhood of Temple Beth El of Rockaway Park, adding, "Any young girl would like a silver bracelet with 'I Love You' in Hebrew."

Synagogue gift shops like the one at Temple Beth El provided an ideal venue for explicitly Jewish consumer behavior, encouraging the purchase of gifts with a pronounced Jewish flavor. Largely a postwar phenomenon, the gift shop's origins lay both in American Jewry's suburbanization and in the general religious revival of the 1950s. In this instance, as in so many others, geography affected not only where people lived but how they lived. "Many towns throughout the country have no facilities for the purchase of Jewish ceremonial objects," observed one suburbanite. Religious-article shops, the traditional outlet for Judaica and "ritual appliances," tended to be clustered in downtown areas, usually at some distance from the suburban neighborhoods to which a steadily growing percentage of second- and third-generation Jews had repaired in the late 1940s and early fifties. Stepping in to fill—and create—the need, the suburban sisterhood gift shop was close to home and convenient. The shop's location also reflected the growing importance of the suburban synagogue. Much more than just a house of worship, it now served a variety of recreational, cultural, and social needs while also providing "the communal setting" for suburban Jewish life. From a logistical as well as a cultural perspective, then, it made sense for the synagogue, the community's most dominant symbol of Jewish identity, to house a small shop, usually located just off the main lobby, to display and sell Jewish ritual objects and novelty goods.

The postwar era's renewed cultural emphasis on religious performance only furthered the gift shop's popularity. "Rabbis are happily now reporting a trend in the modern home to again use Sabbath candlesticks," William B. Meyers, a descendant of the famed eighteenth-century American Jewish silversmith, Myer Myers, observed in 1954. "What is still more gratifying is that laymen are replacing old, unattractive ceremonial objects with home ceremonial silver of a truly artistic conception." Similar observations were made by others of Meyers's generation. Writing a few years earlier, Ruth Glazer, *Commentary*'s astute student of contemporary American Jewish behavior, called for the development of an American Jewish aesthetic commensurate with the tastes and newfound religious inclinations of affluent suburban Jews. With her characteristic blend of mordant humor and sociological insight, she ventured the opinion that American Jews of the 1950s, "tentatively feeling their way back to a half-remembered

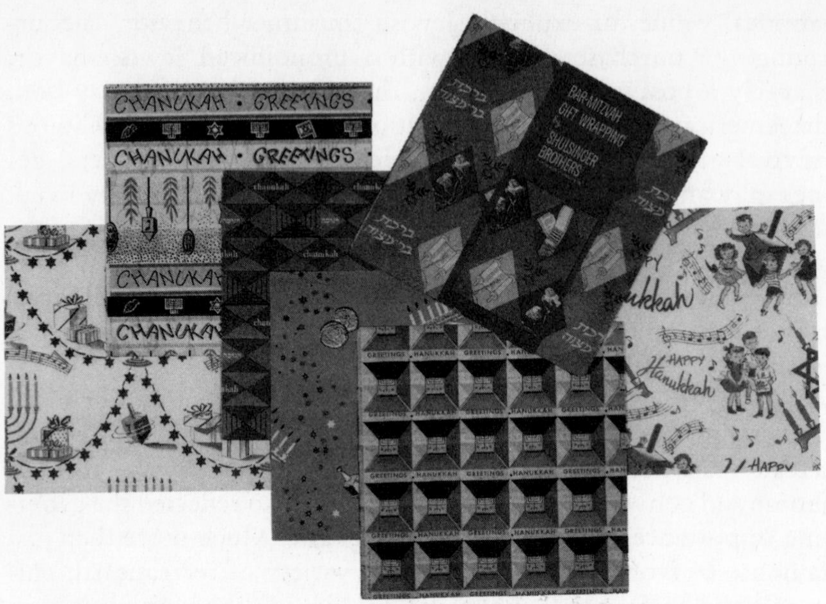

Synagogue gift shops stocked their shelves with a wide array of products, including different kinds of wrapping paper.

religion, will hardly find aesthetic quality as unimportant as their forebears." More to the point, Glazer expressed the hope that, in due course, "we may find a way to be observant and beautiful too." Sisterhood gift shops, numbering in the hundreds by the mid-1950s, rose to that challenge by carrying an array of handsome, widely priced goods. Typically, these included wrapping paper and napkins with a Jewish motif, dreidels, puzzles, kiddush cups, candlesticks, mezuzahs, challah covers and matzoh covers, traditional and ornate yarmulkes, tallesim, and tefillin, and newfangled items like a "yahrzeit bulb and stand." Figurines, etchings, books, and "Palestinian things" also crowded the shelves. Surveying this abundance, one gift-shop customer proudly observed, "We have better facilities to work with than our mothers had."

Gift-shop managers made sure to apply contemporary notions of display and merchandising to their wares in order to secure and retain customers, many of whom, after all, were sophisticated devotees of the department store. Toward that end, carefully worded "directives" on what to stock and how to display it were routinely issued. "Guard against dusty, overcrowded, poorly arranged shelves," gift-shop organizers were told. "Avoid the outdated, and the shabby. . . . Steer clear of the unesthetic appearance of the typical old-fashioned 'Jewish Book Store.' " Brightly lit, well laid out, and attractively decorated, the sisterhood gift shop tangibly illustrated the consonance of modernity, materialism, and an appealing Jewish aesthetic.

Shopping and working in an environment filled with Jewish things, Jewish women not only familiarized themselves with Jewish ceremonial lore and customs but educated others as well. As a popular sisterhood slogan had it, "Educate Through the Gift Shop." Thanks to its purposeful embrace of consumer education, the gift shop was largely responsible for acquainting the American Jewish public with goods from Israel and for familiarizing it, albeit in commercial terms, with the new Jewish state. At a time when few American Jews traveled to Israel, the gift shop's "Israeli corner" provided a firsthand opportunity for encountering that country's exotic mysteries. Insisting that "Every American Jewish Home Should Possess a Lovely Item from Israel," the shop encouraged women to decorate their homes with Israeli *tshatshkes*, a "vigorous tide" of which had begun to enter American markets as early as the mid-1930s. As one enthusiast put it: "Eventually, we hope, this infiltration of tourist imports will affect the *decor* of our Jewish homes and lovely *Betzalel* plaques [so named for the school of modern Israeli design in Jerusalem] and dignified silver Menorahs will take the place of the Meissen and the Minton."

WHILE THE SYNAGOGUE gift shop materialized the American Jewish aesthetic, the "Jewish Home Beautiful," a sort of tableau vivant popular in the early 1930s, dramatized it. In synagogue auditoriums across the country (and, later, on stage at the New York World's Fair), thirty-seven amateur performers, drawn from the ranks of local sisterhoods, literally sang the praises of seven "meticulously set" Sabbath and holiday tables arranged in a semicircle along a raised platform. "This pageant is very effective for a Mothers and Daughters Day program," explained its creators, Betty D. Greenberg and Althea O. Silverman. "A mother and her married daughter, symbolizing the transmission of the tradition from one generation to another, act as hostesses at each table. The mother lights the candles and the daughter reads the description of the holiday represented by the table." Heartwarming, fun, and imaginative, "Jewish Home Beautiful" was intended to inspire modern Jewish women with the richness of Jewish material culture. It is "not presented as a museum piece, as something to admire and then to forget or merely to recall in conversation," Greenberg and Silverman asserted. "Its purpose is rather to urge every mother to assume her role as an artist and on every festival, Sabbath and holiday, to make her home and her family table a thing of beauty as precious and as elevating as anything painted on canvas or chiseled in stone."

Striking an unusually responsive chord among thousands of Jewish women of the interwar and postwar eras, the "Jewish Home Beautiful" pageant swept the country. "Calls for it are constant," related one enthusiast, as synagogue sisterhoods from Reno, Nevada, to Rye, New York, staged their own productions. The publication in 1941 of *The Jewish Home Beautiful*, a compilation of "production notes," photographs, songs, and recipes, not only furthered the show's popularity but showed in abundant detail how this vision of domestic Jewish aesthetics might be enacted in the home. "Jewish mothers of today have not lost their desire to introduce beautiful pageantry into their homes," stated the text, which would go through eleven printings in twenty years. "But they have turned to strange sources for their inspiration. The attractive settings offered by our large department stores and women's magazines for Valentine's Day, Hallowe'en, Christmas and other non-Jewish festive days have won the hearts of many of our women who either through lack of knowledge or of imagination have failed to explore the possibilities of our own traditions." By drawing on the engaging, colorful trappings of American consumer culture and applying them to the domestic celebration of Jewish holidays, the "Jewish Home Beautiful" approach presented Jewish rituals, foods, symbols, and artifacts in ways that appealed to the resolutely modern, aesthetically sensitive Jewish woman: holiday tables featured elaborate floral arrangements, cheerful color schemes, and artistic displays of Jewish ritual objects and foods.

Take, for example, *The Jewish Home Beautiful*'s recommendations for celebrating the spring festival of Shavuoth. Touting the merits of a room festooned with blossoms and flowers, it suggested that the holiday table, resplendent with either yellow or pink appointments, be set for a buffet reception or tea. For a centerpiece, the book proposed several platters of blintzes "arranged like two Tablets of the Law . . . with cinammon outlining five rows on each blintze to suggest the inscriptions on the Ten Commandments." Purim, too, lent itself to flights of fancy. "The holiday closest to the feminine heart," it featured Queen Esther, a "Cinderella-like" character whose courage and devotion to the Jewish people satisfied "the dramatic urge in every woman's soul." In keeping with the holiday's spirit of "masquerade, hilarity and merry-making," the text suggested that the "table should be very gay and colorful," strewn with masks, noisemakers, and figurines. "A small doll richly dressed as Queen Esther may be perched on a tiny throne in the center of the flowers. If a glass horse is available, a figure dressed in purple as Mordecai should be sitting on the horse," it explained.

The "Jewish Home Beautiful" concept enthusiastically embraced consumer culture, turning flowers, china, and even Cinderella to its own advantage. This vision of Jewish life that was simultaneously participatory, fun, and colorful provided a rebuttal to the charge that Judaism was lackluster and ill equipped to withstand the blandishments of modern American society. There's no need to resort to Saint Patrick's Day parties, to Halloween and Christmas parties, Jewish women were told, "when there is so much beauty, so much pleasure, so much of rich spiritual significance to be derived from Jewish holidays properly observed in the home."

YET, DESPITE THE SUCCESS of the synagogue gift shop and the popularity of the "Jewish Home Beautiful" ethos, the American Jewish aesthetic remained consistently, almost stubbornly, second-rate. Critics throughout the 1950s continued to bemoan the absence of an unimpeachably high artistic tradition. "No one has apparently sought to attract the attention of serious artists to the problem of creating Jewish ritual objects of our own time and taste worthy of the tradition they represent," stated one dissatisfied consumer at the time. Speaking before a 1956 Women's League convention on "Jewish Art for the Home and Synagogue," Dr. Stephen Kayser, the curator of New York's Jewish Museum, and his wife, Louise, its resident exhibition designer, also criticized the lack of a fine-arts aesthetic, pointing out that "in the modern Jewish home the selection of ceremonial objects for actual use as well as for beautification is scanty and often in questionable taste."

The Kaysers' appearance at the Women's League convention underscored the long-standing association between Jewish museums and Jewish women's groups. Almost from their inception, national sisterhood organizations featured exhibitions and panel discussions on Jewish artistic matters, such as the one on "Arts and Crafts in the Jewish Home" held at the very first national convention of the Women's League in 1918. A year earlier, the National Federation of Temple Sisterhoods had manifested its own

Recommended table settings for Shavuoth, Purim, and Yom Kippur: from the bounty of Purim to the austerity of Yom Kippur, Jewish ceremonial life afforded many opportunities for aesthetic expression.

commitment to the arts by creating a standing committee to lobby for the creation of a permanent display of Jewish ceremonial objects to be housed at the Cincinnati campus of Hebrew Union College. As a flyer explained, "many objects that were held in high esteem by those who were familiar with their use are today to be found hidden in garrets. You can redeem them from this oblivion by presenting them to the Museum." With considerable enthusiasm, Jewish women throughout the country searched through their attics. They assumed responsibility for enlisting both fiscal and cultural support on behalf of permanent Judaica collections, whether it be the Midwest's Union Museum or the East Coast's Jewish Museum. Raising money, obtaining objects, sponsoring tours, drumming up publicity—they displayed a seemingly natural affinity, or "sentiment," for art and the "beautiful symbols of our faith," the same qualities that gave rise to the gift shop and the "Jewish Home Beautiful." "The Jewish women of this country," explained Stella Freiberg, chair of the National Committee of the Union Museum, "are particularly adapted to preserve this symbolism."

Sisterhoods and other Jewish women's groups regularly scheduled trips to Jewish museums, often timing them to coincide with the Jewish holidays. "Purim and Passover suggest spring," the Women's League observed characteristically. "They also remind us of ceremonials and ceremonial objects. What could be more appropriate on a beautiful spring day than to visit the Jewish Museum?" (Some found a trip to the Metropolitan's Egyptian wing equally appropriate. "The viewing of the remains of the surroundings in which the Hebrews were enslaved will bring the story of Israel in Egypt much closer to the understanding of young and old," Trude Weiss Rosmarin "warmly recommended.") With its appeal to history, emotion, and memory, museum-going was no mere visual experience or even a challenging intellectual exercise but rather a highly charged ritual that tied the visitor to his or her heritage, "deepen[ing] and sweeten[ing] the springs of Jewish sentiment." "A visit to the museum," explained Paul Romanoff, the Jewish Museum's curator in 1933, "is bound to strengthen the tie of the individual Jew to his people and to strengthen his pride in his race." The objects on display, he continued, "bring the past to life, enlighten the present and lend glamour to the wholesome

Jewish museums throughout the country took pride in showcasing the cultural patrimony of previous generations.

patriarchal life of the Jews." In glamorizing the Jewish historical experience, Jewish museums ennobled and inspired their audience even as they objectified and preserved Jewish culture; visitors at the time claimed to have felt the "palpitating life and vitality" of Jewish ceremonial objects and the "dynamic force" of Jewish history. A Jewish museum, one of its supporters related, "makes vivid the episodes and personages of the Jewish past. Its collections show us types and modes of Jewish culture and civilization; and they serve to bring out that our history was continuous."

A powerful medium of moral education and social uplift, the museum also reminded—some might say reassured—Jewish viewers that their distinguished heritage could rightly take its place alongside other great world civilizations whose artifacts and artwork were also publicly, and triumphantly, displayed. At Jewish museums throughout the country, curators placed Jewish ceremonial art on a pedestal (literally and metaphorically), encouraging viewers to admire the decorative surfaces of a repoussé kiddush cup, the complicated embroidery of a tallis bag, and the intricacies of an illuminated Haggadah. "Jewish Art looms up in the craftsmanship of some of the many beautiful objects," a dazzled visitor reported. Within the Jewish museums' cramped galleries, where walls and display cases overflowed with fascinating specimens of the "habits and customs of the Jewish race," the viewer's attention was held by the artistry and the exotic historicity of the objects on display.

Ultimately, the appeal of the curatorial extended beyond the

Designed by Ludwig Wolpert, this kiddush cup epitomized "good taste and contemporary feeling."

gallery into the classroom, the lecture hall, the gift shop, and the private home, coloring the Jewish public's attitude toward its material culture and providing a brand-new incentive for owning and displaying Judaica: connoisseurship. "Have You a Museum Piece?" asked *Outlook* in 1951. "Have you something in your home which could be a museum piece? Today, the Sisterhood Gift Shop has many ritual articles that in beauty are comparable to those we see displayed at the [Jewish] Museum. Perhaps one hundred years from now they will find their way to [that] edifice!" gushed the magazine. Some of the museum's standard-bearers even believed that the experience of visiting a museum could actually inspire a religious revival. Exposure to the treasures of the Jewish Museum "creates a desire to return to practices that had once been alive in the Jewish home and which, for one reason or another, have been neglected in the course of time," stated Louise Kayser in 1956. "Hardly any Jewish woman leaves the galleries without feeling an urge to do something in her home with objects which might add to it the dimension of beauty in Jewish life." It's against this background that the Jewish Museum established a design department under the direction of Ludwig Wolpert, a Bauhaus-trained master craftsman of Judaica. With the opening of the Tobe Pascher Workshop in 1956, the Jewish communal concern with style came full circle. Any number of items could now be purchased at the museum where "good taste and contemporary feeling go hand in hand."

No longer "curiosities" or "ancient relics," Jewish objects had become entirely aestheticized. "We realized how appropriately Jewish ceremonial art of superior contemporary design could enhance the practice of traditional rituals," explained the workshop's patron, Abram Kanof, proudly pointing to the museum's new role as both an agent of cultural continuity and a custodian of history. Eventually, or so it was hoped, the beautifully crafted and resolutely modern Jewish ritual objects fashioned by Wolpert's hand and in accord with elite museological standards would make their way into the average American Jewish home, where their presence would put its inhabitants "well on the road to making the modern Jewish home truly beautiful."

5
Kitchen Judaism

"It has become the fad to sneer at 'kitchen religion' but who can measure the influence upon the child of the gala appearance of the table on Sabbath and holy-days, with its snowy linen, its shining silver, and each holy-day marked by its own special dishes. Surely we who live in a land where Thanksgiving and turkey are synonymous can understand the effect of this association of ideas." As Mrs. Caesar Misch, the author of this 1911 passage clearly understood, the preparation and consumption of food loomed large in the American Jewish home: an integral aspect of everyday life, food provided both the substance and the context in which to express notions of domesticity, ritual, and identity. Within American Jewish circles, this bond between cuisine and culture—a "bond in sanctity"—was so widespread and seemingly inviolate that it gave rise to a brand-new form of Jewish identity known popularly as "kitchen Judaism," or "bagels-and-lox Judaism." Once the ties to the Old World and its cultural heritage loosened, eating became an increasingly important way to recapture and revivify a sense of connection. Eating was also an enjoyable, effortless way to assert one's identity. If American Jewry were to measure its religious commitment in terms of food, one rabbi observed in the 1940s, we'd have a "one hundred percent religious community."

Like so much else associated with American Jewish home life, the relationship between cuisine and culture was rooted in halakha (Jewish law); in this case, kashruth, the Jewish dietary laws, an elaborate system of biblically ordained culinary do's and don'ts, modified over time by custom, dictated the kinds of foods consumed and their modes of preparation. "The simple act of eating has become for us a complicated ceremony, from the preparatory phases of ritual slaughter through milchigs and fleishigs, kosher and treif." For centuries, if not millennia, fidelity to the complicated laws of kashruth was an axiom of faith and practice within the Jewish community, for whom the very definition of a Jewish home was a kosher home. The advent of modernity changed all that as an increasing number of newly emancipated Jews began to question both the legitimacy and the hegemony of distinctive culinary habits. Reform Jews of the early nineteenth century harbored profound doubts about the religious, cultural, social, and even aesthetic significance of a practice that so dramatically set them apart from the rest of the body politic. Judaism, they maintained, was a matter of what one thought and how one behaved rather than what one consumed. In other instances, growing apathy or indifference, rather than fervent ideology, hastened kashruth's fall from grace. It was simply easier not to observe these "dietary injunctions" than to be inconvenienced or embarrassed by them. For some Jews, the price paid for observing kashruth was not only social but economic as well. "It is at the cost of no little sacrifice that a Jew can manage to live kosher under modern circumstances," the *American Hebrew* noted in 1910, pointing to "the extra cost of the meat itself, and of the extra kitchen utensils that are necessary," or what another journal several years later called the "double expense" of kosher housekeeping. In still other instances, kashruth's importance diminished gradually with the passage of time and, with it, one's more religious relatives. "The Friday night candles disappeared, and the two distinct sets of ware, one for meat dishes, one milk, were washed in the same sink."

But even as a steadily growing number of modern Jews came to disregard the laws of kashruth, many retained the distinctive culinary preferences shaped by it in the first place. As one food expert stated categorically, "Practically all of the Jewish people have a natural, inherited repugnance towards certain distinctly *non-Kosher* [or *treyf*] items, such as lard—because of a many-centuries-old antipathy from a religious standpoint toward pig and products derived therefrom." Displaying what Barbara Kirshenblatt-Gimblett has called "selectively *treyf*" behavior, American Jews, as a group, avoided pork and other patently nonkosher food prod-

"What's Cooking" and other food columns in the Yiddish press introduced readers to American cuisine.

ucts while vigorously indulging an appetite for chop suey and ballpark hot dogs whose *treyf*-ness was less overt. At the same time, they held on to their affinity for gefilte fish, brisket, and blintzes, chipping away at the identification between "Jewish" and "kosher" in the process. "Uncertain, in a precarious world, of the articles of their faith, the Jews of the neighborhood could make one affirmation unhesitatingly. Jewish food was good," wrote Ruth Glazer, the daughter of a Jewish delicatessen owner. Following the dictates of convenience rather than those of tradition, American Jews became "selectively kosher" or "kosher-style." This singularly American Jewish invention allowed them to indulge in what another contemporary scoffingly called an "optional Judaism." The gastronomic equivalent of ethnicity, "kosher-style" enabled its adherents to practice kashruth "without pain or effort" by disentangling the food from the traditional restrictions governing its use, a Judaized version of having your cake and eating it too.

Kashruth was not only redefined but repositioned as a growing number of American Jews restricted its observance to the home. The new geography of kashruth promoted a more flexible approach toward dietary constraints, localizing and containing them. "Since the main purpose of these practices is to add Jewish atmosphere to the home," explained Mordecai M. Kaplan in 1935, offering a theological rationale for the everyday behavior of his coreligionists, "there is no reason for suffering the inconvenience and self-deprivation which result from a rigid adherence outside the home." Furthermore, such flexibility would "no longer foster the aloofness of the Jew, which, however justified in the past, is totally unwarranted in our day." As Kaplan realized, "eating *out*"—a phrase riddled with transgressive implications—had developed into a normative American Jewish practice. Comments on the order of "Well, I keep a kosher home as far as possible, but when I go out I eat all sorts of things I don't have at home," emerged, in due course, as a commonplace explanation. With greater elegance, a Conservative rabbi put it this way: "A realistic view of the stubborn facts of American Jewish life will reveal that full kashruth observance outside of the home is freighted with difficulties."

This dichotomy between the public and the private consumption of kosher food was actually one of long standing. Following the lead of their constituents, many Jewish institutions, such as hospitals, orphanages, educational institutions, and even some synagogues, honored kashruth more in the breach, serving nonkosher food at gatherings—a trend that began as early as 1841 in Hamburg, when two hundred supporters of a Jewish boys' school consumed "crabs, oysters and pig's head" at the school's twenty-fifth anniversary dinner with no visible ill effects. Years later, in 1883, American Reform Jews emulated their German cousins by dining on shrimp at a formal banquet celebrating the ordination of America's first group of Reform rabbis, an incident that lived on in infamy as the "trefe banquet." According to one eyewitness account, "the great banqueting hall was brilliantly lighted, the hundreds of guests were seated at the beautifully arranged tables, the invocation had been spoken by one of the visiting rabbis, when the waiters served the first course. Terrific excitement ensued when two rabbis rose from their seats and rushed from the room. Shrimp had been placed before them as the opening course of the elaborate menu." Excitement mingled with indignation as a number of guests—"a surprisingly small minority," according to another eyewitness—took vigorous exception to the menu, waxing eloquent over the perceived affront to Judaism. The menu's defenders stood firm, insisting, after all, that "this *is* the nineteenth century." As legend would have it, the caterer was to blame for the culinary faux pas. Having taken great pains to keep "lard out of the pots, pork in all its shapes from the menu, and cheese and butter from the table," he stumbled by serving shrimp as the first course. While posterity has judged the (anonymous) caterer harshly, he was guilty, at best, of acting on a common misperception of kashruth according to which pork products, not seafood, were taboo; the latter "were so good they had to be kosher."

Despite the public hue and cry that greeted the affair, American Jews persisted in their culinary improvisations on tradition. In 1910, for example, the *Hebrew Standard*, with barely concealed amusement, reported that the approved menu at the Purim Ball of a Long Island synagogue included such "toothsome dainties" as lobster salad, crab meat, and ham sandwiches. "Judaism on Long Island is quite progressive," the paper wryly concluded. Years later, in Maryland, a Montgomery County synagogue's sisterhood inaugurated the season with a "spaghetti party" at which the dietary laws were completely ignored. "No one thought of *kashruth* in advance because most of the members did not keep kosher houses. But a lively and respectful eye observed the cheese on the meat sauce and the cream with the coffee," wrote a reporter, noting that a few days after the party a resolution was passed that "forthwith" all sisterhood functions must be kosher.

As the Maryland incident suggests, not everyone looked kindly upon unkosher behavior, especially once the kosher caterer came into his own and kosher food products lined the grocery shelf; at that point, there seemed to be no excuse for not adhering to the laws of kashruth. An openly *treyf* banquet, insisted Jewish leaders of the interwar years, was inexcusable, a thing of the past. "Such conduct reveals a lack of refinement, an uncouthness on the part of the host which all the floral decorations and all the wines and liquors served in profusion cannot conceal. If Emily Post knew

Jewish social life as well as she knows the general social life, she would undoubtedly include a set of *Kashrut Don'ts* in her rules of etiquette." Despite these admonitions and the threat of Emily Post, a majority of American Jews, dining privately or publicly, continued to display little regard for the traditional dietary proscriptions; by their actions (or inactions) they served notice that being Jewish had little, if anything, to do with keeping kosher.

Statistical evidence, though lamentably slight, gives some indication of the extent of culinary apostasy. Between 1914 and 1924, the consumption of kosher meat in the Greater New York area fell by 25 to 30 percent. Elsewhere throughout the nation, the decline was equally pronounced. By the mid-1930s, according to the *Literary Digest*, levels of kashruth observance had fallen so low that it "makes Jew and Gentile alike wonder that *kosher* is still a word to four million people in the USA." Reviewing *The Royal Table* (1936), a history of the dietary laws, the magazine's anonymous critic took the opportunity to look into the extent of American Jewry's compliance with the ancient requirements. After talking with "authentic sources" at the Jewish Theological Seminary and other national institutions, he claimed to have discovered that no more than 15 percent of the nation's Jews strictly observed kashruth, while 20 percent observed "some of the laws some of the time" and 65 percent ignored virtually "all of the laws most of the time." Based on these tabulations, the *Literary Digest* concluded that the American Jew has "kick[ed] his cumbersome dietary rituals into a cocked hat." Not surprisingly, the reviewer's conclusions, the language in which he couched them, and the statistical acumen on which they rested drew fire. Louis Finkelstein, the president of the Jewish Theological Seminary, vigorously denied the comments that had been attributed to him, insisting they had been misquoted and misunderstood. The Philadelphia *Jewish Exponent* also discounted the author's findings. "Matters of food are such peculiarly personal affairs that it seems virtually impossible to gather statistics regarding them," the paper insisted, noting that what with the large volume of available kosher food products, the *Digest*'s figures were surely "far below the mark." But were they?

Subsequent indices suggest these figures were right on the mark and that, as one postwar observer related, kashruth was "on the way out." In Minneapolis, a local rabbi estimated in 1948 that only 7 percent of the Jews in his city consistently kept kosher; an expanded number, 15 percent at best, kept kosher just at home. Several years later, a Chicago rabbi estimated that over one hundred kosher butchers had recently closed their doors for want of business, a phenomenon duplicated in smaller Jewish communities where the only kosher butcher in town "complains that he cannot make a living from the amount of business available." Meanwhile, detailed sociological studies of ritual behavior among postwar suburban Jews confirmed a pattern of long-term decline: sociologist Marshall Sklare found less than 10 percent of third-generation American Jews maintained a kosher regimen. More damning still were the findings of a 1953 "National Survey of Synagogue Leadership," which revealed that only slightly more than one third of the United Synagogue elite kept the dietary laws; two thirds were inattentive.

AMID SIGNS of kashruth's steady, irrevocable decline throughout the century, many true believers within the American Jewish community sought determinedly to persuade their coreligionists of the practice's merits. Borrowing heavily from anthropology and zoology, its defenders alternately sanitized, domesticated, aestheticized, commodified, and otherwise reinterpreted the practice of keeping kosher. "Kashruth need not be a burdensome affair," stated the editor of the *Jewish Examiner Prize Kosher Recipe Book.* "The substance of kashruth needs only to be made available in terms that are understandable to the young American Jewish housewife, to gain for the Biblical dietary laws the allegiance to which they are entitled." In kosher cookbooks, sermons, and in such upbeat pamphlets as *Yes, I Keep Kosher*, the affinity of kashruth to the modern world was repeatedly and imaginatively invoked.

Many authorities turned to science for its "stamp of approval," arguing that kashruth made empirical, medical, and nutritional sense. "Whoever made the Jewish dietary laws, whether given by Hammurabi in his code, or by Moses in the Thora [*sic*], or by Joseph Karo in the Shulchan Aruch, or by all the old rabbis together, they were not fools, but wise men. Each and every one of them was, as you might say, a bacteriologist, a pathologist," commented Dr. B. Bernheim in 1903. Others, like Detroit physician N. E. Aronstam and Johns Hopkins pharmacologist David Macht, looked less to the ancient past than to the present. Insisting on the inherent rationality of the dietary laws, they equated kashruth with more contemporary notions of freshness, purity, and what we would today call ecological balance. Aronstam, a Darwinian by training and inclination who presented his findings at the 1911 International Exhibition of Hygiene, allowed as how the precepts of kashruth corresponded to an evolutionary food chain in which permissible foods, such as fish with scales, were of "greater nutritive value" because they "stand higher on the ladder of evolution" than fish without. After placing each category of forbidden food within a comparative evolutionary context, Aronstam concluded unequivocally that the Jewish dietary laws "are in accordance with the doctrines of modern sanitation and its regulations compatible with the dictates of hygiene." The Bible, he resoundingly affirmed, "is the pioneer of the sanitary sciences of today."

Like Aronstam, David Macht, the author of over nine hundred scientific articles, drew on the results of numerous pathological, toxicological, and biochemical studies to validate kashruth. In "The Scientific Aspects of the Jewish Dietary Laws" (1930) Macht described in great detail how recent laboratory experiments had detected the presence of deadly germs and poisonous substances in oysters, shellfish, and pork products. Medical arguments touting the digestibility and solubility of kosher cuisine were also widely circulated. Other articles such as "The Jewish Dietary Laws from a Medical Point of View" affirmed the inherent sensibleness of kashruth by drawing on clinical evidence proving that the meat of kosher animals was far easier to digest than that of nonkosher ones; conversely, meat and milk mixed together "make for indigestion and stomach troubles." To those who would argue that the Jewish dietary laws were the vestiges of a primitive "totemism," these findings demonstrated otherwise. When subjected to the "searchlight of science," kashruth seemed to hold its own.

Though penned by male physicians and scientists, this literature was designed to appeal to women who, in their newly assumed role as "home engineers," presided over an environment that more closely resembled a laboratory than the proverbial castle. Thanks to the professionalization of home economics and the popularity

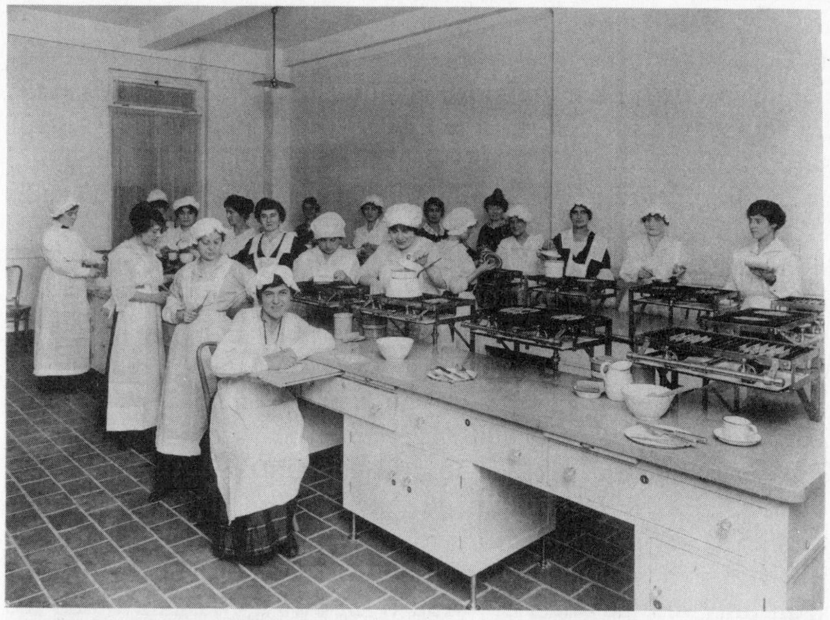

Young Jewish women and their mothers eagerly donned the starched cap and apron of the domestic scientist, hoping to learn "to cook American."

of scientific cookery (a movement that "pursued the science of food, not the sensuality"), women were taught to bring reason and precision to the multiple tasks of feeding a family. In settlement houses, cooking schools, and classrooms across the nation, home economists and their female disciples studied the composition of foods and the physiology of eating. Busy measuring and analyzing everything from baked beans and marshmallow salad to white sauce—three staples of scientific cookery—food missionaries and the women they inspired offered their fellow Americans a new way to think about diet, digestion, and moral well-being, the trinity of concerns central to the "gospel of good cooking."

Immigrant women and their daughters often made up a significant proportion of those in the classroom and at the cast iron stove. "Apt pupil[s]," they absorbed the most up-to-date information on food preparation, preservation, and service; at home they tried out new recipes for toast, casseroles, green vegetables, and rice pudding on unsuspecting family members, sometimes with only limited success. "And right away, Mashah joined the cooking class in the settlement, one evening a week, to learn the American way of cooking vegetables and fixing salads. And soon we all had American salad and American cooked vegetables instead of fried potato latkes and the greasy lokshen kugel [noodle pudding] that Mother used to make." Like Mashah, author Edna Ferber, growing up in Kalamazoo, Michigan, also enrolled in a weekly cooking class offered by her high school. "The dishes we essayed were, however, a shade too smothered in cream sauce for my taste," she recalled. "Goy cooking, we called it. Ours was richer, more sophisticated food." Swallowing their distaste for "goy cooking," many Jewish women attempted to learn the "American way." For advice, they turned to *The Settlement Cook Book*, a staple in Jewish households ever since the early 1900s, when a "little band of Hebrew women," led by Mrs. Simon Kander, established a Jewish Mission in Milwaukee. Helping to familiarize Jewish housewives with the basics of American cuisine, *The Settlement Cook Book* was Jewish by association only; in fact, the text had more in common with *Miss Parloa's Kitchen Companion*, the bible of scientific cooks everywhere, than with the Old Testament. And yet, far from gathering dust on a kitchen shelf, this cookbook was often among the most heavily utilized in the Jewish household, its pages torn and stained by frequent use. Yiddish versions were also available.

Despite their interest in *The Settlement Cook Book* and its recipes for toast and apple pie, Jewish women continued to prepare traditional Jewish dishes, which, when measured by the canons of scientific cookery, fell woefully short. Whereas the laws of kashruth were applauded as scientifically sound, the cuisine itself left much to be desired. According to the exasperated nutritionists and domestic scientists writing about "Jewish dietary problems" in the *Journal of Home Economics* and other professional journals, the eating habits of immigrant Jews posed a veritable health hazard. Overseasoned, briny, and imbalanced in favor of meat rather than milk, the Jewish diet allegedly contributed to the anxiety, constipation, and excess weight commonly found among the grown-up members of the population. "You will quite often meet a woman who likes to eat much and well," a contemporary noted. "This, added to the fact that the Jewish women usually do nothing but housework after marriage, is probably the reason why obesity is more frequently met with among them." The deleterious consequences of Jewish eating habits affected all segments of the population, though, contributing to malnutrition among the young. "The Jewish children," observed Bertha Wood, a dietitian at the Boston Dispensary, "suffer from too many pickles, too few vegetables and too little milk," leaving them high-strung, overexcited, and irritable.

In their encounter with immigrant Jews, domestic scientists sought to refine the Jewish palate, an elusive goal that one participant likened to a "real missionary task." And yet, although one might expect them to rail against kashruth, whose prohibition against mixing meat with milk ran counter to some of their most cherished notions, like having a glass of milk at every meal, domestic scientists did no such thing. Instead, they tried to circumvent these culinary obstacles, acknowledging a certain measure of sympathy for what often appeared to be an illogical ritual. "One has to recognize these prejudices as one recognizes varying tastes and cater to them," cautioned Dr. Max Kahn in the pages of the *Journal of Home Economics*, adding that "if you, at your leisure, will read through Deuteronomy you will become expert in the

Jewish ritual." Off honing their exegetical skills, some nutritionists and home economists would have been better served perhaps by improving communications with their students, or "clients." Novelist Anzia Yezierska described one such encounter between a food missionary, or "friendly visitor," and an immigrant family that was clearly not all peaches and cream. "By pictures and lectures she shows us how the poor people should live. . . . Always it's on the end of my tongue to ask her, 'You learned us to do without so much, why can't you learn us how to eat without eating?' "

Over time, the nutritionists' critique of the Jewish diet elided into a critique of the Jewish mother's feeding techniques and, by extension, of Jewish culture as well. Writing in such influential periodicals as the *American Journal of Orthopsychiatry* and the *Medical Woman's Journal*, experts made much of the maternal relationship to food, suggesting strongly that because "Jews put great emphasis on intellect but also on food," deleterious consequences were bound to follow. Jewish children aged two through five, one study found, tended to be significantly fussier than those of other ethnic groups. Forty-eight percent refused two or more foods, as compared with only 18 percent of Polish and 16 percent of Negro youngsters of the same age. Based on this finding, the study concluded "the taking of food must have a significance in Jewish culture which it lacks in the Polish and Negro. It creates in these mothers so much concern that in spite of medical advice which they follow exceedingly well as to cod-liver oil, time out of doors, sleep, toilet habits, etc., they are unable to establish a healthy attitude towards eating." Another study took the Jewish mother to task for manifesting an "over-protective attitude in the feeding situation." As proof, it cited numerous instances of Jewish mothers who, despite financial constraints, insisted on grade-A eggs and lamb chops for their children when cheaper cuts of meat and grade-B eggs would have done just as well. Empirical evidence went only so far to explain this seemingly irrational behavior; the study's author sought an explanation rooted in the etiology of culture. To her way of thinking, the Jewish mother's clinically demonstrated preoccupation with food was rooted in some kind of mysterious gustatory proclivity: "preoccupation with foods for generations back, the emphasis placed on 'clean' and 'unclean' foods has made the Jewish mother more food conscious. Even when customs relating to dietary practice are ignored by the younger generations, the psychological effects of such preoccupation with foods for generations back *still persist*."

Despite their obvious defects, Jewish mothers, it was widely believed, tended to be attentive and able cooks, not just zealous ones. After all, "who is more careful about vitamins and the seven groups of food essential for good nutrition than the Jewish mother?" "Jewish women are as a whole good cooks," observed dietitian Mary L. Schapiro, explaining that "they have the secret of making a little go a long way." One "beneficiary" of Jewish culinary wizardry, Harry Gersh, a union organizer and the son of an immigrant Jewish woman, did not always agree. Offering a "heretical view of a sacred Jewish institution," Gersh reflected on his mother's inability to cook, an idea, he confessed, that initially shocked him because of its novelty. "Ma's cooking is enshrined in Jewish tradition, as well as in American folklore. Thousands of pretty pictures in magazine ads, subways and billboards had taught me that motherhood was a higher cooking diploma than a *ruban bleu*." His mother's flavorless, heavy, and indigestible cooking, however, seemed to mock that convention, leading him to question whether his culinary plight was idiosyncratic or widely shared. While gathering data and talking to his friends, he discovered an awful truth. "I had found out that my mother was not the only Jewish mother who couldn't cook. Joe's mother wasn't any better and Irving's was definitely worse." Leonard Bernstein's mother, like Harry's, Joe's, and Irving's, was also not too adroit in the kitchen. Admonishing her children "to have some salt," she produced large, bland platters of overboiled and overcooked meat and chicken. "Food to her was meant to be eaten in copious amounts, not necessarily enjoyed for its taste."

SOME JEWISH TABLES made up in tastefulness what they lacked in taste by sentimentalizing kashruth. Despite the weight of science, some kashrut advocates preferred to leaven their arguments on its behalf with emotion, insisting that "kashruth is more than a matter of health and sanitation. It is a state of mind." Here, too, Jewish cookbooks played an important role, popularizing sentiment much as they had popularized science. As much about culture as about recipes, this new genre of Jewish women's literature associated Jewishness with the steaming, fragrant vapors of the kitchen—here was "kitchen Judaism" in the purest and most estimable sense of the term. Through the "humble literature" of cookbooks, women emerged as cultural authorities in their own right, personifications of Jewish knowledge and tradition. While not all Jewish cookbook writers resembled "motherly matrons in steel-rimmed spectacles, their white hair smoothly parted above a red placid face"—some, in fact, prided themselves on being young, trim, and stylish—they likened themselves to the *baleboste*, the traditional Jewish housewife, and derived their authority from her expertise, social significance, and "inherited routine."

Under the *baleboste*'s tutelage, American Jews were encouraged to regard the consumption of kosher food as a way of affirming and celebrating tradition, Jewish identity, and cultural continuity. Evoking such sacred ideals as motherhood, tradition, and history, the sentimental approach endowed them with charm and magic. Heirlooms in their own right, family recipes handed down over the years conjured up memories of a "romantic past" while serving as a tangible link with Jewish history. "Will we be wise enough to recognize the importance of these traditions and to hand them down intact to future generations?" inquired a popular Jewish cookbook of the interwar years. "All we need to remember is that by the beautiful expedient of surrounding certain foods with the halo of religious associations and with the magic charm of 'once in a while,' our mothers were able to preserve these traditions for us down through the ages."

Mordecai Kaplan was perhaps the keenest exponent of this particular approach. Pronouncing the scientific view of kashruth "gratuitous," he urged his followers not to overstate the practical importance of the dietary laws. "By giving them a utilitarian purpose their function as a means of turning the mind to God is bound to be obscured," he wrote in his seminal *Judaism as a Civilization*. Instead, this most original of Jewish thinkers preferred to consider kashruth a "Jewish folkway" that enhanced the quality of modern Jewish life. "But if Jews are not to exaggerate the importance of the dietary practices," cautioned Kaplan, "neither should they underestimate the effect those practices can have in making a home

Jewish. If the dietary folkways are capable of striking a spiritual note in the home atmosphere, Jews cannot afford to disregard them." By turns pragmatic and emotional, Kaplan squarely situated the observance of kashruth within a contemporary framework. Insofar as kosher food, along with Jewish artwork and

---

GEFILTE FISH

3 lbs. fish (pike and white fish or pike and carp)	1 tsp. salt
2 onions	⅛ tsp. pepper
1 egg	a few dashes of cinnamon
½ cup water (approximately)	1 stalk celery
2 tbsp. matzoh meal or bread crumbs	1 carrot
	1 potato (if desired)

If there is any one particular food that might lay claim to being the Jewish national dish, gefilte fish is that food. This may be due to the fact that since it is associated with the Shabbat, it appears on our menus more frequently than do most of the other distinctly Jewish dishes. But the greatest factors making for its popularity are its intrinsically delectable qualities.

Clean and wash the fish thoroughly, salt and place in refrigerator until ready to prepare. Either leave the fish whole or cut it into two-inch slices, as preferred. If the fish is left whole, do not remove the head or the tail. In either case, remove the flesh with the bones, leaving the skin intact. Now clear the flesh from the bones. Put the fish and one onion through the food chopper and then into a wooden bowl. Add the egg, matzoh meal, seasoning and enough water to make a soft light mixture. Chop until smooth and thoroughly blended. Fill the skin with this mixture. If the fish has been sliced, wet the hands with cold water, form oval cakes out of the mixture and fit them into the bands of skin. Place the bones on the bottom of a heavy kettle. Slice the other onion, the carrot, the potato and the celery, place them on the bones and season all with a dash of salt, pepper and cinnamon. On these place the fish and cover with cold water. Cook rapidly at first, then slowly for about two hours. If the sauce has boiled down completely, add a little water. Allow the fish to cool somewhat before removing from the kettle. Serve warm or cold, garnished with the sliced carrot and, if cold, also with the jellied sauce.

Horseradish Relish is an indispensable accessory to gefilte fish. Scrape and grate a horseradish root. Mix with a little vinegar and sugar to taste and color with a little beet juice.

The preparation of gefilte fish required skill and patience, as this recipe from *The Jewish Home Beautiful* attests.

bric-a-brac, infused the middle-class Jewish home with an appropriately Jewish sensibility, it was to be encouraged; by no means, however, was it obligatory.

A way of shoring up sentiment, kashruth was also likened to a "fine art," and aesthetic canons were to be applied to its performance. "Living as a Jewess is more than a matter of faith, knowledge or observance," *The Jewish Home Beautiful* reminded its readers. "To live as a Jewess, a woman must have something of the artist in her." Kashruth, then, became the implied medium and Jewish cuisine the means by which the talent and artistry of the modern Jewish woman could be unveiled. Aestheticizing the practice of kashruth and the celebration of Jewish holidays, this perspective held out the possibility that Judaism could more than hold its own in complexity, tastefulness, and modernity with the best the West had to offer; in the process, the powerful, lingering stereotype of an impoverished Judaism, lacking in grace and charm, was overturned, or at least subdued. "The Jewish bride who starts her career as a home-maker by making provision for the observance of *kashruth* need not feel sorry for herself or envy her friends who do not observe. . . . There is no good reason why she should feel apprehensive lest her menus, which are determined by the laws of forbidden foods and forbidden food mixtures, be monotonous. In culinary perfection and variety the 'kosher kitchen' can well hold its own in comparison with any fare," wrote Trude Weiss Rosmarin encouragingly. Under these circumstances, the prospect of entertaining nonkosher guests could be made into an occasion for culinary delight. "The Jewish woman who entertains guests who are not observers of *kashruth* need not feel self-conscious or apologetic, for if she will serve a good *Jewish* meal, her guests will have a special treat." Where others viewed kashruth as socially restrictive, culinarily inferior, and unduly expensive, Weiss Rosmarin and her cohorts sang its praises, recasting drawbacks as virtues and liabilities as assets. By sleight of hand, even the onerousness of having two sets of dishes now became a fortuitous opportunity, "a welcome change in the setting of the table, a variety in dinnerware which usually only the wealthy indulge in. To own two sets of dishes and silverware is therefore a real privilege, a luxury permitted and commanded, moreover, by Jewish law, which should be gratefully appreciated by the Jewish home-maker."

At times, this conflation of aesthetics and kashruth resulted in confusion. "We have frequently marveled at the ease and independence with which American Jewesses adjust matters religious in order to suit time and place in a modern household," noted the *American Jewess* in 1898, referring to the curious case of a woman who, for Passover, bought special plates for serving oysters, a nonkosher food. While some women might have been troubled by this seeming inconsistency between style and sacrament, others were not. Still others seemed delighted by the challenge of keeping a home that was both kosher and stylish. "Secretly, I suspected that [my mother] kept a kosher house largely because of the difficulties it imposed," wrote Felicia Lamport in her autobiographical novel, *Mink on Week Days*. "To her, the planning and serving of epicurean meals was almost a career. . . . The limitations made her career that much more challenging and her triumphs that much greater. . . . A number of hostesses she knew set good tables, but she was the only one to serve *kosher* ambrosia." Setting a good example as well as a lovely table, Mrs. Lamport and other women of her generation internalized the notion that "in a Jewish home, a perfectly prepared meal, daintily served, is not enough. It may satisfy the physical desires and the esthetic sense but *to be perfect*, it must be kosher."

ULTIMATELY, THE GREATEST INDUCEMENT to keeping kosher was neither aesthetic nor scientific but a practical one: the growing availability of mass-produced kosher food items. Hundreds of ritually permissible foodstuffs, from soup to nuts, made their way onto the table of the "observant Israelite," demonstrating once again that modernity enhanced the possibilities of a religious life simply by expanding the number of goods and services available to the kosher consumer. As the makers of Crisco vegetable shortening exuberantly proclaimed upon its debut as a rabbinically certified product, "The Hebrew Race has been waiting 4,000 years for Crisco." Commercial manufacturers had targeted Jewish consumers as early as 1900, mindful of the profitability of this ethnic

The kosher consumer of the 1940s could choose from a wide array of food products.

marketplace, where the annual food budget ran into the millions of dollars. Through carefully placed advertisements in the Yiddish press, evocative posters in store windows, and the distribution of free product cookbooks, they promoted the tastiness and health-giving properties of Borden's Condensed Milk, Uneeda Biscuits with their "odor repelling" In-Er-Seal packaging, and dozens of other items. As the decade wore on, Procter & Gamble, General Foods, and Heinz 57 Varieties accelerated their efforts, adding explicitly kosher products to their inventory as well. Market research revealed that despite the overall decrease in the number of kosher consumers, the steadfast among them constituted a sufficiently large and profitable pool of patrons to warrant an investment in kosher goods. What's more, come the Jewish holidays, which occurred several times a year, even the unobservant were inclined to purchase kosher foods. "For more than a few Jews," observed one sociologist, "holidays become family and eating festivals (no wonder Manischewitz sells more than eighty kinds of Passover foods)."

Product cookbooks familiarized Jewish consumers with the array of new foodstuffs by providing "tempting" and "ingenious" dishes based on recipes rigorously tested in the manufacturers' "test kitchens." Betty Brown, the home economist at I. Rokeach & Sons, came up with spaghetti made from matzoh, while Manischewitz outdid itself with a recipe for "farfeloons," coconut macaroons constituted from matzoh farfel. These and other treats were developed as a way of broadening the Passover palate and relieving "matzoh monotony," but manufacturers hoped their appeal would be year-round as well. Rumford's *What Shall I Serve? Famous Recipes for Jewish Housewives* and *Crisco Recipes for the Jewish Housewife* offered more familiar and sturdy fare. Drawing on the "unusual recipe-consciousness of the entire Jewish people," the Rumford cookbook offered recipes for strudel and strawberry shortcake; Crisco's taste ran more toward such American culinary

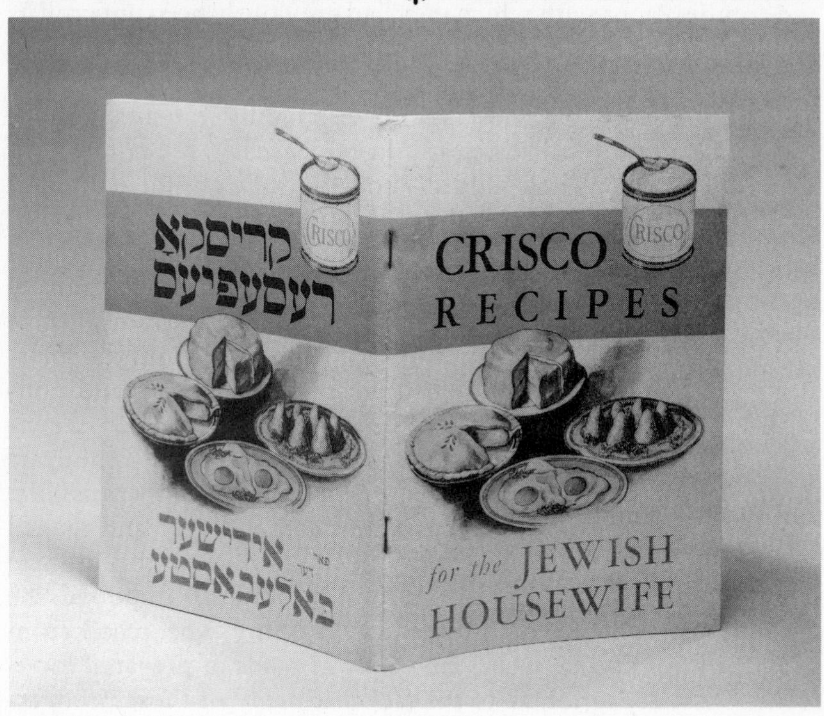

Published in Yiddish and English, this cookbook encouraged two generations of consumers to use Crisco, the "modern" and "digestible" fat.

staples as apple pie. Its bilingual text furthered not just culinary vitality but family solidarity as well by enabling Yiddish-speaking mothers and their English-speaking daughters to cook together.

Recipe contests like the one sponsored by Gold Medal Flour also whipped up interest in new American food products. "Ask your grocer how you can become a Gold Medal woman," the company stated, promising five hundred dollars in prize money as well as the prospect of publication. Choosing from among a thousand entries, the manufacturer published *The Gold Medal Flour Cookbook* (1921), a comprehensive compilation, in Yiddish, of soups, poultry, fish, eggs, cakes, condiments, and ice creams. The cookbook's intention, its foreword made clear, was not simply to familiarize the Yiddish-speaking consumer with Gold Medal products, or even to refresh her understanding of traditional Jewish cuisine. Rather, its mandate was an ecumenical one: to broaden the Jewish palate by introducing housewives to individual foods and combinations with which they had previously been unfamiliar. The cookbook's cover, ironically enough, proclaimed an altogether different message, one that seemed to clash with its stated objectives. Featuring an observant Jewish family seated around the *shabbos* table, two challahs clearly in evidence and the phrase "An Enjoyable Sabbath," in Yiddish, hovering nearby, the iconography identified Gold Medal Flour as nothing less than a key ingredient in Jewish ritual practice. Wolff Brothers, manufacturers of buckwheat groats and other healthful foods, followed suit by publishing the *Yiddish-English Cook Book*, it, too, based on a recipe contest among the "most fastidious" consumers of Wolff products.

By the 1920s, so many food products, both kosher and non-kosher, cluttered the marketplace that the United Synagogue considered publishing *A Guide for Jewish Housewives* to help shoppers distinguish between the ritually permissible and the impermissible. "Today there are so many preparations and packaged and canned goods the consistence of which are unknown to the average woman, that very often Trefah food is bought," reported the Committee on Religious Observance. "Many who recoil from forbidden food go on using the various brands of prepared foodstuffs, blissfully ignorant of the fact that many of those products contain ingredients that are positively not Kosher." Though the publication per se failed to materialize, the appearance of specially

In the New World, age-old foodstuffs like matzoh came in a variety of new, and often daintified, forms.

designed logos bearing a rabbinic seal of approval, or *heksher*, as it was ritually known, helped housewives to ascertain a product's "freedom from trefah ingredients."

When it came to the production and distribution of kosher food items, manufacturers were assisted by marketing and advertising firms like the Joseph Jacobs Organization, which specialized in the "Jewish field." These businesses helped the food giants "promote their products to an important buying group of the American public" by developing a series of broadcast and print campaigns uniquely designed to court the kosher consumer, usually timing the campaign to coincide with the Jewish holidays. On such occasions, "festive meals are the order of the day," manufacturers were told. "The week preceding them, in each instance, is a *big buying period*, when the sale of commodities increases tremendously." Courting reluctant manufacturers was also a part of the organization's mandate as it sought to convince them of the benefits of doing business with those whose religion differed markedly from their own. Through specially produced booklets, such as *Customs and Traditions of Israel, The Jewish Culture—And What It Means to the American Manufacturer in the Marketing of His Products*, and *The Joseph Jacobs Handbook of Familiar Jewish Words and Ex-*

pressions (a text to be used "for making friends with Jewish merchants"), kashruth's peculiarities were explained away and rendered less daunting. "Some of the customs described here may appear bizarre, some even fantastic; but one fact must be stressed . . . they are universally premised upon sound reason and rooted in beautiful sentiment. Superstition, irrational belief, and narrow-mindedness have no place in Jewish observance."

Instead, white bread, mayonnaise, and satiny-smooth Spry gradually assumed pride of place within the kosher kitchen, transforming it from an island of culinary superstition to a common meeting ground for tuna fish sandwiches and oatmeal cookies. In 1927, after protracted negotiations between the United Synagogue and Messing Bakeries, Inc., a kosher white bread was made available for the first time. *The United Synagogue Recorder* eagerly reported the news, hailing it as "one of the most important things that the Religious Observance Committee has done in the past year." Stressing the fact that most white breads contained either lard or milk, and hence were unsuitable for use, the magazine encouraged the Jewish housewife "to make this bread popular. Please ask for this bread and insist that your grocer take it in if he has not as yet done so." Grocers didn't need to be persuaded of the merits of Pillsbury's XXX flour, a popular product, which they widely stocked. "Challoh that you will produce from this flour for your Sabbath and holidays will be very light in weight, big, beautiful and tasty," kosher customers were informed. "It makes a challoh the likes of which you have never dreamed possible and which will make your neighbors jealous." Whether baking challah or pastries, Jewish housewives also availed themselves of Crisco and Spry, two competitive versions of vegetable shortening. "See how smoothly this pre-creamed shortening blends with other ingredients—what light, fluffy cake batter it makes. You'll be amazed how light and fine-textured your cakes are! How flaky and tender your pastries!" Meanwhile, those without a hankering for pastry, cake, or white bread could choose from among Durkee's mayonnaise and salad dressings, Aunt Jemima's buckwheat pancakes, and twenty-six of Heinz's fifty-seven varieties of pickles, condiments, creamed soups, and baked beans, now free of blood-stained eggs, lard, wine vinegar, and other ritual impurities.

With the invention, in the mid-thirties, of "beef frye," a meat product said to look, taste, and smell like bacon and "at the same time to be positively kosher," the wall between kosher and non-kosher crumbled almost entirely. A marvel of technology, beef frye, or "Jewish bacon," so astonished kosher consumers that, according to writer Isaac Rosenfeld, they gathered outside the window of a kosher delicatessen to watch it being sliced by a knowledgeable counterman. "But what is there in bacon, kosher or *treif*, to draw such a crowd?" Might it have to do with beef frye's representation of "food in the form of the forbidden, an optical pun on kosher and *treif*," he wondered. Others attributed the product's allure to its perceived ability "to fortify Jewish merchants, so to speak, against the great American breakfast craving for bacon and eggs." Ultimately, beef frye's value to the kosher consumer was as much symbolic as gustatory: it, too, held out the very real and tantalizing possibility that the observance of kashruth posed no barrier to participation in the wider world, at least in a culinary sense. After all, even kosher Jews could now eat bacon! "Due to misstatements presented in the guise of truth, many non-Jews believe that the 'orthodox' Jew has peculiar idiosyncrasies; that he is definitely set in his ways, requiring none of the necessities of life or its luxuries; that his mode of living and psychological reactions are entirely different from those of the average human being," wrote Jacobs in one of his helpful asides. "Nothing could be further from the truth," as the existence of beef frye so clearly demonstrated. Ultimately, the wholesale kosherization of basic American food products suggested that the constraints of kashruth affected only the way the food was made, not the food itself. "On the few occasions when self-denial might be demanded, American technology is there to eliminate the inconvenience; thus almost every American diet staple is now available in kosher or Passover form," wrote sociologist Herbert Gans in 1956.

Technological advances also increased the availability of traditional kosher food items, enabling manufacturers as diverse as Isaac Gellis ("the first and largest kosher sausage factory in the United States") and Horowitz Bros. & Margareten ("the choice of millions") to satisfy an appetite for kosher cuisine. Tea, coffee, borscht, chicken soup, potato starch, noodles, egg barley, egg flakes, and six different kinds of matzoh, from "Hygienic Mat-

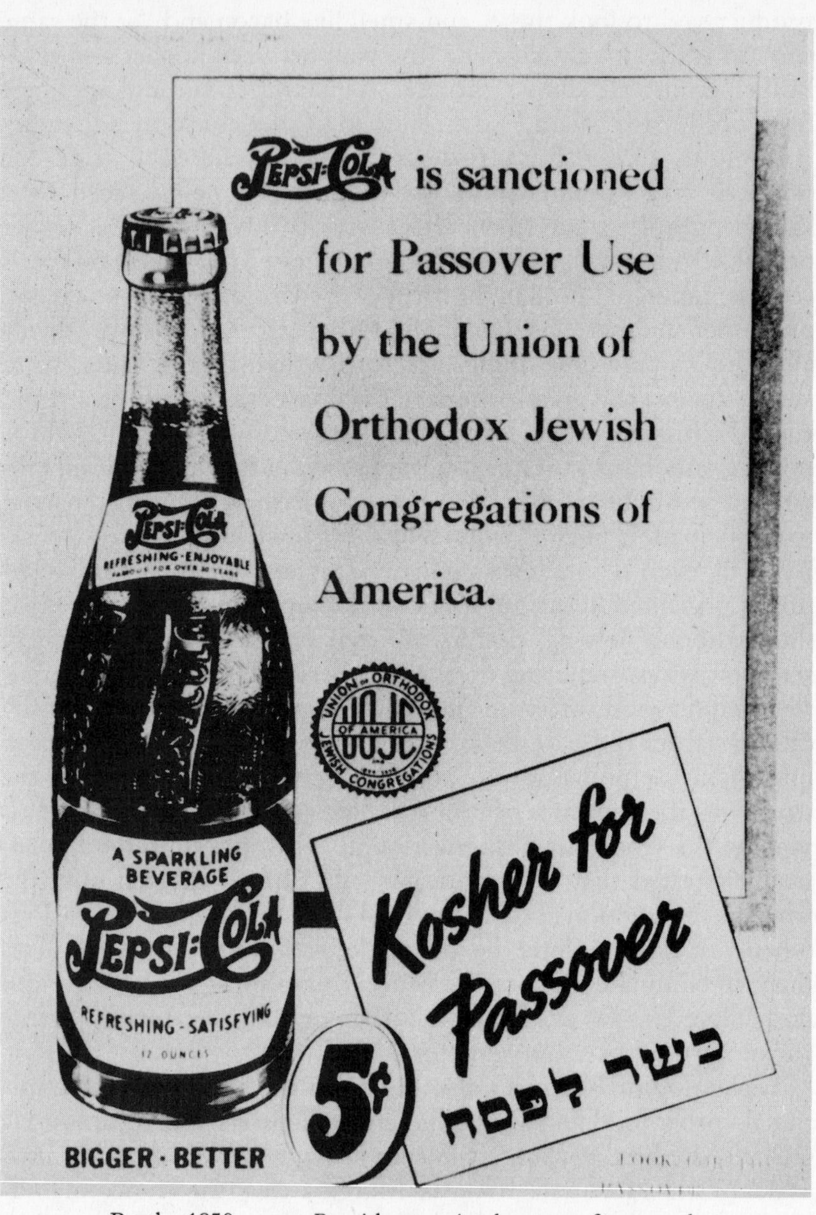

By the 1950s, even Pepsi bore a ritual stamp of approval.

zohs" to "Matzohs (plain)," were now produced yearly, as was gefilte fish, a quintessential Jewish *maychel* (treat) whose pleasures had been sung by legions of consumers, including Israel Zangwill and the members of the Jewish Women's Congress. Reassuring consumers that mass-produced gefilte fish was just as tasty and economical as the kind Mother used to make, Jewish manufacturers turned a steady profit from their traffic in fish. Some, like I. Rokeach & Sons, produced not just fish but also salad oils, soups, soaps, and scouring powders. Established in New York in 1890 by Lithuanian-born Israel Rokeach, this firm pioneered the manufacture of commercial soap whose individual bars proclaimed the word *Kosher* in bold red or blue letters. "Reading correctly the handwriting on the wall, [Rokeach] foresaw that the modern housewife would be at least as interested in sanitation as in Kashruth, and if the old-fashioned methods of cleaning pots, pans and dishes with sand or just elbow-grease, would prove too bothersome, she might be sorely tempted to use the non-kosher soap that was so readily available," explained the company's official history. "[Rokeach] felt, therefore, that he would fill an important need, and perform a great public service, if he could supply the kosher home with kosher soap." Unable to rest until he found a way to make a soap free of animal fat, Rokeach experimented with various chemical combinations until he discovered coconut oil—and "that's how kosher soap started."

Advertising stimulated an appetite for newly created kosher products like Rokeach kosher soap while helping to overcome a general suspicion of packaged goods. In not a few Jewish households, "cans were also objects of dark suspicion. They were poisonous. And if they weren't poisonous they gave food a bad taste." Thanks to brand-name advertising, though, not all cans were tarred with the same brush. "Mother belonged to the modern school. She used canned tomato soup. Only Campbell's of course." Other families felt the same way about such kosher food manufacturers as Horowitz Bros. & Margareten or Rokeach. "You may insure yourself against disappointment by looking and asking for the Package with the Red Shield of David Horowitz inscribed therein," promised Horowitz Bros. & Margareten, whose products claimed to be "kosher in the true sense of the word" and to

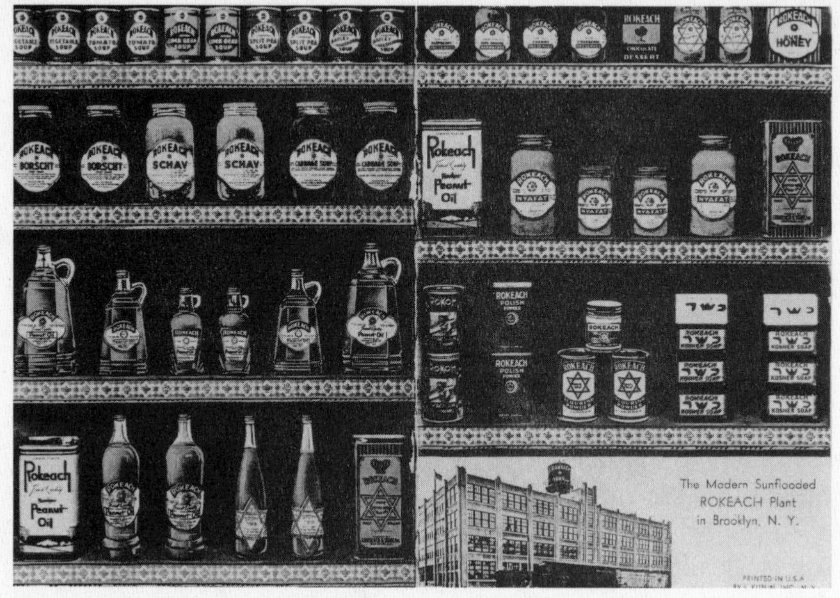

On the grocer's shelf, and at home, hygiene and kashruth went hand in hand.

leave "nothing to be desired in quality or cleanliness." Popular shibboleths such as quality, cleanliness, and sanitation were routinely enlisted on the side of canned goods, packaged matzoh, and kosher butcher shops and bakeries. When, in 1925, Sol Green of Philadelphia called his newly opened South Fourth Street bakery a "most up to date sanitary bakery" and boasted that "it has the most modern baker's improvements, is all white, and is a day light [sic] Bakery," or when Mr. Barsky, his neighbor on South Fifth Street, opened his "first class" butcher shop, "where you will get quality meats," they contributed as much to the rationalizing of kashruth as did the medical literature surveyed earlier.

With its double armor of rabbinical *heksher* and laboratory seal of approval, kosher food connoted healthy food produced in "sun-flooded" factories under the most rigorously hygienic conditions, an association actively exploited by most manufacturers. In language reminiscent of the domestic science movement, Horowitz

Bros. & Margareten, for one, publicly extolled the virtues of its "scientific baking." "We have raised the kneading and baking of Matzoh from haphazard, careless, hit-or-miss process to a science. The temperature of the oven to the exact degree, and the time of the baking in seconds, as well as the thickness of the Matzoh in fractions of an inch, are all noted. We bake by carefully computed formulae." Science also cast its spell over the B. Manischewitz Co., another leading manufacturer of kosher goodies. Like other food giants with an in-house staff of dietary technicians, it maintained the Manischewitz Experimental Kitchens, where recipes using Manischewitz products were tested by the company's very own "Domestic Science Expert and Graduate in Institutional Management."

Occasionally, the often unintentionally humorous encounter of food and science made its way from the experimental kitchen to the television screen. In an episode of *The Goldbergs*, a terrifically popular television program of the fifties, the show's star, Molly Goldberg (the "*baleboste* of the airwaves"), is invited by a leading food manufacturer to whip up a batch of her homemade gefilte fish in his test kitchen. The prospect that her dish might become a nationally produced item excites Molly enormously as she dons a starched white apron and cap and joins the staff of the laboratory kitchen. A spontaneous, old-style cook, more comfortable with a "pinch of this and a pinch of that" than with precise measurements, she is unable to comply with the company's demand that she produce a detailed recipe for her fish, replete with a list of ingredients and the ratio of fish to eggs, sugar, and carrots. After much trial and error, several late-night phone calls to her family, and numerous tastings, Molly reluctantly gives up: old-fashioned cooks like herself, it seems, just can't compete with domestic scientists.

Onscreen and off, manufacturers continued to promote their products by publishing calendars and other handy, abbreviated guides to Jewish ritual life. Diamond Crystal Salt, for example, released *The Jewish Housewife's Guide*, a pocket-sized compendium of Jewish ritual information featuring a five-year Jewish calendar, while the Stuhmer Baking Company published a Jewish almanac whose annual appearance "has become a tradition." In addition to the usual calendrical information, *Stuhmer's Almanac* contained the lyrics to the "Star-Spangled Banner" and "Hatikvah," as well as the texts of assorted prayers, including *yizkor* (the prayer for the dead), grace after meals, the Friday-evening kiddush, and the Torah blessings recited by the bar mitzvah boy. "Our friends tell us that they look forward to its helpful contents each year," the company noted. "We attempt to include within it only that material for which there is a real daily need. We hope you will value your copy and keep it near you throughout the year." Even more than the Stuhmer or Diamond Crystal handouts, the Maxwell House Haggadah, which debuted in the mid-1930s, epitomized the "unique relationship between a product and a people." With more than twenty million copies distributed free of charge over the past half century, the convenient bilingual Haggadah produced by the makers of Maxwell House Coffee has become one of American Jewry's most enduring and popular cultural icons. American Jewish homes might have lacked a lot of things, but the Maxwell House Haggadah was not one of them.

Jewish housewives, picking up a copy of the Haggadah at their neighborhood grocery store, or gazing at a pantry stocked with kosher pancake mix and jars of gefilte fish, no doubt responded with "unalloyed joy" to the growth of the kosher-food industry. Although kosher food cost approximately 8 to 10 percent more, the kosher consumer was prepared, for the most part, to absorb the extra cost. For the Jewish housewife, "the question of Koshruth arises above the monetary question at all times." From time to time, though, her forbearance gave way, resulting in what has become known, somewhat dramatically, as the Kosher Food Riots. This term, one reporter was quick to explain, had nothing to do with rabbinical approval of boisterous public behavior but rather was coined by the police. "Some linguistic genius of an Irish policeman pronounced it 'kosher,' not by virtue of any 'hehksher,' or certificate of fitness issued by a rabbi, but because of the descriptive quality of the term 'Kosher' as an adjective to the particular kind of riot." In 1902, and again in 1917, when several hundred butchers in New York and Chicago announced that they were raising the price of kosher meat by a few cents a pound, the "thread of endurance snapped." Loyal customers, feeling the pinch, confronted their neighborhood butchers, demanding they readjust prices to an earlier, and more equitable, level.

Stuhmer's purveyed tradition along with its pumpernickel bread.

When the retailers refused, the women called for a boycott. At first sporadic and "desultory," the boycott spread throughout both cities. As housewives and butchers squared off, tempers flared, fistfights erupted, meat was ruined; in short order, the boycott "degenerated into a good sized riot which kept the police busy for several hours." Unable to withstand both the wrath of their customers and the loss of their patronage, the butchers met their demands and rolled back prices to pre-boycott levels. Butchers were not the only ones to bear the brunt of consumer anger. In 1916, Jewish women in Pittsburgh, angered by an "unjust" increase in the price of kosher bread, took on local bakers. Their boycott proved so successful that bakers restored prices to what they had been prior to the boycott. This show of spirit, observed the *American Jewish Chronicle*, demonstrated conclusively that "when it comes to fighting for principle, [Jewish women] can do it just as well as men."

* * *

נייע ערעפענונג

נייעס פאר דאון-טאונער פובליקום

מר. בארסקי מאכט בעקאנט וועגען זיין נייע ערעפענונג פון איין פוירסט קלעסס סעניטערי, קלינע אונד גרויסארטיגע

כשר בוטשער סטאר

שבת אווענד, דעצעמבער 8טען, 1934

אונטער דער השגחה פון הרב לעווינטאל

2130 סויט 5טע סטריט

איהר וועט צו יעדער צייט בעקומען די בעסטע כשרה פלייש און איך פרישע געקילעטע טשיקענס קומט און איבערצייט זיך, איהר וועט אויך זיין צופרידען מיט די בילינע פרייזען.

	פונט		פונט
טשאק - -	16ס	ברוסט - -	25ס
סטייק - -	25ס	ריב סטייק -	30ס
וויעל קאטלעטס	25ס	וויעל ברוסט -	16ס
לעמב טשאפס	30ס	לעמב שאלדערס	25ס

פרעזענטען וועלען געגיבען ווערען צו יעדען קאסטאמער בא דער ערעפענונג

אירדערס ווערען דעליוועט פריי — מיר נעמען אן פוד ארדערס

NEW OPENING MR. BARSKY announces the new opening of a first class Kosher Butcher Store where you will get quality Meats at very Reasonable Prices. In our Store you will at all times get the Finest and Best Meats in the City also a selection of Freshly Killed Chickens -- Strictly Kosher under the supervision of RABBI LEVINTHAL.

Souvenirs will be given to All on Opening Day

Saturday Evening, December 8th, 1934

AT 2130 S. 5TH STREET

ORDERS DELIVERED FREE -- -- FOOD ORDERS ACCEPTED

Kosher butchers were easy to find in some neighborhoods and rare in others.

In fighting for their principles, butchers in New York and Chicago insisted that they were as much the victims of rapacious packers and distributors as were the consumers. While in no way excusing their behavior, this explanation did reflect fundamental imbalances in the distribution of kosher food whose availability was not evenly apportioned throughout the country. Simply put, when it came to kashruth, geography was destiny. In some cities with a decent-size Jewish population, like Denver and Minneapolis, one could easily find a range of kosher foods, but in others, like Johnstown, Pennsylvania (the "Jewish Middletown"), even kosher meat was difficult to obtain. And under the best of circumstances, kosher eateries were scarce. "The difficulties of finding kosher refreshment outside of the home form a series of temptations which require a very strong will to resist," noted the *American Hebrew* as early as 1910; nor had the situation improved a decade later when the United Synagogue sought, unsuccessfully, to create a "United Synagogue Restaurant" in every town. "Unless we do that," explained a spokesman, "under the present mode of life, we shall bring to pass a condition of affairs in which the observance of the dietary laws will be limited to the home."

Of course, one didn't need to consult the United Synagogue's pocket-sized *Directory of Kosher Hotels, Boarding Houses and Restaurants in the United States*, a 1919 publication, to know that the greatest concentration of kosher retail outlets and "racial restaurants" anywhere in the United States could be found in New York City. Home to America's largest Jewish population, the Big Apple contained thousands of food institutions—butcher shops, delicatessens, and dairy, vegetarian, and meat restaurants—that catered to the Jewish client eager to "serve his stomach and his faith." While some might have taken for granted Cohen's Dairy Restaurant or Felix's Kosher Restaurant (the "Jewish Delmonico's"), such diligent students of New York history and culture as the Federal Writers Project team did not as they explored the eating habits of New Yorkers in the early 1940s. Thanks to their copious field notes, cartons of which may be found in New York City's Municipal Archives, a detailed map of the Jewish culinary capital and of "Jewish food customs" can be drawn. "The Jews are fond of good food, and when their circumstances permit, they eat well—very well, and with discriminating taste. . . . This chapter, therefore, offers a chance to talk about food here with the same reverence, enthusiasm and gusto that a Jewish Escoffier, Savarin or George Rector might write about the sort of food of which Jewish people are most fond," wrote one researcher to a member of the project team, outlining his ideas for a chapter on Jewish culinary practice. "It isn't all garlic!" he added enthusiastically.

Fish topped the list of known Jewish culinary preferences. "The Jews are one of the largest homogene fish-consuming elements of the public of New York," noted researcher Adam Gostony in his 1942 essay "Jews as Fish-Consumers." "If the writer hesitates to name them as the largest single fish-consuming group," Gostony explained, "it is only due to the consideration that the Jews are not permitted to eat . . . every kind of fish." He then went on, at great length, to identify such representative Jewish food "delicacies" as gefilte fish, bismarck herring, roll mops, matjes herring, salted herring, homemade schmaltz herring, homemade pickled herring, homemade fried herring, smoked herring, chopped herring, herring salad ("a gray looking material"), whitefish, and salmon. Back in Russia, he explained, herring was often the cheapest food the Jews could find; upon emigrating to the New World, they continued to enjoy its pleasures. "They got so used to it they still kept their preference for its taste." An Old World food, herring and other piscine delicacies were sold in a brand-new setting: the appetizing store, an "outgrowth of New York City's special trading inventions and creations." Although the origins of its name remains a mystery which neither historical records nor recent conversations with the members of Local 338, the counterman's union, has succeeded in clearing up, the store's appeal as a source of "delicious table delicacies" is not hard to understand. "Attractively furnished with beautifully arrayed windows in which food products, mostly in tins, are arranged in symmetrical order," the appetizing store featured dozens of smoked and dried fishes, "home-made salads," European tinned goods, cheeses, bulk candy, and a variety of domestic and imported nuts. Four to five hundred of these stores—for example, Saperstein Brothers and Barney Greengrass, "a New York tradition since 1908"—took root in New York's residential neighborhoods, where it was not uncommon to find several clustered together on one block; in 1936, the Lower East Side alone boasted thirty-six appetizing emporia. "Although people of every nationality patronize the retail appetizing stores, the Jewish people are by far the greatest customers," reported a contemporary observer. "This may be attributed to their peculiar love for highly seasoned foods."

As much a neighborhood institution as the appetizing store, the local delicatessen, or "deli," also laid claim to both ethnic pride and culinary loyalty. Whether kosher or merely kosher-style, its neatly arranged rows of salami, chubby frankfurters (known as "specials"), triple-decker pastrami sandwiches, and mustard in distinctive paper cups proclaimed it to be a representative Jewish culinary institution. "The Jews, because of their more delicate taste, have taken to delicatessens more readily than the others and they are the ones who contribute most to the spread of the article amongst the general population," observed David Pater in the pages of the *Mogen David Delicatessen Magazine*, the house organ of the Mogen David Delicatessen Owners' Association, as he described the "delicatessen field" in 1931. Though inextricably identified with New York, which in the mid-1930s boasted approximately five thousand delis, both the food and the institution (the word referred to both) spread throughout the United States, from Baltimore, Richmond, and Memphis in the South, and Chicago, Detroit, and Minneapolis in the Midwest, all the way to California. "We get a good deal of Jewish delicatessen in Hollywood," wrote Orson Welles. "Without pastrami sandwiches there could be no picture-making. And I understand there is a project afoot to pipe the borscht across the continent from Lindy's."

More of a novelty than borscht, delicatessen was not always so beloved. At first, Jewish housewives had too many qualms about its nutritive value, doubtful that something as highly spiced as, say, salami or pastrami could possibly be good for their children. Tenaciously they adhered to "the first principle of any Bronx housewife—namely, No Delicatessen," breaking that rule only in cases of "extreme emergency" or fatigue. "At other times a coalition of all other members of the household can temporarily so overpower her that she will look the other way when the provisions are brought onto the premises." The neighborhood deli owner, determined to gain the housewife's confidence and "to inculcate in the public mind the word delicatessen as synonym with such words as appetite, pleasure, purity, etc.," joined forces with a coalition of manufacturers, jobbers, restaurateurs, and other retailers to cultivate a public taste for their products, which they staunchly believed to be "nutritious, digestible, nourishing." For starters, they beefed up their own image by dressing themselves, their countermen, and their stores in white, the color of sanitation and hygiene. The coalition also retained the services of Ada C. Calkins, an "expert household economist," to create economical and healthful recipes likely to appeal to the nutrition-conscious housewife; Calkins's efforts, which resulted in such "Delicious Delicatessen Dinners" as frankfurters and mashed potatoes and peppers stuffed with pastrami, allegedly convinced numerous Jewish housewives of deli's value. "I run my house on a very small budget and I find the delicatessen is just as inexpensive as the meat markets because there is no waste at all in the meat from the delicatessen," Mrs. Green proudly informed her sister-in-law, Mrs. Abramson. "Well," replied an impressed Mrs. Abramson, pointing to the pastrami-pepper concoction, "this dinner has convinced me!" If sampling a "Delicious Delicatessen Dinner" were not enough, the promotional literature of the Mogen David Delicatessen Owners' Association went to great lengths explicitly to highlight the economy, health, modernity, and sophistication found in a frankfurter or a corned-beef sandwich. "They are more concentrated, more filling and serve as both an appetizer and a meal. They save time, for they can be eaten ready made, without any extra work on the part of housewife or host. And they go well with all kinds of drinks, hot or cold, mild or strong. They are ideal for all occasions and must grow in favor with the rise and spread of culture. . . . Nothing else can take their place in the menu of the people, once they have tasted them."

"Deli" did indeed take its place in the "menu of the people," becoming an established part of American Jewish cuisine, a treat as hallowed and highly regarded in some quarters as the Sabbath was in others. "When Milton . . . thought of feasting, he thought of the corner delicatessen, near his folks' cleaning and dyeing plant in Detroit: hot pastrami sandwiches, mustard in a paper twist," a character in a *Commentary* story recalled. In some families, Thursday night was reserved for eating out at the neighborhood deli; in others, Sunday afternoon provided the appropriate "occasion." Growing up in Brownsville, Alfred Kazin looked forward with

HEBREW®
NATIONAL
KOSHER DELICATESSEN
PRESENTS
31 ways to make
hot meals out of
hot dogs!

The American consumer found it hard to resist the taste of a kosher hot dog.

In New York City, the deli was a neighborhood institution.

great relish to Saturday night at the neighborhood delicatessen. "And now, as the electric sign blazed up again, lighting up the words *Jewish National Delicatessen*, it was as if we had entered into our rightful heritage." Highly seasoned and tantalizing, "this was food that only on Saturday nights could be eaten with a good conscience."

In some neighborhoods, the deli was as much an outpost of Jewish culture as of Jewish cuisine, freely dispensing ritual information along with the mustard and the corned beef. "Say it with food," advertised Halpern's Delicatessen of Memphis, which specialized in "parties, condolence expression, or welcome neighbor," while in suburban New York, the kosher-style delicatessen owned by Ruth Glazer's parents served as a recognizable "symbol of traditional Jewish living." In the suburbs, explained Glazer, "the important word to the community was not 'delicatessen' but 'Jewish.' " Glazer's humorous and insightful portrait, "The Jewish Delicatessen: The Evolution of an Institution," which she pub-

A $10.00 Present to the First Customer

With great pleasure I announce to the people of Down-town that in order to give my customers better service I have remodeled the Store at 7th and Cantrell Sts. as a modern Delicatessen Store and can say with pride that it will be the most beautiful store in this section with up-to- date fixtures.

Grand Opening

OF THE

DELICATESSEN

... ... STORE ... ...

Saturday, Sept. 20th

STORE OPENS AT 2 P. M. SHARP

Five Good Reasons for Patronizing this Store

1. Best and Finest Groceries at very Low Prices.

2. Fresh Foods in Delicacies every day to be had in this Store, all kinds of Smoked Fish and fresh Pastrama and Corned Beef, Pickled Tongues of the greatest variety -- "the kind you want to taste".

3. This store will be managed by an expert in the Delicatessen Line and you can be assured of courteous treatment at all times.

4. Presents for $500.00 will be given away on the Opening Day. Don't miss this opportunity. Every customer that spends a dollar at our store will get a Souvenir that's worth 39c wholesale.

5. Your money's worth or your money back.

COME AND CONVINCE YOURSELF

AT

2114 South 7th Street

Corner 7th and Cantrell Sts.

(לעזט די אנדערע זייט)

Philadelphia, too, was not without its own modern delis.

lished in *Commentary* in 1946, suggested something of the deli's cultural significance; the outpouring of letters and phone calls generated by her essay confirmed it. "No article yet printed in *Commentary* has elicited as many comments, oral and written, as Ruth Glazer's 'The Jewish Delicatessen,' " the magazine's editors explained several months later as they published a representative sample. "Of the many communications of praise, amplification, and correction, we present a few in a kind of informal symposium on a subject that seems to strike a responsive chord in the—shall we say—hearts of so many." Orson Welles, though on a diet, declared himself an authority on pastrami and lox; Daniel Bell, then a young instructor at the University of Chicago, lamented his inability, at the culmination of a five-mile walk, to find a decent hot pastrami sandwich in the Windy City. Historian Joshua Starr offered a few pungent historical observations on the origins of the "Jewish weakness for delicatessen," which he dated to the third century, while Louis Berg reminisced about the Virginia deli operated by his father. Charles Yale Harrison had the last word. Concerned lest he be thought a "callithumpian, one who thinks more of food and the grosser pleasures than he does of loftier matters," the novelist offered the observation that delicatessen was to the Jews what frog's legs was to the French and suet pudding to the British. "And so it is with us Jews who frequently speak of the heritage of Israel when what we really have in mind is—yes—Jewish delicatessen."

While the deli was given over to meat, the dairy restaurant scrupulously adhered to a menu of dairy products, grains, fish, and soups. "A place where nothing but the most palatable dishes built out of milk and milk products were to be had, and where no morsel that had been in the vicinity of meat could be obtained for love or money," the dairy restaurant—and its cousin, the vegetarian restaurant (in some instances these designations were used interchangeably)—was initially located in immigrant neighborhoods, where it provided a hearty, inexpensive lunch ("and much black bread") to working-class customers. Though its pleasures were practical ones, on occasion it offered a bit more. In his memoir of the immigrant Jewish experience, Kazin fondly recalls "our one Emma Bovary, Mrs. E, whose wild longing for a nicer world than this led her to abandon her housework for half an hour every morning to sit *at a table* in the empty vegetarian restaurant; it made her feel so distinguished." The majority of customers, perhaps less finely wrought than Mrs. E., came simply to eat. And eat they did. In the 1940s, Ratner's, the granddaddy of dairy restaurants, "in good taste since 1905," served 2,500 customers daily, dispensing 100 portions of gefilte fish a day (200 on weekends), 60 to 70 portions of blintzes and potato pirogen, 80 to 100 portions of borscht, 20 portions of kashe varnitchkes—"doughy things soaked in butter and buckwheat"—and 300 cups of coffee. "Synthetic foods," like the fancifully named Protose or Nuttose steak and the mushroom cutlet, were also on the menu. Providing a satisfying, filling alternative to meat, these dishes contributed to the idea that the dairy and vegetarian restaurant was not only a tasty but a healthy venue as well.

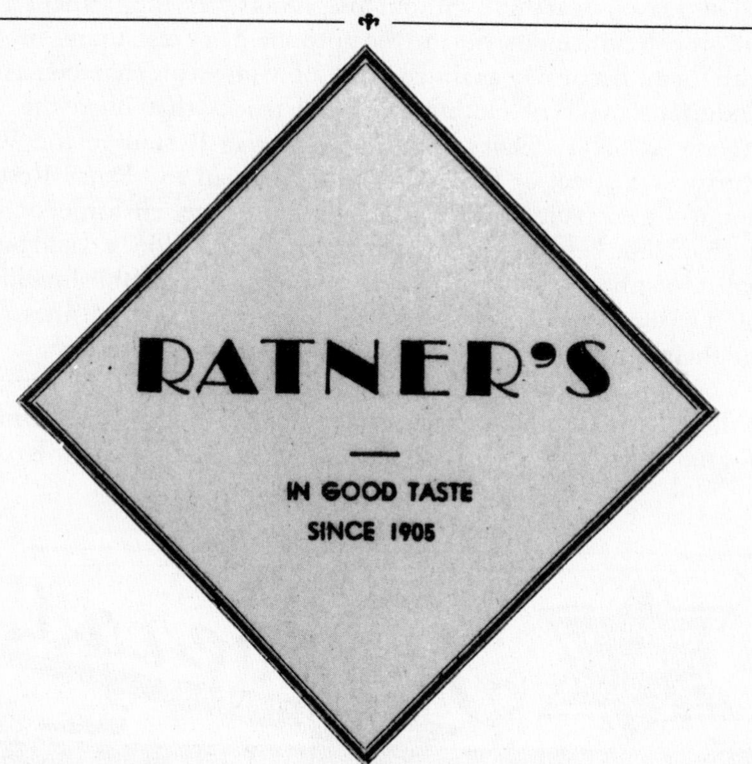

With its mouth-watering onion rolls and nutritious soups, Ratner's has become a culinary legend.

Take, for example, the official history of Ratner's, "the East Side's premier dining place," whose origins unfolded against a mysterious epidemic of stomach ailments believed to have been caused by rotten meat, or so the owners told WPA researchers more than a generation later. That epidemic, coupled with "a desire to be helpful," reportedly led to the establishment of a tiny dairy restaurant, first on Pitt Street and later on Delancey, the Lower East Side's main east-west thoroughfare. From twelve dishes, the menu expanded to one hundred and fifty, "none of which," according to the WPA writers, "are known to have ever caused anybody stomach trouble." Despite its downtown location, Ratner's continued to draw a diverse crowd. "It is especially crowded on weekends when housewives tend to take a day off from their kitchen chores. Venerable patriarchs who refuse to touch food at their children's home for religious reasons, eat there without misgivings." As the garment trade and other Jewish industries moved uptown, dairy restaurants moved with them, becoming as much a part of Midtown's character as the ubiquitous racks of clothing and the trucks that lined the side streets. At S&H's Dairy Kosher Vegetarian Restaurant on West Thirty-first Street or the Vitamine Vegetarian and Dairy Restaurant at Twenty-eighth Street and Fifth Avenue, customers could lunch on "the best and most nutritious foods that money could buy"; and at Steinberg's Dairy Restaurant, an Art Deco establishment located in the heart of the residential Upper West Side, businessmen and their families could dine on "dairy food served at its best."

The lure of a swell Midtown address also affected the fortunes of the superior class of kosher restaurant like Felix's Kosher Dining Room, touted as the "Jewish Delmonico's," or Garfein's Kosher

Generations of Upper West Side residents fondly remember Steinberg's for its filling food and homey atmosphere.

Family Restaurant, an "East Side Waldorf-Astoria" whose silverware, table linens, chandeliers, wall hangings, table lamps, and cuisine provided an elegant atmosphere for dining. "Among the happiest moments of your life you will recollect those spent in Garfein's Kosher Family Restaurant," promised its advertisements, noting reassuringly that Garfein's service was the "equal to any restaurant in the Times Square section" of town. Trotzky's Dining Room, Lou G. Siegel, "America's largest kosher restaurant," and Paramount Kosher Restaurant, situated in the heart of Midtown, made similar claims, trumpeting the "elegance—atmosphere—beauty" of their establishments, whose rich wood paneling, restful lighting, and shiny Art Deco accessories proclaimed sophistication and modernity at every turn. Touting "the combination of excellent food, beauty and service that will meet the demands of the most discriminating," these strictly kosher restaurants played up their affinities with other stylish eateries while downplaying that which set them apart. In these establishments, kashruth was rendered subtle and invisible, both literally and metaphorically. Where a bold Hebrew sign that included the word *Kosher* unmistakably identified other kosher restaurants, Lou G. Siegel, remarked a restaurant-goer of the 1940s, "is marked plainly if inconspicuously by a small English legend bearing the words: Dietary Laws Strictly Observed." That many of Siegel's one thousand customers daily were "non-Jews who come to enjoy the distinctive Jewish cooking" furthered its cosmopolitan aspirations.

Commercial ventures, New York's kosher restaurants were owned and operated by businessmen determined to profit from the distinctive eating habits of their coreligionists. Perhaps the sole exception, and certainly the most interesting, was the Brooklyn Jewish Center Restaurant, a full-scale eatery run by and housed on the premises of the Brooklyn Jewish Center in Crown Heights during the early thirties. (The Jewish Center on Manhattan's West Eighty-sixth Street also maintained a restaurant during the same period but the unavailability of records makes it difficult to relate its history.) Both the center's membership and the Brooklyn Jewish community as a whole were encouraged to "Make the Center Restaurant the place to take your family whenever you decide to dine out." Open several nights a week and on weekends, as well as on Thanksgiving, it provided full-course kosher dinners at reasonable prices in a conveniently located and handsomely appointed dining room presided over by a seasoned maître d' with years of experience at Delmonico's.

After a few years, the restaurant languished and finally closed, a victim of the Depression, which dramatically curtailed such leisure pursuits as dining out *en famille*. Chances are, however, that even under better economic circumstances the Center Restaurant would have had a hard time sustaining customer loyalty, a problem increasingly faced by the more established Midtown eateries as well. By the mid-1930s, there were simply not enough kosher restaurant-goers to fill Paramount's or Garfein's dining room on a regular basis—though non-Jews and nonkosher Jews with an occasional yen for kosher brisket did supplement their thinning ranks. Moreover, the Jewish restaurant-goer was notoriously fickle in his or her culinary allegiances, especially when unhampered by kashruth. With thousands of restaurants to choose from, from Chinese to Czech, competition was fierce. "The temptation to 'eat out' is great; the City offers an alluring array of eating places and the desire 'to get away from the kitchen once in a while' is not uncommon among housewives," related a WPA writer of the

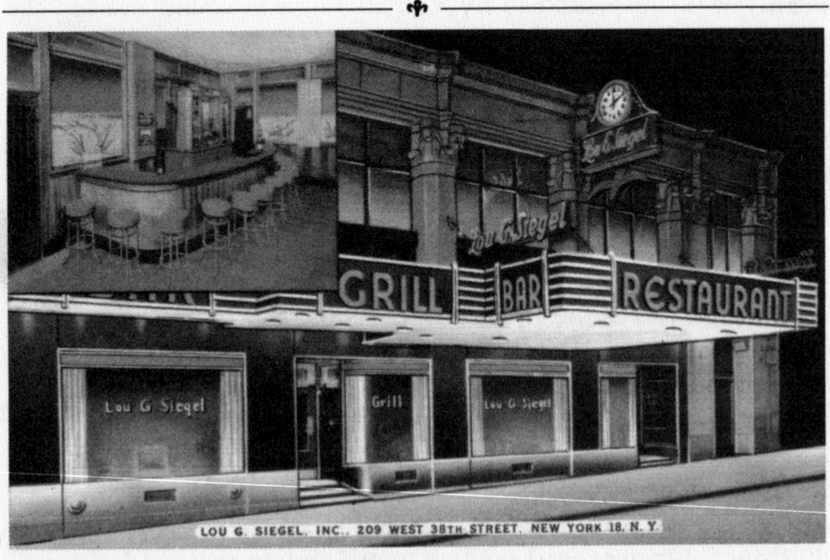

Lou G. Siegel represented the acme of sophisticated kosher dining.

209 WEST 38th STREET • NEW YORK, N.Y.

Siegel's menu contained "a complete line of the choicest foods and delicacies."

early 1940s. The East Side Chamber of Commerce, dedicated to the "rehabilitation of the Lower East Side," played on that temptation. Throughout the thirties and forties, it worked tirelessly to promote tourism, dining, and shopping in the old Jewish neighborhood. " 'Come downtown and let's have a good old-fashioned East Side meal.' That's what 1000's of people from other parts of New York and suburbs still say every week," stated the *East Side Chamber News* in 1936. "Others also feel that shopping tours on the Lower East Side are never complete without having at least one meal at any one of the many fine eating places in this neighborhood. The dairy restaurants along the leading business thoroughfares are particularly popular with shoppers."

While extolling the virtues of dairy restaurants and other kinds of classic Lower East Side eateries, the *East Side Chamber News* mentioned in passing that a number of Chinese restaurants had sprung up recently in the area. Once foreign to the neighborhood, at least eighteen Chinese "tea gardens" and chop suey places could now be found within walking distance of Ratner's. Chinese restaurants also took root in the Bronx, Harlem, and Brooklyn, where they became as much a fixture of the New York Jewish neighborhood as the appetizing store and the corner deli. Brownsville, home of Alfred Kazin's adored Jewish National Delicatessen, was also the place where in 1917 the World Chop Suey Restaurant opened its doors at 1774 Pitkin Avenue, promising every customer a free Chinese souvenir. Within ten years, Brownsville's main street contained no less than six chop suey houses, which were particularly favored by the neighborhood's younger element. "They are the last places to close, and a picture of Pitkin Avenue after two o'clock at night is a blot of darkness riven by six dazzling chop suey signs," Felix Mayrowitz, a local resident, observed in 1928. Then as now, contemporaries seemed puzzled by the Jewish affinity for chow mein and bok choy. To Mayrowitz, "eating Chinese" was a form of overt religious and cultural rebellion in which the younger generation manifested its disregard for the old-fashioned ways of its elders. For others of Mayrowitz's generation, it bespoke sophistication and worldliness. Much like Ma-ch'iau P'ai, or mah-jongg, the "beautifully picturesque, enchanting . . . and fascinating" Chinese tile game that captivated the country in the years following World War I, Chinese foods had also become very fashionable of late, related a Yiddish journalist as the Roaring Twenties came to a close. Still others confessed to being thoroughly bewildered. Writing in *Der Tog* on "The War Between Chop Suey and Gefilte Fish," another journalist, his tongue firmly planted in his cheek, investigated the recent Jewish conversion to Chinese food. Not too long before, East Side Jews who could not manage without a piece of herring and who were more than willing to sell their soul for a slice of gefilte fish or a bowl of kasha became devotees of chow mein and other delicacies with strange names. What accounted for this? And what did it mean? Local storekeepers and restaurateurs, he found, shrugged their shoulders in disbelief and incomprehension at the thought of a *hashek*, a hankering, for Chinese dishes. Others, especially those who equated Jewish cuisine with tradition, were less inclined to be quite so tolerant; to their way of thinking, abandoning gefilte fish for chop suey signaled a form of assimilation. Did this portend a new movement, *Der Tog*'s reporter wondered, musing over the possibility of placards reading "Down with chop suey! Long live gefilte fish!"

In New York or Arizona, an appetite for kosher-style cuisine was hard to quell.

* * *

GIVEN ALL THE CHANGES in Jewish culinary behavior, it's no wonder that "the question of kashruth is today a mooted one," related Mrs. Jesse Bienenfeld in 1939. "So many of us disregard the Jewish dietary laws, yet have no personal misgivings on that account nor do we seem to have our status as Jews questioned, nor our membership in the Jewish community challenged. But," she hastened to add, "there are others among us who look askance at this general disregard." Rabbi Max Arzt, for one, not only looked askance at his coreligionists' relaxed attitude toward kashruth but also sought to make a last-ditch effort to maintain some degree of consistency. "I feel that a complete break with these laws outside of the home makes of their home observance a mockery," he asserted. Determined to align the halakhic proprieties of kashruth with American Jewry's culinary proclivities, the Conservative rabbi looked for a way—consistent with both rabbinic literature and contemporary American restaurant practices—to legitimate the consumption of broiled fish and vegetables in nonkosher restaurants. The modern restaurant, Arzt observed in a 1940 responsum, typically used different utensils to broil fish and cook meat, thus obviating the danger that meat ingredients would find their way into a vegetable or fish dish. And the continuous scouring of all dishes and silverware, meanwhile, rendered them fit for use. Based on these and other considerations, Arzt forcefully argued on behalf of the "halachic permissibility" of eating cooked vegetables and broiled fish in otherwise nonkosher establishments. Such behavior, he maintained, is not only "within the bounds of Jewish law," but also of great practical benefit. "Our preaching and teaching on the subject of Kashruth will be more realistic and more challenging if we will be in a position to claim that the observance of Kashruth outside the home is not at all impossible."

Despite his far-reaching conclusions, Arzt's solution came a bit too late for most American Jews, who, when it came to dining out, had already fashioned their own highly idiosyncratic arrangements. "It becomes almost pointless, therefore, to present a code of Jewish practice to our people," Meyer Kripke, one of Arzt's colleagues, noted resignedly. "If you will tell them now that they may eat fish in an un-kosher restaurant, they will say they are *already* eating lobster and shrimp."

In the years that followed, however, American Jews took a surprising turn. Amid signs of a postwar religious revival, kashruth enjoyed a sudden burst of popularity in the kitchens of suburban Jewish housewives. "Mama's cooking" came into its own, leading some contemporary observers to wonder if perhaps the "eggbeater is today the most effective weapon for propagating the faith." Ironically enough, a younger generation, nourished on tuna casseroles and salmon croquettes, developed a hunger for gefilte fish and traditional Jewish dishes, causing what a student of "informal Judaica" called "added bustle in the kitchen." Whether symptom or cause, a galaxy of new Jewish cookbooks met that need as publishers throughout the 1950s released *The Molly Goldberg Cookbook*, Jennie Grossinger's *The Art of Jewish Cooking, The Jewish Holidays and Their Favorite Foods, The Jewish Holiday Cookbook*, and *Aunt Fanny's Junior Jewish Cook Book*, a book "which every child should have." These handsomely produced texts assembled recipes of time-honored Jewish dishes, which they accented either with folksy humor or with simplistic comments—one critic called it "innocent sociology"—concerning the Sabbath, Jewish holidays, and the Jewish people.

While most cookbook authors deviated not a whit from tradition, one or two succumbed to the temptation to adorn the old standbys, adding peanut butter to chopped liver ("Variation No. 2"), mayonnaise to boiled chicken, and, worse still, using jarred gefilte fish. At first blush, these adaptations smacked of heresy, for they ran counter to the impulse to preserve the inviolability and sanctity of the Jewish kitchen, an impulse characteristic of the postwar Jewish cookbook as a whole. Upon closer inspection, though, these playful modifications appear to underscore food's very malleability as a source of cultural identity.

In a way, what counted was not the authenticity of the recipe but its symbolic power and presentational value as a touchstone of authentic Jewish culture. "Jewish Cooking is here to stay," American Jews now insisted, staking claims to its relevance—if only at home and on special occasions. Locating Jewishness within a domestic context, on the holiday dinner table, American Jews reinforced the organic Jewish connection, that "bond of sanctity," between food, family, domesticity, and identity. And yet, despite its constancy in Jewish history, the meaning of that bond had changed significantly under the circumstances, the "stubborn facts," of modern American Jewish life. Increasingly, it mattered little whether one kept kosher throughout the year as long as one consumed a few kosher or kosher-style foods on the holidays. Socially acceptable, even normative, the ceremonializing of Jewish cuisine blinded American Jewry to kashruth's larger cultural meaning: "A balanced Jewish diet involves more than food," one kosher-keeping housewife affirmed. "It calls for the intake and transmission of the heart of Judaism, the everyday spiritual values."

6
The Call of the Matzoh

"LADIES, IT'S TIME to modernize the kitchen end of this holiday. No longer need you hide behind those heavy 'meat and matzoh' menus, bemoaning the effects upon your family's waistlines and digestive systems. Passover means spring time, so let's bring the garden to the dinner table. . . . Let's make this, in culinary terms, a modern Pesach." In the modern era, holidays like Passover (or Pesach, its Hebrew name) called forth the creative energies of the Jewish housewife, providing her and her family with opportunities for dramatizing Judaism within the home. The Jewish calendar contained many such moments. In addition to the Sabbath, or *shabbos*, which came once a week, hardly a month went by without some kind of Jewish holiday or commemorative occasion, from the High Holy Days in the fall and Chanukah in the winter, to Passover in the spring and Shavuoth on the cusp of summer. Given the inroads made by acculturation, it's remarkable how many Jews actually set their clocks by these distinctive moments, which, of course, they marked in their own unique fashion. In lieu of going to *shul* or attending temple, the overwhelming majority of American Jews honed their sense of ritual not in the sanctuary but in the dining room, where they believed, along with Rose Goldstein, that "the array of traditional foods which accompanies the observance of the richly significant Jewish calendar festivals is the flour which nourishes Judaism." Eating, shopping, cooking, dressing up, and visiting with family constituted the major elements of the American Jewish encounter with sacred time.

A "Jewish calendar," usually supplied by the neighborhood kosher butcher, a national food manufacturer, or the local synagogue, ordered the sequence of the year. It hung discreetly in the kitchen, where its compilation of dates and candle-lighting times enabled housewives, the guardians of birthdays and anniversaries, to keep tabs on the imminent arrival of a holiday. Dutiful and straightforward, the Jewish calendar betrayed no signs of favoritism; in its scheme of things, all holidays were equal. American Jews, on the other hand, were nothing if not selective in their preferences, favoring Chanukah and Passover at the expense of Purim and Shavuoth, and honoring the Sabbath in a singularly abbreviated manner. A variety of external factors—consumerism, child-centeredness, leisure, and even style—shaped these preferences and values, giving rise to yet another form of vernacular Judaism.

Of all the Jewish holidays, Passover received the most attention. Its array of built-in culinary restrictions, which prohibited the consumption of bread and other leavened items, no doubt compelled an unusual degree of compliance. But to focus exclusively on these restrictions is to miss the holiday's spiritedness and fun, characteristics embodied by, though not limited to, its special foods. "Passover, the prince of Jewish festivals, has arrived," trumpeted the *Hebrew Standard* in March 1915. "It is the festival par excellence, *sans pareil*; no other yom tov [holiday] can compete with it or claim so large a share in the Jew's affection. On this festival every nook and corner in the Jewish house bespeaks festivity, and every member of the household, in festive garb and festal humor is doing his or her level best to give Passover a right royal welcome." Passover provided a bounty of tangible pleasures, from seldom-consumed dishes and the equally (and increasingly) rare opportunity of an extended family gathering to such artifacts as colorful Haggadahs, sparkling stemware, memory-laden seder plates, and even a gift or two. "Passover was the giant of Jewish holidays and had much to say for it. The story was good and the food was good," Edgar, the protagonist of E. L. Doctorow's novel *World's Fair*, fondly recalls, echoing (if more prosaically) the *Hebrew Standard*'s enthusiasm. "Passover involved getting dressed up and taking an enormous journey with packages and flowers."

It also involved a great deal of work. Using the holiday as a pretext for spring cleaning, Jewish housewives busied themselves with the ardors of housekeeping, exhuming dirt and dust from their customary hiding places, airing bed linens, washing and ironing the drapes, and discarding a year's accumulation of odds and ends. In some quarters, the frenzy of activity that accompanied the pre-Passover period was so pronounced that newspapers, in their own annualized ritual, sent out reporters to cover the "Jewish matrons' week of trial." "It is not unreasonable that more dirt shall be gathered up [in this week] in a single block on the East Side than on a mile of Fifth or Madison Avenues," commented the *American Hebrew*. "This annual housekeeping, even though it taxes the resources of the street cleaning department, should be welcomed as a sanitary measure." Jewish housewives also busied themselves with shopping, stocking up on matzoh, new dishes, and clothing. "Where other nationalities spend the bulk of their money at weddings, funerals and processions," observed the *Tageblatt*, "the Jew has his Passover, which makes a hole in his pocket every year." Merchandisers took advantage of the retail opportunities implicit in Passover by commercializing the *yontef*, or holiday. "We supply everything for the Passover season," boasted Bloomingdales as early as 1900, while Macy's, not to be outdone, set aside a portion of its fifth floor for a "Passover Department," which supplied "groceries, wine, etc., for the Feast of Passover." All of its products, Macy's assured consumers, "strictly comply with the Mosaic Dietary Laws." In Brooklyn, Loeser's Linen prominently advertised its line of table linens designed to "insure a perfect setting for the Passover table," while on the Lower East Side, shoppers thronged the crowded side streets and "curb markets" to avail themselves of the special sales *lekavod Pesach* (in honor of Passover). "While this section is always alive with business, the Passover holiday has multiplied this to a degree hardly conceivable save to those who have witnessed this trade centre," wrote one astonished reporter as he surveyed the spurt of holiday activity. The *New York Times*, in turn, accompanied its investigation of "Passover Eve on the East Side" with deftly rendered drawings of determined shoppers while the *News* featured "Last Minute Photos" of the downtown holiday scene.

Not every Jewish housewife took to shopping and housecleaning with the same energy and enthusiasm. Then as now, quite a few regarded Passover as more of a burden than a joy and balked, or at the very least fumed, as the holiday generated a steadily

MACY'S FOR

PASSOVER FOODS

DEPARTMENT OPENS MARCH 28TH–5TH FLOOR

Macy's Passover Department will be open from Thursday, March 28th to Wednesday, April 24th, inclusive, on the Fifth Floor. There you will find a Seder Table authoritatively set in the proper manner with appointments befitting the occasion. Macy's is taking special pains to provide foods strictly in accordance with Hebraic traditions and dietary laws: Matzohs, meals, smoked meats, honeys, dried fruits, teas, coffees, cakes, and spices. Well known products from Goodman, Manischewitz, Horowitz Bros., and Margareten, Meyer London, Federation of Yeshivoth and Talmud Torahs. Also Macy's own imports of Cheeses, Chocolate, and Cocoas from Holland and Switzerland, and Palestine products, all packed under the strictest supervision.

Macy's Wine and Liquor Store, 7th Ave. between 34th and 35th Streets carries a complete assortment of Kosher California Wines, Slivovitz and Palestine Wines. The china, glassware and linens featured at this time are selected to meet every requirement. The readers of the AMERICAN HEBREW will welcome this opportunity of providing for Pesach at Macy's low prices.

SEND FOR SPECIAL PASSOVER GROCERY PRICE LIST

IRISH LINEN DOUBLE DAMASK, hand hemmed. 72 x 90 inches____**5.59.** Napkins to match, 22" x 22", doz.____**6.53.** Other size cloths proportionately priced. *Macy's Sixth Floor*

FORMAL DINNER SERVICE FOR 12 Wide maroon, blue or green bands with elaborate gold decorations. Most unusual for **27.95.** (*Usually would be 39.95*). *Macy's Eighth Floor*

SILVERWARE—"Wilshire," a simple modern design, **10¢** each, and "Narcissus," a perfect reproduction of a fine sterling pattern in an all-over flower design, each **17¢**. Open stock. *Street Floor*

THE CUT CRYSTAL WATER GOBLETS, champagnes, clarets, wines, sherbets, cordials, cocktails in the lovely "Lucille" pattern, **22¢** each. Decanter to match, **99¢.** *Macy's Eighth Floor*

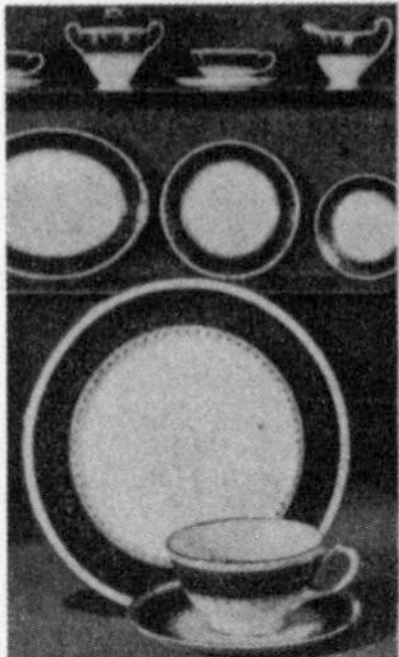

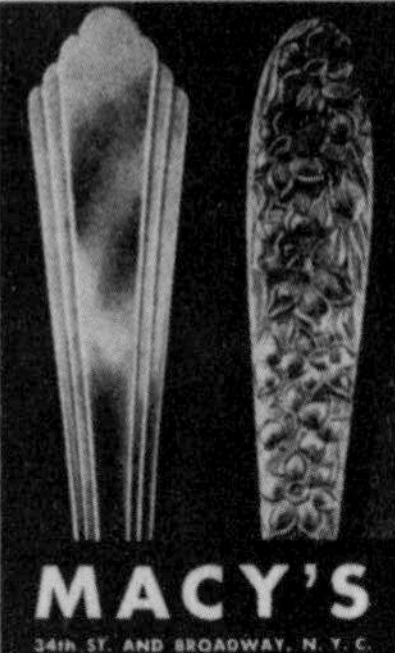

We sell only for cash. Resulting economies including efficiency and volume save, we estimate, six per cent. We endeavor to have the prices of our merchandise reflect this saving, subject to limitations over which we have no control.

THIS ISSUE, 15c. Entered as second-class matter January 9, 1903, at the Post Office at New York, N. Y., under the act of March 3, 1879. The American Hebrew and Jewish Tribune, published weekly at The American Hebrew Publishing Co., 212 Fifth Avenue, New York. Copyright, 1935, by The American Hebrew Publishing Company. Subscription rates: In the United States, $5.00; Canada, $6.00, and foreign, $6.00. VOL. 136. NO. 22

Department stores, America's "cathedrals of commerce," heavily promoted Passover.

---

increasing pile of responsibilities. "Yes! Pesach is coming! Don't frown! Be glad!" exhorted Mrs. Samuel Spiegel in the pages of the *United Synagogue Recorder*, encouraging her coreligionists to partake happily in the festive spirit by offering an engagingly new rationale for ritual behavior. "What if it does entail a little more work? The new dishes and new kinds of food make of Pesach a party lasting eight days, because with the new dishes which you haven't seen for a year, and with the new food which you haven't eaten for a year, also come new clothes. Let us begin to call them again Pesach clothes, and not Spring clothes," she suggested, appealing to the ever-present sartorial impulse. "Pesach is a joyous and happy holiday. The house takes on a festive appearance. There is freedom and sunshine in the air as well as in the Seder service."

Some housewives interpreted "freedom" literally, by going away for the holiday, an increasingly popular pre–World War I phenomenon that caused much consternation among American Jewry's cultural custodians. "Avoid Household Cares, Spend Passover at Arverne," urged the owners of Stone's Cottage in 1915, while Eisenberg's Wave Crest Hotel, in nearby Far Rockaway, invited potentially fatigued women to "celebrate the Passover festival amid delightful country surroundings by the sea, avoiding the usual annoyance of ritual household preparation." A boon for housewives, the idea of spending Passover by the sea or in the mountains troubled their rabbis, and quite a few sisterhood leaders as well, who believed it mocked "the true Passover emotion" and diminished the holiday's true meaning. "The family is lost in a multiplicity of families; instead of a home ceremony, Passover calls up thoughts of travel and ease," they complained. By their lights, Passover was not intended as a glorious week-long vacation to be spent in the company of strangers one encountered in the hotel lobby; instead, Passover was meant to be spent at home, in the company of family and friends. "Do not close your home for that week," implored one sisterhood leader, contrasting the modern-day behavior of her coreligionists with its more distinguished, lustrous antecedents. "In those days of long ago Pesach was a holiday that young and old helped to prepare for in the home. Will you bring that Pesach back again? Prepare for it yourself."

American Jewry's cultural authorities also discouraged the practice of attending a public seder, whose sponsors and organizers typically included either a local synagogue, community center, or kosher caterer. Although its origins date back to the early years of the century when charitably minded Jewish organizations hosted a seder for those financially unable to mount one of their own, the public seder gained in both popularity and respectability

The traditional way to make a Seder

1 CANDLES are lighted by the mother of the house to usher in the festival of Passover. The benediction which she pronounces over the candles gives a religious meaning to this simple act. An abundance of light symbolizes joy and festivity, and the soft candle-glow adds an aura of spirituality to the Seder table.

2 A CUP OF WINE is placed at each table setting. The sanctification of the Holiday is pronounced over the first cup. Three additional cups are drunk during the course of the Seder, making a total of four, to symbolize the four expressions of the Lord's promise to redeem the children of Israel and deliver them from bondage.

3 THE HAGGADAH (literally "the telling") contains the complete Seder ceremonies in their prescribed order *(seder)*. The first part of the book, concerned mainly with the story of the Jews' deliverance from Egypt, is read before the meal. After dinner follows the second portion consisting of prayers of praise and thanks to the Almighty.

4 MATZOH represents the "bread of affliction" eaten by the Jews in Egypt, and also the bread that had to be baked during their hasty flight when there was no time for leavening. Three *matzot* are placed in the Seder tray. Half the middle *matzoh*, saved for the *Afikomon* (dessert), is playfully "stolen" by a child and ransomed for a prize.

5 THE Z'ROAH, a roasted shank bone, is placed on the Seder tray. It represents the ancient sacrifice of the Paschal lamb *(Pesach)* which had to be eaten roasted. *Pesach*, the Hebrew name for Passover, also refers to the Lord's passing over *(posach)* the Jewish homes during the plague visited upon the Egyptian first-born.

6 THE BEITZAH, a roasted egg placed left of the *Z'roah*, symbolizes the required offering brought on all festivals in the Temple. The egg, while not itself sacrificed, is used in the Seder as it is the Jewish symbol of mourning (in this case for the loss of the Temple where the sacrifices were brought).

7 THE MAROR or "bitter herbs" (usually horseradish) is placed in the middle of the tray and symbolizes the Jews' bitter suffering under the Egyptian yoke. Directly below is the *Chazereth*, another piece of bitter herbs, commemorating the custom of eating *Maror* sandwiched between two pieces of *Matzoh*.

8 THE CHAROSET, placed beneath the *Z'roah*, is a mixture of chopped apple, nuts, cinnamon, and wine designed to look like the mortar used by the Jews in building the palaces and pyramids of Egypt during centuries of forced labor. Before the *Maror* is eaten, it is dipped into the *Charoset*.

9 THE KARPAS, a piece of parsley or lettuce placed to the left of the *Charoset*, symbolizes the meager diet of the Jews in Egyptian bondage. It is dipped into salt water in remembrance of the tears they shed in their misery. The *Karpas* also signifies Springtime, the season of Passover.

10 THE CUP OF ELIJAH, filled with wine, is kept on the table throughout the Seder in the hope that the Prophet Elijah may appear as a messenger of the Almighty and announce the coming of the Messiah. Thus, in the midst of their memories of the past, the Jews look forward to the day of universal peace, love, and brotherhood.

© 1957 Barton's Candy Corporation. Published originally in the New York Times in full page size by Barton's Bonbonniere Continental Chocolate Shops as a community service. Reprints available without charge at any Barton store.

BARTON'S products are manufactured under supervision of the Union of Orthodox Jewish Congregations of America. Barton's factory, offices, and 65 owner-operated Continental Chocolate Shops are closed on the Sabbath and all Jewish Holidays.

For brochures illustrating BARTON'S Passover chocolate assortments and baked delicacies ask at any BARTON shop or write to BARTON'S Dept PS, 80 DeKalb Avenue, Brooklyn 1, N. Y.

Barton's products are also available at leading Department Stores in principal cities. (Consult telephone directory).

Modern American Jews needed explicit instructions on how to assemble a seder.

---

during World War I. At that time, when thousands of young Jews, stationed far away from home, had no place to go for the seder, public institutions stepped into the breach by opening their facilities to "our boys." Long after the war ended, the practice stuck, this time appealing to middle-class families who were attracted by its convenience and ready-made ease. "That most characteristic of all home celebrations, the Seder service, shows some signs of migrating from the home into the banqueting hall," lamented Rabbi Jacob Kohn in 1932, attributing its appeal to the small size of the contemporary Jewish family and the inability of its members to conduct the service. Jewish leaders such as Kohn regretted the conditions that contributed to this "vogue" and encouraged their coreligionists to stay home. "The growing generation cannot permit its Jewishness to subsist on the haziest of childhood memories. Fathers and mothers may consider that their spark of Judaism is derived from a recollection of ceremonialism in their *own* youthful homes; and similar recollections must be passed on to their still susceptible offspring," editorialized the *United Synagogue Recorder*.

In alluding to the past, the proponents of the home-centered Passover resorted to an extremely powerful argument for ritual behavior. Memory and its claims enveloped the holiday, sustaining its spirited distinctiveness. As one housewife put it, Jews "may forget the furnishings of the home but they will never forget the Seder." Memory insinuated itself into every nook and cranny of the festivities, from the recitation of the Haggadah, a ritualized exercise in collective memory, to the physical appearance of the seder table. Assembled over time and place and from a variety of sources—Grandmother's cupboard, Aunt Sadie's basement—the items displayed on the table served as tangible, physical embodiments of family history and collective memory. As much an opportunity for the display of family history as of elegance, the seder fostered a unique aesthetic. On any other night, those assembled around the table might have frowned on the visual incoherence and mixed provenance of the table appointments in which kiddush cups brought from the Old World mingled with the "good dishes" and the Community Silver (actually, silverplate) purchased in the New. But Passover was different: on seder nights, these seeming eccentricities of taste and eclecticism were welcomed, eagerly anticipated, and sanctioned as critical elements of the holiday spirit. Home movies constituted an equally personal, though far more novel, way of recalling and preserving the past. Surely it's no coincidence that the Passover seder ranked with first birthdays as one of the most popular subjects to be captured on film. Typically, the camera panned from the well-dresssed table, crowded with ritual appointments, to the well-dressed guests, vividly and kinetically capturing the exuberance and warmth of the occasion. Smiling into the camera, celebrants assume one of three characteristic poses: waving hello, pretending to recite a passage from the Haggadah, or eating.

The traditional Passover seder meal and the chanting of the Haggadah gave structure and form to these quotidian pleasures, hallowing them. Energetic, if not always liturgically correct, renditions of the centuries-old text, the ceremonial consumption of four cups of wine, and the presence of children, momentarily resplendent in holiday attire, contributed to the high spirits. "The children were amused at the curious olden pictures in the Haggadahs," recalled publisher Philip Cowen. "Some of the young

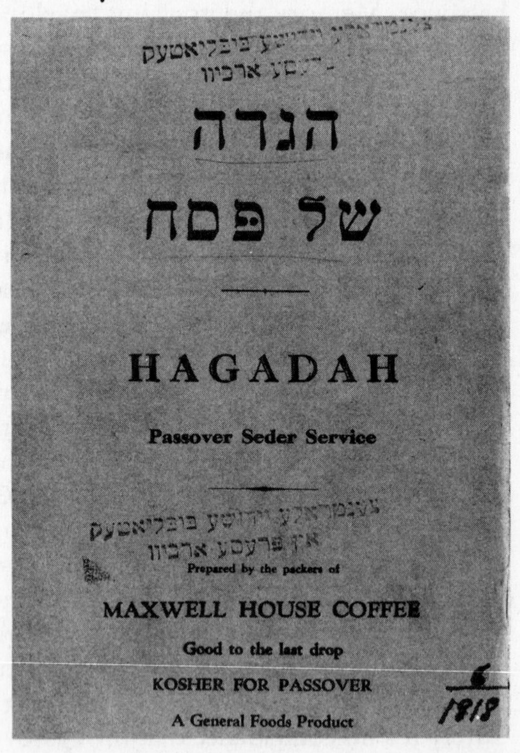

Found in thousands of Jewish homes throughout the country, the Maxwell House Haggadah demonstrated the "unique relationship between a product and a people."

ones gave vent to their surprise that the Lord couched his instructions to Moses in such awful English." The prospect of a delicious meal also contributed to the merriment and in some (perhaps all?) cases, was actually its cause. In households across the country, the cry "When do we eat?" invariably punctuated the protracted seder routine, becoming, in its own way, as much of a ritual as those set forth in the Haggadah. Making their way through course after course of "sumptuous" and "ambrosial" Jewish dishes, seder celebrants brought a "certain playful solemnity" to the table, ceremonializing Jewish cuisine. "People who during fifty-one weeks of the year care nothing for the dietary laws, listen to the call of the matzoh and the special dishes that share with it the place of honor in the Passover menu and forgo their usual haunts, their oysters and ham, etc., and insist on things 'yontefdik,' " commented the *American Hebrew* in 1911. "This may not seem to mean much for Judaism or 'Jewishness' . . . but it does for it gives the Passover a place in the life of the indifferent Jew."

That American Jews valued Passover above all other Jewish festivities has become both a statistical and an emotional truth. As far back as the 1920s, statistical surveys of Jewish ritual behavior, like those regularly issued today, pointed out that more American Jews celebrated a Passover seder than kept kosher, observed *shabbos*, or lit Chanukah candles. In making sense of this affinity, some contemporary observers likened Passover to the Fourth of July, for both celebrated the ideal of independence. Others, freely mixing their metaphors, compared Moses, "the other great Emancipator," with Lincoln, and the Exodus with the freeing of the slaves. However lovely and resonant, these associations had little to do with American Jewry's collective affection for Passover. For them, its meaning lay not so much in freedom as in family. Passover's appeal rested on a foundation of domesticity and sentiment; it was "a time for family reunion and for strengthening of home ties." This "picturesque ceremonial [not only] streaks with color the dull drab monotony of daily life. . . . Far more important are its associations with what may be called family unity," explained the *Tageblatt* more than twenty years before the first statistical survey was conducted, accurately summarizing the holiday's hold on the American Jewish imagination. Building on the organic

A SONG OF SEDER
Sing a song of *Seder*,
A table without rye;
Four and twenty visitors,
And not a single pie.
The father is the king tonight,
Filling all the *Kosos;*
The mother, though a queen,
Is making the *Charoses;*
The children in the parlor
Are planning lots of fun;
They'll hide the *Afikoman*
When the *Seder* is begun.
40

American Jews viewed Passover as one of the most spirited of Jewish holidays.

connection between family, memory, and the seder narrative, American Jews infused the rituals of the seder with those of the family reunion. No wonder, then, that Passover developed into the quintessential American Jewish holiday of "kinship" and togetherness.

* * *

WHILE PASSOVER'S POPULARITY in America was bound up with food and family, Chanukah's success was tied to commercialization and a search for religious parity. "It is the good fortune of Hanukkah to become the first [Jewish holiday] to revive in an American setting," noted one American Jewish parent in the 1950s, while another, musing over this shift in fortunes, allowed as how Chanukah was no mere Jewish holiday but a "major competitive winter sport." One of the few Jewish ritual practices actually to grow rather than diminish in popularity, the winter festival enjoyed an unprecedented burst of attention in the years following World War II, when it emerged not only as the Jewish antidote to Christmas but as its functional equivalent. Pressures from within and without, from the marketplace and the suburban neighborhood, combined to make Chanukah, the commemoration of an ancient victory by the Maccabees, increasingly relevant and attractive to

Memories of Passover seders past lingered long after the last piece of matzoh had been consumed.

modern urban Jews. A study in cultural improvisation and ritual renewal, the history of Chanukah in America, as one observer presciently pointed out in the 1930s, "is a step in the evolution of what the future Jewish historian will refer to as American Judaism."

For much of its history, Chanukah fared poorly in the New World, a victim of neglect. "The customary candles disappear more and more from Jewish homes," noted Dr. Gustav Gottheil, a leading Reform rabbi, as early as 1884; the same trend was ruefully confirmed several decades later by the *American Jewish Chronicle*, which, with considerable alarm, pointed to the diminishing number of Chanukah celebrants. "Not even the Zionists make such a fuss about Chanukah," the paper noted, adding that most Jews, Zionist or not, simply had no idea when to celebrate the Maccabean victory by lighting the menorah. By contrast to Christmas, whose advent was energetically mapped out weeks in advance, Chanukah's arrival was a mystery: "We must ask 'the old man' when it comes." "I was losing track even of the calendar," confessed a recently arrived immigrant, homesick for the Old World. "Did I know that last week was the Feast of the Maccabees? How could anyone know it in America?" Although statistics on the declining number of celebrants in the years prior to World War I are hard to come by, the frequency of exhortations to light the menorah, which surfaced annually during the holiday season in both the contemporary Anglo-Jewish and Yiddish presses, suggest the extent to which that practice had fallen off. "Kindle the Chanukah lights anew, modern Israelite! Make the festival more than ever before radiant with the brightness and beauty of love and charity," urged Kaufmann Kohler, a leading Reform rabbi; the *Jewish Messenger*, in turn, suggested "try[ing] the effect of the Hanukkah lights. If just for the experiment, try it."

At the time, more American Jews, it seems, were inclined to experiment with Christmas than with Chanukah. Beguiled by its charms, they adorned their homes with greenery and parlor illuminations and eagerly exchanged gifts. "Jewish young folks give and accept Christmas presents," wrote one baffled student of holiday behavior in 1916. "Christmas is an occasion for extra shopping, purchase of new clothes, going out to parties and special

Children's books like Jane Bearman's 1943 *Happy Chanuko* emphasized the festival's playful qualities.

---

entertainments." Along with millions of other Americans, American Jews ignored the holiday's "theological implications" in favor of its secularized, commodified, and mirth-filled dimensions, claiming that "no one who has an eye for beauty and sweetness can withstand the marvelous charm exercised over young and old by the advent of [Christmas] night." Christmas's appeal was not limited to well-heeled and well-established Jews either; it trickled down as well to the immigrant Jewish population, which encountered the yuletide spirit on the streets and in the marketplace, in the public school and town square. The Yiddish press also contributed to an awareness of Christmas. With its keen sociological imagination, it took great pains to familiarize readers with the peculiarities of the commodified American Christmas. In editorials and feature articles—such as "Christmas Presents," an extended discussion of holiday shopping practices; "How Christmas Became a Christian Holiday," an analysis of the historical Jesus; and "Christmas and Yom Kippur: Fantasy and Reality," a comparative look at the philosophies behind these two holidays—Yiddish newspapers made sure their readers understood the American Christmas spirit.

Some readers, in fact, may have understood the Christmas spirit all too well. According to the *Jewish Daily Forward*, a startlingly large proportion of new arrivals took quickly to the custom of giving Christmas presents, a practice allegedly as widespread as the exchange of *shalakh-mones*, Purim gifts. "Who says we haven't Americanized," the paper quoted several immigrants as saying. "The purchase of Christmas gifts is one of the first things that proves one is no longer a greenhorn."

Not all American Jews looked kindly on the blossoming of Christmas spirit in their midst; some even took offense. "How can the Jew, without losing self-respect, partake in the joy and festive mirth of Christmas? Can he without self-surrender, without entailing insult and disgrace upon his faith and race, plant the Christmas tree in his household?" Other detractors focused less on issues of self-respect and more on theology. If American Jews understood the origin of Christmas, "they in all probability would not find as much joy in the Christmas tree as they seem to do now," wrote one critic, urging American Jews to pay heed to the holiday's deeper meaning. Still others insisted that the vagaries of the calendar were no excuse for substituting Christmas for Chanukah. Writing in the pages of the *Ladies Home Journal*, Rabbi Emil Hirsch argued that the "synagogal calendar provides at the identical season of the year an occasion for as intense a manifestation of joy." From Hirsch's perspective and that of his colleagues,

Chanukah's similarities with Christmas were substantive as well as calendrical: the Jewish holiday, much like the Christian one, provided a "vigorous story, dramatic incidents, strong personalities, fine home-scenes, abundance of imagery, plenty of traditional customs, home-cheer."

Still, no amount of rhetorical excess could disguise the fact that Chanukah's charms paled in comparison with those of Christmas. "How humble and insignificant does the one appear by the side of the other," Kohler remarked, perpetuating (unintentionally) the image of Chanukah as pallid, enervated, and even meek. With its exuberance and profound family spirit, with its decorations and Santa Claus, Christmas "gives a zest to life that all the Chanukah hymns in the world, backed by all the Sunday-school teaching and half-hearted ministerial chiding, must forever fail to give," acknowledged Esther Jane Ruskay, author of the acclaimed *Hearth and Home Essays*. Though mindful of Christmas's charms, she remained steadfast in her loyalty to Chanukah and fierce in her opposition to the presence of a Christmas tree in a Jewish home. Those who celebrate Christmas, Ruskay insisted, not only betray their own faith but, perhaps worse still, commit an unforgivable breach of etiquette. Such people, she wrote, are characterized by an "ignorance of racial properties, and ill breeding so rank, so utterly un-American, not to say un-Jewish, as must always place them beyond the pale of civilized notice."

"Modest" Chanukah, meanwhile, stayed its course as a quaint and "unassuming" holiday. By the 1920s, though, it began to come into its own as a notable Jewish domestic occasion and an exercise in consumption, a transformation documented vividly in the Yiddish press. By contrast to the pre–World War I era, when holiday-related promotions were in short supply, Yiddish newspapers of the interwar era carried dozens of tempting advertisements for Chanukah gifts, from automobiles to waffle irons. "A Chanukah Present for the Entire Family—The Greatest Bargain [*metsiah*] in the World," trumpeted an advertisement for a Hudson motorcar in a December 1925 issue of *Der Tog*, while the *Morgen Zhurnal* carried a series of ads from the Colgate Company extolling such "Chanukah Pleasures" and novelties as perfumes, shaving emollients, and dental creme. Consumers were also encouraged to use a wide range of food products "*lekavod Chanukah*" (in honor of Chanukah), from Canada Dry ginger ale and Goodman's noodles to Aunt Jemima pancake flour, "the best flour for latkes," and Crisco shortening, which successfully allied "Chanukah latkes and Modern Science." Subtly but firmly, advertisements for consumer goods played on the "time-hallowed" practice of distributing "Chanukah *gelt*," or holiday money, disguising the overtly monetary nature of that exchange by extending its purview to include the amenities of modern life. Some advertisements, though, were far more explicit. "Save for Chanukah," advised the East River Savings Institution, suggesting that depositors take advantage of its popular Christmas plan to put some cash aside for Chanukah gifts. And the Libby Hotel Corporation offered consumers a modern-day version of *Chanukah gelt*: stock shares, which they claimed in an ad in *Der Tog* make the "nicest Chanukah present."

Editorials accompanied these overtly mercantile solicitations, encouraging parents, particularly mothers, to add the exchange of

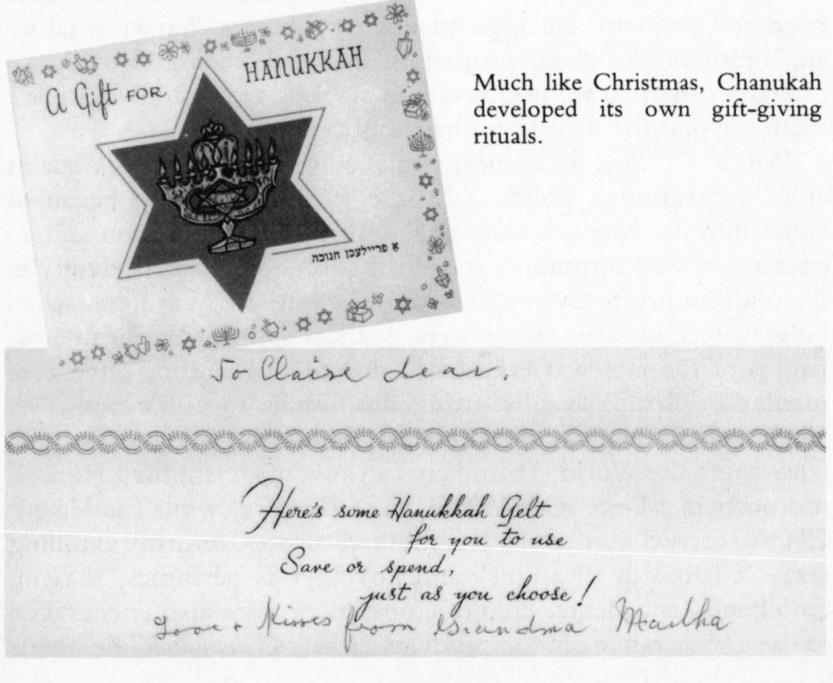

Much like Christmas, Chanukah developed its own gift-giving rituals.

presents to the roster of "Chanukah *minhagim* [customs]." Recounting the heroic exploits of the Maccabees is not enough, counseled the *Morgen Zhurnal*; to command the attention and affection of Jewish children, the holiday must become an occasion for storytelling, gift-giving, and merrymaking. Jewish children's books, then in their infancy, also reflect the growing popularity of gift-giving. Take, for example, a poem entitled "Aunt Mollie Came for Chanukah," an entry in *Mother Goose Rhymes for Jewish Children.*

> *Aunt Mollie came for Chanukah*
> *She brought me two new toys,*
> *A* Mechonis [*car*] *and a big* Kadur [*ball*]
> *Just the thing for boys.*
>
> *Aunt Mollie came for Chanukah*
> *She made me pretty curls,*
> *She brought me a new* Booba [*doll*]
> *Just the thing for girls.*

Poems like these legitimated gift-giving while also solidifying gender norms. Toy manufacturers and Judaica importers quickly capitalized on both trends by developing an array of *boobas* for girls and *kadurim* for boys, as well as games, records, books, papier-mâché decorations and menorahs. "Chanukah is Gift Time at M. Wolozin, 28 Eldridge Street, The House of a Thousand Traditional Hebrew Gifts," this Judaica distributor proudly related. By the 1940s, gift-giving had become an integral aspect of the holiday. "If ever lavishness in gifts is appropriate it is on Hanukkah," advised the authors of a guidebook to modern Jewish living. "Jewish children should be showered with gifts, *Hanukkah gifts*, as a perhaps primitive but most effective means of making them immune against envy of the Christian children and their Christmas presents." Although children remained the chief beneficiaries of holiday largesse, grown-ups were not immune to its pleasures. As the *Hadassah Newsletter* pointed out, "Mah-jong sets make appreciated Chanukah gifts."

Through their production of a wide array of menorahs fashioned from tin, chromium, silverplate, and silver, Judaica manufacturers

PRETTY LITTLE BOOBAH

See my little *Boobah!*
She's pretty as can be;
Looks just like a *Tinok,*
As far as I can see.
Her *Rosh* is full of curls,
Aynayim, very blue,
She dances and says, "*Imma*",
And always smiles at you.

CHANUKAH

Judah had a little lamp,
With branches bright as gold;
And every night on *Chanukah,*
When it was very cold,
He put it on the window-sill,
When he came home from school,
And lit the little blinking lights,
Just like they do in *Shool.*

Mother Goose Rhymes for Jewish Children shed light on the traditional candle-lighting ceremony.

furthered the Chanukah spirit for both children and adults. Where once American menorahs had been limited in style, shape, and material, they now came in all sizes and shapes. In one Brooklyn Jewish household of the 1920s, for instance, a simple wooden ruler did double duty as a Chanukah menorah: the family's matriarch would affix the holiday candles to the wood and light them in a row, from right to left. "At least the candles were evenly spaced," quipped a member of the family as she recalled her grandmother's inventiveness. By the 1940s, rulers and other improvised materials had given way to "many new and beautiful Hanukah lamps of modern design," including electrified menorahs, musical menorahs, menorahs from the Jewish homeland, and even "authentic plastic" menorahs. "Every home," insisted one affluent Jewish homemaker, surveying the market's surfeit of menorahs, "should own at least one." The success of a musical menorah fashioned from chromium, an inexpensive metal whose luster resembled that of silver, attests both to the inventiveness of Judaica manufacturers and the receptivity of the consumer. Created by Ziontalis, a leading American manufacturer of Jewish ritual products, this newfangled menorah, which played fragments of either "Hatikvah" or "Rock of Ages," was available in forty-seven different styles. More to the point, perhaps, it "always gleams, needs no polish and will not tarnish." Throughout the interwar years, the wholesale introduction into the American Jewish market of mass-produced Palestinian—and then, after 1948, Israeli—menorahs made of greenware or patinated bronze, further legitimated the transformation of Chanukah into a gift-giving occasion. Meanwhile, kosher chocolate manufacturers indulged American Jews' fascination with Israel by producing a line of overtly nationalistic games to accompany their line of Chanukah candies. Loft's Chocolates, for example, introduced a spinwheel game entitled "Valor against Oppression" which featured such latter-day "Maccabees" as Moshe Dayan; Barton's introduced the "Barton's Race Dredel," an Israelized version of Monopoly whose board featured a map of Israel, miniature Israeli flags, menorahs, and the following text: "Every Jewish boy and girl thrills to the heroic story of the Maccabees. . . . We light the candles every night, . . . recite the blessings, sing the songs, play chess, go to parties and dance the hora."

A. W. Binder's songbook *Chanukah Songster* and guidebooks such as Emily Solis-Cohen's *Hanukkah: The Feast of Lights* enhanced the spirit of improvisation and fun. Binder's compilation imparted "a real live character" to Jewish music by providing the lyrics and sheet music to such holiday standards as "Rock of Ages," a melody to be sung "very marked and singingly," and to new tunes such as "Chanukah Candles," a "musical vision" to be sung "slowly and languidly." With detailed suggestions for "A Hanukkah Party," and descriptions of costumes, props, puppet shows, and dances for such characters as "The Top," "The Pancakes," and "The Spirit of Giving," Solis-Cohen's book identified Chanukah as a lively, fun-filled, child-centered occasion, a notion that spread quickly throughout the Jewish community. "The Jewish woman who would want to make Hanukkah loom large in her children's minds as a festive season would be wise to give a children's party at her home," mothers were advised. Much the same can be said of *The Jewish Home Beautiful*'s approach to the holiday. This guidebook to Jewish ritual practice enthusiastically championed the merits of a home "bright with candle lights and gay with parties and the exchange of gifts." Advising would-be celebrants to create place cards in the shape of a hammer to symbolize the might of the Maccabees, it designated the holiday a

MENORAH VEGETABLE SALAD

6 hard boiled eggs
black or green olives
14 asparagus tips (green)
½ inch of tips removed

Put the whites of the eggs through a coarse sieve and spread solidly on a large flat platter as the background for the Menorah. Lengthwise across the center of the platter place three asparagus tips, end to end. Using this as a base, place eight asparagus tips vertically to represent the eight candles. To form the base of the Menorah, place under the lengthwise line of tips, in the center, two half pieces of asparagus, side by side vertically, and underneath these, one asparagus tip horizontally. Mash the yolks with melted butter and form into tiny balls, with a point at one end, to represent the tip of the flame. Place these balls above the eight asparagus tips in the row and sprinkle a little paprika on each ball. Use the remainder of the yolk alternately with the olives to form a frame around the edge of the platter.

Jewish cookbooks of the 1940s and 1950s were filled with imaginative holiday recipes.

"period for mirth and for spreading of good-will." The consumption of appropriate holiday foods contributed to the merriment. "Maccabean sandwiches" composed of either tuna fish or egg salad and shaped to resemble a bite-sized Maccabee warrior, or the "Menorah fruit salad," a composition of cream cheese and fruit that, when molded, resembled a menorah, were deemed essential to the holiday's success, especially among young children. Potato pancakes, or latkes, were also popular. "It goes without saying that the Jewish woman will not neglect the culinary aspects of the festival; especially she will not fail to treat her family to 'Latkes,' the traditional Hanukkah delicacy," one holiday manual enthused. Noted another: when it came to building Jewish memories, the "value of latkes" could never be overestimated. In speaking of latkes, most holiday specialists had in mind the traditional tuber kind but there's no doubt that the invention of chocolate latkes must have generated quite a few memories of its own. Barton's first introduced consumers to its innovative product in 1951, when it offered a box of fifteen chocolate spheres—"Just in Time for Chanukah"—for $1.19. Jewish homemakers eagerly took to these and other celebratory conceits, applauding the development of chocolate latkes and related candies. "It is conceivable that chocolate elephants and lions will be as common in Jewish homes at Chanuko [sic] time as chocolate rabbits are in Christian homes at Easter time," predicted one delighted rabbi. Equally thrilled by Chanukah's prospects, a California Jewish woman offered the following advice in 1951: "Let this be our guiding principle: Keeping within the framework of our own tradition, using a color scheme of blue and silver and yellow and gold, let us adorn our homes inside and outside as beautifully as we can for *Hanukkah*, enlarging upon the old-time Feast of Lights."

By the late 1950s, Chanukah's accoutrements had grown to include paper decorations, greeting cards, napkins, wrapping paper, ribbons, chocolates, games, and phonograph records. What with all these goodies, no longer did the American Jew have cause to dread the "cruel month" of December. Chanukah, with its range of "better facilities," could now serve as a fulfilling and viable cultural substitute. Admittedly, many American Jews continued to celebrate some form of Christmas, sharing in the "loveliness of the day." A survey of holiday practices among middle-

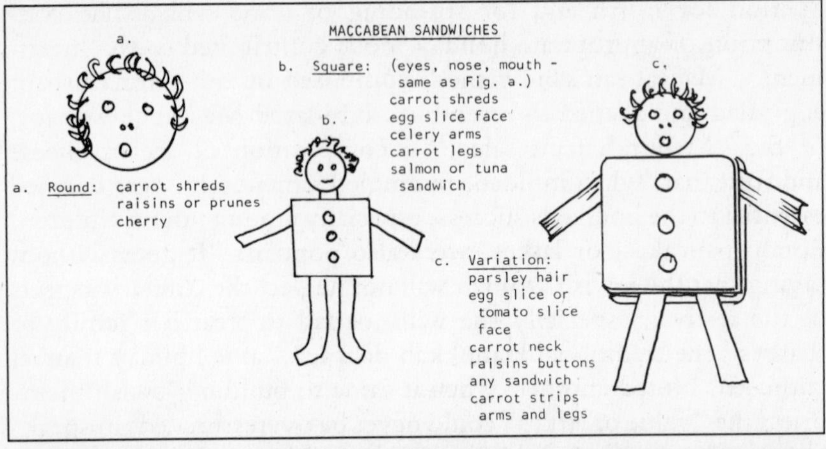

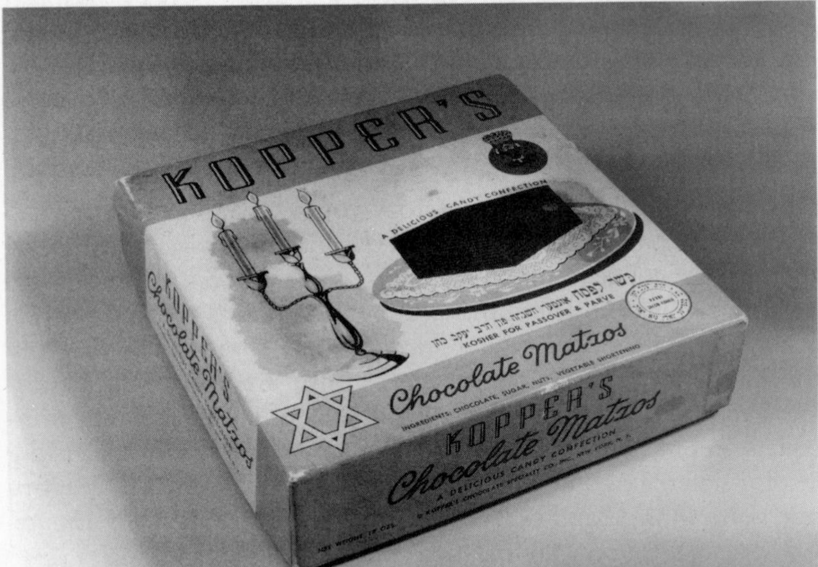

Inventive new dishes and food products added zest to Chanukah and Passover celebrations.

class Chicago Jews of the time found, for example, that close to 40 percent decorated their homes with a Christmas tree. And yet, the confluence of social and market forces ensured that Chanukah could serve as a powerful "antidote" to Christmas. "Hanukkah is only one of our festivals, and a minor one at that; but we exalt it above all our holidays," a writer in *The Reconstructionist* noted critically in 1948. "We magnify it beyond all reason, and establish it as a major holiday in our children's minds." Sociologist Marshall Sklare, studying Jewish life on the "suburban frontier," confirmed Chanukah's latter-day allure. "Hanukkah, in short, becomes for some the Jewish Christmas," he stated categorically. Interestingly enough, the outside world in the years following World War II came increasingly to share that assessment, freighting Chanukah with the same cultural and social significance as Christmas and yoking the two together in demonstration of America's "cultural oneness."

Joint Christmas-Chanukah observances in the public schools were the most apparent, and far-reaching, indication of the growing parity between the two holidays. Although settlement-house workers as far back as 1913, if not earlier, had invented an ecumenical "Midwinter Festival" that featured such "common symbols" as a Yule log, a lit Christmas tree, a Chinese lantern, and a Chanukah menorah, such displays did not become institutionalized until the post–World War II era. Public school educators then developed the strategy of convening a "holiday assembly" on a "compromise date" in December in which a Christmas tree and a "Menorah candle" and the singing of Chanukah hymns and Christmas carols figured prominently. The postwar spirit of ecumenism and neighborliness extended beyond the classroom and the assembly hall, carrying over into the new medium of television. Special holiday broadcasts like those produced by the Jewish Chautauqua Society in conjunction with the Central Conference of American Rabbis underscored the essential harmony between Christmas and Chanukah by showing scenes of Christian and Jewish neighbors exchanging gifts and visting one another's homes during the holiday season.

Many within the Jewish community lamented Chanukah's "transfiguration" into a "Jewish Christmas," deriding both the process and the end product as a pallid and inappropriate imitation of non-Jewish practices or, worse still, as a "back-door means to participation in a Christian festival." Chanukah "needs no apology and will sustain no borrowings," stated *Jewish Life*, an Orthodox Jewish publication, urging its readers to infuse the holiday with an authentically Jewish spirit. While those more traditional in outlook tended to be the most outspoken in their criticism, a more liberal element within the American Jewish community shared their concern. "It should be made clear to members," advised the leadership of the Young Judea youth movement, "that Xmas, unlike Thanksgiving and Lincoln Day, is not a National American holiday. It is rather a purely Christian religious festival. It may also be necessary to explain that Chanukah is not the Jewish Xmas. There is not the slightest similarity between the two." Parents, too, increasingly gave voice to a sense of frustration as they competed with Christmas. "The character of the holiday has been transfigured by an accident of timing; what used to be a festival of freedom becomes a festival of refuge."

Despite the pressures of conformity and the "need to compensate Jewish children for the glory and glamour of the Christmas season," American Jews in search of a more authentically Jewish rationale for and expression of Chanukah did not have to look too far afield. They could draw on Zionism, then in its heyday, to legitimate the Chanukah experience and to provide a more positive, less compensatory, role for the holiday. Although the overwhelming majority of American Jews seemed to relate their celebration of Chanukah to that of Christmas, Zionism had the potential to supply an appropriately Jewish idiom and context for the display of Chanukah spirit while lessening the reliance on external "borrowings." "Recently, the observance of Chanukah has gained added vitality," the editors of *Outlook* observed in 1935, pointing to the promise of "Modern Zionism." "Color is given to Jewish life by the development of a new art, drama, music, and literature in Palestine." In fact, the association between Zionism and Chanukah was an old one whose origins date back to the pre–World War I era. At the time, as editorials in the religiously oriented Yiddish press made clear, the public linked the Maccabean festival to the donation of *sheqalim* to the Zionist cause, casting the holiday as a philanthropic occasion. Subsequently, the flowering of cultural Zionism and then, in 1948, the establishment of the State of Israel, enabled Chanukah to acquire a new symbolism and relevance. American Jews now identified the Maccabees not with *shekel* collectors but with the "modern brave warriors" of the newborn state.

Whether cherishing the legacy of latter-day Maccabees or competing with contemporary Christians, American Jewry's embrace of Chanukah illuminates the process of ritual change and adaptation; it also suggests something about the cultural ingenuity and determination of the folk. "It all goes to show," observed one suburban rabbi fascinated by the degree of attention his congregants lavished on Chanukah, "that if you work away at it, you can revive a holiday."

BETWEEN THE WINTER SEASON of Chanukah and the spring season of Passover, the remaining Jewish festivals languished for want of attention. With the exception of the Orthodox community and the more observant members of Conservative Jewry, who, with varying degrees of vigor, observed all of the calendrically mandated holidays, the majority of American Jews treated holidays other than Passover and Chanukah with benign neglect. They turned a deaf ear to the reminders of their clergy that Purim, for instance, was a delightful holiday worth celebrating, or that Shavuoth abounded in floral charm. When it came to marking moments on the Jewish calendar, denominational differences, muted in so many other respects, came sharply to the fore. The failure of these moments to take hold more generally within the American Jewish community not only reflects those differences but throws into bold relief the critical importance of commercialization, sentiment, domesticity, and logistics in determining ritual practice and "holiday consciousness."

Taken as a whole, Purim, Shavuoth, and Sukkoth suffered from an "accident of timing." Purim, the Jewish festival of lots, tended to get lost in the shuffle between Chanukah and Passover; Shavuoth (or Pentecost) fell prey to a "too close proximity to summer," while Sukkoth, the holiday of booths that came quick on the heels of the High Holy Days, succumbed to a bout of post-holiday ennui that logistical difficulties only compounded. The holiday's central ritual, building a small outdoor booth, a sukkah, clashed head-on with the realities of modern life. The practice, observed one of its partisans sadly, "has regrettably been neglected in this country, especially in the large metropolitan centers. No doubt, building a Sukkoh in a city like New York is connected with difficulties, but the booth, rich in historical memories, is well

In some Jewish homes, a miniaturized centerpiece took the place of the large outdoor booth, or sukkah.

worth the price." For some, Sukkoth offered an opportunity to encounter nature (under controlled circumstances); for others, it provided yet another colorful alternative to Christmas. "Jewish mothers who pity their children for missing 'the fun of decorating the Christmas tree' should not deprive them of the joy of decorating the Sukkoh, which offers much greater opportunities to the children to exercise their skills, inventiveness and artistic taste," suggested one guidebook. By far the most realistic and imaginative solution to the urban dweller's dilemma was offered by Rabbi Samuel Harrison Markowitz in his manual, *Leading a Jewish Life in the Modern World.* Why not construct a miniaturized sukkah, he proposed. When placed on the buffet or dining room table as a centerpiece or decorative ornament, it would make a lovely, as well as practical, addition to the holiday spirit. Markowitz was so taken with the idea of the dollhouse sukkah that he provided detailed illustrations and instructions for its construction. Despite these suggestions and inventive strategies, Sukkoth failed to claim the loyalty of the modern American Jew. Quite apart from the technical problems its observance presented, this autumnal festival rendered Jewishness much too visible, distinctive, and quirky. "Now that we are so conscious of ourselves, so prim, and always on our good behavior before our neighbors . . . we have quite forgotten the gentle manners and lovely customs of an old-fashioned Judaism," lamented one of its champions, longing for the days when numerous sukkahs dotted the great out doors.

Along with Sukkoth, Purim and Shavuoth exemplified "old-fashioned Judaism." Enacted largely within the synagogue rather than the home, their observance lacked both the spirit and the objects necessary to the continued vitality of Jewish holiday observance in the modern era. During the closing years of the nineteenth century and the opening ones of the twentieth, Jewish hospitals and other charitable organizations hosted lavish "Purim balls" to drum up financial and social support, leading the American Jewish public to associate Purim more with philanthropically induced partying than anything else. In New York, Beth Israel Hospital staged its annual Purim Ball, reportedly "the most brilliant Jewish social function of the year," at Madison Square Garden. Later, as this practice fell out of favor, American Jewry's cultural custodians attempted diligently to awaken a more general interest in Purim by defining it as a "holiday of merriment, jolliness and buffoonery," in which children attended a synagogue service dressed up as Queen Esther, Mordecai, and other historical personalities associated with the holiday. When that interpretation failed to muster much enthusiasm, a new perspective was offered that focused on its womanly associations. Purim was hailed as "the Jewish women's special holiday," and women were encouraged to "make the most of it." They didn't. Even the tradition of exchanging *shalakh-mones*, or Purim gifts, remained a lovely, quaint, and decidedly low-key affair, a "womanly practice," instead of lending itself to the quickening pulse of commercialization and to parallels with other commodified holidays. "It is quite appropriate to point out to [the children] that, while their Christian friends get gifts only on Christmas, the Jewish calendar has two holidays—Hanukkah and Purim—when gifts are the order of the day," crowed a Purim enthusiast, seeking to make Purim as much a competitive sport as Chanukah. This, too, fell wide of the mark.

Much like Purim, Shavuoth, a springtime festival commemorating the giving of the Ten Commandments, never commanded the degree of devotion intended by tradition. Despite its short-lived association with Mother's Day, the holiday was more of a stately synagogal affair than anything else and lacked the affective qualities and domestic rituals that endeared Passover to so many. For this reason, Reform and Conservative circles paired Shavuoth with confirmation ("season and sentiment were all in its favor"), hoping the excitement and pageantry associated with the modern-day ceremony would enliven the ancient holiday. At the very least, the conjunction of the two momentarily halted the exodus of congregants who, with increasing affluence and mobility, actively cultivated the "vacation habit." For one day, they stayed in town and attended services, even if they were motivated less by religious fervor than by familial pride. Still, despite the temporary surge in synagogue attendance, Shavuoth remained a somewhat lonely and lackluster moment on the Jewish calendar. Its supporters liked to claim that Shavuoth was a "happy holiday in which the abstract and the concrete elements of Judaism and Jewishness are harmoniously blended," but it possessed little in the way of attractive material benefits. Apart from the gifts distributed to the confirmants and a holiday repast of blintzes, its physical aura was limited to the sanctuary, freshly bedecked with flowers and transformed by greenery.

Though a pleasing sight, the floral synagogue did not provide enough of an incentive to draw, or retain, worshipers. "Holiday consciousness is on the wane," observed Emil Lehman, the author of a national survey of synagogue attendance in 1950, in his dutiful tabulation of the declining number of holiday worshipers on Shavuoth and throughout the year. Indeed, American Jews, never the most avid of worshipers, filled the sanctuary to capacity only on the autumnal holidays of Rosh Hashanah (the Jewish New Year) and Yom Kippur (the Day of Atonement), giving rise, as early as the turn of the century, to the much-derided notion of the "Yom Kippur Jew." Such Jews, with their "neither-here-nor-there attitude," lamented the *American Hebrew*, "have no use for congregational worship, may even deride it, and yet when the fall holidays arrive, are not manly enough to persist in their indifference."

Casually observant most of the year, the American Jewish folk bestowed on Rosh Hashanah and Yom Kippur the reverential-sounding title of the "High Holy Days," underscoring their prominence. A show of consumerism heightened the holidays' importance. With space suddenly in short supply, would-be worshipers scrambled to purchase tickets to ensure their place either in the main sanctuary or in the "overflow" service. Outfitted in brand-new suits and dresses, they crowded the synagogue, listening attentively as the plaintive sounds of the ram's horn, the shofar, filled the air. The drama of the moment, though compelling, was not the only reason behind the High Holy Days' overwhelming popularity. Memory and its claims on the community also pulled American Jews into an embrace with sacred time and into the pews of the synagogue. The liturgical opportunity to recall the names, and lives, of deceased family members enabled worshipers to keep alive a sense of the past—if only once or twice a year.

Outside of the synagogue, the exchange of New Year's greeting cards further highlighted the season's significance. Much like Americans everywhere who, as early as the 1880s, eagerly marked the Christmas season with elaborately printed holiday messages, American Jews created a parallel vogue for Jewish New Year cards,

Dress Up... for the Holidays!

Rosh Hashanah—Sept. 21 & 22
Yom Kippur—Sept. 30

Richman Bros.
Quality Clothes for Men
Suits
Overcoats
Topcoats

One quality
One price

$22.50

Richman Bros.
329 Market St. • Harrisburg, Pa.

Admit M ....
Seat No. L. C. F. 4 ...... *Price* ....

בית הכנסת עץ חיים
קאָנגרעסס סטריט
לראש השנה ויום הכפורים הבע"ל, שנת ת"ש

Congregation "ETZ CHAIM"
CONGRESS STREET
5700 - New Year Days and Day of Atonement - 1939
SEPTEMBER 14—15 and 22—23

Mens' Ticket מענ'ס מקום

Name ....
Seat No. L- C F 4 ....
Price ....

American Jews bought tickets to and new clothes for High Holy Day services.

or *shana tovas*. When communities were small and contained, explained the *American Hebrew* in 1905 as it surveyed the popularity of this "new custom," there was little call for greeting cards. "It was then both practical and possible to convey all the personal greetings of the festivals, as well as the social news of the home circle, by word of mouth." But as communities grew in size and opportunities for personal, informal exchange diminished, American Jews came increasingly to rely on the mails to convey the appropriate seasonal sentiments of good health, prosperity, and peace.

Shana tovas came in a variety of styles, from the "tawdry and bedizened" to the subdued and restrained, and featured a variety of motifs: handshakes, floral garlands, evocations of the Old Country, and scenes of smiling, multigenerational families gathered round the holiday table were among the most common. In an effective pictorial way, the Jewish greeting card bound together the family, memory, and Jewish tradition even as it popularized the connection between them. Capitalizing on the Jewish greeting card's popularity, several Jewish communal organizations, such as the National Federation of Temple Sisterhoods, even developed their own product. "It seems absurd to spend large sums upon fancy Rosh Hashanah cards," stated the sisterhood group in 1919, urging members to "fill the mails with 'Uniongrams,' " its version of a telegram. At once a practical and a philanthropic gesture, the purchase and subsequent use of a booklet of "Uniongrams" not only diffused holiday cheer but supported the Federation's efforts on behalf of Hebrew Union College, the flagship of Reform educational institutions. "The complete successs of the 'Uniongram' can come only when Jews will think of [it] as readily as they do of the 'telegram,' " stated its supporters.

Flooding the post office, the costly and time-consuming exchange of cards and "Uniongrams" often entangled senders and recipients alike in a web of etiquette. Should they be sent to business associates or just friends and family? And what of cousin Max, who, for three years running, hasn't reciprocated? Should he be dropped from the list? "New Year presents the same difficulty as the issue of wedding invitations," wrote a student of American Jewish social life. "We have to debate where one can safely draw the line." Classified greetings provided a

Jewish New Year cards freely mixed their metaphors, combining seasonal salutations with patriotism.

Consumers fancied sentimental scenes like this one in which an aging grandfather blesses his young grandson.

satisfyingly communal solution. "The only way in which to reach all your friends," advised the *Jewish Times*, was to advertise in the New Year Greetings section of the paper. For one dollar per entry, a family could widely and inexpensively extend its best wishes to thousands of coreligionists or, as the paper predicted, "from one end of Maryland to the other end, they will *all* see your New Year's announcement." Businesses, too, seized on the opportunity to wish their Jewish customers well. Banks, restaurants, retail emporia, even hairdressers like Alfred, "The Creator of Distinctive Bobs," extended their hopes for a "happy and prosperous New Year to Friends and Patrons."

American Jewry's cultural elite, though, did not quite share the folk's enthusiasm for seasonal expressions of friendship and religiosity. Speaking before the annual convention of the Council of Jewish Women in 1911, Mrs. Caesar Misch noted how "we are too prone to magnify one or two days in the year, to become

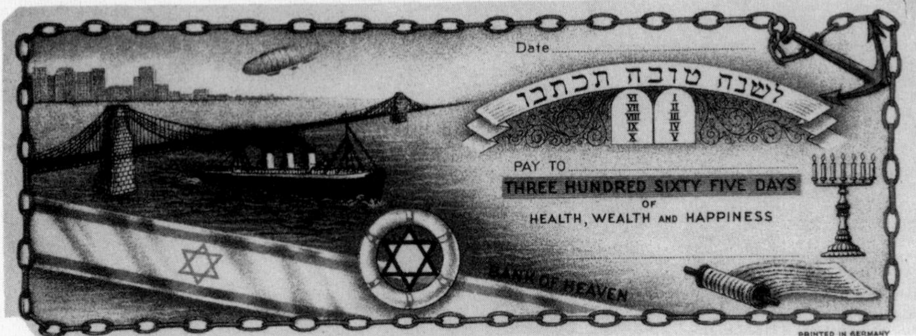

Some greeting cards, drawing on the imagery of a ship ticket, wished family and friends a healthy and prosperous "voyage" in the year ahead.

'Yom Kippur Jews' and to forget that the Sabbath which comes every week is as holy to the Lord as are the festivals and Holydays which come only once a year." Thirty years later, another influential American Jewish woman, Trude Weiss Rosmarin, felt compelled to reiterate that point. "It is a sign of the degeneration of Jewish community and religious life that Rosh Ha-Shonoh and Yom Kippur occupy such a prominent place in the calendar of present-day Jews," she commented in 1941. "Although these holidays have a solemn and serious air all their own, still their observance is nowhere in Jewish law commanded more emphatically than the keeping of the other holidays and, especially, the Sabbath observance." No matter how elegantly or frequently enunciated, condemnations of the "Yom Kippur Jew" changed nothing. American Jews poured into the synagogues in the fall, eager to memorialize their deceased and to pray (however briefly) for the continued well-being of the living; they then absented themselves for the better part of another year.

NO AMOUNT OF CHEERLEADING about the importance of the Sabbath could sway the laity to alter its customary "sabbathless" behavior. Though aware (perhaps) of Achad Ha'am's famous pronouncement, "More than the Jews have kept Sabbath, the Sabbath has kept them," the overwhelming majority of American Jews remained utterly impervious to its celebrated charms. At first, economic hardship and the necessity to work long hours compelled many to violate the Sabbath. "Not all Jewish working men work on Saturdays because they are no longer religious," noted the *American Jewish Chronicle* in 1916. "Thousands of our working men go to shops on Saturdays very reluctantly. They would rather go to synagogue." The burden of work also fell heavily on independent retailers and shopkeepers, compelled to keep open their stores late on Friday evening and all day on Saturday, the biggest sales opportunities of the week. Jennie Grossman's husband, the owner of a grocery store, "had to work *shabbos*. He had to because he was in business. . . . If you wanted to make a living you had to do it. It bothered him, but he couldn't help it. He wanted to make a living. He wanted on account of me." The Depression accentuated these difficulties, keeping an unprecedentedly large number of Jews from their Sabbath rest. In a Wilkes-Barre, Pennsylvania, synagogue, for instance, only six men out of a membership of 250 were able to keep the Sabbath in 1936; everyone else had to work.

Still, the clash of economic imperatives with the sanctity of *shabbos* only partially explains its tenuous grip on the American Jewish imagination. American Jews found lots of other reasons to avoid resting on the Sabbath, using it instead for errands, dancing lessons, sleeping late, and myriad activities that passed for leisure. In fact, by the eve of World War I, a tradition of *non*observance had set in, one that effectively rendered "Sabbath consciousness" obsolete and neglect of the Sabbath "habitual." Like other Americans, Jews rested on Sunday. "Alas, today, in many quarters, the Sabbath is but a memory," lamented one rabbi at the time. "No honest observer can deny that the Jewish Sabbath in this country faces virtual extinction."

By the early twenties, fewer than 20 percent of American Jews attended a Sabbath service of any kind, a percentage that dipped precipitously to 2 percent a generation later. Of that tiny percentage, virtually all were women. "Our rabbis are finally admitting that were it not for the women, the synagogues might close their doors," observed one female temple-goer, Hannah G. Solomon, attaching a positive meaning to this demographic reality. Others were a bit more ambivalent, even troubled, by the preponderance of women worshipers, fearful lest the synagogue become too much of a "woman's institution." Whatever one's views, there was no denying that women kept *shabbos*, men did not. "Under modern conditions, it is the mother who becomes the guardian of the Sabbath and its interpreter," explained Deborah Melamed in her 1927 guidebook, *The Three Pillars*, noting how she created "an atmosphere of Sabbath peace and leisure" by preparing Sabbath delicacies, dressing the children and herself in "Sabbath garb," and making sure that the entire family sat down together to eat a lovely dinner. The Jewish woman, added another guidebook, "must 'educate' her husband to leave his store or office a little earlier, and, if possible, to bring home some flowers for the Sabbath Eve table." Admittedly, it was not easy to educate one's husband and family in the charms of the Sabbath, to prepare its special foods, and to coordinate the family's activities so that everyone would gather together on Friday evening around a table set with the good china and silver. "It requires hard thinking and much effort to make the traditional Sabbath a weekly occasion for the family," admitted one female Sabbath observer.

It goes without saying that not all women attended services or tended to their candle-lighting and culinary duties with the requisite enthusiasm; if the sermonic and prescriptive literature is to be taken at its word, a goodly number apparently preferred to shop. As early as 1904, Mathilde Schechter, acutely attuned to the social climate in which middle-class Jewish women like herself moved, publicly disapproved of "the Jewess who does her shopping and makes her dressmaker's appointments on the Sabbath." That kind of Jewess, she insisted gently, does "herself a spiritual wrong." Other religious authorities, like Israel Levinthal, took to the pulpit to rail against violations of the Sabbath. "You too must lead the way to the finer things in life," he told the women of his Brooklyn congregation, urging them not to go "shopping on Shabbos." During the interwar years and the immediate postwar era as well, women were repeatedly taken to task for spending their Saturdays at the department store, that so-called cathedral of commerce, rather than in their local synagogue. "We pledge ourselves to urge all our members to realize that it is one of our solemn duties as Jewish women to abstain from shopping, diversions and secular preoccupations that interfere with our religious duties," resolved the women of the National Federation of Temple Sisterhoods, a resolve shared by their Conservative and Orthodox sisters as well. Despite the best of intentions, however, the resolve not to shop was hard to maintain. A statistical survey conducted in 1948, for example, revealed that of 163 women surveyed, 140 indicated they shopped on *shabbos*. Of the same group, an equally substantial number, it's worth pointing out, also claimed to light Sabbath candles, thus suggesting that the one activity did not necessarily preclude the other. In any event, even allowing for those whose inclinations ran more to clothes than prayer, women accounted for a disproportionately larger segment of the "temple-going" population than men or children. "The principal thing for the rabbis to do to-day is to fight the indifference of the men," notes a male character in Leah Morton's popular 1926 novel, *I Am a Woman—And a Jew*. "The men pay their dues to the synagogue and feel it's enough. You can't get them to come to services. . . . The women come and they bring the children. But the men stay home."

American Jewry's overwhelming resistance to attending Sabbath services *en famille* frustrated and angered those who presided over them. "When preaching to our people on behalf of Synagogue attendance . . . we often feel as if we were a King Canute attempting to hold back the ocean's tide," sadly noted Simon Greenberg, a leading Conservative rabbi and a president of the Rabbinical Assembly. For Greenberg and his fellow clergy, attending *shabbos* services was "the *sine qua non* of Jewish spiritual loyalty." Repeatedly, they conflated Sabbath observance with synagogue attendance, seeking determinedly "to cultivate the temple-going habit." Those of a more realistic cast, though, doubted the efficacy of such efforts. Attendance at a Saturday-morning service seemed to be a "lost cause." Some Reform rabbis went so far as to transfer the Sabbath service to Sunday, arguing that what mattered in the long run was the spirit of sanctification and restfulness associated with the Sabbath; the date on which that spirit showed itself was, if not immaterial, then certainly interchangeable with the day on which all Americans rested. "On Sunday mornings, the thing to do was to go to the Jewish Temple on Grand Boulevard to hear Rabbi Emil Hirsch hold forth," recalled Edna Ferber. "Finding the Saturday-morning congregation too largely feminine he had arbitrarily switched to the Christian Sabbath for his main service. Crowds packed the place."

Other rabbis found a "late" Friday-evening service followed by an "informal social hour" to be a far more congenial way to mark the Sabbath—and draw a crowd. Conservative clergy placed much stock in this innovation, hoping its convenient hour and swiftly paced service would attract the entire family where the traditional Sabbath-morning service could not. By the mid-1940s, virtually every Conservative synagogue and quite a number of modern Orthodox ones as well held a Friday-evening service, the "next best" thing to a traditional Sabbath gathering, yet it hardly qualified as a total success. "In the pews of the synagogue," observed Leah Morton, "the congregation sat as if at a lecture, immovable, well-bred. This might have been a group at a Chautauqua lecture. . . . One almost expected well-bred applause at the conclusion [of the service]." Even on Friday nights, the audience consisted largely of women. Of Conservative Jewish families surveyed in 1950, less than one-third attended the late Friday-evening service as a "unit." In synagogue after synagogue, women constituted close to three-quarters of those in attendance. Dressed to the nines, "they wore expensive and knowing hats. Their shoes were beautifully put together and cut. Their hair was marcelled, their hands were jewelled. They wore much too much jewelry." Over time, women's ranks thinned as well; different social activities competed for their attention. "Paradoxical and outrageous as it may seem, Friday night services in this day and age have been placed in sharpest competition with a variety of opportunities in the fields of entertainment," noted one outraged observer in 1950. "Television is only a latest newcomer to the series of distractions."

Determined to woo contemporary Jews away from the television set and to reintroduce them to the manifold pleasures of the Sabbath table, Conservative leaders of the 1950s launched the "National Sabbath Observance Effort." American Jews across the country were actively and publicly encouraged "to avoid all avoidable work on the Sabbath, specifically not to shop, not to cook, and not to do any laundry," but instead to light candles, partake of a Sabbath meal, and to attend services. In Norwich, Connecticut, the local Conservative synagogue conducted a "Sabbath In-

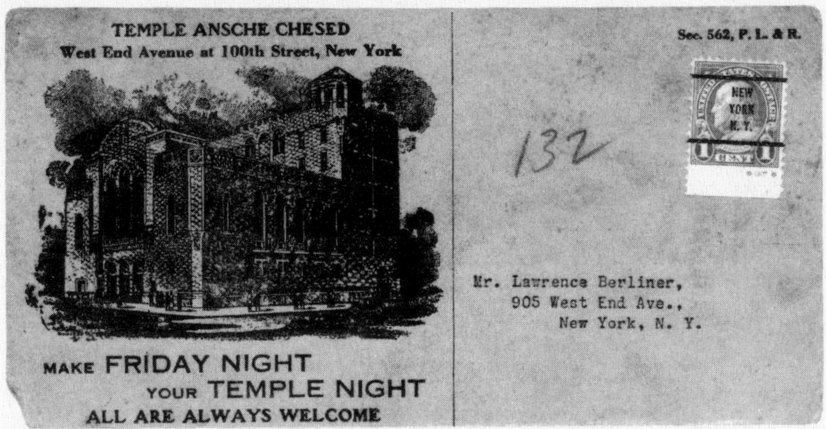

TEMPLE ANSCHE CHESED
West End Avenue at 100th Street, New York
Sec. 562, P. L. & R.
132
Mr. Lawrence Berliner,
905 West End Ave.,
New York, N. Y.
MAKE FRIDAY NIGHT
YOUR TEMPLE NIGHT
ALL ARE ALWAYS WELCOME

CONGREGATION B'NAI SHOLOM, TEMPLE ISRAEL
MICHIGAN AVENUE AT FIFTY-THIRD STREET
CHICAGO

IMPORTANT NOTICE

Please take notice that our Friday evening services will be resumed on October 12, 1917.

The services as usual, will start at 8:15 P. M. promptly. Please be in your seats on time so as to avoid unnecessary confusion.

We hope that every member will make it his duty to attend these services regularly and take advantage of the privilege of listening to the interesting and instructive discourses delivered by our able and learned Rabbi and Leader.

Bring your friends with you. We want every seat occupied at these services.

Yours very truly,

BOARD OF DIRECTORS
CONGREGATION B'NAI SHOLOM, TEMPLE ISRAEL
P. A. GROSSMAN, Secretary.

Congregations across the country transformed the twenty-five-hour Sabbath into a nocturnal event.

stitute" at which a "typical Sabbath lunch and food demonstration with *halle* and gefilte fish" was held following Saturday-morning services. At a Sabbath Institute in Miami, attendees were taught the "four basic steps" of Sabbath preparation; they also received a seven-page leaflet, *Making Our Home Shabbosdik*. Elsewhere, sisterhood women convened workshops and spring conferences on the subject, hoping not only to "highlight the Sabbath observance in a big way," but also to supply the "know-how and know-why" of ritual practice. The grassroots response to these events, reported *Outlook*, was "heartwarming and gratifying."

By far the most controversial contribution to the Sabbath's "revitalization" was the Conservative movement's decision to permit driving on the Sabbath, provided the car was headed in the direction of the synagogue. "Large segments of the population regard riding to the locale of their activities—economic, social, recreational and religious—as a normal feature of modern life," suburban rabbis acknowledged. "To continue unmodified the traditional interdiction of riding on the Sabbath is tantamount to rendering attendance at the synagogue on the Sabbath physically impossible for an increasing number of our people." Taking into account the geographical and vehicular "realities of modern life," and hoping to lessen the spiritual distance between postwar American Jewry and its synagogue, the proponents of change maintained that "the positive values involved in the participation in public worship on the Sabbath outweigh the negative values of refraining from riding in an automobile."

The opponents of change, however, were not nearly so sanguine. Doubtful that lifting the age-old prohibition against the use of technology on the Sabbath would result in a greater number of worshipers, they wondered about its potential for abuse and misuse. "Actually, the question is not whether [American Jews] should ride to the service or stay home; it is, rather, should they ride to the synagogue or should it be to the movies," stated one disheartened Conservative rabbi. Another wanted to know if lifting the ban on driving had actually effected change. "I have been waiting . . . for the Jew who would tell me that *because* of the Rabbinical Assembly Responsa he started to attend the Sabbath service," stated Rabbi Greenberg. "That would have been much more conclusive validation of our action." Such proof was not immediately forthcoming; even today, more than forty years later, the long-range effects of this decision continue to be debated.

In legitimizing driving to *shul*, the Conservative rabbinate no doubt thought it was meeting the folk halfway, on their own turf (or driveway); but the fact is they had fundamentally misread the popular attitude toward ritual performance. It's not that the folk were inclined to jettison the Sabbath entirely or that they were hostile to the idea of being "Sabbath-minded." Rather, they preferred to experience *shabbos* on their own temporal terms and to accommodate its distinctive, sacral rhythms to the rhythms of their household. What appeared, then, to the elite as a flagrant violation of the Sabbath had more to do with competing notions of time, or what sociologist Eviatar Zerubavel has termed a "temporal map." Where the Conservative clergy and other cultural elite defined their Jewish temporal map in terms of sacred and profane and created a network of institutions that reflected these separate spheres, the folk's temporal map either blurred or made little allowance for such distinctions. What's more, at the grassroots level of American Jewish life, *shabbos* was not experienced in devotional terms but in domestic, culinary, and sentimental ones. The notion that "although the Sabbath may not be observed in other respects, for Friday night and Saturday one buys *chaleh*" probably came closer to characterizing the Sabbath behavior of more American Jews than did any edict regarding public worship. In those homes touched by the presence of the proverbial Sabbath Queen and her angels, American Jews gave the Sabbath its due by setting aside a few hours for "spiritual nourishment" during which they lit the Sabbath candles, enjoyed a leisurely Friday-evening dinner with challah and much conversation, and then went about their business. "All week we're rushing about to board meetings, committee meetings, Temple meetings. . . . But tonight, we catch up with one another . . . we're brought up to date as to 'what's new and with whom,' " one mother wrote, explaining why she treasured Friday evenings at home. "Let us keep the Sabbath by beginning to keep the Friday night sacred to the family," suggested another, furthering the Sabbath's links with domesticity. "Let us all celebrate it by making the evening at home for ourselves and all our children. Let all the married children have a weekly reunion at their parents' home." In some households, charm provided the incentive for keeping Friday evening sacred. "Kindling the Sabbath lights is a charming ceremony," noted one Reform rabbi as he urged his coreligionists to adopt the practice. "In our electrically lighted homes it has double significance. Light is always attractive and the soft glow of the candles has a charm that is only enhanced by modern lighting."

However illuminated, the Sabbath enjoyed a "jolly welcome"

when defined and experienced in modern terms. Just like the dietary laws, *shabbos* lent itself to reinterpretation. "It seems to me that the only way we can produce the Sabbath and start changing the pattern of behavior on that day is to sell it to a group of young, intelligent mothers and their children and make them feel so good about it, [because] they are setting a new fashion for the Sabbath Day, giving it the 'new look' so to speak," a Sabbath observer wrote at the time of the revitalization campaign, drawing unabashedly on notions of taste and style derived from the commercial world of fashion. Belief in the Sabbath's therapeutic value also proved to be a big selling point. Leaning heavily on psychology, modern-day Sabbath champions emphasized the regenerative qualities of a day spent at rest and at home. The Sabbath alleviated strain, anxiety, and fatigue, or so they claimed, and also restored one's equilibrium and sense of moral balance. "Mental uneasiness and ennui which are so often characteristic of modern man result not only from a gnawing sense of futility but also from the atrophy of the spiritual, creative and imaginative faculties with which he has been endowed. . . . The Sabbath brings release." Some believed that the benefits of Sabbath rest were as much physical as psychological. One Brooklyn rabbi, extolling the importance of the Sabbath to his congregants, shared the startling statistic that Jews numbered "two to four times as many brain-sufferers" as non-Jews. Why was this? "It's because where Christians have Sunday, Jews without Shabbos have nothing."

Where advocates of the health-oriented Sabbath highlighted its benefits to the individual, others emphasized its benefits to the entire family, asserting that "the Sabbath quickens the spirit and fortifies the meaningful cohesiveness of the Jewish family." For Leon Lang, the author of numerous articles on modern Jewish life, the Sabbath provided an extended exercise in emotional gratification. "Affection is a living, functioning experience on the Sabbath, for every member of the family," he wrote. "The dress for the Sabbath is of the best, by adult and child; the food for the Sabbath caters to the delights of all members of the family. A special sensitiveness reigns in the home that no one in the family shall say the unkind word, shall raise a dispute which may lead to quarreling. . . . Here is a family situation, in which affection, in its deepest meaning, becomes an experienced reality." In some

SABBATH
TO MARKET FOR SHABBOS
To market, to market,
To buy a big fish
For *Shabbos*, for *Shabbos*;
Oh my, what a dish!
To market, to market,
To buy *Chalos* two,
For *Shabbos*, for *Shabbos*;
My work is all through.
9

Jewish parents sought diligently to give the Sabbath a "new look."

families, though, the experienced reality of the Sabbath was cause for frustration, not joy, as younger members chafed under its special brand of discipline. To ensure that there "never be a dull Sabbath in the home," families were encouraged to come up with imaginative alternatives to the usual round of youthful pursuits. A columnist in *Helpful Thoughts*, a Jewish children's magazine, devised what is arguably one of the more creative solutions to Sabbath ennui: a Sabbath club. "So start your little club, elect your own officers, mark your own regulations," the paper advised, hoping that a number of Sabbath-observing boys and girls would follow suit. "But remember the real objective of the club must be to make you *remember the Sabbath day*." Setting aside special toys, games, and activities for *shabbos* play was yet another much-touted way to "ward off that deadening, all too familiar complaint, 'You can't *DO* anything on Shabbas,' " as was visiting with relatives or inviting friends to spend the afternoon. "Let them have a party on Saturday," suggested one Jewish mother. "Every child loves a party. Let the Sabbath be connected in the child's mind with joy and happiness."

Whether associated with happiness or with health, the modern Sabbath, it seemed, could endure as long as its adherents muted its formerly distinctive qualities, trading holiness and sanctity for relaxation, amiable conversation, fun, and games. Only then was there reason to believe that "the prospect is bright to regain our Saturdays."

As THE YEAR ROLLED BY, American Jews, then as now, heeded the call of the matzoh and popularized the whirl of the dreidel but disregarded the Purim masquerade and downgraded the Sabbath. On the surface, it appeared that their actions were motivated entirely by caprice, ignorance, and sheer laziness. At best, these choices betrayed little by way of either logic or consistency. And yet, beneath the surface, barely discernible, one can make out the pattern that explains, or at least shapes, American Jewry's expressed holiday preferences. American Jews wanted their holidays to be just like everyone else's holidays and, where possible, reconfigured them accordingly, emphasizing their affective quality. Holy moments once consecrated to God or Jewish history were transformed into occasions of domestic expression and consumerism; sacred time became family time. Proceeding intuitively, American Jews did to the Jewish calendar what they had done to the dietary laws, infusing the sacred with the vernacular and the transcendant with the quotidian. From time to time, the community's religious authorities would plead for the importance of constancy in Jewish life or, as Mrs. Henry Gichner of Washington, D.C., put it, comparing Judaism to fine silver, "the more we use it in our daily lives, the more beautiful lustre it takes on." But these exhortations fell on deaf ears. American Jews steadfastly preferred the occasional, the "once in a while," approach to modern Jewish living to one which, like fine silver, required continuous attention.

7
A Last Farewell

In Sholom Aleichem's classic short story "Beryl Isaac and the Wonders of America" the title character, infatuated with the New World, rhapsodizes about its size, its scale, its exceptional bounty. Asked by a skeptical friend, "Don't people die in America . . . Or do they live on and on?" he responds: "Of course they die, but the *way* they die—that's what's wonderful." For Beryl Isaac, as for thousands of his more worldly coreligionists, death provided an opportunity for "sham and show," for honoring the dead through a display of affluence and status. When it came to mourning, American Jews "created their own death-style, as they had their own life-style," noted one real-life skeptic. "Ostentation replaced modesty, and instead of simplicity, extravagance ruled the day."

In most instances, the American Jewish way of death had more to do with inexperience than with a yearning for extravagance. "When Death strikes, we often find ourselves faced with a multiplicity of vexing questions and problems concerning these traditional practices for which we have no immediate answers," noted a sympathetic rabbi, excusing the often ill-informed choices made by most of his congregants. By contrast, Orthodox Jews and "revolutionary" Jews knew exactly how to conduct a funeral, or so it seemed to Yiddish journalist B. Z. Goldberg, who, in a 1949 issue of *Der Tog*, explored contemporary American Jewish funerary practices. The traditionalists, he wrote, follow the letter of the (Jewish) law, from ritually purifying the body (*taharah*) and dressing it in a white linen shroud to reciting certain Psalms and saying kaddish, the mourner's prayer for the dead, at the funeral service. The revolutionaries, in turn, have their own customs, or *minhagim*: they find solace in the words of Marx and in the stirring cadences of the Internationale. "The free-thinking, non-partisan funeral, however, has no recognizable form or content," Goldberg asserted. "One never knows whether to wear a hat or to go bare-headed; whether to play music or recite a *kapitel tehillim*, a few Psalms."

The Jewish funeral director, a title increasingly preferred to that of undertaker or mortician, leaped into the breach, ordering the chaos of loss. "When death occurs, the funeral director assumes every responsibility," explained the owners of the Riverside Memorial Chapel, the nation's largest chain of Jewish funeral parlors, urging consumers to "select a funeral director with the care you would a physician." This trained—and paid—professional relieved the bereaved family of the "annoying details" associated with dying. He secured the death certificate and burial permit, prepared the body for burial, arranged the funeral, placed obituary notices in the newspaper, and orchestrated the cemetery service. "To move people about in a vehicle is a service relationship," observed one student of the American funeral industry, referring to the funeral cortege. "But to organize and direct a procession which must be profoundly ceremonial, which cannot be rehearsed or repeated, and in which mistakes are always magnified by a high level of emotional intensity . . . elevates the funeral director's work beyond and above that of the craftsman, tradesman, or purveyor of petty personal services." Efficient, organized, and helpful, the modern funeral director also brought tact and sensitivity to his work, "that quality of considerateness which spiritualizes his acts, and renders consolation. In a very real sense, his is a 'personal service,' " one such professional proudly acknowledged. Added another: "It is a comfort to know that during those trying hours of sorrow you can place your confidence" in a trained professional.

Placing their trust in the funeral director, the folk embraced the "American way of death" with all of its "ritual novelties." At one time, traditional American Jewish funerals were known for their unassuming modesty, especially when compared with those of other ethnic groups. A widely cited study of funeral costs conducted in 1928 by the Metropolitan Life Insurance Company found that American Jews "were unusually economical in funeral ex-

Telephone LUdlow 7-4800

SINGLE GRAVES AND PLOTS FOR SALE IN ALL CEMETERIES

M. HELLMAN

UNDERTAKER and FUNERAL DIRECTOR

MAIN OFFICE:

1532-34 GRAND CONCOURSE

New York, July 16 1937

Funeral Expenses of Deceased W Agner

Cemetery

Society

		Removing Body			15	—
		Embalming Body			25	—
		Freezing Body				
		Man Watching.....Nights.....Days			5	-
		Candles and Candelabra				
		Camp Chairs				
		Coffin or Casket	5		30	-
		Shrouds			5	
		..........Yards Linen				
		Sewing Set				
		Use of Parlors			15	-
		Tara	1		5	-
		Pallbearers				
		Hearse			12	-
	2	Cars	2		22	-
		Opening Grave			12	-
		Metal Grave Marker				
		Box Mattress				
		Advertisements				
		Permit Expenses			1	-
		Transcripts	$147.			
		Hosp. Morgue Expenses				
		Grave	[illegible]		45	
		Reverend Services	#102 -			
		Tips as Directed [illegible]				

Rec Payment July 17, 1937

M. Hellman

Funeral directors took care of everything.

penditures while the Irish and the Italian were inclined to be more extravagant." It attributed this show of fiscal restraint to a "religious tradition of simplicity in burial customs." But like so much else associated with the American Jewish experience, that, too, would change. With the exception of Orthodox funerals, which, by and large, remained scrupulous in their fidelity to tradition, the American Jewish funeral gradually lost much of its distinctiveness. A sizable, and constantly growing, proportion of American Jews took to dressing the departed in his tuxedo or her "good" dress rather than in the simple white linen shroud prescribed by tradition for both men and women. Even embalming, a practice once anathemized, took hold. "In the early days all people objected to having any cosmetics used on the body or having it fixed up in any way. Today they no longer object. In fact they would, I am sure, remark if I didn't do these things as a matter of course," reflected a Jewish funeral director in Minneapolis in the 1940s.

As they cultivated a funeral aesthetic that closely resembled that of their neighbors, American Jews prettified not only the corpse but the coffin as well. Much like other Americans, they believed that "the presence of flowers at a funeral serves as a fitting tribute to the deceased. It is a mark of respect as well as of beauty." Despite the fact that Jewish tradition unequivocally frowned on "funeral offerings" as un-Jewish and inappropriate, American Jews as early as the 1880s placed multicolored and beribboned floral baskets, sprays, wreaths, and special floral emblems such as lyres, harps, anchors, gates ajar, and broken wheels at the brass feet of increasingly ornate mahogany caskets, having rejected also the humble pine box, once intrinsic to Jewish burials, as aesthetically unpleasing. "It is the essence of the modern funeral service to put the burial of the dead in a context of things pleasant and beautiful, and to consider the comfort of the bereaved," explained a historian of the American funeral industry, underscoring its wholesale "cosmetization."

Anything but funereal, the funeral home furthered death's aestheticization, banishing gloomy, morbid thoughts with those of a more lofty and elevating nature. "In architecture, in appointments, in its very atmosphere of strengthening tenderness, it consoles," noted Riverside Memorial Chapels whose flagship Manhattan facility, the latest in Moorish moderne, epitomized the progressive

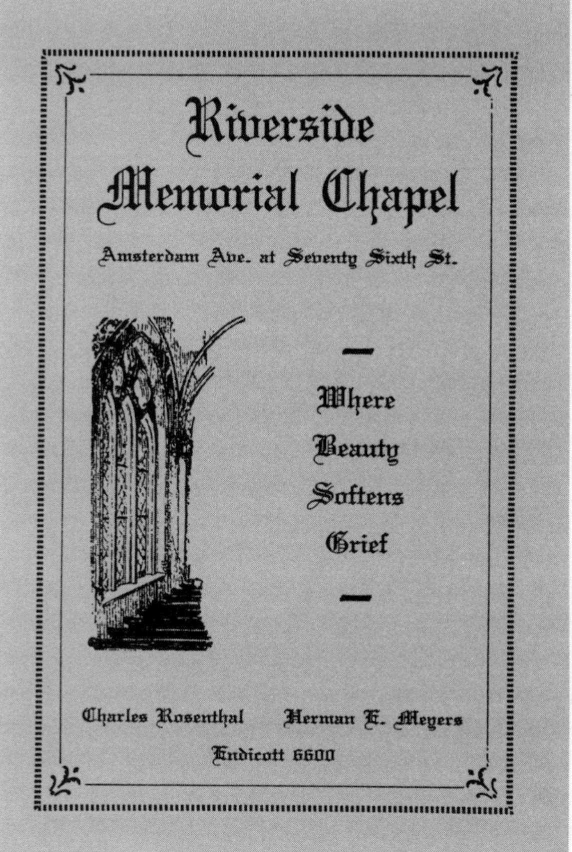

American Jews, like Americans everywhere, came to prefer the commercial funeral parlor to their own private parlor when saying their final farewells.

funeral establishment where "beauty softens grief." "This building contains many modern conveniences installed with one purpose in mind—the comfort of those in sorrow. Private driveway, rest rooms, arrangement room, minister's room where family and minister may confer in privacy, and roof garden where mourners may relax in comfort far above the noises of the busy city, are provided for." The funeral home also actively attended to the needs of friends, family, and business associates who had come to pay their respects. Seated in the chapel, whose high domed ceiling, burnished wood pews, and stained-glass windows reflected "dig-

The funeral home prided itself on its sensitivity and efficiency.

nified beauty" and facilitated contemplation, they said their "last farewell."

With its emphasis on professionalism and its promise of consolation, the Jewish funeral home developed into the preferred ceremonial site for collective mourning. A product of the 1890s, it eventually superseded the private home, synagogue, *khevre kadisha* (Jewish communal burial society), and *landsmanshaft* (Jewish mutual aid society). "This development can scarcely be wondered at," wrote one observer in the 1930s as he surveyed the proliferation of commercial facilities in virtually every major city, from

Los Angeles and New York to Minneapolis, Detroit, and New Orleans. "For in the funeral chapel the solemn beauty of the last service is most properly set." While some challenged this view, arguing that, as a religious service, the funeral deserved to take place in the sacred setting of the synagogue, most Jews sought comfort instead in the funeral chapel. As the latter took hold, it transformed what had once been a lay, communal undertaking into an exclusively male-dominated business enterprise. "Our modern equipment makes our efficient and understanding service as near as your telephone, anytime, anywhere—a service within the means of all," explained Brooks Funeral Service of Bridgeton, New Jersey, whose personnel were committed to "serving Jewish tradition in the modern manner." Yet another concern put it even more directly, appealing to the mourner's most atavistic fears. "With cherished memories of the departed, shall there mingle the thought that, at the last, all was not as it should have been?"

The implication that only the commercial funeral home could ensure a fitting Jewish burial profoundly disturbed American Jewry's cultural custodians, who sharply criticized the funeral director for his assumption of ritual responsibility. "All too frequently, well meaning members of the family or friends will offer their counsel, claiming to be authorities on Jewish law," noted Minneapolis Rabbi Albert Gordon, referring delicately, if obliquely, to the neighborhood funeral director. "Their advice, more often than not, may be based upon some superstitious practice or purely local custom which they may happen to remember. It seldom has any authoritative basis in law." Funeral directors, in turn, frequently turned the tables, attributing ritual confusion to the rabbis. "I cannot find any real laws governing burials," wrote Sam Piser, a Chicago funeral director, in 1930. "In my [fourteen years of] experience I have noted that there is more chaos in America than in any country in the world as to funeral rites. It seems that every rabbi here interprets his own burial laws. . . . It is high time that our rabbis in this country should once and for all times provide a minhag America [a standardized code] for our people."

The rabbinate, seeking to clarify the situation, recommended a division of labor: it alone would interpret Jewish funerary law and funeral directors would see to its execution. But that solution didn't always work, especially when funeral homes took to hiring a "funeral parlor rabbi," a freelance religious specialist, oftentimes a "cantor, teacher or just an ordinary citizen," to preside at funeral services. "It is just this species of easy going rabbis who function at rites-de-passage—which for most people spell the sum and substance of religion—that are the main cause of a civilization's or religion's decadence," fulminated Mordecai Kaplan. Tension between the pulpit rabbi, the "funeral parlor rabbi," and the funeral director came to a head in the early 1960s, when an interdenominational coalition of Massachusetts congregations, determined to eliminate funeral "abuses," established a nonprofit communal burial society akin to the old-style *khevre kadisha*. Threatened with the loss of both face and income, local funeral directors fought back, appealing to the community in the name of democracy and freedom. "Would you allow such restrictions to apply to your every day living—to your purchase of homes, furnishings, clothing, automobiles and the other necessities in everyone's life?" they asked, insinuating that the formation of a communal burial society endangered American Jewry's basic rights. But the Massachusetts rabbinate held firm and succeeded in opening and operating a communal burial society devoted to "simplicity and equality in funerals."

The clergy's critique of the funeral industry did not stop with the funeral director. Together with sisterhood groups, the rabbinate launched a "vigorous protest in behalf of simplicity and common sense," condemning the laity's preference for physical extravagance and recommending instead that the funeral be kept simple, tasteful, and in accord with Jewish precepts. From the pulpit and the printed page, the two railed against excess, showiness, and "senseless extravagance," insisting that "display of every kind should be eliminated." Flowers bore the brunt of communal criticism. "From the Jewish custom of simple funerals, we have dashed into style and pomp, and we are confronted with a display that is as heathenish as it is offensive," wrote the National Federation of Temple Sisterhoods, urging its members to distinguish between the appropriate use of flowers at the dinner table and in the sanctuary pulpit and their ill-advised use at a funeral. Instead of spending money on meaningless floral displays, Jewish women were encouraged to make a charitable contribution in memory of the deceased. "Let the women of Israel again come forward to be the pioneers to abolish this abused custom and the flag bearers to this beneficent end," the sisterhood organization ringingly stated, endorsing charity as a "charming courtesy." In much the same spirit of charm, restraint, and tastefulness, the elite championed the virtues of a brief, but heartfelt, service. "A funeral should not be like a meeting. . . . A word from one appropriate person should be enough," noted one inveterate funeral-goer; others went still further. "Propriety should rule both as to the nature of the remarks and the length of time consumed in making them," suggested Chicago rabbi Joseph Stolz. "Ordinarily a funeral sermon lasting more than fifteen or twenty minutes is an *agmas nefesh*, a torture and a cruelty. And furthermore, the spoken word should not be prostituted into fulsome praise of the living or the dead, nor should it aim at opening anew the foundation of tears and be the cause for those sudden outbursts of grief that remind us of the professional wailers of the Orient."

When it came to the cemetery, modern American Jews abandoned all pretense of restraint by spending lavishly on elaborate "sarcophagus monuments." "I presume there is enough money superfluously spent on monuments every year in every fair-sized Jewish community of this country to maintain a professorship at the Hebrew Union College," observed one strongly inclined advocate of funeral reform writing at a time when endowing a chair in Rabbinics or Semitics cost dearly. "Deeds, not stones, are the best and most enduring monuments," he chided. Time and again, the clergy made a point of stressing that "simplicity is the outstanding feature of Jewish laws concerning the honor due to the dead. . . . It would be very regrettable if we should give this up." And, time and again, American Jews listened respectfully and then hired firms such as the New England Granite Works or the Grey-Conkendall Company to make "beautiful mortuary memorials of every description, executed by the best sculptors in the country devoted to this art." In 1878, for instance, Solomon Rich's widow, Mathilda, spent $2,300, then an enormous sum of money, to erect a monument in memory of her German-born husband. Fashioned out of the finest granite and designed to resemble a Greek temple, it also featured a traditional Hebrew inscription that read: "Here are buried the remains of the pious man, Solomon, son of Joseph

Rich, who was born on the 23rd of Sivan 5577 and died 27th of Tebeth of the year 5638. May his soul be included in everlasting life!"

Hundreds of extravagant, visually heterogeneous monuments like the one erected by the Rich family ornamented the well-groomed landscape of Jewish cemeteries, vexing the clergy and bewildering new arrivals to America. "A strange place, Columbus' Land," mused a former inhabitant of the Old World who had expected to see the characteristically humble and modest Jewish burial grounds, with their jagged, uneven rows of headstones and eerie ambiance, reproduced in America. "Here Protestant cemeteries with their simple gravestones . . . appear much more Jewish than the Jewish cemeteries." Elaborate iron gates and stone arches erected by groups like the Morris L. Kramer Family Circle and the Progressive Brethren of Nieshwish, a Jewish mutual aid so-

Solomon Rich's family erected this dignified mauseoleum in his memory.

In death, as in life, Jewish family circles and mutual aid societies made ample room for their own members.

ciety, added to the cemetery's novel appearance—as well as to the inflaming of passions. "Most of the complaints, and most of the business of the meetings," observed a guest at a "society" meeting, "have to do with the cemetery or sick benefits." That plots were allotted on a first-come, first-served basis enlivened the proceedings, especially when a "bad spot—against a fence or overlooking a dump or factory"—fell to the uncle of an important or outspoken member. In such instances, we are told, the ensuing discussion took one of two forms: "for the uncle and against." Democracy of a different sort found a home in Montefiore's Temple of Rest, an "imposing, yet not gaudy or proud" communal mausoleum. "Come and plan for a Future over which you have no control," urged Mausoleum Associates in 1930, promoting the crypt as an alternative to the "old method" of in-ground burial. This innovation, its sponsors trumpeted, not only "fittingly typifies the democracy of death," but is "built for and by Far-Thinking Men and Women who appreciate the tempo of this Modern Age and who are progressive enough to plan their Future as they protect their Now."

Whatever their orientation, many Jewish cemeteries—Acacia, Cypress Hills, King Solomon Memorial Park, Salem Fields, Woodlawn—seemed more inspired by a putative association with gardening than with the *beit olam*, the eternal resting place, of tradition. Drawing on the model and nomenclature of the American landscape cemetery which placed a premium on the restorative and contemplative attributes of a well-ordered physical environment, cemetery promoters emphasized how their properties were "beautifully laid out along park-like plans . . . surrounded by picturesque scenery," and located on "high, dry and level ground." In their appeals to potential customers, they focused more on the cemetery's scenery and greenery than its role as a quasi-sacred repository of history. "Its light and comfort, its personal care and upkeep, its seclusion and exclusiveness . . . are the things you ought to know," advertised Mausoleum Associates, while Woodlawn Cemetery sent prospective customers a "book of views upon request." Other facilities, like Mount Carmel, a cemetery maintained by the Workmen's Circle, a Jewish Socialist fraternal order, boasted of their distinguished clientele. Home to literati and labor leaders like Sholom Aleichem and Meyer London, this cemetery was nothing less than a Jewish "Valhalla, or Pantheon."

A "new country—a world by itself" to which mourners came as "pilgrims," Mount Carmel and other modern Jewish cemeteries were located at a considerable distance from the city. Once a familiar feature of any village, town, or neighborhood, the cemetery came to be what historian Kenneth Ames has called a "separate, specialized landscape to accommodate the dead." As it moved farther and farther to the city's outskirts, mourners had to travel by ferry, trolley, subway, and, in later years, a private car to get there. Infrequent pilgrimages to the cemetery only height-

APRIL 4, 1930 777

MONTEFIORE

TEMPLE *of* REST

New York's Exclusively Jewish MAUSOLEUM

. . . . . . At the Feast of Passover

An eternal shrine to the memory of your beloved ones is being erected, stone upon stone. . . . And, on this festive occasion of Passover, YOU and all of YOU can give thanks to the far-sighted Men and Women who are making this Temple of Rest possible. . . . They've looked ahead and liberated themselves from the old method of ground burial with the same keen sense of freedom as did our ancient forefathers when they forsook Egypt.

But you must investigate Montefiore Temple of Rest immediately. Fill out the coupon NOW and find out about New York's first and exclusively Jewish Mausoleum. Its light and comfort, its personal care and upkeep, its seclusion and exclusiveness, its actual low cost (within the reach of all) are the things you ought to know. . . . The feast of Passover . . . let it plan YOUR FUTURE for YOU . . . TODAY!

Your Copy of our Beautifully Descriptive Booklet is waiting for you!

MAIL THIS COUPON—TO-DAY!

MAUSOLEUM ASSOCIATES, INC.
1170 Broadway, New York City
(Ashland 1985-1986)

Name ....

Address ....

Address ....

A.H. 4-4-30

Montefiore's Temple of Rest and other Jewish cemeteries proudly advertised in the Jewish press.

ened the sense of distance. Families, following Jewish custom, limited their visits to the month of Elul, the period preceding the High Holy Days, and to Mother's and Father's Day, a "purely American" concession to parental memory. Not surprisingly, a cemetery's accessibility became one of its major assets. "Reached by Brooklyn 'L' or trolleys," advertised Salem Fields while Riverside Cemetery, a New Jersey competitor, boasted of being "nearer to the center of New York City than any other Jewish cemetery." Businessmen like Sidney Jackier, the proprietor of the Euclid Hotel, also capitalized on cemetery geography. His establishment, adjacent to Salem Fields and Cypress Hills cemeteries, offered mourners a wide range of related services, including free transportation to and from the burial grounds, "special accommodations" for those inclined to stay the night, and "special prices for funeral parties."

In offering to provide a "funeral party," the Euclid Hotel anticipated the Jewish caterer's entry into the mourning business. "We Cater Shivahs," read one advertisement, referring to the traditional seven-day mourning period that immediately followed the burial service. Returning either to the home of the deceased or their own residence, mourners (in the immediate family) were expected to give themselves over completely to their grief. According to Jewish law, they were not to wash or attend to worldly affairs for seven days—the term *shivah* derives from the Hebrew word for "seven," *shevah*. A highly elaborated Jewish code of behavior governed the shivah period, from personal expressions of mourning and the conventions of the condolence call to the appearance of the "shivah house." Much like black crepe streamers and mourning wreaths, the presence of memorial candles, covered mirrors, prayerbooks, and "shivah benches," low stools on which the mourners reposed, identified the Jewish home as a site of mourning; secular appurtenances such as folding chairs, coat racks, and hangars, often supplied by the funeral home to accommodate the large number of callers, also bore witness to the presence of death. The mourner, in turn, was identified by a noticeable rent in his or her clothing, a tangible symbol of grief.

So much for tradition. Then, as now, American Jews observed their own kind of shivah, transforming this doleful occasion into an exercise in conviviality. Unable fully to inhabit the traditional

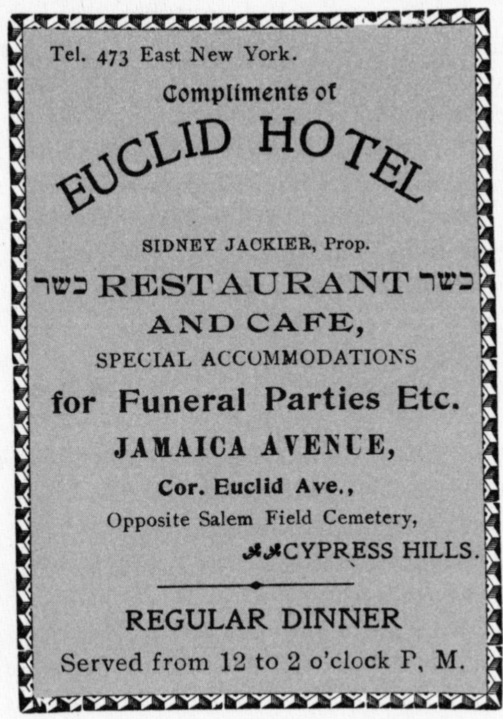

In the early 1900s, the Euclid Hotel distributed this complimentary calendar to its patrons.

role of mourner, they became hosts instead. "Shiva has developed into an atmosphere of the afternoon cocktail party," lamented the rabbi of a Mount Vernon congregation, noting how "potato chips, fruit, cigarettes and drinks are spread for the entertainment of the visitor. Smoke is generally so thick and the din of conversation so loud, one could well wonder what is taking place." That business associates sent ornately wrapped fruit baskets and condolence callers brought cake also added to the party spirit. In fact, condolence-inspired gift-giving had become so widespread by the 1950s that one American Jew actually inquired of an authoritative body of Conservative rabbis whether he had to bring something when paying a "shivah call." "I know that people bring gifts to people who are sitting [shivah]. Is that a *Jewish Custom*? If not whos [sic] Custom is it?" wondered Mr. C. Weinberg of Alabama Avenue in Brooklyn. "The custom to bring gifts to people who are sitting shivah is not a Jewish custom and should be discouraged," responded Rabbi Michael Higger. "The Jewish custom is to bring to people food which they need for regular meals only."

As this exchange suggests, notions of customary shivah practice varied widely. Within Reform circles as well as secular ones it was de rigueur to observe only three days rather than an entire week and to dispense with such conventions as tearing one's garment, wearing slippers in lieu of leather shoes, covering the mirror, and sitting on or close to the ground; such practices were seen as examples of outmoded, Oriental superstitions. "Inasmuch as we have practically abolished all Orientalism from the synagog, and in everyday life have altogether ceased to express our feelings after the pattern of Orientals, it is out of all reason to retain Oriental modes of mourning," a leading Reform rabbi stated in 1898, urging his congregants to display restraint and discretion throughout the mourning period. "It is as much a virtue to exercise self-control at the coffin as at the banquet table. Indeed, it is by this self-restraint that a man betrays true culture."

In time, Jews affiliated with other denominations also began to modify their mourning practices. "Do you encourage the practice of covering mirrors at the home of mourners?" Conservative rabbis were asked in the late 1930s. A majority of those surveyed did not. Some failed to "stress it," while others claimed the practice was "immaterial." One particularly imaginative rabbi mediated between these two positions by recommending "the use of Bon Ami if they ask [for] it." Rather than cover the mirrors and interfere with the home's aesthetic, he symbolically erased the mirrors by whitewashing their surface with the popular cleanser. Sitting shivah for its prescribed length also underwent a whitewash of sorts, becoming increasingly a one-sided, gendered affair. Many otherwise traditional congregations looked kindly upon male mourners who, owing to economic exigencies, returned to work after observing only three days of mourning; women, by contrast, were expected to observe shivah in its entirety.

Distinctive mourning garb also changed over time, in line with American sartorial conventions of grieving. For much of the nineteenth century, American mourners were swathed from head to toe in black, lusterless fabrics that conspicuously advertised the sense of inner loss. Later, as the forms of "fashionable tribulation" multiplied, an increasing number of Americans rejected them altogether, acting out of what historian James Farrell calls a "cultural revulsion against the extended effects of death." The imperatives of restraint similarly affected Jewish mourning attire. While wearing black was never a particularly Jewish practice, rending one's clothing or what was known in Hebrew as *keriah* served as the traditional way by which a mourner outwardly represented his or her grief. "The rite of *keriah* is well grounded in Jewish literature, law and practice," explained one rabbinical authority. "It is not only compatible with the mourner's need for giving vent to his feelings but also helps him to release suppressed emotions by physical means."

Despite its touted therapeutic value, this practice, too, gave way to the more modern, resolutely genteel custom of discreetly substituting a black ribbon or armband for a glaringly ripped blouse, tie, or suit jacket, a substitution energetically promoted by the funeral director and taken up enthusiastically by the folk. "The mores of our day do not always permit resorting to methods of performing *keriah* which were employed in previous generations," conceded the Conservative movement's Committee on Jewish Law and Standards. "Therefore, we recognize *keriah* with a [black] ribbon as valid." In this instance, as in so many others, American Jews struck off in a new direction: reversing age-old patterns of Jewish mourning behavior, they now opted for emotional restraint and material extravagance.

Within many households, mourning did not stop with shivah but continued for an additional eleven months in Conservative and Orthodox circles and twelve months in Reform society as the bereaved men of the family assumed the daily ritual obligation of reciting the mourner's kaddish at synagogue services. (Since Jewish law relieved women of the responsibility of time-bound worship, they were not obligated to recite kaddish in public and most traditional Jewish women did not.) To be sure, ardent freethinkers "avoided kaddish like the whirlwind," but a strikingly high proportion of otherwise ritually inattentive men did not. Isolating this one particular ritual from hundreds of others, they seemed to believe that reciting the ancient Aramaic prayer "constitutes the chief duty that the Jew owes to his religion." Whatever their motivation—family loyalty, superstition, the bonds of memory, or a composite of all three—men took time out from their worldly affairs and raced to the synagogue. "All day long a [Midtown

---

THE MOURNERS' KADDISH

Reader and Mourners

Yisgadal v'yiskadash sh'me rabbo, b'olmo deevro chiruseh v'yamlich malchuseh, b'chayechon uvyomechon, uv'chayey d'chol beys yisroel, baagolo uvizman koreev, v'imrue omen.

Congregation

Y'he sh'meh rabbo m'vorach l'olam ulolmey olmayo.

Reader and Mourners

Yisborach v'yishtabach v'yispo-ar v'yisromam v'yisnaseh v'yis-hador v'yisa-ley v'yishal-loi sh'meh d'kud-sho b'reech hu l'elo min col birchoso v'shiroso tushb'choso v'nechemoso daamiron b'olmo, v'imru omen.

Y'he sh'lomo rabbo min sh'mayo c'chayim olenu v'al col yisroel, v'imru omen.

Oseh sholom bimromov, hu ya-aseh sholom olenu v'al col yisroel v'imru omen.

5

Transliterations of the Mourners' Kaddish enabled those unfamiliar with the language to fulfill their ritual obligations.

synagogue] is shaken by traffic; all day long there is a hasty coming and going of sayers of the Prayer for the Dead—chauffeurs, businessmen, shoeblacks, policemen, lawyers, gangsters, drug-store clerks, bell-boys—on foot and in cars," the writer and social critic Maurice Samuel acidly observed in 1932. "Once a day during the first year of mourning, once a year thereafter, they hurry from their stores, offices and hackstands, tumble into the synagogue, wait for a quorum to go through the prayers, then at the signal stand up and gabble something beginning *Yisgadal veyiskadash sheme rabo . . .*" If another eyewitness is to be taken at his word, noise seemed to be as much a part of the kaddish-saying experience as speed. "Every mourner present shouts the kaddish at the top of his voice apparently trying to drown out every body else's voice until the noise, especially in the larger congregations . . . becomes almost deafening," observed Rabbi Elias Solomon, much disturbed by the din.

The folk's apparent preference for (hastily and noisily) reciting kaddish reflected, at bottom, a basic misunderstanding about its purpose. "The influence of Catholicism has doubtless colored these prayers," complained one rabbi, pointing out that many Jews, ignorant of its history and meaning, equated kaddish with a mass for the dead. But safeguarding the souls of the deceased and ensuring their eternal rest had nothing whatsoever to do with the liturgy. Its focus, and objective, lay elsewhere: with the mourner and his acknowledgment of the divine presence. The prayer was intended to heighten the worshiper's awareness of the "Author of all things," not to summon up thoughts of heaven or hell. That kaddish was written, and recited, in Aramaic, a language known by few American Jews, surely contributed to the disjunction between intent and understanding and fostered what Omaha rabbi Leo Franklin called "a spirit of blind superstition." Urging that kaddish "be made intelligible to the people," he, together with many of his colleagues, strongly recommended its translation into the commonly spoken vernacular. Were American Jews to recite the prayer in English, the rabbi argued, "misapprehension and consequent superstition would be absolutely impossible."

But the folk preferred to stumble over the unfamiliar sounds of the "authentic" text rather than use a literal English translation or a contemporized adaptation. Transliterations "printed in Latin letters . . . like an answer to an algebra problem," facilitated the encounter between the mourner and the ancient words. The transliterated kaddish, which appeared as early as the 1890s in Jewish prayerbooks, as well as mourning guides and convenient-sized "kaddish cards," enabled the mourner to overcome seemingly insurmountable linguistic difficulties and to find consolation in the lilting, exotic, and mournful cadences of an ancestral language. Closer to a mantra than a mass, kaddish's power derived from its evocativeness and historicity, not from its literal meaning. Kaddish's power also derived from its link to family. A form of parental piety practiced by generation after generation of Jews, saying kaddish enabled the mourner to affirm the bonds of family and to feel both the presence of ancestors long since gone and the spirit of the recently departed.

While kaddish remained a male institution, the appeal of *yizkor*, the memorial service for the dead, seemed more evenly distributed. Several times a year, on Yom Kippur and the holidays of Shmini Atzeret, Passover, and Shavuoth, crowds of male and female worshipers known by the 1920s as "*yizkor* Jews" gathered together in the synagogue to recall the lives of loved ones and to give voice to the centrality of domestic Judaism. Responsive readings, often in English, coupled with kaddish and a series of traditional prayers individually memorializing one's parents, grandparents, and friends allowed for an enhanced sense of participation and belonging. For a few solemn moments, the individual and the collective came together, bound by memory and family.

Such charged moments did not last long. Having tended to their ritual obligations, "*yizkor* Jews" then exited the service en masse, much to the consternation of the men in the pulpit and the regulars in the pews. "In a large number of congregations, many of the worshippers, despite the plea by the rabbi, leave immediately after the Yizkor . . . so that the service is interrupted," complained one worshiper. Congregation B'nai Israel of Red Bank, New Jersey, went a step further. In a specially published brochure, it firmly admonished the occasional worshiper: "The Yizkor Service you are privileged and permitted to take part in is only a part of a complete service and when you leave the Synagogue immediately after the Yizkor, you are breaking the sanctity and violating the holiness of a sacred occasion and disturbing the quiet and dignity

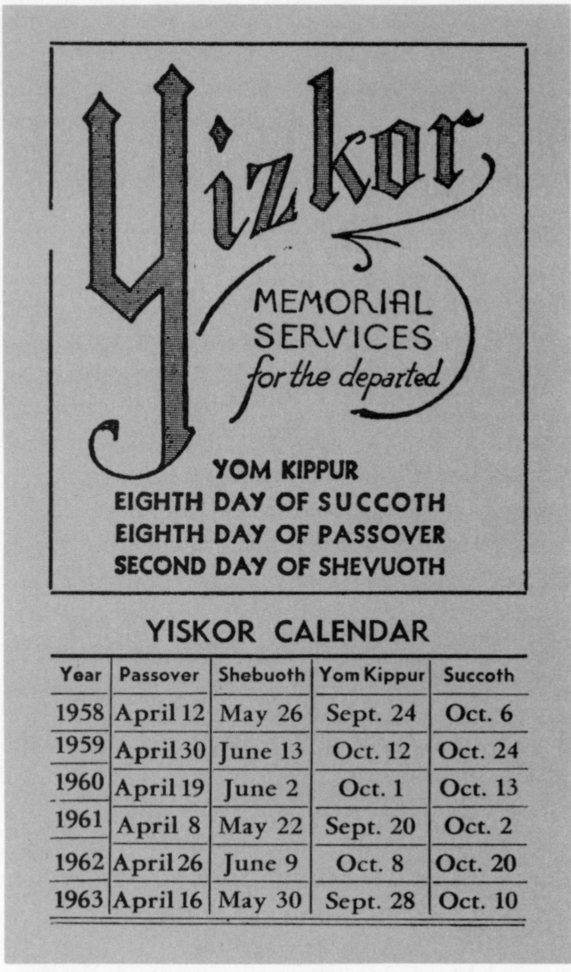

Year	Passover	Shebuoth	Yom Kippur	Succoth
1958	April 12	May 26	Sept. 24	Oct. 6
1959	April 30	June 13	Oct. 12	Oct. 24
1960	April 19	June 2	Oct. 1	Oct. 13
1961	April 8	May 22	Sept. 20	Oct. 2
1962	April 26	June 9	Oct. 8	Oct. 20
1963	April 16	May 30	Sept. 28	Oct. 10

Yizkor Memorial Services attracted a large crowd.

of a Congregation whose hospitality you have accepted." Visitors were encouraged to remain in their seats until the end of the service.

Though a potential source of disturbance, the *yizkor* Jew was also a potential source of revenue. Many synagogues publicly advertised "Yizkor Memorial Services," hoping to increase attendance and, in turn, to create a more abiding and permanent affection for organized religion. "How many have through filial piety been awakened to become religious Jews?" wondered Kaufmann Kohler, urging his rabbinic colleagues not to look deprecatingly at those brought to the synagogue by "affliction." An even greater number of synagogues expressly associated *yizkor* with fund-raising through what one congregation called "Rolls of Remembrance." Linking money to memory, the modern American synagogue invigorated the time-honored Jewish tradition of giving charity, or *tsedakah*, in honor of the dead. At some point during the service, generally following an emotion-laden sermon, synagogue officials and ushers passed out small cards bearing such phrases as "I reverently cherish the memory of (fill in the blank)," inviting worshipers to make a memorial "offering." Many did, either making an on-the-spot contribution or mailing one in at a later date. "Experience has shown us," noted a veteran Jewish fund-raiser, "that this truly Jewish method of honoring a loved one is often a source of far greater satisfaction . . . than any other."

Memorial tablets also allowed for a public display of private memory. Traditionally, most tablets were made of paper on which gentle lions, flowers, Torah crowns, and other Jewish symbols were painstakingly calligraphed and sweetly illustrated. They hung on the walls of the synagogue or *landsmanshaft* meeting room, humbly attesting to the passage of time and personality. By the early 1920s, if not sooner, mass-produced, electrified metal versions came into vogue, superseding the handmade artifact. With its individualized lightbulbs, the "Bronze Yahrzeit Memorial Electric Tablet," boasted its manufacturer, provides "a new source of income for your Congregation . . . at the same time commemorating the memory of your beloved ones." Congregants would pay as much as a hundred dollars to enshrine and illuminate the names of their deceased loved ones on a bronze tablet. "We unveil these plates not in some private sanctuary, not in some unknown hidden corner of a field, or a home, but in the very midst of our community," declared Rabbi Simon Greenberg as he presided over the unveiling in 1938 of a suite of memorial tablets at his Philadelphia synagogue. "These beloved dead belong no longer to their families alone. In shedding their mundane vestments their souls join the company of the infinite number of noble men and women who have preceded them. Their memories become part of the heritage of the people of Israel."

Domestic memento mori ensured the vitality of memory in the home as well. Within many immigrant households, brightly colored paper *yorzeit* plaques or "pictures" served as chromolithographs of death. Valued both for their artistry and for their practicality, they infused the humdrum routine of record-keeping, of remembering the Hebrew anniversary of a family member's death, with an aesthetic sensibility that combined elements of Victorian and Jewish mourning iconography. Black-veiled urns, weeping willows, and grief-stricken women mingled with Hebrew sayings and stylized depictions of *Kever Rahel* (the cave of the matriarch Rachel) to form a decorative border around the name of the departed and the "date of decease."

Popular among the immigrant generation that often framed and hung them on the wall, *yorzeit* plaques disappeared into the desk drawers of their children or were replaced altogether by a pocket-sized calendar. Increasingly, death became less an open subject of

Yorzeit plaques provided a colorful way to memorialize the dead.

Some chromolithographs inclined toward Victorian themes; others favored a more traditional Jewish aesthetic.

artistic endeavor than the discreet object of routinization. "You do not need the old style yarzeit tablet on the wall any more. The corresponding date-calendar in book form takes its place. It is accurate and handy," advertised the publishers of the *Corresponding Date Calendar and Family Record* whose silk-bound compilation of Hebrew and "civil" dates was destined "for every Jewish home." Reverend E. M. Myers, author of *The Centurial: A Jewish Calendar for One Hundred Years, 1890–1990*, put forth a similar claim. "This handy volume should be in every Jewish household," he asserted in 1918. "By its use one is enabled to ascertain the date of *every Jewish holiday* for the hundred years between 1890 and 1990 inclusive. Explicit directions are also given how to ascertain the date of *Jahrzeit*."

Funeral homes also published practical guides, or "yahrzeit memorandums," to assist Jewish families in "solemnizing" the occasion. "If you give us the name and date of the death of your departed, we will be glad to prepare and mail, without charge, a table showing the Hebrew date of the Yahrzeit for the next five years and a Yahrzeit candle," wrote the directors of Riverside Memorial Chapel, whose slender volume *Prayers and Meditations* contained both practical and liturgical advice. With a kind of mathematical fervor, these handy compendia squared the Hebrew calendar with the American one, reconciling lunar and solar time. "Suppose a death to have occurred on the 4th day of *Nissan*; to know what English date that will be in the year 1897, look when *Rosh-Chodesh Nissan* will be in that year," advised one such text. "You will find it to be April 3rd. That being the first day of the month, the 4th would be three days later; and the *Jahrzeit* in that year will be April 6th."

Why all the calendrical excitement over *yorzeit* dates? Much like *yizkor* and kaddish, the marking of a *yorzeit* loomed large in American Jewry's collective ritual imagination. Through a small number

As a courtesy to their clients, funeral homes often published pocket-sized booklets filled with relevant ritual information.

of manageable and highly sentimentalized ritual activities, American Jews could experience, if only for a moment, the rhythms of sacred time. More to the point, *yorzeit* ritualized a sense of family. Unlike the stark and somber mourning rituals associated with, say, Tisha B'Av, a historic fast day commemorating the destruction of the Temple, whose meaning tended to elude modern American Jews, *yorzeit*'s immediate, personal mourning rituals invited compliance. Those able successfully to ascertain the appropriate Hebrew date of death (no mean feat, apparently) would first congregate at the synagogue to say kaddish; returning home, they would then light a memorial candle, or *yorzeit licht*, a time-honored Jewish tradition. Perched atop the refrigerator or on the living room mantelpiece, it flickeringly recalled the memory of the dearly departed.

The "Standard Yahrzeit Lamp," to use one of its brand names, could be easily purchased at the local grocery store and supermarket, where, encased in a ridged glass container bearing thinly incised Jewish stars and menorahs, it nestled on the shelves alongside boxes of matzoh and jars of gefilte fish. Whether made domestically or imported from the Holy Land, the candle carried one bilingual label warning consumers to place the item on a plate, away from flammable surfaces, and another indicating "this glass is kosher for household usage." This somewhat curious comment reflected, even as it legitimated, the common practice of utilizing the glass once the candle had been thoroughly extinguished. Less a matter of ecology or frugality than a fear of sacrilege—it just didn't seem right to toss the quasi-sacred object into the garbage—saving the memorial candle container often became as much a part of the *yizkor* ritual as lighting it. Many Jewish families would transform the newly obsolete ritual implement into an ordinary household glass from which they drank milk, juice, and other nonsacramental beverages, ensuring its afterlife. Later, technological change solved the problem of disposability. By the 1940s, electrified yahrzeit candles, known commercially as "Flame Glo," competed with those made of paraffin while plastic and patinated metal containers vied with glass jars. With its "pretested bulb designed for beauty and long life," the electric candle provided 120 volts of illumination as well as what its manufacturer

A greeting card celebrating the Jewish life cycle.

called "quality, elegance and performance." Simulated wax drippings on the candle's base underscored the product's modernity. When these novelties first appeared in the display cases of synagogue gift shops and Judaica retailers, they caught the eye of sociologists and historians like Abraham Duker, who marveled at the wondrous union of American know-how and Jewish ritual. "Many innovations can be traced back to American mechanical ingenuity and the present progress of the plastics industry," he wrote in 1950, only barely restraining his bemusement at the inventiveness of contemporary Jewish life.

Where Duker discerned imagination, others worried about "Judaism reduced to a *memento mori*," and, in a flurry of phrases and prognoses, expressed profound concern over the popularity of "kaddish Judaism," "mortuary Judaism," and "moribund Judaism." The synagogue, complained Rabbi Robert Gordis in 1946, has been "emptied of one function after the other . . . forced to be little more than a mortuary chapel for Kaddish and yizkor." Admittedly, American Jews did seem to expend great effort in attending to the dead and summoning up old family memories rather then revivifying and resurrecting their own ongoing lives as Jews. And yet, as one American Jew presciently told another way back in the 1890s, "death sustains the life of American Judaism."

Conclusion

Over a century ago, in the spring of 1893, Rabbi Maurice Harris ascended the podium of Chicago's imposing Zion Temple to discuss the state of contemporary American Jewry. With intermarriage on the upswing and synagogue attendance in decline, the community's distinctiveness, the rabbi feared, was fast losing ground. "Can a minority move among a majority without being absorbed by it?" he wondered, glumly pointing out that "our distinctive characteristics are going, one by one; we are becoming more and more like our neighbors and less distinguishable from them." In the ghetto, Harris continued, waxing nostalgic for a bygone era, "it was so simple. . . . To keep the Sabbath, to attend divine services, was to flow with the tide. *Not* to observe the ceremonial law was to single oneself out for uncomfortable mistrust and social ostracism." In America, though, the tide seemed to be moving swiftly and inexorably away from tradition and toward new and uncharted avenues of expression. "This is the age of freedom, this is the land of freedom. Are we Jews ready for it? Are we brave enough to walk alone? Can we trust ourselves?"

Designed to provoke and challenge rather than reassure, the issues Harris raised underscored the anomalousness of American Jewish life, at once liberating and constraining. Citizens of a new world, America's Jews flourished to a degree unprecedented in Jewish history; Judaism, however, fared less well. What was once a comprehensively ordered, fully integrated system of beliefs and behaviors had come undone, its constituent parts disaggregated and reassembled. In the alchemy of America, a new form of Jewish identity emerged—Jewishness—whose expression had as much, and perhaps more, to do with feeling "Jewish at heart" than with formal ritual. Detached from the recurring rhythms of the traditional Jewish calendar, this modern version of Jewish identity anchored itself in the life cycle, with its punctuation marks of birth and death, the onset of puberty, and the exchange of marital vows. Meanwhile, Jewish holidays such as Passover and Chanukah, newly recast as exercises in domestic felicity, furthered the association between family, sentiment, and tradition, as did a growing affection for Jewish cuisine, an increasingly resonant "symbol of allegiance."

The fragmented, highly selective nature of American Jewishness troubled the community's cultural custodians, who were accustomed, after all, to equating authenticity with an earlier model of theological rigor and behavioral consistency. "Looking at Jewish homes today from the Jewish point of view, as we know Jewish homes used to be," lamented Mrs. Jacob Gittleman, a stalwart member of her synagogue sisterhood, in 1937, "we see many ghost-houses, grim skeletons of former religious vitality." Such bleak comparisons between the present and the past, between the old-time Jewish order, on which "memory feasts," and the more disordered realities of the modern era, proved extremely compelling to Mrs. Gittleman and her likeminded coreligionists, inspiring them to redouble their efforts on behalf of a "renascence" of tradition. As Gittleman herself put it, "There is a huge task confronting our organizations, the rehabilitation of our old traditions, the rebuilding of the homes of our people to make them Jewish."

More often than not, such campaigns either fell wide of the mark or missed it entirely. Animated by a vision of the past, calls for inserting traditional Jewish values and behaviors into the present obscured the extent to which Jewishness had become a malleable and protean social construct. The clergy and the sisterhood might rail against the popular inclination to "relegate [traditional rituals] to an attic or cellar, as defunct heirlooms," or to identify Judaism solely with "bagels and lox and gefilte fish," but the folk saw things differently. Little troubled by inconsistencies or contradictions or the burdens of the past, they fashioned a homegrown American Jewishness. Heavy on sentiment and light on ritual, their version came closest to a singularly modern understanding of American religious culture.

Can we survive freedom, asked Rabbi Maurice Harris in 1893. Since then, each generation has attempted to answer that question. The wonder of it all—and of America—is that the answer remains the same.

Notes

ABBREVIATIONS

AH	*American Hebrew*
CCAR	Central Conference of American Rabbis
JDF	*Jewish Daily Forward*
NYT	*New York Times*

PAGE

INTRODUCTION

3 **"folklore can be scooped up":** Y. L. Cahan cited in Barbara Kirshenblatt-Gimblett, "The Folk Culture of Jewish Immigrant Communities: Research Paradigms and Directions," in Moses Rischin, ed., *The Jews of North America* (Detroit, 1987), p. 82.

"maligned for its vulgarity": Barbara Kirshenblatt-Gimblett, "The Folk Culture," p. 84.

"transculturation": Abraham G. Duker, "Emerging Culture Patterns in American Jewish Life: The Psycho-Cultural Approach to the Study of Jewish Life in America," *Proceedings of the American Jewish Historical Society*, vol. 39, Sept. 1949–June 1950, p. 353.

4 **"inventory of Jewishness":** I. Steinbaum, "A Study of the Jewishness of Twenty New York Families," *YIVO Annual*, vol. 5, 1950, p. 232.

"freedom to observe": Dr. Maurice Harris, "The Dangers of Emancipation," *CCAR Year Book*, vol. 4, 1893, p. 58.

"carries his own shulkan arukh": Duker, "Emerging Culture Patterns," p. 376.

"The fact that": I. Steinbaum, "A Study of the Jewishness," p. 253.

5 **"piano playing":** I. Steinbaum, "A Study of the Jewishness," p. 243.

"Jews should believe": I. Steinbaum, "A Study of Jewishness," p. 253.

"all that we had left": Irving Howe, "A Personal Reminiscence," in Susan Braunstein and Jenna Weissman Joselit, eds., *Getting Comfortable in New York: The American Jewish Home, 1880–1950* (New York, 1990), p. 16.

6 **"inexhaustible reservoir":** Miriam Isaacs and Trude Weiss Rosmarin, *What Every Jewish Woman Should Know: A Guide for Jewish Women* (New York, 1941), p. 5.

"flickering to life": Howe, "A Personal Reminiscence," p. 16.

"The Jewish God": Rabbi Joseph Blau, "Who Will Question?" *Hebrew Standard*, May 6, 1910, p. 8.

"new adventure in Jewishness": Morris Freedman, "A New Jewish Community in Formation," *Commentary*, vol. 19, no. 1, Jan. 1955, p. 37.

CHAPTER ONE: KISSING BUSINESS

9 **"wedding-ring":** Sisterhood and Mothers' Club (Temple Mishkan Tefila), *The Center Table* (Boston, 1922), p. 1.

covenant with posterity: Sidney Goldstein, *Meaning of Marriage and Foundations of the Family: A Jewish Interpretation* (New York, 1940), p. 1.

"Transmitting a civilization": Jacob Kohn, *Modern Problems of Jewish Parents: A Study in Parental Attitudes* (New York, 1932), p. 79.

10 **"nursery" of identity:** Joseph Stolz, *President's Message,* CCAR publication, July 3, 1907, p. 8.

"The primary . . . locus": Mordecai M. Kaplan, *Judaism as a Civilization* (New York, 1934), p. 416.

"chief functions": Steven Mintz and Susan Kellogg, *Domestic Revolutions: A Social History of American Family Life* (New York, 1988), p. 45.

"custodian" of moral values: Mary P. Ryan, *Cradle of the Middle Class: The Family in Oneida County, New York, 1790–1865* (New York, 1981), p. 238.

"ministering priests": Charles S. Levi, "Problems of American Judaism," *CCAR Year Book,* vol. 23, 1913, p. 290.

"no Jewish old maids": "The Jewish Old Maid," *American Jewish Chronicle,* vol. 1, no. 18, Sept. 8, 1916, p. 556.

11 **"the intelligence of American Jewry":** *American Jewish Chronicle,* vol. 1, no. 1, May 12, 1916, back page.

"numbers of Jewesses": "The Jewish Old Maid," p. 556.

"The marriage standards": "The Jewish Old Maid," p. 557.

"undignified method": "The Cost of a Husband," AH, Nov. 18, 1910, p. 63.

12 **"bearded cupids":** Meyer Berger, "Profiles: Bearded Cupid," *The New Yorker,* June 11, 1938, pp. 16–21.

"Timid clients": Berger, "Bearded Cupid," p. 16.

social ecology of courtship: JDF, Nov. 29, 1916, p. 4.

Harkavy: Alexander Harkavy, "Letters of Love," *American Letter Writer and Speller* (New York, 1901), pp. 138–51, esp. pp. 143, 147, 148–49.

14 **"Dear Constance":** "Heart to Heart Talk by Constance," *Froyen Zhurnal,* vol. 3, no. 5, Oct. 1923, p. 49.

15 **"two different things":** Hayim Malits, "Religion and Family Life," *The Home and the Woman* (New York, 1924; Yiddish), p. 200. I'd like to thank Jeffrey Shandler for sharing this text with me.

"The chances are ten to one": Malits, "Religion and Family Life," p. 202.

"the kissing-business": Malits, "Religion and Family Life," p. 200.

God himself: *Etiquette: A Guide to Proper Behavior, Politeness, and Good Manners for Men and Women, Assembled According to the Best Authorities by Tashrak* (New York, 1912; Yiddish), p. 145.

***"mayles,"* or qualities:** *Etiquette,* p. 155. See also pp. 155–62 for a discussion of a potential husband's virtues and pp. 162–68 for those of a wife.

17 **"It's not necessary":** *Etiquette,* p. 166.

"Schoolteachers don't go": Berger, "Bearded Cupid," p. 19.

"etiquette of masculinity": Beth Bailey, *From Front Porch to Back Seat: Courtship in Twentieth-Century America* (Baltimore, 1989), p. 98.

"not the true article": *Etiquette,* p. 156.

"Ten Commandments": *Froyen Velt,* vol. 1, no. 3, June 1913, p. 1.

18 **"Ten Rules":** *Froyen Zhurnal,* vol. 2, no. 1, March 1923, p. 15.

"Health, character, background": Kohn, *Modern Problems,* pp. 96–97.

"just as serious": Goldstein, *Meaning of Marriage,* p. 1.

19 **"If young men would look":** Israel Levinthal, "The Jewish Conception of Marriage," March 16, 1928, Sermons and Addresses, Israel H. Levinthal Collection, Ratner Center Archives for the Study of Conservative Judaism, Jewish Theological Seminary, New York (hereafter Ratner Center Archives).

"We prepare the young woman": Leo Jung, *The Jewish Way to Married Happiness* (New York, 1930), p. 3.
"Young people": Goldstein, *Meaning of Marriage*, p. 11.
"Now more than ever": Goldstein, *Meaning of Marriage*, p. 14. See also Ernest R. Groves, "Report of Committee on Education for Marriage and Family Living," *Living*, vol. 2, Spring 1940, pp. 47–48.
"Chances for happiness": Jerome Beatty, "Taking the Blinders off Love," *American Magazine*, Dec. 1937, p. 22.
rationalization of love: See Bailey, "Scientific Truth . . . and Love," in *Front Porch*, pp. 119–40.
20 **lecture topics:** "Jewish Institute on Marriage and the Family," *CCAR Year Book*, vol. 48, 1938, p. 99.
"to cope more adequately": "The Jewish Institute on Marriage and the Family—A Service Organization," ca. 1940, p. 3, "Subject and Organizational Files O–S," Sidney Goldstein Papers, Archives of the Stephen Wise Free Synagogue, New York (hereafter Goldstein Papers).
"Wedding knell?": Samuel Glasner to Sidney Goldstein, Oct. 2, 1939, "Marriage," Goldstein Papers.
Bossard: James Bossard to Sidney Goldstein, March 4, 1940, "Marriage," Goldstein Papers.
"Along with the Pope's": May 1945 clipping from *Social Forces* in "Marriage and Family Counseling, 1943–47," Goldstein Papers.
"I congratulate you": Ernest Burgess to Sidney Goldstein, Sept. 25, 1939, "Marriage," Goldstein Papers.
"social science laboratories": "The Jewish Institute on Marriage and the Family—A Service Organization," ca. 1940, p. 3.
"wisdom of centuries": Goldstein, *Meaning of Marriage*, p. 4.
21 **"Love must not become":** Jung, *The Jewish Way*, p. 3.
"Judaism develops the proper attitude": Jung, *The Jewish Way*, p. 2.
"When you hear the word": Jung, *The Jewish Way*, p. 4.
22 **"printed in . . . luxurious":** Abraham Cahan, "A Ghetto Wedding," *The Imported Bridegroom and Other Stories of the New York Ghetto* (New York, 1898), p. 230.
"genuine Jewish ceremony": "Going Under the Chupah—By An Immigrant," *American Jewess*, vol. 7, no. 1, April 1898, p. 13.
"When I had a few dollars saved": Irving Howe, *World of Our Fathers* (New York, 1976), p. 220.
23 **"respectable wedding":** Cahan, "A Ghetto Wedding," p. 226.
24 **"That was all":** Cahan, "A Ghetto Wedding," p. 232.
"Goldy looked": Cahan, "A Ghetto Wedding," p. 236.
Purchase a diamond ring: *Etiquette*, pp. 196–200.
"a *minhag* is a *minhag*": *Etiquette*, p. 196.
"foolish schnorring": *Etiquette*, p. 220.
"white, shimmering and cloud-like": "Society's Sphere," *American Jewish Chronicle*, vol. 2, no. 24, April 20, 1917, p. 788.
25 **"Mr. Hirsch lived":** Samuel Chotzinoff, *A Lost Paradise: Early Reminiscences* (New York, 1955), pp. 152–53.
"electric *khupe*": Howe, *World*, p. 221.
"I had known chicken": Chotzinoff, *A Lost Paradise*, p. 154.
26 **"An East-side family":** *Hebrew Standard*, March 4, 1910, p. 9.
The groom claimed: JDF, Dec. 3, 1916, p. 1.
"bigger and better neighborhoods": Sarah Schack, "O'Leary's Shul—And Others," *The Menorah Journal*, vol. 16, no. 5, May 1929, p. 464.
27 **"Wedding temples":** Abraham G. Duker, "Emerging Culture Patterns in American Jewish Life: The Psycho-Cultural Approach to the Study of Jewish Life in America," *Proceedings of the American Jewish Historical Society*, vol. 39, Sept. 1949–June 1950, pp. 379–80.

"Prof. . . . Goldberg": *Jewish Times*, Sept. 5, 1930, p. 16.
"richness and comfort": AH, Nov. 21, 1924, p. 42.
"The club and the hotel": "Religious," *CCAR Year Book*, vol. 20, 1910, p. 59.
"This occasion": *Outlook*, vol. 25, no. 1, Sept. 1954, p. 11.

28 **"All one had to do":** Bezalel Kantor, "Simchas in America," *Jewish Spectator*, vol. 14, no. 5, March 1949, p. 16.
Photographer's antics: Kantor, *Simchas in America*, p. 17.
"everything that goes with the ceremony": Marriage Permit Number 622, July 19, 1925, Ansche Chesed Collection, box 11, folder 22, Ratner Center Archives.
"Professional help": Ruth Jacobs, *The Jewish Wedding: An Explanation of Its Ancient Rituals and Modern-Day Etiquette with Suggestions for Proper Dress, Procedure, Arrangements* (New York, 1955), p. 3. I'd like to thank Peter H. Schweitzer for bringing this document to my attention.
"Parents used to ask the rabbi": Albert Gordon, *Jews in Transition* (Minneapolis, 1949), p. 135.
"the most preferred drinks": Jacobs, *The Jewish Wedding*, pp. 2–6.

30 **"There is another . . . meaning":** Jacobs, *The Jewish Wedding*, p. 10.

31 **"the Lowenstein Catering Company's number-one wedding":** Herman Wouk, *Marjorie Morningstar* (New York, 1955), pp. 555–57.

32 **"Jewish weddings are often":** Stuart Rosenberg, *The Real Jewish World* (New York, 1984), p. 157.
"cultural heritage": Kantor, "Simchas in America," p. 17.
"tend to theatricalize": "Some Seasonal Thoughts on Marriage," *The Reconstructionist*, vol. 22, no. 10, June 29, 1956, p. 5.
"It isn't proper": "Marriage and the Family: A Wedding Pageant," *Proceedings of the Biennial Convention, National Women's League, 1950–52* (1952), p. 118.

33 **"Marriages may be wrought in heaven":** Saul Ellenbogen, "Weddings in the Synagogue," *The Synagogue Center*, vol. 2, no. 2, Sept. 1941, p. 4.
"splendid accommodations": Israel H. Levinthal, "Hotel and Public Hall Marriages," *Brooklyn Jewish Center Review*, vol. 25, no. 7, March 1957, p. 4.
"Excellent Service": "To June Brides," *Brooklyn Jewish Center Review*, vol. 16, no. 33, April 1933, p. 22.
the "marriage rite": Levinthal, "Hotel and Public Hall Marriages," p. 4. See also Sidney Greenberg, "Canopies and Canapes," *United Synagogue Review*, vol. 14, no. 1, Spring 1961, pp. 14–15.
"definite appointment": Irving J. Yeckes to Sidney Flatow, Jan. 10, 1954, Ansche Chesed Collection, box 14, folder 66, Ratner Center Archives.
"The synagogue must be careful": Ellenbogen, "Weddings in the Synagogue," pp. 5–6.

34 **"I realize . . . that customs":** Levinthal, "Hotel and Public Hall Marriages," p. 4.
"Please remember": Ellenbogen, "Weddings in the Synagogue," p. 6.

35 **"The changes which have taken place":** "Responsum 2: Propriety of Using Discarded Practices in Reform Services—Answer," *CCAR Year Book*, vol. 65, 1955, p. 89.
"quaint" provisions: "Of Interest to Women," AH, Oct. 13, 1911, p. 747.
This act . . . is a "landmark": Theodore Friedman, "The New Marriage Contract," *Outlook*, vol. 25, no. 4, June 1955, pp. 8–9.
"map of history": Louis Finkelstein quoted in "The Steering Committee of the Joint Law Conference, 1953–54," *Proceedings of the Rabbinical Assembly of America*, vol. 18, 1954, p. 75. See also "The Problem of the Agunah," *Outlook*, vol. 6, no. 2, Dec. 1935, pp. 5, 11.
"the crude . . . performance": "Propriety of Using Discarded Practices," p. 89.

36 **ring survey:** "Findings of Committee on Ritual Survey," 1939, p. 13, RG 27-2-16, Ratner Center Archives.

"These ladies stated": Joseph Aub, "One or Two Wedding Rings," in Gunther Plaut, *The Rise of Reform Judaism* (New York, 1963), pp. 217–18.

"full equality of woman with man": CCAR, *Rabbi's Manual* (Cincinnati, 1928), p. 181.

38 **"Divorce is an evil":** J. Leonard Levy, "The Modern Problem of Marriage and Divorce," *CCAR Year Book*, vol. 23, 1913, p. 342.

"My aunt was divorced": Personal communication.

"You stuck it out": Burton Bernstein, *Family Matters: Sam, Jennie and the Kids* (New York, 1982), p. 59.

mistaking "liberty for license": Morris D. Waldman, "Family Desertion," *Jewish Charity*, vol. 5, nos. 3–4, Dec. 1905/Jan. 1906, p. 54.

"poor man's divorce": See, for example, Reena Sigman Friedman, "Send Me My Husband Who Is in New York City: Husband Desertion in the American Jewish Immigrant Community, 1900–1926," *Jewish Social Studies*, vol. 64, no. 1, Winter 1982, pp. 1–18.

"a very undesirable woman": Marvin Bressler, "Selected Family Patterns in W. I. Thomas' Unfinished Study of the 'Bintel Brief,'" *American Sociological Review*, vol. 17, Oct. 1952, p. 568.

"a poor manager, a coffee addict": Isabel Lonison, "A Study of Background Factors in Eighty Cases of Desertion Closed in 1932, Known to the Jewish Social Service Association of New York," M.A. thesis, Graduate School for Jewish Social Work, New York, 1934, p. 124.

39 **Family desertion . . . "has continued to grow":** Waldman, "Family Desertion," p. 51.

"recreant husbands": "Handling Deserting Husbands," *Jewish Charities*, vol. 2, no. 3, Oct. 1911, p. 1. See also Oscar Leonard, "Family Desertion," *Jewish Charities*, vol. 4, no. 4, Nov. 1913, pp. 14–15.

"domestic virtues": Waldman, "Family Desertion," p. 51.

"Divorce has increasing incidence": Leon Lang, "Jewish Values in Family Relationships," *Conservative Judaism*, vol. 1, no. 2, June 1945, p. 17.

40 **"Never before have wives and mothers":** Goldstein, *Meaning of Marriage*, pp. 1–2.

"Judaism has the same view": Israel H. Levinthal, "Companionate vs. Jewish Conception of Marriage," Jan. 9, 1931, Sermons and Addresses, Israel H. Levinthal Collection, Ratner Center Archives.

"blunders are possible": "The Orthodox View of the Jewish 'Get'," AH, Dec. 9, 1910, p. 160.

"marital mishaps": Levy, "Modern Problem," p. 344.

41 **"The only way . . . to get a divorce":** "Secular and Rabbinical Divorces," AH, Sept. 4, 1903, p. 498.

42 **"eccleciastical divorce":** "Rabbinical Divorce," AH, Sept. 11, 1903, p. 535.

"menace to the reputation": "Secular and Rabbinical Divorces," AH, Sept. 4, 1903, p. 498.

"campaign of education": "Rabbinical Divorce," AH, Sept. 11, 1903, p. 535.

"Be it resolved": "Jewish Ministers on Jewish Divorces," AH, Nov. 25, 1910, p. 107.

"unregulated giving of *get*": "Other Orthodox Views on the Divorce Question," AH, December 31, 1910, p. 248.

"are in every respect unnecessary": Levy, "Modern Problem," p. 346.

43 **"It creates the most":** David Aronson, "The Agunah Question," *Proceedings of the Rabbinical Assembly of America*, vol. 7, 1940, p. 302.

"knee breeches": Mel Scult, *Judaism Faces the Twentieth Century: A Biography of Mordecai M. Kaplan* (Detroit, 1993), p. 299.

"I wanted a new thing": Leah Morton, *I Am a Woman—And a Jew* (New York, 1926), p. 16.

"no Biblical Rebecca": Morton, *I Am a Woman*, p. 64.

"As yet, marriages": Esther Jane Ruskay, *Hearth and Home Essays* (Philadelphia, 1902), p. 58.

44 **"A few anthropologists":** Editorial, *Jewish Times*, April 25, 1930, p. 10.

"a sort of *yichus*": "Religious Life," *American Jewish Chronicle*, vol. 1, no. 3, May 26, 1916, p. 79.

"Are certain . . . American Jews": "Is There a 'Jewish Intermarriage'?" *Der Tog*, Sept. 2, 1928, p. 3. I'd like to thank Daniel Soyer for bringing this article to my attention.

45 **Lauterbach nuptials:** JDF, Oct. 17, 1902, p. 4.

the "imagination of New York": Morton, *I Am a Woman*, p. 62.

front-page news: NYT, April 6, 1905, p. 1.

"Utmost cordiality": NYT, June 21, 1905, p. 1.

"East Side settlement workers": "East Side's Poetess Is Now Mrs. Stokes," NYT, July 19, 1905, p. 7.

46 **"newspaper misnomer":** "Communication," AH, July 29, 1905, p. 235.

"practicability": Ruskay, *Hearth and Home Essays*, p. 58.

"Let Jewish girls beware": "Just Between Ourselves, Girls," *Hebrew Standard*, April 14, 1905, p. 6. See also "Intermarriage," *Hebrew Standard*, April 21, 1905, p. 8.

47 **a "growing tendency":** Celia Silbert, "Intermarriage on the East Side," *American Jewish Chronicle*, vol. 1, no. 15, Aug. 18, 1916, pp. 456–57.

"John Manning the millionaire": Anzia Yezierska, *Salome of the Tenements* (New York, 1923), p. 14.

"a vivid exotic": Yezierska, *Salome*, p. 171.

"a nobody from nowhere": Yezierska, *Salome*, p. 17.

"the oriental and the Anglo-Saxon": Yezierska, *Salome*, p. 209.

48 **"the story of the girl":** "Who's Who in Literature—1926," AH, Dec. 3, 1926, p. 208. See also Elma Ehrlich Levinger, "The New Jew in Fiction," AH, Jan. 2, 1925, p. 247.

"an American institution": Clipping from the *Philadelphia Ledger*, Feb. 28, 1928, Billy Rose Theater Collection, Library for the Performing Arts, Lincoln Center, New York. I'd like to thank Jennifer Myer for bringing this and other relevant newspaper clippings to my attention.

"America's third largest industry": Clipping from the *New York Herald Tribune*, Jan. 9, 1927, Billy Rose Theater Collection.

"subway public": Unidentified *Time* clipping, n.d., Billy Rose Theater Collection, Library for the Performing Arts, Lincoln Center, New York. See also Maurice Samuel, "The Mnemonic of Oblivion," in *Jews on Approval* (New York, 1932), esp. p. 228.

"Judaism's undoing": Kaplan, *Judaism as a Civilization*, p. 418.

"the coffin of the Jewish race": David Einhorn quoted in Moshe Davis, "Mixed Marriage in Western Jewry," *Jewish Journal of Sociology*, vol. 10, no. 2, Dec. 1968, p. 181.

"sounds the death knell": Ruskay, *Hearth and Home Essays*, p. 62.

the prospect of "loss": Goldstein, *Meaning of Marriage*, p. 73; Julian Morgenstern, "Report on Mixed Marriage and Intermarriage—Discussion," *CCAR Year Book*, vol. 57, 1947, p. 178.

49 **"the opposition . . . to intermarriage":** "Intermarriage," *Froyen Zhurnal*, vol. 2, no. 9, Jan. 1923, p. 65.

"Every religious group": David De Sola Pool, "Intermarriage," *Hebrew Standard*, Feb. 7, 1919, pp. 5–6.

Drachsler findings: Julius Drachsler, *Democracy and Assimilation: The Blending of Immigrant Heritages in America* (New York, 1920), esp. pp. 102, 121–22, 133, 147. On Drachsler himself, see Charles Bernheimer, "Julius Drachsler—An Appreciation," *Jewish Social Service Quarterly*, vol. 4, no. 1, Sept. 1927, pp. 220–25.

"social psychology": Milton Barron, "The Incidence of Jewish Intermarriage in Europe and America," *American Sociological Review*, vol. 11, Feb. 1946, p. 12. See also Reuben B. Resnik, "Some Sociological Aspects of the Intermarriage of Jew and Non-Jew," *Social Forces*, vol. 12, no. 1, Oct. 1933, pp. 94–104.

50 **"the reluctant" . . . the "emancipated":** Maria H. Levinson and Daniel J. Levinson, "Jews Who Intermarry," *YIVO Annual*, vol. 12, 1958–59, pp. 128–29.

"they may be used in classifying": Barron, "Incidence of Jewish Intermarriage," p. 13.

"What's the matter": Silbert, "Intermarriage on the East Side," p. 456.

51 **"a good sociological basis":** Samuel Mayerberg, "Report on Mixed Marriage and Intermarriage," *CCAR Year Book*, vol. 57, 1947, p. 181.

"a checkered existence": Silbert, "Intermarriage on the East Side," p. 457.

Fishberg and Ruppin's studies: Cited in Drachsler, *Democracy and Assimilation*, p. 157. See also "Intermarriage," *The Jewish Encyclopedia* (New York, 1904), p. 612.

"nature herself stamps her . . . disapproval": Mendel Silber, "Intermarriage," *CCAR Year Book*, vol. 18, 1908, p. 275.

"serious hazards to success": Judson T. Landis and Mary C. Landis, *Building a Successful Marriage* (New York, 1948), p. 162.

"All couples have some problems": Landis and Landis, *Building a Successful Marriage*, pp. 132–33.

52 **"different household customs":** JDF, Feb. 15, 1925, p. 3.

"a *goy* was a *goy*": Quoted in James S. Slotkin, "Jewish-Gentile Intermarriage in Chicago," *American Sociological Review*, vol. 7, no. 1, Feb. 1942, p. 346.

"They'd never known a Jew": Quoted in James S. Slotkin, "Adjustment in Jewish-Gentile Intermarriage," *Social Forces*, vol. 21, Dec. 1942, p. 230.

"heredity of civilization": Ludwig Bernstein, "Intermarriage and Jewish Social Service," *Jewish Social Service Quarterly*, vol. 5, 1929, p. 238.

"Why, even in cases where": Quoted in Bernstein, "Intermarriage and Jewish Social Service," p. 239.

53 **"We dare not rest the whole weight":** Kohn, *Modern Problems*, pp. 108–12.

"There are two tendencies": Emily Solis-Cohen, "The Jewish Girl's Thoughts on Jewish Life," *United Synagogue Recorder*, vol. 5, no. 4, Oct. 1925, p. 11.

54 **"reliably estimated":** Hershel Shanks, "Jewish-Gentile Intermarriage: Facts and Trends," *Commentary*, Oct. 1953, p. 370.

"shackling of Cupid": AH, June 16, 1905, p. 69.

"In each of us is stored up": Israel Levinthal, "What Intermarriage Means to the Jew," March 25, 1932, Sermons and Addresses, Israel H. Levinthal Collection, Ratner Center Archives.

"In true and happy marriage": Silber, "Intermarriage," p. 275.

"sanctuary of love": Morton, *I Am a Woman*, p. 186.

CHAPTER TWO: *YIDISHE NACHAS*

55 **"bewildering display":** Felix Mayrowitz, "Golden Jubilee: The Story of Brownsville," *The Menorah Journal*, vol. 14, no. 6, June 1928, p. 583.

56 ***Pricing the Priceless Child:*** Viviana A. Zelizer, *Pricing the Priceless Child: The Changing Social Values of Children* (New York, 1985).

"there is no family": Rabbi Dr. Leon S. Lang, "Our Changing Jewish Family," typescript address to the Women's League of the United Synagogue of America, New York, 1939, p. 7, 1939 Convention Folder, Women's League Archives.

"the Jewish family is child-centered": Natalie F. Joffe, *The American Jewish Family: A Study* (National Council of Jewish Women, 1954), p. 7.

"forerunner of Montessori": James Crichton-Browne, "Introduction" to W. M. Feldman, *The Jewish Child: Its History, Folklore, Biology and Sociology* (London, 1917; New York, 1918), p. xxv.

"fly[ing] to the doctor": Feldman, *The Jewish Child*, pp. 383, 409.

"Even from the very cradle": Feldman, *The Jewish Child*, pp. 277 ff.

"Happy the children": Esther Jane Ruskay, *Hearth and Home Essays* (Philadelphia, 1902), p. 90.

"unobtrusive charity and religious well-doing": Ruskay, *Hearth*, p. 48.

58 **"temperate and well-ordered life":** Ruskay, *Hearth*, p. 95.

"presiding genius": Irene Wolff, "The Jewish Woman in the Home," in Leo Jung, ed., *The Jewish Library*, third series (New York, 1934), p. 93.

"The ideal Jewess": "Five Essential Qualifications of the Ideal Jewess," *United Synagogue Recorder*, vol. 5, no. 1, Jan. 1925, p. 37.

"The greatest part": Rose Goldstein, "Woman's Share in the Responsibility for the Future of Judaism," *Outlook*, vol. 8, no. 4, May 1938, p. 13.

real-life pedestal: "Report of the National Committee on the Union Museum," *Proceedings, 4th Biennial Assembly of the National Federation of Temple Sisterhoods*, May 1921, p. 28.

"higher calling": Mrs. Grace P. Mendes, "Mother's Own Life Must Be an Example," AH, Sept. 10, 1915, p. 470.

"world-historical importance": Linda Kerber, "Separate Spheres, Female Worlds, Woman's Place: The Rhetoric of Women's History," *Journal of American History*, vol. 75, June 1988, p. 21.

"Age of Mother-Power": "The Age of Mother-Power," *Bookman*, vol. 39, June 1914, pp. 451–52.

society "deeded" mothers: Wolff, "The Jewish Woman in the Home," p. 95.

"money-getter": Ernest Groves and Gladys Hoagland Groves, *Parents and Children* (New York, 1928), p. 130.

"moral stamina": "The Jewish Home," *The Center Table* (Boston, 1929), p. 1.

"mothercraft": "Mothercraft: A New Profession for Women," *Good Housekeeping*, vol. 59, Dec. 1914, pp. 672–78.

"motherhood now is regarded": "Frills or Health for Baby?" *American Jewish Chronicle*, vol. 1, no. 9, July 7, 1916, p. 272.

59 **"sacred duty":** "Chanukah Lights and Christmas Candles," *American Jewish Chronicle*, vol. 2, no. 7, Dec. 22, 1916, p. 210.

"scientific study": Mrs. Edward W. Hooke, "To Save All Babies," 1914, Mitchel Papers, New York City Municipal Archives.

"meaning of motherhood": "The Meaning of Motherhood," *Woman's Home Companion*, vol. 40, Nov. 1913, p. 13.

"Baby Week Colors": NYT, May 8, 1916, p. 11.

"Baby Sabbath": NYT, April 30, 1916, p. 5; May 6, 1916, p. 9.

"Little Mothers Aid Associations": NYT, June 22, 1914, p. 9.

"as much fun as dolls": NYT, June 23, 1914, p. 11.

"conceded fact": Mrs. Edward W. Hooke, "To Save All Babies," 1914, Mitchel Papers, New York City Municipal Archives.

61 **"Milk Has Its Day":** NYT, June 24, 1914, p. 10.

milk stations: Julie Miller, "To Stop the Slaughter of the Babies: Nathan Straus and the Drive for Pasteurized Milk, 1893–1920," *New York History*, vol. 72, no. 2, April 1993, pp. 159–84. I'd like to thank Ms. Miller for bringing this article to my attention.

"Milk Don'ts for Mothers": NYT, June 22, 1914, p. 9.

"model babies": NYT, April 28, 1914, p. 7; May 14, 1914, p. 7; JDF, May 11, 1916, p. 8.

festive parade: NYT, June 26, 1914, p. 7; May 12, 1916, p. 8.

"motherhood unified": NYT, May 12, 1916, p. 8.

"facts": JDF, May 14, 1916, p. 2. See also "Baby Week and the Jewish Mother," *American Jewish Chronicle*, vol. 1, no. 2, May 19, 1916, p. 49; "Baby Week," JDF, May 9, 1916, p. 8; "Baby Week and Childhood Diseases," *Der Tog*, May 10, 1916, p. 4.

"If there is anything": NYT, May 7, 1916, p. 15.

62 **"when unable to nurse":** Maurice Fishberg, "Leaves from a Doctor's Note-book," *Jewish Charity*, vol. 3, no. 4, Jan. 1904, p. 95.

"The women are not obliged to dress up": "A Day with the Mothers in Brownsville," *Hebrew Standard*, Feb. 7, 1919, p. 2.

"The Importance of a Fresh and Clean Food Supply": AH, Nov. 18, 1910, p. 81.

"Cheating the Garbage Pail": Dora Askowith, *Three Outstanding Women* (New York, 1941), p. 47.

"A series of health talks": Leah Leonard, "Recreation for Mothers," *Jewish Charities*, vol. 9, no. 9, Jan. 1919, p. 181.

muttershaft: See, for example, "The Young Mother," *Froyen Zhurnal*, vol. 1, no. 1, May 1922, p. 48.

"The printed page": "Yiddish Handbook for Mothers," *Jewish Charities*, vol. 3, no. 1, Aug. 1912, p. 7.

"role of the modern mother": *Froyen Zhurnal*, vol. 1, no. 1, May 1922, p. 48.

Mutter und Kind: Jacob Mayerson, *Mutter und Kind* (New York, 1912), esp. p. 36.

63 **"This little book":** "Yiddish Handbook for Mothers," p. 7.

What No Girl Should Know: "Editorial Comment," *Birth Control Review*, vol. 1, no. 5, Dec. 1917, p. 16. See also Margaret Sanger, *Vos Yede Meydel Darf Visn* (New York, 1916; 1921).

Unser Gezund: See, for example, vol. 3, no. 11, March 1915, pp. 336–38; vol. 5, no. 10, Feb. 1917, p. 381; vol. 5, no. 12, April 1917, p. 481. See also Eli Lederhandler, "Guides for the Perplexed: Sex, Manners, and Mores for the Yiddish Reader in America," *Modern Judaism*, vol. 11, no. 3, Oct. 1991, pp. 321–41.

64 **"Forget not, dear friends":** Editorial, *Unser Gezund*, vol. 3, no. 11, March 1915, p. 1.

"The Truth about Sexuality": Advertisement in *Unser Gezund*, vol. 3, no. 12, April 1915, n.p.

Birth Control or Race Suicide: JDF, July 19, 1916, p. 7. See also the Lawrence Marwick Collection of Copyrighted Yiddish Plays, Library of Congress. I'd like to thank Zachary Baker of the YIVO Institute and Peggy Pearlstein of the Library of Congress for sharing this material with me.

A Woman's Duty in Birth Control: Marwick Collection, Library of Congress.

"tangled jungle": Elizabeth Stuyvesant, "The Brownsville Birth Control Clinic," *Birth Control Review*, vol. 1, no. 2, March 1917, p. 8. See also Elsa G. Herzfeld, "Superstitions and Customs of the Tenement-House Mother," *Charities*, vol. 14, July 22, 1905, pp. 983–86.

"I found my doctors": Susan Cotts Watkins and Angela D. Danzi, "Women's Gossip Networks: Information Exchange and Social Support among Italian and Jewish Women in the United States, 1910–1940," unpublished paper presented at the Eastern Sociological Society, April 1991, p. 20. I'd like to thank Professor Watkins for generously sharing her work-in-progress.

Bobba Hannah: Ida Selavan, "Bobba Hannah, Midwife," *American Journal of Nursing*, vol. 73, part 4, April 1973, pp. 681–83.

65 **"busier than doctors":** "Jewish Midwives in New York," JDF, Sept. 13, 1902, n.p. I'd like to thank Daniel Soyer for bringing this article to my attention.

"midwife problem": Grace Abbott, "The Midwife in Chicago," *American Journal of Sociology*, vol. 20, no. 5, March 1915, p. 693.

"Never before had Jewish mothers": "Safeguarding Children at Birth," AH, Feb. 27, 1925, p. 473.

comparative birth statistics: Cited in Abbott, "The Midwife in Chicago." See also Lara Vivienne Marks, "Irish and Jewish Women's Experience of Childbirth and Infant Care in East London, 1870–1939: The Response of Host Society and Immigrant Communities to Medical Welfare Needs," unpublished Ph.D. thesis, Oxford University, 1990.

"Expectant mothers from all over . . . New York": AH, Feb. 27, 1925, p. 473.

66 **"will not be obliged to break the Dietary Laws":** *19th Annual Report, The Jewish Maternity Association of Philadelphia*, 1892, p. 12.

"From the day they register": "Safeguarding Children at Birth," AH, Feb. 27, 1925, p. 473.

68 **"mental occupation":** "Report of Obstetric Clinics," *40th Annual Report, Jewish Maternity Hospital* (Philadelphia, 1914), p. 17.

"Family limitation is so acutely desired": Harry L. Lurie, "The Sex Hygiene of Family Life," *Jewish Social Service Quarterly*, vol. 3, no. 2, Dec. 1926, p. 22.

"They will jump from chairs": "Criminal Abortions—Abortions, Etc.," Jan. 9, 1914, file no. 856, Records of the New York Kehillah, Judah Magnes Collection, Central Archives for the History of the Jewish People, The Hebrew University, Jerusalem, Israel.

"Everywhere we were received": Elizabeth Stuyvesant, "The Brownsville Birth Control Clinic," p. 8.

"The removal of the fear of pregnancy": Harry L. Lurie, "The Sex Hygiene of Family Life," p. 24.

"a superb store of admonishments": Zena Smith Blau, "In Defense of the Jewish Mother," *Midstream*, vol. 13, no. 20, Feb. 1967, p. 47.

evil eye: Leah Rachel Yoffie, "Popular Beliefs and Customs among the Yiddish-Speaking Jews of St. Louis, Mo.," *Journal of American Folklore*, vol. 38, 1925, pp. 375–99.

69 **"The malnutrition, marasmus and rickets":** Maurice Fishberg, "Health Problems of the Jewish Poor," AH, Aug. 7, 1903, p. 374.

health statistics: quoted in Maurice Fishberg, *The Health and Sanitation of the Immigrant Jewish Population of New York* (New York, 1902), pp. 20–21.

"assiduity": Fishberg, "Health Problems of the Jewish Poor," p. 374.

"passionate assertions" of affection: Jacob Kohn, *Modern Problems of Jewish Parents: A Study in Parental Attitudes* (New York, 1932), p. 11.

"blind and unreasoning love": "Jewish Mother Love," *Froyen Zhurnal*, vol. 3, no. 5, Oct. 1923, p. 50.

"The Jewish mother . . . "betray[s]": Ethel Maslansky, "Cultural Factors Influencing the Attitudes of Jewish Mothers towards Eating Habits," *Medical Woman's Journal*, vol. 48, no. 4, April 1941, p. 114.

70 **Cultural anthropologists:** Martha Wolfenstein, "Two Types of Jewish Mothers," in Margaret Mead and Martha Wolfenstein, eds., *Childhood in Contemporary Cultures* (Berkeley, 1955), pp. 424–40; Ruth Landes and Mark Zborowski, "Hypotheses Concerning the East European Jewish Family," *Psychiatry*, vol. 13, 1950, pp. 447–64.

"known for nagging": Landes and Zborowski, "Hypotheses," p. 454.

"Suffering is the major theme": Wolfenstein, "Two Types of Jewish Mothers," p. 434.

Landmarks in the field: See, for example, David M. Levy, "Maternal Overprotection," *Psychiatry*, vol. 1, no. 4, Nov. 1938, pp. 561–91; "The Dangerous Mother," in Ernest Groves and Gladys Hoagland Groves, *Parents and Children* (Philadelphia, 1928), pp. 115–24.

"Jewish mother's *prime* function": "The Jewish Home," *The Center Table* (Boston, 1929), p. 1.

71 **"classroom in Judaism":** Mrs. David Goldstein, "A Chat on Education," *Outlook*, vol. 21, no. 1, Sept. 1950, p. 13.

"great and noble responsibility": "Chanukah Lights and Christmas Candles," p. 210.

"repository of our family past": Philip Roth, *Patrimony* (New York, 1991), p. 36.

"double responsibility": "Suggestions for a Talk by Mother," typescript, May 7, 1948, p. 1, Temple of Aaron Congregation of St. Paul, Minnesota Collection, Ratner Center Archives, Jewish Theological Seminary, New York (hereafter Ratner Center Archives).

"new obligations": "Greeting by Dr. Kaufmann Kohler, President, Hebrew Union College," *Proceedings of the Council of Jewish Women, Fifth Triennial Convention,* Dec. 1908, p. 23.

"we need woman": Israel Levinthal, "The Jewish Woman—A Purim Sermon," March 2, 1917, Sermons and Addresses, Israel Levinthal Collection, Ratner Center Archives. See also Levinthal's "Woman's Influence on Judaism, or What Judaism Owes to the Jewish Woman," Nov. 16, 1917.

"The religious training of my children": Jacob Kohn, *Modern Problems of Jewish Parents: A Study in Parental Attitudes* (New York, 1932), p. 121. See also Strauss, "An Informal Talk upon the Psychological Problems in the Bringing Up of Jewish Children," *Outlook,* vol. 1, no. 4, April 1931, p. 1.

72 **"aboriginal God-appointed educator":** Jeannette Miriam Goldberg, "Religion Should Be Taught in the Home," AH, Sept. 10, 1915, p. 470.

"folk-fancies and superstitions": Rose B. Goldstein, "Women's Share in the Responsibility for the Future of Judaism," *Outlook,* vol. 8, no. 4, May 1938, p. 13.

"ABC of Jewishness": Miriam Isaacs and Trude Weiss Rosmarin, *What Every Jewish Woman Should Know* (New York, 1941), p. 21.

"Our men are so driven": Abraham E. Hirschowitz, *Religious Duties of the Daughters of Israel,* third ed. (New York, 1917), preface.

The Three Pillars: Deborah M. Melamed, *The Three Pillars of Wisdom: Thought, Wisdom and Practice* (New York, 1927), preface. See also Deborah M. Melamed, "The Modern Woman and Traditional Judaism," *United Synagogue Recorder,* vol. 1, no. 1, Jan. 1921, pp. 9–10.

"what a Jewish woman ought to know": Advertisement cited in *Outlook,* vol. 3, no. 2, Dec. 1932, p. 2.

"The position of responsible leadership": Isaacs and Weiss Rosmarin, *What Every Jewish Woman Should Know,* p. 20.

73 **"symposium":** AH, Jan. 3, 1930, p. 355.

"Mother's Class": "Har Zion Temple: A Quarter Century of Service, 1924–1949," p. 95, Har Zion Temple Collection, box 1, Ratner Center Archives.

"feminine Paul Reveres": "Mrs. Joseph Leblang: Ardent Advocate of Jewish Education," AH, Nov. 26, 1926, p. 85.

National radio: "Cultural Papers and Radio Talks," *Outlook,* vol. 4, no. 4, May 1934, p. 7. See also "Utilizing a New Art," *United Synagogue Recorder,* vol. 8, no. 1, Feb. 1928, p. 7.

"we need no Mother's Day": Mrs. Max Leopold Margolis, "Woman's Place in Preserving Traditional Judaism," *Outlook,* vol. 11, no. 1, Sept. 1940, p. 5. See also Israel Levinthal, "Mother's Day," Sermon Notes, May 10, 1930, Levinthal Collection, Ratner Center Archives. On the history of Mother's Day, see Leigh Eric Schmidt, "The Commercialization of the Calendar: American Holidays and the Culture of Consumption, 1870–1930," *Journal of American History,* vol. 78, no. 3, Dec. 1991, pp. 887–916, esp. pp. 900–13.

"mass celebrations": Jewish Welfare Board, "Bulletin on the Observance of Mother's Day," May 14, 1922, typescript, p. 2.

74 **"the floral emblem of mother love":** Jewish Welfare Board, "Bulletin," p. 9.

75 **"Mother's Night Service":** "Mother's Day Material, 1928–1948," Congregation Shaare Zion of Sioux City, box 1, folder 4, Hyman Rabinowitz Papers, Ratner Center Archives.

"I speak on behalf of all daughters": "Daughter's Speech," May 2, 1937, "Mother's Day Material," Ratner Center Archives.

Temple of Aaron: "Mother's Day Service and Program," *Temple of Aaron Bulletin,* May 18, 1944.

cultural synthesis: "Shevuouth: The Jewish Mother's Festival," *Froyen Zhurnal,* vol. 1, no. 2, June 1922, p. 66.

"to become better boys and girls": *Helpful Thoughts,* vol. 1, no. 1, Feb. 1896, p. 4.

76 **"a little paper all their own":** *Helpful Thoughts*, vol. 1, no. 10, Feb. 1897, p. 110.
"sacred cause of Judaism": *Helpful Thoughts*, vol. 1, no. 10, Feb. 1897, p. 4.
"Foundation Stones of Judaism": *Helpful Thoughts*, vol. 1, no. 2, March 1896, p. 15.
three thousand grandchildren: "Foundation Stones of Judaism," *Helpful Thoughts*, vol. 1, no. 5, June 1896, p. 43.
"to make Jewishness attractive": "From a Teacher to Parents," *The Jewish Child*, vol. 1, no. 1, Jan. 31, 1926, p. 4.
"non-Jewish environment": "To Our Mothers: Greetings!" *The Jewish Child*, vol. 1, no. 1, Jan. 31, 1926, p. 7.
78 **"Jewish Tom Thumb":** "A New Book for a Jewish Child," *Outlook*, May 1935, p. 12. See also "Children's Corner," *Outlook*, vol. 1, no. 1, Sept. 1930, p. 9.
"Why, that's me!": "Book Corner of Especial Interest to Our Women," *United Synagogue Recorder*, vol. 9, no. 1, Jan. 1929, p. 23.
79 **Yiddish primers:** Jeffrey Shandler, " 'We Can Read and Understand': A Semiotic Analysis of the American Yiddish Primer and the Transformation of Literacy," in David Goldberg, ed., *The Field of Yiddish, Fifth Collection: Studies in Language, Folklore, and Literature* (Evanston, 1993), pp. 263–93, esp. p. 269. I'd like to thank Mr. Shandler for sharing this article with me.
80 **"Shabbos box":** Mrs. Reuben Weilerstein, "Living a Jewish Life Through Your Children," *Outlook*, vol. 1, no. 5, June 1931, p. 2.
"Every child loves a party": Mrs. S. J. Winer, "Coordinating Jewish Teaching in the Home and School," *Outlook*, vol. 3, no. 1, Sept. 1932, p. 2.
oversized dreidels: Press Release, The Dra-Dell Corporation, n.d., YIVO Archives.
81 **"A year ago":** "Chanukah Presents," *Outlook*, vol. 8, no. 2, Dec. 1937, p. 4.
82 **"doll with a purpose":** Mrs. Max L. Forman, "The Bible Doll: A New Tool in Our Visual Education Program," typescript, ca. 1947, p. 4, Barr Forman Collection. Dr. Barr Forman of New Haven, Connecticut, generously provided this document and dozens of others relating to his mother's work.
"authentic" biblical garb: Clipping from Forman interview with Mildred Wang, "Bible Doll Lady," *Hong Kong Tiger Standard*, n.d., Barr Forman Collection.
"People spend a lot of money": Quoted in Wang, "Bible Doll Lady."
84 **"The Doll creates happy experiences":** Mrs. Max L. Forman, "Presenting the Bible Dolls: Dolls That Teach a Lesson: Character, Democracy, Religion," typescript, n.d., p. 1, Barr Forman Collection.
"Seeing the doll": Mrs. Max L. Forman, "Presenting the Bible Dolls," p. 2. In 1991, The National Museum of American Jewish History in Philadelphia mounted an exhibition of Mrs. Forman's dolls entitled "Diana Forman: 'The Bible Doll Lady.' " Curated by folklorist William Westerman, the exhibition featured 131 different Bible Dolls.
"shining, twinkling ornaments": Label copy for the Bible Dolls, n.d., Donna Forman Collection.
"storyette": "This Rebbetzin Makes Bible Dolls," *Long Island Jewish Press* clipping, n.d., n.p., Donna Forman Collection.
"You ought to hear her": "Mothers and Children," *American Jewish Chronicle*, vol. 1, no. 7, June 23, 1916, p. 210.
85 **"subjective disharmony":** Alter Landesman, "The Adolescent: Some of His Interests and Conflicts," *Proceedings of the Rabbinical Assembly*, vol. 5, 1936, p. 312.
"Sometimes he would insist": James Atlas, *Delmore Schwartz: The Life of an American Poet* (New York, 1977), p. 3. See also Marvin Bressler, "Selected Family Patterns in W. I. Thomas' Unfinished Study of the 'Bintel Brief,' " *American Sociological Review*, vol. 17, Oct. 1952, p. 570.
"lifelong attachment": Rabbi Gabriel Schulman, "The Child and the Synagogue," in New York Board of Jewish Ministers, *Problems of the Jewish Ministry* (New York, 1927), p. 94.
"Jewish Music and Games": *Outlook*, vol. 2, no. 4, April 1932, p. 11.

"parent educators": See, for example, Mrs. M. F. Schwab, "Jewish Child Study Circles," *Proceedings of the Sixth Biennial Assembly of the National Federation of Temple Sisterhoods*, 1925, p. 153; Mrs. Alexander Langsdorf, "Child Study in 1933," *Proceedings of the Tenth Biennial Assembly of the National Federation of Temple Sisterhoods*, 1933, pp. 112–14.

"They flocked to child study classes": "Discussion—The Needs of the Adolescent," Rabbi A. Herbert Fedder, *Proceedings of the Rabbinical Assembly*, vol. 5, 1936, p. 323.

86 **"In fact, our time":** Mrs. Alexander Marx, "Modern Problems of Jewish Parents," *Outlook*, vol. 3, no. 2, Dec. 1932, p. 2.

"fully adjusted": Landesman, "The Adolescent," p. 311.

"Now you might ask": Israel Strauss, "An Informal Talk Upon the Psychological Problems in the Bringing Up of Jewish Children," *Outlook*, vol. 1, no. 4, April 1931, pp. 1, 11.

87 **"If the concerns of Judaism":** Kohn, *Modern Problems*, p. 125. See also Robert L. Griswold, *Fatherhood in America: A History* (New York, 1993).

"If the man does not live": Kohn, *Modern Problems*, p. 130.

"Of all the problems": Rabbi Israel Goldfarb, "The Child and the Synagogue," in New York Board of Jewish Ministers, *Problems of the Jewish Ministry*, p. 85.

"laboratories of character-building": Goldfarb, "The Child and the Synagogue," p. 87.

"special devices": Goldfarb, "The Child and the Synagogue," p. 85.

"apex of the child's impressionable period": Goldfarb, "The Child and the Synagogue," p. 88.

"Wise parents": Kohn, *Modern Problems*, p. 32.

CHAPTER THREE: RED-LETTER DAYS

89 **"The year of":** Milton Klonsky, "The Trojans of Brighton Beach," *Commentary*, May 1947, p. 466.

"most important milestone": Isaac Levitats, "Communal Regulation of Bar Mitzvah," *Jewish Social Studies*, vol. 10, no. 2, April 1949, p. 153.

"no ceremony": Jacob Kohn, *Modern Problems of Jewish Parents: A Study in Parental Attitudes* (New York, 1932), p. 28.

90 **"advantage of antiquity":** M. M. Eichler, "Confirmation—Pro and Con," *United Synagogue Recorder*, vol. 2, no. 3, July 1922, p. 3.

"punctuation mark": Albert S. Goldstein, "Let's Bar Bar Mitzva," *CCAR Journal*, vol. 3, Oct. 1953, p. 21.

"no ceremony at all": Stuart E. Rosenberg, *The Real Jewish World: A Rabbi's Second Thoughts* (New York, 1984), p. 18.

"greatest of holidays": Moses Weinberger, *People Walk on Their Heads: Moses Weinberger's Jews and Judaism in New York*. Translated from the Hebrew and edited by Jonathan S. Sarna (New York, 1982), pp. 14–15.

"As for phylacteries": Weinberger, *People Walk on Their Heads*, p. 76.

91 **"aleph-bais to bar mitzvah":** Samuel Joseph, "Israel Konovitz: Pioneer Jewish Educator in America," unpublished manuscript, n.d., p. 4. See also Robert Gordis, "Jewish Education in New York City—Its Chaos and a Possible Remedy," *The Menorah Journal*, vol. 17, no. 2, Nov. 1929, p. 133.

"bar mitzvah factories": Samuel Sussman, "Bar-Mitzvah Drops," Jan. 26, 1942, p. 1, Har Zion Temple Records, box 1, folder 2, Ratner Center Archives, Jewish Theological Seminary, New York (hereafter Ratner Center Archives).

"procedure of public prayers": Solomon Uselaner, *Jewish Laws and Customs, or Bar-Mitzvah Guide* (New York, 1927), pp. 47–48.

92 **"Even those who":** Kalman Whiteman, *Bar Mitzvah: Speeches Based on the Sidra and Haftarah of Every Sabbath in the Year, Together with the Most Essential Laws of Tefillin and the Appropriate Instructions to Teachers* (New York, 1931), p. v.

bar mitzvah texts: Prof. G. Selikovitsch, *The Jewish-American Orator* (New York, 1908); S. Druckerman, *Bar Mitzvah: A Selection of Confirmation Speeches in Hebrew, Yiddish, English* (New York, 1907); Solomon Uselaner, *Jewish Laws and Customs, or Bar-Mitzvah Guide* (New York, 1927); Simon Glazer, *The Bar-Mitzvah Pulpit: Sermonettes for Bar-Mitzvah Boys and Others* (New York, 1928); Jacob Katz, *Attaining Jewish Manhood* (New York, 1931); Reuben Kaufman, *Bar Mitzvah Manual: The Piano Method* (New York, 1936).

bar mitzvah speeches: See especially "Forms for the Introduction of The Speeches," in Whiteman, *Bar Mitzvah*, pp. 1–3.

93 **"red-letter day":** William M. Feldman, *The Jewish Child: Its History, Folklore, Biology and Sociology* (London, 1917), p. 234.

"Dear Rabbi": Handwritten Bar Mitzvah Speech, General Family History—Silver, folder 39.6, YIVO Archives.

Joe and Paul's: Audiotape of Advertisement by Joe & Paul, WPNX and Brooklyn Broadcasting Company, ca. 1940s, Max and Frieda Weinstein Archives of Recorded Sound, YIVO Institute.

"outstanding clothing": Transcription of Stanton Street Clothiers Association Ad," cited in liner notes of LP recording, *Dave Tarras: Yiddish-American Klezmer Music, 1925–1956*, Yazoo Records, 1992.

94 **"household of Israel":** AH, April 17, 1925, p. 761.

"revel[ed] in the feeling": Kohn, *Modern Problems*, p. 29.

"We request the pleasure": Alexander Harkavy, *American Letter Writer and Speller* (New York, 1902), p. 191.

96 ***Jewish Times:*** Masthead, *Jewish Times* (Baltimore), March 14, 1930.

its Social Page: See, for example, "Announcements," AH, Dec. 2, 1910, p. 149; Dec. 30, 1910, p. 263.

"better class bar mitzvah": Samuel Chotzinoff, *A Lost Paradise: Early Reminiscences* (New York, 1955), p. 115.

"The main event": Rosenberg, *Real Jewish World*, pp. 19–20.

"We will conduct the catering": Draft Agreement between Kotimsky & Tuchman and Congregation B'nai Jeshurun, Aug. 19, 1948, B'nai Jeshurun Records, box 7, folder 4, Ratner Center Archives.

97 **"bar mitzvah party reception":** "Menu—A Bar Mitzvah Party Reception Given in Honor of Leon Alexander," Jan. 17, 1928, Bar Mitzvah Invitations, Philadelphia Jewish Archives.

"the child was . . . unacquainted": Kohn, *Modern Problems*, p. 31.

98 **"murmuring orchestra":** Herman Wouk, *Marjorie Morningstar* (New York, 1955), p. 89.

"club dates": Personal communication from Henry Sapoznik, July 15, 1993. See also Bruce Alan MacLeod, "Music for All Occasions: The Club Date Business of Metropolitan New York City," Ph.D. thesis, Wesleyan University, 1979.

"anything larger than a trio": Personal communication from Henry Sapoznik, July 15, 1993.

Food, not the . . . boy himself: "Menu—A Bar Mitzvah Party Reception Given in Honor of Leon Alexander," Jan. 17, 1928, Bar Mitzvah Invitations, Philadelphia Jewish Archives.

"Petit-four la Sylvan": Menu from Sylvan M. Tobin's Bar Mitzvah, June 20, 1942, Philadelphia Jewish Archives.

"Jewish niceties": Leslie Prosterman, "Food and Celebration: A Kosher Caterer as Mediator of Communal Traditions," in Linda Keller Brown and Kay Mussell, *Ethnic and Regional Foodways in the United States: The Performance of Group Identity* (Knoxville, 1984), p. 130.

"great angle they got": Wouk, *Marjorie Morningstar*, p. 89.

99 **"Supreme in the Art":** Proposal from Newman Caterers to Congregation B'nai Jeshurun, March 7, 1945, B'nai Jeshurun Records, box 7, folder 4, Ratner Center Archives.

"ultra-fashionable in food": *Jewish Times* (Baltimore), May 16, 1930, p. 12.
"The caterers had given": Wouk, *Marjorie Morningstar*, p. 86.
100 **"make it nicer":** Prosterman, "Food and Celebration," p. 133.
"The caterer demonstrates": Prosterman, "Food and Celebration," p. 140.
"One of my vivid memories": Comment in Visitor's Book, "Getting Comfortable in New York: The American Jewish Home," The Jewish Museum, New York, Nov. 11, 1990.
candle-lighting ceremony: Abraham G. Duker, "Emerging Culture Patterns in American Jewish Life: The Psycho-Cultural Approach to the Study of Jewish Life in America," *Proceedings of the American Jewish Historical Society*, vol. 39, Sept. 1949–June 1950, p. 382.
Levenson comic sketch: *The Story of a Bar Mitzvah Boy*, Apollo Records, ca. 1940s, Max and Frieda Weinstein Archives of Recorded Sound, the YIVO Institute. Benny Bell's *Bar Mitzvah Speech—Today I Am a Man*, Bell Records, ca. 1950s, was also well known.
102 ***Encyclopaedia Britannica:*** AH, April 12, 1935, p. 466.
"gifts of Jewish significance": Kohn, *Modern Problems*, p. 30.
bar mitzvah certificates: *The Orthodox Union*, vol. 13, no. 2, Dec. 1945, p. 17; *Jewish Life*, vol. 21, no. 4, March–April 1954, p. 83.
the "fantastic" reception: Kohn, *Modern Problems*, p. 31.
"disintegration of Jewish life": Mordecai M. Kaplan Diaries, May 4, 1935, Jewish Theological Seminary Archives.
"vulgarities . . . of American Jewish life": Norman Podhoretz, "The Jew as Bourgeois," *Commentary*, Feb. 1956, p. 188.
103 **"deterioration":** H. P. Mendes, *Bar Mitzvah for Boyhood, Youth and Manhood* (New York, 1938), p. ix. Thirty years later, Hattie Eisenberg published *How to Have a Happy Bar Mitzvah* (New York, 1968), which contained numerous suggestions on how to arrange a tasteful and restrained celebration.
"in keeping with child psychology": Kohn, *Modern Problems*, p. 30.
104 **"the proper uses of a party":** Abraham Segal, "Reconstructing Bar Mitzvah," *The Reconstructionist*, vol. 10, no. 19, Jan. 26, 1945, p. 106.
"Every effort": "Standards for Synagogue Practice—United Synagogue Biennial Convention Recommendations," *Brooklyn Jewish Center Review*, vol. 37, no. 36, May 1956, p. 15.
105 **"these celebrations":** Kohn, *Modern Problems*, p. 31.
"founding fathers": Goldstein, "Let's Bar Bar Mitzva," p. 20.
"part of the pattern of Reform Judaism": Roland B. Gittelsohn, "Bar Mitzvo Practice in Liberal Jewish Congregations," in CCAR, *Confirmation Practices in Liberal Jewish Congregations* (Chicago, 1946), p. 27.
Rabbi's Manual: CCAR, *Rabbi's Manual* (Cincinnati, 1928), p. 152. See also Joseph Krauskopf, "A Change of Confirmation Day," *CCAR Year Book*, vol. 22, 1912, p. 326.
"troops" of girls: "Shabouth and Confirmation," AH, May 4, 1915, p. 36.
106 **"floral offerings":** Marion Spitzer, *Who Would Be Free* (New York, 1924), p. 17. See also "Large Numbers Participate in Confirmation," *American Jewish Chronicle*, vol. 1, no. 5, June 19, 1916, p. 157; Henry Berkowitz, "The Crown of a Good Name: A Service of Confirmation for Shebuot" (New York, n.d.), p. 6.
107 **"to shine in public":** Horace J. Wolf, "Time to Cry 'Halt,' " AH, April 23, 1915, p. 707.
First Prize Winner: "Confirmation Essay Prize Winners," AH, May 23, 1930, p. 15.
108 **"The confirmation has become":** *Proceedings of the Council of Jewish Women, Third Triennial Convention*, 1902, p. 227.
"one of the most popular ceremonials": "Shabouth and Confirmation," p. 36.
"All over the land": Wolf, "Time to Cry 'Halt,' " p. 707.

"For weeks in advance": "President's Page," *Outlook*, vol. 17, no. 4, May 1947, p. 2.

"Dr. Hirschberg wanted": Spitzer, *Who Would Be Free*, p. 19.

109 **"exchange its . . . character":** Wolf, "Time to Cry 'Halt,' " p. 707.

"loot-gathering": "Abuses of Confirmation—Rabbi Horace J. Wolf Responds to Criticisms of His Article on Modern Practices," AH, May 14, 1915, p. 28.

"Would it be possible to limit": Wolf, "Time to Cry 'Halt,' " p. 707. See also "Editorial Comment," AH, April 23, 1915, p. 717.

the "shams, the pomp": Dr. Nathan Krass, "Abuses of Confirmation—Prominent Rabbis Discuss Rabbi Wolf's Article on Modern Practices," AH, April 30, 1915, p. 747.

"It is wrong when children": Edward N. Calisch, "My Little Boy," *Helpful Thoughts*, vol. 3, no. 3, May 1898, p. 38.

110 **"Ada's Confirmation Presents":** Julia Richman, "Ada's Confirmation Presents," *Helpful Thoughts*, vol. 1, no. 3, April 1896, pp. 20–21.

"promiscuous giving": "Report of National Committee on Religion," *Proceedings of the Fifth Biennial Assembly, National Federation of Temple Sisterhoods*, 1923, p. 64.

confirmation Bible: "An Appropriate Gift for Confirmation, Bar Mitzvah, Birth Day, Etc.," *Jewish Home*, vol. 10, no. 10, June 1904, p. 394.

charitable contribution: See, for example, *Proceedings of the Sixth Biennial Assembly, National Federation of Temple Sisterhoods*, 1925, p. 35.

"simple dresses": "Abuses of Confirmation—Prominent Rabbis Discuss Rabbi Wolf's Article on Modern Practices," p. 747.

112 **"simplicity in dress":** Louis Egelson, "Confirmation Practices in the Jewish Religious School," *CCAR Year Book*, vol. 41, 1931, p. 382.

"the externals of dress": Egelson, "Confirmation Practices," p. 385.

"abuses of Confirmation": "Abuses of Confirmation—Rabbi Horace J. Wolf Responds to Criticisms of His Article on Modern Practices," AH, May 14, 1915, p. 28.

The "evils" Wolf complains about: Rabbi Joseph Silverman, "Abuses of Confirmation—Prominent Rabbis Discuss Rabbi Wolf's Article on Modern Practices," p. 747.

"robbing life": Rabbi Hyman Enelow, "Abuses of Confirmation—Prominent Rabbis Discuss Rabbi Wolf's Article on Modern Practices," p. 742.

113 **"principles of American democracy":** "Shabouth and Confirmation," p. 36.

"confirmation costume": "Shabuoth and Confirmation," p. 36.

Szold's critique: Henrietta Szold, "The Education of the Jewish Girl," *The Maccabaean*, vol. 5, no. 1, July 1903, p. 6.

114 **"raising woman to man's level":** Louis Feinberg, "Objections to Confirmation," *United Synagogue Recorder*, vol. 2, no. 3, July 1922, p. 4.

"feminine indulgence": See, for example, Hannah G. Solomon, *Proceedings of the Council of Jewish Women, Second Triennial Convention*, 1900, p. 20.

"girls' business": Leon Lang, "What Have We Done with Confirmation?" *Proceedings of the Rabbinical Assembly of America*, vol. 5, 1936, p. 294.

Reform bar mitzvah: Gittelsohn, "Bar Mitzvo Practice," p. 27.

115 **"inglorious anticlimax":** Goldstein, "Let's Bar Bar Mitzva," p. 21.

"rescued the Saturday morning service": Eugene Sack, "The Mitzva in Bar Mitzva," *CCAR Journal*, vol. 3, Oct. 1953, p. 24.

116 **"salesmanship":** Gittelsohn, "Bar Mitzvo Practice," p. 28.

"nostalgic indulgence": "Report of the Committee on Responsa," *CCAR Year Book*, vol. 44, 1954, p. 83.

"little more than a concession": Goldstein, "Let's Bar Bar Mitzva," p. 20.

frivolity: Gittelsohn, "Bar Mitzvo Practice," p. 27.

"atavistic restoration": Goldstein, "Let's Bar Bar Mitzva," p. 20.

117 **"two figments":** "Report of the Committee on Responsa," *CCAR Year Book*, vol. 44, 1954, p. 83.

"In the liberal temple": Goldstein, "Let's Bar Bar Mitzvah," p. 21.
118 "strong popular appeal": Lang, "What Have We Done," p. 289.
"the ceremony . . . has taken root": "Synagogue Ritual Survey," *Proceedings of the Rabbinical Assembly of America*, vol. 12, 1948, p. 107.
"*necessary*, formal induction of the youth": Lang, "What Have We Done," p. 293. My emphasis.
"we should be wary": Feinberg, "Objections to Confirmation," p. 4.
119 "warmth and . . . color": Lang, "What Have We Done," p. 307.
"We find that": Lang, "What Have We Done," p. 291.
"ritual of discontinuity": Stuart Schoenfeld, "Folk Judaism, Elite Judaism, and the Role of the Bar Mitzvah in the Development of the Synagogue and Jewish School in America," *Contemporary Jewry*, vol. 9, no. 1, Fall–Winter 1987–88, p. 69.
120 "There are enough Jews": Isaac Landman, "Issues that Confront American Israel," *CCAR Year Book*, vol. 43, 1933, p. 148.
"Upon becoming a bar mitzvah": Segal "Reconstructing Bar Mitzvah," p. 10.
"mortality": Reuben J. Magil, "The Rabbi in a Small Community," *Proceedings of the Rabbinical Assembly of America*, vol. 13, 1949, p. 170.
"bar-mitzvah drops": Sussman, "Bar-Mitzvah Drops," p. 1.
bar mitzvah "lads": Minutes of the Ritual and Religious Services Committee, Brooklyn Jewish Center, March 9, 1953, Brooklyn Jewish Center Collection, box 28, Ratner Center Archives.
"speaking to God": "Official Prayer to Be Recited by a Bar Mitzvah at the Services of the Brooklyn Jewish Center," n.d., Brooklyn Jewish Center, Minutes of the Ritual Committee, Brooklyn Jewish Center Records, box 28, Ratner Center Archives.
"criteria": "Minutes of the Meeting of a Special Committee on the Music Situation," May 13, 1956, Minutes of the Ritual Committee, Brooklyn Jewish Center, Brooklyn Jewish Center Records, box 28, Ratner Center Archives.
121 "Finis to the book": Goldstein, "Let's Bar Bar Mitzva," p. 21.
"something earned": Israel Goldstein, "Comment—The Child and the Synagogue," in New York Board of Jewish Ministers, *Problems of the Jewish Ministry* (New York, 1927), p. 108.
"No boy": "To Members Planning Bar Mitzvahs," *Brooklyn Jewish Center Review*, vol. 37, no. 25, Feb. 1956, p. 22.
compelled . . . to take a speed test: "Requirements for Confirmation—Har Zion School Report," no. 9, Jan. 15, 1946, Har Zion Records, box 1, folder 5, Ratner Center Archives. Students were expected to be able to read "eight lines, per minute, small type."
"The rub": Segal, "Reconstructing Bar Mitzvah," p. 11.
"The adolescent craves fun": Hyman Chanover, "The Rabbi in a Small Community," *Proceedings of the Rabbinical Assembly of America*, vol. 13, 1949, p. 176. See also Solomon S. Bernards, "The Bar Mitzvah and the Synagogue," *The Synagogue Center*, vol. 2, no. 2, Sept. 1941, p. 13.
122 "adolescent tendencies": Chanover, "The Rabbi in a Small Community," p. 177. See also Hyman Chanover, "Conducting a Sunday *Tefilin* Club," *The Synagogue School*, vol. 7, no. 1, Sept. 1948, pp. 6–10.
"boyology": Joseph Kett, *Rites of Passage: Adolescence in America, 1790 to the Present* (New York, 1977), p. 224.
"post–Bar Mitzvah clubs": Israel Goldfarb, "The Child and the Synagogue," *Problems of the Jewish Ministry*, p. 89.
"a sort of revolt": Simon Greenberg, "Lecture XI—Confirmation Classes," May 2, 1925, Simon Greenberg Papers, Har Zion Confirmation Class Lectures, box 1, Ratner Center Archives.
"cultivate attitudes": Lang, "What Have We Done," p. 295.
"*kehillah*-mindedness": David Aronson, "What Jewish Equipment Ought We to Give the Bar Mitzvah or Confirmant?" *Proceedings of the Rabbinical Assembly of*

America, vol. 5, 1936, p. 328. Some enterprising rabbis included sex education in the curriculum. "One day," recalled Rabbi A. Herbert Fedder, "a Bar Mitzvah group of 20 boys instead of learning 'brochos' [prayers] received a talk on the biology of sex and its relation to the sacredness of life." In short order, this innovation generated controversy. "Needless to say," writes Fedder, "a furor was created in the community for a while but the youngsters responded with a new sense of confidence in the rabbi . . . because they felt that someone was eager to listen to their intimate problems" (A. Herbert Fedder, "Discussion—The Needs of the Adolescent," in *Problems of the Jewish Ministry*, p. 322).

"equipment": Aronson, "What Jewish Equipment," p. 324.

"bar mitzvah minded": Sussman, "Bar-Mitzvah Drops," p. 3.

123 **"a matter for girls only":** Harry Halpern, "Comment—The Child and the Synagogue," *Problems of the Jewish Ministry*, p. 97.

Neuman's consecration service: Abraham A. Neuman to Israel H. Levinthal, May 28, 1931, p. 1., Brooklyn Jewish Center Records, box 11, "Consecration Services for Girls, 1938," Ratner Center Archives.

"There was no active opposition": Neuman to Levinthal, May 28, 1931, p. 2.

"with the same dignity": Israel H. Levinthal, "Initiating Girls in Jewish Religious Life," *Brooklyn Jewish Center Review*, vol. 15, no. 25, Feb. 1935.

"new experiment": Benjamin Kreitman to the East Midwood Jewish Center, April 22, 1955, Brooklyn Jewish Center Records, box 4, Ratner Center Archives.

"Precisely at eleven": *Brooklyn Jewish Center Review*, vol. 17, no. 35, May 1937, p. 15. See also "Consecration Classes 1936–1937," Brooklyn Jewish Center Records, box 10, Ratner Center Archives.

125 **"What most impressed":** "Center's First Consecration Services Acclaimed by Congregation," *Brooklyn Jewish Center Review*, vol. 16, no. 43, June 1936, p. 3.

"There was a want": M. M. Eichler, "Confirmation—Pro and Con," p. 3.

"The Jewish girls of today": Miriam Isaacs and Trude Weiss Rosmarin, *What Every Jewish Woman Should Know* (New York, 1941), p. 20.

"the problem of the young girl": Beatrice S. Genn, "The Religious Training of the Adolescent Girl," *Jewish Forum*, vol. 9, no. 10, Dec. 1926, p. 545.

"Less thought has been given": Genn, "The Religious Training," p. 542.

126 **"In this way":** Israel H. Levinthal, "The Value of the Consecration Service," *Brooklyn Jewish Center Review*, vol. 17, no. 35, May 1937, p. 3.

murky statements: See, for example, Rabbi Jacob Bosniak," Comment—The Child and the Synagogue," *Problems of the Jewish Ministry*, p. 104.

"The cry that": Feinberg, "Objections to Confirmation," p. 4.

127 **"I was excited":** "It's Back to the 'Bima' for This History Maker," *Jewish Week*, March 26, 1992, p. 2. See also Mordecai M. Kaplan Diary, March 28, 1922 and May 31, 1933, Jewish Theological Seminary Archives. I'd like to thank Rabbi Dr. Jacob J. Schacter for bringing these references to my attention.

"It is very interesting": "Shall Women Be Ordained as Rabbis?" *CCAR Year Book*, vol. 32, 1922, p. 171.

early bat mitzvahs: "What Our Sisterhoods Are Doing," *United Synagogue Recorder*, vol. 5, no. 1, Jan. 1925, p. 34; Louis Levitsky, "Conduct of Religious Services," *Proceedings of the Rabbinical Assembly of America*, 1927, p. 80.

1931 survey: Morris Silverman, "Report of Survey on Ritual," *Proceedings of the Rabbinical Assembly of America*, vol. 4, 1932, p. 331.

128 **"farce":** Silverman, "Report of Survey on Ritual," p. 330.

"planning to institute": Morris Goodblatt, "Synagogue Ritual Survey," *Proceedings of the Rabbinical Assembly of America*, vol. 12, 1948, p. 107.

129 **"without infringing on the Shulchan Aruch":** Jerome Tov Feinstein, "The Bas Mitzvah Comes to Our Synagogue," *Orthodox Union*, vol. 12, no. 1, Oct. 1944, p. 25. What follows is drawn from Feinstein's account.

"logical consequence" of bar mitzvah: Ahron Opher, "The Case for Bas Mitzvah," *CCAR Journal*, vol. 3, Oct. 1953, p. 25.

130 "Frankly, I am puzzled": "Report of the Committee on Responsa," *CCAR Year Book*, vol. 44, 1954, pp. 81–82.
"Bas mitzvah has no place": Israel Bettan, "Responsa: Bas Mitzvah Has No Place in Reform Jewish Practice," *CCAR Journal*, vol. 6, June 1954, p. 26.
"a *briah hadasah* [a new being]": Josiah Derby, "The Present Status of Jewish Education in the Conservative Movement," *Proceedings of the Rabbinical Assembly of America*, vol. 19, 1955, p. 195.
"suggested ceremonies": "Committee on Rituals and Ceremonies," *Proceedings of the Rabbinical Assembly of America*, vol. 16, 1952, p. 90.
"wider latitude": Aaron H. Blumenthal, "The Bat Mitzvah Ceremony," *The Synagogue School*, vol. 7, no. 3, Feb. 1949, p. 4.
bat mitzvah's varied manifestations: Paula Hyman, "The Introduction of Bat Mitzvah in Conservative Judaism in Postwar America," *YIVO Annual*, vol. 19, 1990, pp. 133–46.
131 "equal footing": Blumenthal, "The Bat Mitzvah Ceremony," p. 5.
"How many parents": Derby, "The Present Status," p. 195.
"Hollywood ballyhoo": Levitats, "Communal Regulation," p. 153.
"femininity self-concept": Sanders A. Tofield, "Woman's Place in the Rites of the Synagogue and with Special Reference to the Aliyah," *Proceedings of the Rabbinical Assembly of America*, vol. 19, 1955, pp. 188–89, note 32.
132 "wearied": Adele Bildersee, "The Jewish Adolescent," *Thirteenth Annual Convention, Bar Mitzvah Jubilee of the Young People's League of the United Synagogue of America*, 1937, p. 24.
"The cultural emphasis on precise age": Howard Chudacoff, *How Old Are You?: Age Consciousness in American Culture* (Princeton, 1989), p. 126.
"garlanded milestones": Margaret Sangster, *Winsome Womanhood: Familiar Talks on Life and Conduct* (New York, 1900), p. 133.
133 "coming-out party": Rosenberg, *The Real Jewish World* (New York, 1984), p. 20.
"symbolic Judaism": Herbert Gans, "American Jewry: Present and Future," *Commentary*, May 1956, p. 429.

CHAPTER FOUR: HOME SWEET *HAYM*

135 "As soon as one steps": Miriam Isaacs and Trude Weiss Rosmarin, *What Every Jewish Woman Should Know: A Guide for Jewish Women* (New York, 1941), p. 7.
Diana Forman's house: Diana Forman, "What Makes a Home Jewish," typescript, n.d., Collection of Donna Forman.
137 "architecture of visible health": Gwendolyn Wright, *Moralism and the Model Home: Domestic Architecture and Cultural Conflict in Chicago* (Berkeley, 1980), p. 119.
"in fitness and cleanliness": *The Settlement Journal*, vol. 1, no. 1, April 1904, p. 9.
"Gospel of Simplicity": Bertha H. Smith, "The Gospel of Simplicity as Applied to Tenement Homes," *The Craftsmen*, vol. 9, Oct. 1905, pp. 83–90. See also Bertha Holden, "Tenement Furnishings," *The House Beautiful*, vol. 7, no. 5, April 1900, pp. 307–12.
"wholesome and orderly": *Proceedings of the Council of Jewish Women, Second Triennial Convention*, 1900, p. 137.
"suitable furnishings": Mabel Hyde Kittredge, *Housekeeping Notes: How to Furnish and Keep Home in a Tenement Flat* (Boston, 1911), pp. 2–4.
Henry Street Settlement: "The Flat," *The Settlement Journal*, vol. 1, no. 4, Oct. 1904, p. 14.
139 "housewifely wisdom": "Report of the Chairman of Philanthropy," *Proceedings of the Council of Jewish Women, Third Triennial Convention*, 1902, p. 192.
the "Three D's": Minnie Louis, "Mission-Work Among the Unenlightened Jews," *Papers of the Jewish Women's Congress* (Philadelphia, 1894), p. 177.
"how to arrange the rooms": "The Flat," p. 14.

Plant, Fruit and Flower Guild: "Flowers for the Slums," AH, April 17, 1905, p. 602.
"Home-making Center": "Report of the Brooklyn (New York) Section," *Official Report of the Council of Jewish Women, Seventh Triennial Convention*, 1914, p. 60.
"debris": Jenna Weissman Joselit, "A Set Table: Jewish Domestic Culture in the New World," in Susan Braunstein and Jenna Weissman Joselit, eds., *Getting Comfortable in New York: The American Jewish Home, 1880–1950* (New York, 1990), p. 28. See also Lizabeth Cohen, "Embellishing a Life of Labor: An Interpretation of the Material Culture of American Working-Class Homes, 1885–1915," *Journal of American Culture*, vol. 3, no. 4, Winter 1980, pp. 752–75.
utterly "deficient": "Report of the Pittsburgh (Pa.) Section," *Proceedings of the Council of Jewish Women, Sixth Triennial Convention*, 1911, p. 564.
"laws of health and hygiene": "Report of the Syracuse Section," *Proceedings of the Council of Jewish Women, Sixth Triennial Convention*, 1911, p. 577.
140 **"hub of the home":** *The Settlement Journal*, vol. 1, no. 1, April 1904, p. 9; Smith, "Gospel," p. 88.
kitchen design: "Gospel," pp. 88–90; Kittredge, *Housekeeping Notes*, p. 11.
"Mrs. A.": "New Phase of Domestic Science," *Jewish Charities*, vol. 7, no. 7, Nov. 1916, p. 144.
141 **"floppy wallpaper":** Anzia Yezierska, *Bread Givers* (New York, 1925), p. 14. See also Anzia Yezierska, "Where Lovers Dreamed," in *Hungry Hearts* (New York, 1920), p. 149.
"Our small apartment": Samuel Chotzinoff, *A Lost Paradise: Early Reminiscences* (New York, 1955), p. 122.
142 **"Packed with furniture":** Yezierska, *Bread Givers*, p. 8.
"The number and variety": Chotzinoff, *A Lost Paradise*, p. 63.
"More than simply commodities": Andrew Heinze, *Adapting to Abundance: Jewish Immigrants, Mass Consumption and the Search for American Identity* (New York, 1990), pp. 4–5.
"My mother was very adroit": Chotzinoff, *A Lost Paradise*, p. 113.
143 **Kramer and Wagner:** *Froyen Zhurnal*, vol. 2, no. 10, Feb. 1923, p. 45.
Hebrew Free Loan Society: Jenna Weissman Joselit, *Lending Dignity: The First One Hundred Years of the Hebrew Free Loan Society of New York* (New York, 1992), p. 21.
"More than 80%": *American Jewess*, vol. 2, no. 1, Oct. 1895, p. 69.
144 **"The fact that women":** "The Forward Leads in Advertising Appealing to Women," in JDF, *The Fourth American City—The Jewish Community of New York: A Book of Facts about the Jewish Field, New York, Chicago and National* (New York and Chicago, 1927), p. 25. I would like to thank Shulamith Berger for bringing this document to my attention.
Levinthal's sermons: "Flapperism in Civilization and Religion," March 9, 1923, and "Style," Dec. 29, 1916, Addresses and Sermons, Israel Levinthal Collection, Ratner Center Archives, Jewish Theological Seminary of America, New York (hereafter Ratner Center Archives).
B. V. Cantor: *Froyen Velt*, vol. 1, no. 4, July 1913.
"Grand Rapids Furniture": See, for example, Advertisement for Copeland & Perlmutter in *Froyen Zhurnal*, vol. 1, no. 3, May 1923, p. 23.
Saul Birns: Birns advertised frequently in the Yiddish press. See, for example, *Der Tog*, Feb. 28, 1917.
145 **"a quality-market par excellence":** JDF, *Fourth American City*, p. 30.
"Their annual expenditures": JDF, *Fourth American City*, p. 5.
"There is nothing strange": "How to Start and Carry On a Merchandising and Advertising Campaign in the Jewish Field," in JDF, *Fourth American City*, n.p.
"parlor sets of velvet": Marcus Ravage, *An American in the Making* (New York, 1917), p. 82.

"Practical and Contemporary Kitchens": *Froyen Zhurnal*, vol. 1, no. 2, June 1922, p. 53.

"How to Beautify Your Home": *Froyen Zhurnal*, vol. 1, no. 1, May 1922, p. 46.

146 **"doctor of home decor":** "Home Decorations," *Froyen Zhurnal*, vol. 1, no. 8, Dec. 1922, p. 38.

"Many years ago": "Home Decorations," *Froyen Zhurnal*, vol. 2, no. 10, Feb. 1923, p. 45.

148 **stolid as a "*masevah*":** "How to Beautify Your Home," *Froyen Zhurnal*, vol. 1, no. 1, May 1922, p. 46. On cut glass crystal, see also Joselit, "A Set Table," p. 49.

"the dignified concept of a 'set' ": Isa Knapp, "By the Waters of the Grand Concourse: Where Jewishness Is Free of Compulsion," *Commentary*, Sept. 1949, p. 273.

The Bernsteins: Burton Bernstein, *Family Matters: Sam, Jennie, and the Kids* (New York, 1982), pp. 67–68.

"upholstered surface": Ruth Glazer, "West Bronx: Food, Shelter, Clothing," *Commentary*, June 1949, p. 583. See also "Not Bronx, but America—Letters to the Editor," *Commentary*, Aug. 1949, pp. 194–95.

"cultivate interiors": Knapp, "By the Waters," p. 272.

"the right books": Aaron M. Frankel, "Back to Eighty-sixth Street," *Commentary*, August 1946, p. 171.

A 1931 survey: Union of American Hebrew Congregations of America, *Reform Judaism in the Large Cities: A Survey* (Cincinnati, 1931). See also Arthur L. Reinhart, *The Voice of the Jewish Laity: A Survey of Jewish Laymen's Religious Attitudes and Practices* (Cincinnati, 1928).

"manifestations of Jewishness": *Reform Judaism*, p. 13.

"curiosities": "The President's Chat," *Outlook*, vol. 7, no. 2, Dec. 1936, p. 6. Why do we make of our Jewish symbols "objects to be exhibited like the relics of the Tomb of Tutankamen," the president of Women's League wondered plaintively.

"Zayda was relegated": Milton Klonsky, "The Trojans of Brighton Beach," *Commentary*, May 1947, p. 465.

149 **"Chances are only fifty-fifty":** Abraham N. Franzblau, "Reorientation of Jewish Religious Education," *CCAR Year Book*, vol. 46, 1936, p. 285.

"an emblem of the past": Elizabeth Stern, *My Mother and I* (New York, 1919), p. 166.

"sleazy" white satin: Ruth Glazer, "The Jewish Object—A Shopper's Report," *Commentary*, July 1951, p. 64.

"The average . . . *mezuzah*": Nathan Kollin, "Religion and the Home—Discussion," *Proceedings of the Rabbinical Assembly of America*, vol. 7, 1940, pp. 204–5.

"Pause on the threshold": Esther Fain, "Life in a Conservative Jewish Home," *Outlook*, vol. 25, no. 2, Dec. 1954, p. 27.

"charm and beauty": "Address of Dr. Jacob Kohn," in *Services in Memory of Mrs. Solomon Schechter, November 13, 1924* (New York, 1925), p. 37.

"Go to at least": Mrs. Reuben Weilerstein, "Living a Jewish Life Through Your Child," *Outlook*, vol. 1, no. 5, June 1931, p. 2.

150 **Jewish Home Institute:** "Synagog Extension in Reform Judaism," *CCAR Year Book*, vol. 40, 1930, pp. 411–12; "Make Your Home Jewish," *Pesach Guide for Associate Teacher*, publication of The Jewish Home Institute Department of Information and Service (New York, 1928), frontispiece.

Mordecai M. Kaplan: Mordecai M. Kaplan, *Judaism as a Civilization* (New York, 1934), p. 457; Mordecai M. Kaplan, "The Place of the Rabbi in American Jewish Life," *Proceedings of the Rabbinical Assembly of America*, vol. 7, 1940, p. 279.

"ethics of home decoration": James R. Miller, "The Ethics of Home Decoration," in *Week-day Religion* (Philadelphia, 1880), see chap. 27, pp. 265–74.

151 **"teem[ing] with . . . possibilities":** Isaacs and Weiss Rosmarin, *What Every Jewish Woman*, p. 10.

"place of honor": Isaacs and Weiss Rosmarin, *What Every Jewish Woman*, p. 8. See also "Branch News," *Outlook*, vol. 18, no. 2, Dec. 1947, p. 14.

"JNF Box": Nathan Kollin, "Religion and the Home—Discussion," p. 206.

clarion calls: See, for example, "The United Synagogue of America and the Women's League: Their Ideals," 1920, Women's League Archives, pp. 11–12; Fain, "Life in a Conservative Jewish Home," p. 27; "Chanukah Presents," *Outlook*, vol. 8, no. 2, Dec. 1937, p. 4.

"The arrangement of": Isaacs and Weiss Rosmarin, *What Every Jewish Woman*, p. 8.

152 **"queen of the drawing room":** Audiotape of Interview with Mrs. Adele Ginzberg, Fortieth Anniversary Reception and Tea of National Women's League, Jan. 22, 1958, Women's League Archives.

baleboste: Mel Scult, "The Baale Boste Reconsidered: The Life of Mathilde R. Schechter," *Modern Judaism*, vol. 7, no. 1, Feb. 1987, pp. 1–27.

Szold eulogy: Henrietta Szold, "The Lineaments of Mathilde Roth Schechter," *Services in Memory of Mrs. Solomon Schechter, November 13, 1924* (New York, 1925), p. 13.

"American way": Ginzberg Audiotape.

"The American-Jewish woman": Isaacs and Weiss Rosmarin, *What Every Jewish Woman*, p. 6.

154 **Kohn critique:** Jacob Kohn, *Modern Problems of Jewish Parents: A Study in Parental Attitudes* (New York, 1932), pp. 51–52.

"The first and only": *Der Tog*, Dec. 3, 1919, p. 3.

"makeshift" stuff: "President's Page," *Outlook*, vol. 19, no. 2, Dec. 1948, p. 2.

155 **"ceremonial object day":** "Report of the National Committee on the Union Museum," *Proceedings of the Fourth Biennial Assembly, National Federation of Temple Sisterhoods*, 1921, p. 103.

"a sentiment" for Jewish . . . artifacts: "Report of the National Committee on the Union Museum," *14th Annual Report of the National Federation of Temple Sisterhoods*, 1926, p. 113.

"Art Calendar": "Report of the National Committee on Religion," *Proceedings of the First Biennial Meeting of the National Federation of Temple Sisterhoods*, 1915, pp. 60–61.

"Rembrandt Calendar": "Report of the President," *13th Annual Report, National Federation of Temple Sisterhoods*, 1926, p. 12.

157 **"art's ability":** Mrs. Abraham Simon, "President's Annual Message," *Proceedings of the Second Biennial Meeting, National Federation of Temple Sisterhoods*, 1917, p. 25.

Joint Committee on Ceremonies: "Report of the Joint Committee on Ceremonies," *CCAR Year Book*, vol. 58, 1948, p. 91.

"exquisite work of art": "Report of the Joint Committee," p. 88.

"philosophy of presents": "Philosophy of Presents," *Harper's Weekly*, vol. 54, Nov. 1910, p. 21. See also Viviana A. Zelizer, *The Social Meaning of Money* (New York, 1994), chap. 3, pp. 71–117.

158 **"Symbols count":** "Symbols Count," *Outlook*, vol. 1, no. 1, Sept. 1930, p. 2.

"For Jewish occasions": Althea O. Silverman, "Jewish Gifts for Jewish Occasions," *Outlook*, vol. 6, no. 3, March 1936, p. 7.

"Readers . . . who are puzzled": Isaacs and Weiss Rosmarin, *What Every Jewish Woman*, p. 9.

"A silver talis clip": "Speaking of Gifts," *Outlook*, vol. 22, no. 4, May 1952, p. 18.

159 **"Many towns":** "Have You a Museum Piece?" *Outlook*, vol. 22, no. 2, Dec. 1951, p. 14.

"ritual appliances": "The Society of the Jewish Museum: An Outline for a Prospectus," Dec. 28, 1917, unpublished manuscript, p. 2, John Weichsel Papers,

Archives of American Art, Smithsonian Institution. I'd like to thank Norman Kleeblatt for sharing this document with me.

"the communal setting": Jack Wertheimer, "The Conservative Synagogue," in Jack Wertheimer, ed., *The American Synagogue: A Sanctuary Transformed* (New York, 1987), p. 125.

"Rabbis are . . . reporting a trend": William B. Meyers, "The Art of Living and the Living Arts," *Outlook*, vol. 25, no. 2, Dec. 1954, p. 11.

"tentatively feeling their way": Glazer, "The Jewish Object," p. 63.

160 **"observant and beautiful":** Glazer, "The Jewish Object," p. 67.

"Sisterhood gift shops": Mrs. Max Fink, "The Sisterhood Gift Shop," *Outlook*, vol. 19, no. 4, May 1949, p. 15. See also "Report of the National Committee on Jewish Ceremonials and Art," *29th Annual Report, National Federation of Temple Sisterhoods*, 1942, p. 296; "Report of the National Committee on Jewish Ceremonials and Art," *36th Annual Report, National Federation of Temple Sisterhoods*, 1947–48, p. 164.

"we have better facilities": Sarah L. Kopelman, "President's Page," *Outlook*, vol. 20, no. 2, Dec. 1949, p. 3.

carefully worded "directives": "Directives for Sisterhood Book and Gift Shop Chairmen," *Outlook*, vol. 21, no. 2, Dec. 1950, p. 11.

161 **"Guard against dusty":** "The Gift Shop—Function—Project—Or What?" *Outlook*, vol. 25, no. 2, Dec. 1954, p. 28.

"Educate": "What's Your Gift Shop E.Q.?" *Outlook*, vol. 27, no. 2, Dec. 1956, p. 29.

"Israeli corner": "What Articles Do You Sell in Your Sisterhood Gift Shop?" *Outlook*, vol. 23, no. 3, March 1953, p. 11.

"vigorous tide": Isaacs and Weiss Rosmarin, *What Every Jewish Woman*, p. 8.

"Eventually, we hope": Sarah L. Kopelman, "President's Page," *Outlook*, vol. 19, no. 4, May 1949, p. 3.

"meticulously set" . . . tables: Betty D. Greenberg and Althea O. Silverman, *The Jewish Home Beautiful* (New York, 1945), third ed., p. 67.

"This pageant": Greenberg and Silverman, *The Jewish Home Beautiful*, p. 38.

162 **"not presented as a museum piece":** Greenberg and Silverman, *The Jewish Home Beautiful*, pp. 13–14.

"Calls for it are constant": Dora Spiegel, "The President's Chat," *Outlook*, vol. 11, no. 3, March 1941, p. 2; "Our Eighteen Branches," *Outlook*, vol. 21, no. 4, May 1951, p. 20. See also "Report of the National Committee on Jewish Ceremonials and Art," *29th Annual Report, National Federation of Temple Sisterhoods*, 1942, p. 296.

"But they have . . . strange sources": Greenberg and Silverman, *The Jewish Home Beautiful*, p. 14.

163 **"Tablets of the Law":** Greenberg and Silverman, *The Jewish Home Beautiful*, p. 72.

"The holiday closest to the feminine heart": Greenberg and Silverman, *The Jewish Home Beautiful*, p. 27.

"A small doll": Greenberg and Silverman, *The Jewish Home Beautiful*, p. 71.

There's no need: *Outlook*, vol. 11, no. 3, March 1941, p. 10.

"No one has . . . sought": Glazer, "The Jewish Object," p. 64.

164 **Kayser's speech:** "Jewish Art for the Home and Synagogue," *Proceedings, National Women's League*, 1956, p. 89, Women's League Archives.

166 **"many objects . . . held in high esteem":** "Union Museum for Jewish Ceremonial Objects," *The Union Bulletin*, vol. 4, no. 2, March 1914. I'd like to thank Grace Cohen Grossman for bringing this document to my attention.

"beautiful symbols of our faith": "Report of the National Committee on the Union Museum," *Proceedings of the National Federation of Temple Sisterhoods*, 1922, p. 71.

"Purim and Passover": "Visit the Jewish Museum," *Outlook*, vol. 6, no. 3, March 1936, p. 4.

Egyptian wing: Isaacs and Weiss Rosmarin, *What Every Jewish Woman*, pp. 89–90.
"deepen[ing] . . . the springs": *Proceedings of the First Biennial Meeting of the National Federation of Temple Sisterhoods*, 1915, p. 50.
"A visit to the . . . museum": "The Jewish Museum of the Jewish Theological Seminary," *Outlook*, vol. 3, no. 4, May 1933, p. 11.
167 "makes vivid": "Report of the Assembly Committee on the Union Museum," *Proceedings of Sixth Biennial Assembly, National Federation of Temple Sisterhoods*, 1925, p. 167.
"Jewish art looms up": "Report of the National Standing Committees," *20th Annual Report of the National Federation of Temple Sisterhoods*, 1923, p. 79.
168 "habits and customs": "The Jewish Museum," p. 9.
169 "Have You a Museum Piece?": "Have You A Museum Piece?", p. 14.
"creates a desire to return": Louise Kayser, "Creating Antiques for Our Descendants," *Outlook*, vol. 27, no. 3, March 1957, p. 7.
"good taste and contemporary feeling": Kayser, "Creating Antiques," p. 21.
"We realized": Abraham Kanof, "The Tobe Pascher Workshop, 1956–1986," in Nancy Berman, ed., *Moshe Zabari: A Twenty-Five Year Retrospective* (New York and Los Angeles, 1986), p. 6.
"well on the road": Kayser, "Creating Antiques," p. 21.

CHAPTER FIVE: KITCHEN JUDAISM

171 "kitchen religion": Mrs. Caesar Misch, "Address of the National President," *Proceedings of the Council of Jewish Women, Sixth Triennial Convention*, 1911, p. 54.
"bond in sanctity": Mary M. Cohen, "The Influence of the Jewish Religion in the Home," *Papers of the Jewish Women's Congress* (Philadelphia, 1894), p. 116.
gastronomic [Judaism]: Samuel Silver, "The Translation of That Impact in the Life of the Synagog," *CCAR Year Book*, vol. 56, 1940, p. 340; Mrs. Anna Bear Brevis, "Judaism in the Home Enters Second Phase," *Proceedings of the Biennial Convention, National Women's League*, 1950–52, Women's League Archives, p. 82. See also Cohen, "The Influence of the Jewish Religion in the Home," p. 119.
"one hundred percent": Hyman Rabinowitz, "Response—The Future of the American Jewish Community," *Proceedings of the Rabbinical Assembly of America*, vol. 12, 1948, p. 215.
172 "The simple act": Isaac Rosenfeld, "Adam and Eve on Delancey Street," *Commentary*, Oct. 1949, p. 386.
"dietary injunctions": David Macht, "The Scientific Aspects of the Jewish Dietary Laws," in Leo Jung, ed., *The Jewish Library*, second series (New York, 1930), p. 219.
"no little sacrifice": "Kosher Meat," AH, Dec. 16, 1910, p. 199.
"double expense": "The Housewife's Problem," *American Jewish Chronicle*, vol. 2, no. 9, Jan. 5, 1917, p. 276.
"The Friday night candles": Milton Klonsky, "The Trojans of Brighton Beach," *Commentary*, May 1947, p. 465.
"inherited repugnance": Joseph Jacobs, *The Jewish Culture—And What It Means to the American Manufacturer in the Manufacturing of His Products* (New York, 1941), p. 19. I'd like to thank David Koch of the Joseph Jacobs Organization for bringing this document to my attention.
"selectively treyf": Barbara Kirshenblatt-Gimblett, "Kitchen Judaism," in Susan Braunstein and Jenna Weissman Joselit, eds., *Getting Comfortable in New York: The American Jewish Home, 1880–1950* (New York, 1990), p. 80.
173 "Uncertain, in a precarious world": Ruth Glazer, "The Jewish Delicatessen: The Evolution of an Institution," *Commentary*, March 1946, p. 63.
"kosher-style": Glazer, "The Jewish Delicatessen," p. 60. See also Milton Matz, "The Meaning of the Christmas Tree to the American Jew," *Jewish Journal of Sociology*, vol. 3, no. 1, June 1961, pp. 131–32.

"optional Judaism": Max J. Routtenberg, "Report of the Vice President," *Proceedings of the Rabbinical Assembly of America*, vol. 15, 1951, pp. 34–35.

"without pain": Herbert Gans, "American Jewry: Present and Future," *Commentary*, May 1956, p. 429.

174 **"Since the main purpose":** Mordecai M. Kaplan, *Judaism as a Civilization* (New York, 1934), p. 441.

"Well, I keep a kosher home": Marshall Sklare, *Conservative Judaism: An American Religious Movement* (Glencoe, 1955), p. 204.

"A realistic view": Max Arzt, "Is It Permissible to Eat Cooked Vegetables and Broiled Fish in Non-Kosher Restaurants?" undated manuscript, p. 1., RG 27, box 1, folder 6, Ratner Center Archives, Jewish Theological Seminary, New York (hereafter Ratner Center Archives).

Hamburg boys' school menu: Michael Meyer, *Response to Modernity: A History of the Reform Movement in Judaism* (New York, 1988), p. 114.

eyewitness account: Cited in "The First Ordination and the Terefa Banquet, 1883," *American Jewish Archives*, vol. 26, no. 2, Nov. 1974, p. 130.

175 **"a surprisingly small minority":** Henrietta Szold, cited in "The First Ordination," p. 131. Szold's account first appeared in the *Jewish Messenger*, July 27, 1883, pp. 14–15.

"this *is* the nineteenth century": "The First Ordination," p. 132.

to keep "lard out of the pots": "Correspondence—That Banquet," *Jewish Messenger*, Aug. 10, 1883, p. 5.

"were so good": "The First Ordination," p. 128.

"toothsome dainties": *Hebrew Standard*, March 11, 1910, p. 8.

"spaghetti party": Evelyn D. Wittman, "The Story of a New Sisterhood," *Outlook*, vol. 26, no. 1, Sept. 1955, p. 7.

"Such conduct": Israel H. Levinthal, "Just Between Ourselves," *Brooklyn Jewish Center Review*, vol. 20, no. 13, Nov. 1938, p. 4.

176 **culinary apostasy:** Harold Gastwirt, *Fraud, Corruption and Holiness* (New York, 1974), p. 7.

"makes Jew and Gentile . . . wonder": "Literary Digest Finds Only 15% of Nation's Jews Eat Kosher Foods," *Brooklyn Jewish Center Review*, vol. 17, no. 28, March 1937, p. 4.

The Royal Table: Jacob Cohn, *The Royal Table: An Outline of the Dietary Laws of Israel* (New York, 1936).

Kashruth statistics: "Literary Digest Finds," p. 4.

"Matters of food": "An Answer to Literary Digest's Kashruth Survey," *Brooklyn Jewish Center Review*, vol. 17, no. 31, April 1937, p. 4.

"far below the mark": "An Answer," p. 23.

"on the way out": "Kashrut in Chicago," *The Reconstructionist*, vol. 21, no. 8, May 26, 1955, p. 32.

177 **Minneapolis rabbi:** Albert Gordon, "Towards a Philosophy of Conservative Judaism," *Proceedings of the Rabbinical Assembly of America*, vol. 12, 1948, p. 158.

"complains that he cannot": Mordecai Brill, "Wanted: A Study of Jewish Middletown," *The Reconstructionist*, vol. 10, no. 18, Jan. 12, 1945, p. 11.

Sklare study: Marshall Sklare and Joseph Greenbaum, *Jewish Identity on the Suburban Frontier: A Study of Group Survival in the Open Society* (New York, 1967), pp. 50–55, esp. p. 52.

"National Survey": Cited in Jack Wertheimer, "The Conservative Synagogue," in Jack Wertheimer, ed., *The American Synagogue: A Sanctuary Transformed* (New York, 1987), p. 131.

"burdensome affair": "Why the Kosher Cookbook?" *The Jewish Examiner Prize Kosher Recipe Book*, ed. by "Balabusta" (New York, 1937), p. iv.

Yes, I Keep Kosher: *Jewish Life*, vol. 1, no. 1, Sept.–Oct. 1953, p. 85.

"stamp of approval": N. E. Aronstam, *Jewish Dietary Laws from a Scientific Standpoint* (New York, 1912), p. 5.

"Whoever made the . . . laws": Dr. B. Bernheim, "The Dietary Laws and Health," AH, July 31, 1903, p. 337.

178 **"greater nutritive value":** Aronstam, *Jewish Dietary Laws*, p. 14.

"are in accordance": Aronstam, *Jewish Dietary Laws*, p. 24.

David Macht: David Macht, "The Scientific Aspects of the Jewish Dietary Laws," in Leo Jung, ed., *The Jewish Library*, second series (New York, 1930), pp. 205–25.

"indigestion and stomach troubles": Dr. Louis Launer, "The Jewish Dietary Laws from a Medical Point of View," *Outlook*, vol. 6, no. 1, Sept. 1935, p. 9.

"totemism": Meyer, *Response to Modernity*, p. 273.

"searchlight of science": Aronstam, *Jewish Dietary Laws*, p. 4.

"home engineers": Leah Leonard, *The Jewish Holiday Cook Book* (New York, 1955), p. v.

180 **"pursued the science of food":** Laura Shapiro, *Perfection Salad: Women and Cooking at the Turn of the Century* (New York, 1986), p. 47.

"gospel of good cooking": Shapiro, *Perfection Salad*, p. 128.

"Apt pupil[s]": Bertha M. Wood, *Foods of the Foreign-Born in Relation to Health* (Boston, 1922), p. 95.

"Mashah joined the cooking class": Anzia Yezierska, *Bread Givers* (New York, 1925), p. 56.

"Goy cooking": Edna Ferber, *A Peculiar Treasure* (New York, 1939), p. 90.

"little band of Hebrew women": "New Settlement Plan," *Hebrew Standard*, March 30, 1900, p. 3. See also Kirshenblatt-Gimblett, "Kitchen Judaism," pp. 96–98.

181 **"Jewish dietary problems":** Mary L. Schapiro, "Jewish Dietary Problems," *Journal of Home Economics*, Feb. 1919, pp. 47–59.

"You will . . . often meet": Maurice Fishberg, *The Health and Sanitation of the Immigrant Jewish Population of New York* (New York, 1902), p. 17.

"too many pickles": Wood, *Foods of the Foreign-Born*, p. 91.

"real missionary task": Schapiro, "Jewish Dietary Problems," p. 53.

"One has to recognize": Dr. Max Kahn, "Problems of the Dietitian in the Care of Outpatient Poor Suffering from Diseases of Metabolism," *Journal of Home Economics*, vol. 12, no. 5, May 1921, p. 215.

182 **"clients":** Bureau of Jewish Social Research, *Notes and News*, no. 28, June 1, 1935, p. 25.

" 'You learned us' ": Anzia Yezierska, "My Own People," *Hungry Hearts* (New York, 1920), p. 245.

"Jews put great emphasis": Dorothy E. Hall, "Health Habits," *American Journal of Orthopsychiatry*, vol. 8, no. 4, Oct. 1938, p. 622.

"the taking of food": Hall, "Health Habits," p. 621.

"over-protective attitude": Ethel Maslansky, "Cultural Factors Influencing the Attitudes of Jewish Mothers Towards Eating Habits," *Medical Woman's Journal*, vol. 48, no. 4, April 1941, p. 114.

"preoccupation with food": Maslansky, "Cultural Factors," p. 115. My emphasis.

183 **"who is more careful":** Rose Goldstein, "A Balanced Jewish Diet," *Outlook*, vol. 27, no. 4, May 1957, p. 25.

"Jewish women are . . . good cooks": Schapiro, "Jewish Dietary Problems," p. 55.

"heretical view": Harry Gersh, "Mama's Cooking: Minority Report," *Commentary*, Oct. 1947, p. 367.

"I had found out": Gersh, "Mama's Cooking," p. 369. Several readers disagreed strongly with Gersh's observations. "No, Mr. Gersh," wrote A. J. Rongy, "your verdict about Jewish cooking would not be upheld by a jury of Jewish housewives, composed of many other ma's and their friends." "You remain a prisoner of your infantilism," added Irwin Nussbaum. "We proclaim to the world that we have returned to Ma's cooking. Not only that, but in the process of returning, have brought with us hordes of converts. If you don't believe this, Harry, just take a stroll down Broadway and gaze at the menu in Lindy's" ("In Defense of Mama," letters from readers, *Commentary*, Dec. 1947, pp. 586–87).

"have some salt": Burton Bernstein, *Family Matters: Sam, Jennie, and the Kids* (New York, 1982), p. 155.

"state of mind": *Jewish Examiner Prize Recipe Book*, p. iii.

184 "humble literature": Kirshenblatt-Gimblett, "Kitchen Judaism," p. 77.

"motherly matrons": Ferber, *A Peculiar Treasure*, p. 351.

"inherited routine": Ruth Glazer, "West Bronx: Food, Shelter, Clothing," *Commentary*, June 1949, p. 581.

"romantic past": The Rumford Company, *What Shall I Serve?: Famous Recipes for Jewish Housewives* (n.p., 1931), p. 2.

"All we need to remember": Betty D. Greenberg and Althea O. Silverman, *The Jewish Home Beautiful* (New York, 1945), p. 88.

"gratuitous": Kaplan, *Judaism as a Civilization*, p. 441.

"By giving them": Kaplan, *Judaism as a Civilization*, pp. 441, 443.

186 "fine art": "Cookery," *Jewish Encyclopedia* (New York, 1904), p. 254.

"To live as a Jewess": Greenberg and Silverman, *Jewish Home Beautiful*, p. 13.

"The Jewish bride": Miriam Isaacs and Trude Weiss Rosmarin, *What Every Jewish Woman Should Know: A Guide for Jewish Women* (New York, 1941), p. 73. The kosher kitchen also held its own when it came to the very latest in scientific cookery. See, for example, Mildred Bellin's *Modern Kosher Meals* (New York, 1934), a cookbook designed to fill the "need of the modern Jewish housewife who would combine the dishes 'that mother used to make' with a regard to modern dietetics" (*Outlook*, vol. 5, no. 1, Sept. 1934, p. 13).

"The Jewish woman who entertains": Isaacs and Weiss Rosmarin, *What Every Jewish Woman*, p. 73.

"a welcome change": Isaacs and Weiss Rosmarin, *What Every Jewish Woman*, p. 80.

187 "We have . . . marveled": "Each According to Her Taste," *American Jewess*, vol. 7, no. 3, June 1898, p. 156.

"To her, the planning": Felicia Lamport, *Mink on Week Days* (New York, 1950), p. 9.

"in a Jewish home": Deborah Melamed, *The Three Pillars of Wisdom: Thought, Wisdom and Practice* (New York, 1927), p. 41.

"observant Israelite": *Hebrew Standard*, April 1, 1910, p. 4.

"The Hebrew Race": Quoted in Susan Strasser, *Satisfaction Guaranteed: The Making of the American Mass Market* (New York, 1989), p. 14.

188 "odor repelling": Advertisement for Uneeda Biscuits, AH, April 15, 1910, p. 725.

"eating festivals": Herbert Gans, "American Jewry: Present and Future," *Commentary*, May 1956, p. 429.

189 "tempting": "Free Booklet for Passover," *Outlook*, vol. 22, no. 3, March 1952, p. 14. See also The B. Manischewitz Co., *Tempting Kosher Dishes*, third ed. (1930).

"matzoh monotony": Gella Block, "Pesach Means Springtime," *Jewish Life*, vol. 18, no. 4, April–May 1951, p. 61.

"unusual recipe-consciousness": The Rumford Company, *What Shall I Serve?* p. 2.

190 "Ask you grocer": JDF, Aug. 3, 1921, p. 2. See also "$500 in Prizes for the Best Jewish Recipe," JDF, May 4, 1921, p. 2.

Gold Medal cookbook: Washburn-Crosby Co., *The Gold Medal Flour Cookbook* (Minneapolis, 1921), p. 5, collection no. 85/33, Yeshiva University Archives, New York.

"most fastidious": Wolff Brothers, *Yiddish-English Cook Book* (n.p., 1925), Preface.

"A Guide for Jewish Housewives": "Report of Committee on Religious Observance," *Eighth Annual Report, United Synagogue of America*, 1920, p. 85.

"Many who recoil": "Report of the Convention Committee on Religious Observance," *Eighth Annual Report, United Synagogue of America*, 1920, p. 88.

191 **"freedom from trefah":** "Report of Committee on Religious Observance," p. 85.
"promote their products": Clarence Frances, "Foreword" to Jacobs, *The Jewish Culture*.
"The week preceding": Jacobs, *The Jewish Culture*, p. 16.
192 **"for making friends":** Joseph Jacobs, *The Joseph Jacobs Handbook of Familiar Jewish Words and Expressions* (New York, 1954, sixth printing), cover page.
"Some of the customs": General Foods Corporation, *Customs and Traditions of Israel* (New York, 1934), p. 3.
kosher . . . white bread: "Do You Know That," *United Synagogue Recorder*, vol. 7, no. 1, Jan. 1927, p. 28. See also Samuel M. Cohen, "The Great Work of the United Synagogue Reviewed on the Eve of a New Year," *United Synagogue Recorder*, vol. 5, no. 4, Oct. 1925, pp. 18–19.
"Challoh that you will produce": "Introducing the Jewish Housewife to Pillsbury's Best XXX Flour," *Hebrew Standard*, Feb. 14, 1919, p. 10.
"It makes a challoh": *Hebrew Standard*, Feb. 21, 1919, p. 10.
"See how smoothly": "Orthodox Women Hail New White Kosher Shortening," *Orthodox Union*, vol. 3, no. 11, July–Aug. 1936, p. 7; and *Orthodox Union*, vol. 3, no. 12, Sept. 1937, p. 18, where the caption reads: "The Rebetzin [rabbi's wife] also uses Spry."
193 **"beef frye":** Irving Davidson, "Kashruth in the Day of Paper Plates and 'Beef Frye,'" *Brooklyn Jewish Center Review*, vol. 16, no. 9, Oct. 1935, p. 14.
"But what is there in bacon": Rosenfeld, "Adam and Eve on Delancey Street," p. 385.
"to fortify Jewish merchants": Davidson, "Kashruth," p. 14.
"Due to misstatements": Jacobs, *The Jewish Culture*, p. 21.
"American technology": Gans, "American Jewry," p. 429.
Isaac Gellis: Advertisement, *Brooklyn Jewish Center Review*, vol. 16, no. 33, April 1933, p. 15.
Horowitz Bros.: Advertisement, *Outlook*, vol. 5, no. 3, March 1935, p. 12.
195 **"Reading correctly":** "How Kosher Soup Started," March 1975, Clipping from I. Rokeach & Sons, Inc., Rokeach Company Files; "History and Description of Business," typescript manuscript, n.d., Rokeach Company Files; "I. Rokeach Now Celebrating Its 99th Year," Clipping from *B'nai B'rith Messenger*, Oct. 4, 1968. I'd like to thank Mr. Isaac Levine for sharing this material with me.
canned food: Gersh, "Mama's Cooking," p. 368.
"You may insure yourself": "Has Matzoh a Taste?" *Hebrew Standard*, Feb. 20, 1920, p. 7; "The Case for Horowitz Matzoh," *Hebrew Standard*, March 26, 1920, p. 7.
"kosher in the true sense": Advertisement, United Synagogue of America, *Directory of Kosher Hotels, Boarding Houses and Restaurants in the United States* (New York, 1919), p. 8.
196 **baker and butcher quotes:** Advertising fliers, Peter Schweitzer Collection.
"sun-flooded factories": I. Rokeach & Sons, *The Rokeach Recipe Book* (New York, 1933), n.p. See also Kirshenblatt-Gimblett, "Kitchen Judaism," p. 95. Manischewitz's factory, in turn, was touted as a "Temple of Kashruth, a palace of cleanliness" (*Hebrew Standard*, March 19, 1920, p. 9).
"We have raised": *Hebrew Standard*, Feb. 20, 1920, p. 7.
197 **Manischewitz Experimental Kitchens:** Kirshenblatt-Gimblett, "Kitchen Judaism," p. 93.
The Goldbergs: "Molly's Fish," *The Goldbergs*, 1955–56, National Jewish Archive of Broadcasting, T686, The Jewish Museum. In the mid-fifties, an estimated forty million viewers tuned in once a week to watch Molly Goldberg overcome a seemingly unending series of domestic mishaps. "She has sociology, at least, on her side," observed a fan of the show, attempting to explain its popularity. "There must be many Molly Goldbergs about." (Morris Freedman, "The Real Molly

Goldberg: Baalebosteh of the Airwaves," *Commentary*, April 1956, pp. 359–64, esp. p. 364).

"has become a tradition": Stuhmer Baking Co., *Stuhmer's Almanac, 1939–1940* (New York, 1939), p. 77

198 **"unique relationship":** Jenna Weissman Joselit, "A Set Table: Jewish Domestic Culture in the New World, 1880–1950," in Susan Braunstein and Jenna Weissman Joselit, *Getting Comfortable in New York: The American Jewish Home, 1880–1950* (New York, 1990), pp. 57–58, esp. p. 58.

"unalloyed joy": "Introducing the Jewish Housewife to Pillsbury's Best XXX Flour," p. 10.

"the monetary question": "The Housewife's Problem," *American Jewish Chronicle*, vol. 2, no. 9, Jan. 5, 1917, p. 276.

"Kosher Food Riots": Paula E. Hyman, "Immigrant Women and Consumer Protests: The New York City Kosher Meat Boycott of 1902," *American Jewish History*, vol. 70, no. 1, Sept. 1980, pp. 91–105.

"Some linguistic genius": "Kosher Riots," *American Jewish Chronicle*, vol. 2, no. 22, April 6, 1917, pp. 732–33.

199 **"unjust" increase in the price of bread:** "Women Win Over Bakers," *American Jewish Chronicle*, vol. 1, no. 3, May 26, 1916, p. 94.

201 **"kosher refreshment":** "Kosher Meat," AH, Dec. 16, 1910, p. 199.

"United Synagogue Restaurant": "Report of Committee on Religious Observance," p. 85.

"racial restaurants": "Ratner's Restaurants," unpublished manuscript, Aug. 8, 1940, p. 1, Feeding the City, Works Progress Administration, Historical Records Survey, Federal Writers Project, New York City Municipal Archives (hereafter WPA Collection).

"serve his stomach": Marcus Ravage, *An American in the Making: The Life Story of an Immigrant* (New York, 1917), p. 89.

"Jewish Delmonico's": Advertisement in *Helpful Thoughts*, vol. 3, no. 2, April 1898, p. 31.

"Jewish food customs": Mary L. Schapiro, "Kugel and Zimes," *Jewish Charities*, vol. 9, no. 12, April 1919, p. 267.

"The Jews are fond of good food": Mr. Winans to Mr. Baldwin, April 20, 1932, Jews of New York—Restaurant, Etc., Food, WPA Collection.

202 **"If the writer hesitates":** Adam Gostony, "Jews as Fish-Consumers," unpublished manuscript, Feb. 16, 1942, p. 1, Jews of New York—Restaurant, Etc., Food, WPA Collection.

"special trading inventions": "New York Jews in the Food Industry," unpublished manuscript, ca. 1940, p. 32, Jews of New York—Restaurant, Etc., Food, WPA Collection.

"delicious table delicacies": Storefront Sign, Saperstein Brothers, 1936, Photographic Views of New York, Number 0899-C6, New York Public Library.

"Attractively furnished": "The Appetizing Stores of New York," unpublished manuscript, ca. 1940, p. 1, Jews of New York—Restaurants, Etc., Food, WPA Collection.

"home-made salads": Glazer, "West Bronx," p. 582.

Lower East Side: "Seventh Annual Report on Business and Store Occupancy on the Lower East Side," *East Side Chamber News*, vol. 9, no. 7, July 1936, p. 17.

203 **"Although people of every nationality":** "Appetizing Stores of New York," p. 1.

"their . . . delicate taste": David Pater, "The Delicatessen Field," *Mogen David Delicatessen Magazine*, vol. 1, no. 4, Feb. 1931, p. 11.

"Jewish delicatessen in Hollywood": Orson Welles, "From Mars," *Commentary*, July 1946, p. 70.

"first principle": Glazer, "West Bronx," p. 582. Earlier in the century, Jewish immigrant women were among the first to recognize the utility of delicatessen.

"My mother had noticed the increasing tendency of housewives to spare themselves the labor of cooking by patronizing the delicatessen store," Samuel Chotzinoff recalled in connection with his mother's decision to establish a downtown deli. While her disapproving husband insisted that delicatessen was only a "temporary deviation from normal Jewish eating habits," Mrs. Chotzinoff held her ground. "Only a housewife," she replied, "can have an authoritative opinion on the future of delicatessen." (Samuel Chotzinoff, *A Lost Paradise: Early Reminiscences* [New York, 1955], pp. 182–83).

"appetite, pleasure, purity": "Twenty One Years," *Mogen David Delicatessen Magazine*, vol. 5, no. 6, April 1935, p. 5.

204 "Delicious Delicatessen Dinners": *Mogen David Delicatessen Magazine*, vol. 1, no. 11, Sept. 1931, p. 5; vol. 1, no. 12, Oct. 1931, p. 11.

"I run my house": *Mogen David Delicatessen Magazine*, vol. 1, no. 11, Sept. 1931, p. 11.

"They are more concentrated": Pater, "The Delicatessen Field," p. 11.

"When Milton . . . thought of feasting": Hamlen Hunt, "Today We Eat Leaning," *Commentary*, April 1948, p. 340.

the appropriate "occasion": Glazer, "West Bronx," p. 582.

206 "And now, as the electric sign": Alfred Kazin, *A Walker in the City* (New York, 1951), p. 34.

"Say it with food": *Jewish Folklore and Ethnology Review*, vol. 9, no. 1, 1987, p. 1.

"symbol of . . . Jewish living": Glazer, "The Jewish Delicatessen," p. 63.

208 "No article yet printed": "One Touch of Delicatessen: Symposium on a Jewish Institution," *Commentary*, July 1946, p. 67.

Orson Welles: "From Mars," p. 70.

Daniel Bell: "Chicago, Chicago," *Commentary*, July 1946, p. 71.

Joshua Starr: "Genealogical Note," *Commentary*, July 1946, pp. 70–71.

Louis Berg: "From the Magnolia Country," *Commentary*, July 1946, p. 71.

Charles Yale Harrison: "The Silver Cord," *Commentary*, July 1946, p. 70.

"A place where": Ravage, *American in the Making*, p. 89.

"and much black bread": Typescript notes, "Feeding the City—Jewish," 1940, p. 4, Feeding the City, WPA Collection.

"Mrs. E": Kazin, *Walker*, p. 35.

209 Ratner's portions: "Ratner's Restaurants," p. 2.

210 "the East Side's premier dining place": Advertisement for Ratner's in *East Side Chamber News*, vol. 2, no. 2, Sept. 1928, p. 12.

"desire to be helpful": "Ratner's Restaurants," pp. 1–3.

S & H's: JDF, April 29, 1928, section one, p. 5.

"the best and most nutritious": *Der Tog*, Feb. 28, 1922, p. 7.

Steinberg's: AH, Dec. 9, 1938, p. 24.

211 "Among the happiest moments": *Hebrew Standard*, Dec. 12, 1919, p. 7.

"equal to any": *Hebrew Standard*, Dec. 26, 1919, p. 7.

"elegance—atmosphere—beauty": Advertisement for Paramount Kosher Restaurant, *Orthodox Union*, vol. 12, no. 2, Dec. 1944, p. 20.

"most discriminating": Advertisement for Trotzky's Dining Room, AH, March 27, 1925, p. 602.

"plainly if inconspicuously": "Impressions of Jewish Restaurants," unpublished manuscript, Aug. 9, 1940, p. 1., Feeding the City, WPA Collection.

Brooklyn Jewish Center Restaurant: "Restaurant, 1930–1931," Brooklyn Jewish Center Records, box 27, Ratner Center Archives.

"Make the Center Restaurant": *Brooklyn Jewish Center Review*, vol. 14, no. 12, Nov. 1933, p. 19. See also *Brooklyn Jewish Center Review*, vol. 14, no. 13, Dec. 1933, p. 19.

212 "The temptation": "Eating In," unpublished manuscript, ca. 1940, p. 1, Feeding the City, WPA Collection.

214 " 'Come downtown' ": Joseph Platzker, "Million Dollar Industries on the Lower

East Side—Restaurants," *East Side Chamber News*, vol. 9, no. 1, Jan. 1936, p. 9.

Chinese restaurants: See, for example, Joseph Platzker, "Store Survey of the Lower East Side," *East Side Chamber News*, vol. 8, no. 8, Aug. 1935, p. 17.

World Chop Suey Restaurant: Advertisement in *Der Tog*, March 16, 1917, p. 6.

"dazzling chop suey signs": Felix Mayrowitz, "Golden Jubilee: The Story of Brownsville," *The Menorah Journal*, vol. 14, no. 6, June 1928, p. 589. See also Gaye Tuchman and Harry Gene Levine, "New York Jews and Chinese Food: The Social Construction of an Ethnic Pattern," *Journal of Contemporary Ethnography*, vol. 22, no. 3, Oct. 1993, pp. 382–407.

mah-jongg: Ly Yu Sang, *Sparrow: The Chinese Game Called Ma-Ch'iau: A Descriptive and Explanatory Story* (New York, 1923), p. 19; Frederick Lewis Allen, *Only Yesterday: An Informal History of the 1920s* (New York, 1931), pp. 82–83, 190–91.

215 **"The War":** *Der Tog*, Aug. 20, 1928. I'd like to thank Daniel Soyer for bringing this reference to my attention.

216 **"the question of Kashruth":** Mrs. Jesse Bienenfeld, "Observance of Jewish Dietary Laws," *Outlook*, vol. 9, no. 3, March 1939, p. 7.

"But . . . there are others among us": Max Arzt, "Dr. Kaplan's Philosophy of Judaism," *Proceedings of the Rabbinical Assembly of America*, vol. 5, 1935, p. 215.

"halachic permissibility": Max Arzt, "Is It Permissible to Eat Cooked Vegetables and Broiled Fish in Non-Kosher Restaurants?" undated manuscript, p. 8, RG 27, box 1, folder 6, Ratner Center Archives. See also Julius H. Greenstone, "Report of Committee on Jewish Law," *Proceedings of the Rabbinical Assembly of America*, vol. 5, 1934, p. 102.

"Our preaching": Arzt, "Is It Permissible," p. 9.

"If you will tell them": Meyer Kripke, "Discussion—Towards a Philosophy of Conservative Judaism," *Proceedings of the Rabbinical Assembly of America*, vol. 12, 1948, p. 164.

217 **"eggbeater":** Ruth Glazer, "Holiday Cook," *Commentary*, March 1956, p. 294. Another reviewer, referring several years earlier to Leah Leonard's *Jewish Cookery*, allowed as how "there will be no temptation to serve non-kosher recipes after reading the tempting dishes to be found in this volume" ("Outlook on Books," *Outlook*, vol. 20, no. 3, March 1950, p. 22).

"informal Judaica": "Book Reviewers in This Issue," *Commentary*, March 1956, p. 299.

"added bustle": Glazer, "Holiday Cook," p. 294.

"every child should have": Advertisement for *Junior Jewish Cook Book*, in *Outlook*, vol. 22, no. 3, March 1957, p. 23.

"Innocent sociology": Glazer, "Holiday Cook," p. 294.

variations: Leah Leonard, *Jewish Holiday Cook Book*, cited in Glazer, "Holiday Cook," p. 295.

"Jewish cooking is here to stay": Rose B. Goldstein, "A Balanced Jewish Diet," *Outlook*, vol. 27, no. 4, May 1957, pp. 25–26.

CHAPTER SIX: THE CALL OF THE MATZOH

219 **"Ladies, it's time":** Gella Block, "Pesach Means Springtime," *Jewish Life*, vol. 18, no. 4, April–May, 1951, p. 61.

"the array of . . . foods": Rose B. Goldstein, "A Balanced Jewish Diet," *Outlook*, vol. 27, no. 4, May 1957, p. 25.

220 **"prince of Jewish festivals":** *Hebrew Standard*, March 26, 1915, p. 1.

"giant of Jewish holidays": E. L. Doctorow, *World's Fair* (New York, 1985), pp. 102–3.

221 **"matrons' week of trial":** AH, April 9, 1909, p. 611.

"where other nationalities": *Tageblatt*, April 20, 1910, p. 4.

Bloomingdales: AH, April 6, 1900, p. 667.

Macy's: AH, March 12, 1915, p. 507; March 13, 1925, p. 560.
Loeser's Linen: AH, April 14, 1930, p. 730.
"alive with business": "The Business in the Jewish District," *Hebrew Standard*, April 6, 1900, p. 6.
"Passover Eve on the East Side": Cited in *Hebrew Standard*, April 21, 1905, cover page and p. 8.
"Last Minute Photos": Jenna Weissman Joselit, "A Set Table: Jewish Domestic Culture in the New World, 1880–1950," in Susan Braunstein and Jenna Weissman Joselit, eds., *Getting Comfortable in New York: The American Jewish Home, 1880–1950* (New York, 1990), p. 43.
222 **"Pesach is coming!":** Mrs. Samuel Spiegel, "How Swiftly the Seasons Roll!" *United Synagogue Recorder*, vol. 8, no. 2, April 1928, p. 20.
223 **"Avoid Household Cares":** *Hebrew Standard*, March 19, 1915, p. 11.
"avoiding the usual annoyance": *Hebrew Standard*, March 19, 1915, p. 5.
"true Passover emotion": "The Seder," *United Synagogue Recorder*, vol. 8, no. 2, April 1928, p. 1.
"Do not close your home": Spiegel, "How Swiftly," p. 20.
225 **"That most characteristic of . . . celebrations":** Jacob Kohn, *Modern Problems of Jewish Parents: A Study in Parental Attitudes* (New York, 1932), p. 98. See also Max Arzt, "President's Message," *Proceedings of the Rabbinical Assembly of America*, vol. 7, 1940, p. 81; Charles J. Freund, "Character-Building and the Home," *CCAR Year Book*, vol. 25, 1915, p. 320.
"The growing generation": "The Seder," p. 1.
Jews "may forget the furnishings": Mrs. Nathan Lubin, "Passover, a Joy or a Burden," *Outlook*, vol. 16, no. 3, March 1946, p. 7.
226 **"The children were amused":** Philip Cowen, *Memories of an American Jew* (New York, 1932), p. 410.
227 **"sumptuous" . . . "ambrosial":** Betty D. Greenberg and Althea O. Silverman, *The Jewish Home Beautiful* (New York, 1945), pp. 71, 109.
"a certain playful solemnity": Ruth Glazer, "West Bronx: Food, Shelter, Clothing—The Abundant Life Just Off the Grand Concourse," *Commentary*, June 1949, p. 579.
"call of the matzoh": "Passover Cooking," AH, April 15, 1911, p. 725.
"the other great Emancipator": Spiegel, "How Swiftly," p. 20.
"Family reunion": Mrs. David A. Goldstein, "My Mother's Passover," *Outlook*, vol. 22, no. 3, March 1952, p. 17.
"Picturesque ceremonial": *Tageblatt*, April 13, 1900, English-language page.
228 **holiday of "kinship":** Esther Jane Ruskay, *Hearth and Home Essays* (Philadelphia, 1902), p. 76.
229 **"It is the good fortune":** Mrs. David Goldstein, "More about Hanukkah in the Home," *Outlook*, vol. 22, no. 2, Dec. 1951, p. 16. An earlier version of this material appeared in Jenna Weissman Joselit, "Merry Chanuka: The Changing Holiday Practices of American Jews, 1880–1950," in Jack Wertheimer, ed., *The Uses of Tradition: Jewish Continuity in the Modern Era* (New York, 1992), pp. 303–25.
"competitive winter sport": Grace Goldin, "Christmas-Chanukah: December Is the Cruelest Month," *Commentary*, Nov. 1950, p. 417.
230 **"is a step":** "Hanukkah in American Judaism," AH, Dec. 20, 1935, p. 1.
"The customary candles": Gustav Gottheil, "What Christians Owe the Maccabees," *Jewish Messenger*, Jan. 4, 1884, p. 6.
"Not even the Zionists": Nathan H. Lemowitz, "Jewish Pupils in Public Schools," *American Jewish Chronicle*, vol. 1, no. 17, Sept. 1, 1916, p. 521.
"I was losing track": Marcus Ravage, *An American in the Making* (New York, 1917), p. 118.
"Kindle the Chanukah lights": Kaufmann Kohler, "Chanuka and Christmas," *The Menorah*, vol. 9, no. 6, Dec. 1890, p. 306.

"just for the experiment": "Hanukkah Lights," *Jewish Messenger*, Dec. 3, 1880, p. 4. See also *American Jewish Chronicle*, vol. 2, no. 7, Dec. 22, 1916, p. 195.

"Jewish young folks": Lemowitz, "Jewish Pupils."

231 **"theological implications":** Maurice Harris, "Why Should Jewish Children Not Have Christmas Trees?" *Helpful Thoughts*, vol. 6, no. 4, Dec. 1900, pp. 140–41.

"no one who has": Kohler, "Chanuka and Christmas," p. 306.

232 **The Yiddish press on Christmas:** See, for example, JDF, Dec. 24, 1910, p. 6; Dec. 25, 1910, p. 5; Dec. 26, 1910, p. 4.

"Who says we haven't": "Pious They May Be but They Still Observe Christmas," JDF, Dec. 25, 1904, p. 4.

"How can the Jew": Kohler, "Chanuka and Christmas," pp. 307 ff.

"joy in the Christmas tree": *American Jewish Chronicle*, vol. 2, no. 7, Dec. 22, 1916, p. 195.

no "excuse": Emil G. Hirsch, "How the Jew Regards Christmas," *Ladies Home Journal*, vol. 24, no. 1, Dec. 1906, p. 10.

233 **"vigorous story":** Louis Grossman, *The Hanukkah Festival: Outline of Lessons for Teachers* (Cincinnati, 1914), p. 9.

"How humble": Kohler, "Chanuka and Christmas," p. 305.

"gives a zest to life": Esther Jane Ruskay, *Hearth and Home Essays*, p. 37.

"ignorance of racial properties": Esther Jane Ruskay, *Hearth and Home Essays*, p. 40.

"Modest" Chanukah: *Tageblatt*, Dec. 19, 1900, p. 4.

"The Greatest Bargain": *Der Tog*, Dec. 12, 1925, p. 7.

"Chanukah Pleasures": *Morgen Zhurnal*, Dec. 8, 1920, p. 10.

234 **"best flour":** *Der Tog*, Dec. 9, 1925, p. 6.

"latkes and Modern Science": *Der Tog*, Dec. 19, 1919, p. 10.

"time-hallowed practice": Miriam Isaacs and Trude Weiss Rosmarin, *What Every Jewish Woman Should Know: A Guide for Jewish Women* (New York, 1941), p. 50.

"Save for Chanukah": *Der Tog*, Dec. 14, 1925, p. 6.

Libby Hotel stock: *Der Tog*, Dec. 14, 1925, p. 6. See also Viviana Zelizer, *The Social Meaning of Money* (New York, 1994), esp. chap. three, pp. 71–118.

Editorials accompanied: "Chanukah Must Become a True Children's Holiday," *Morgen Zhurnal*, Dec. 14, 1925, p. 5.

235 **"Aunt Mollie Came for Chanukah":** Sara G. Levy, *Mother Goose Rhymes for Jewish Children* (New York, 1945), pp. 28–29. See also Abraham Burstein, *Too Much Noise: A Chanukah Play for Boys* (New York, 1924).

"Chanukah is Gift Time": *Jewish Life*, vol. 20, no. 2, Nov.–Dec. 1952, pp. 68 ff.

"If ever lavishness": Isaacs and Weiss Rosmarin, *What Every Jewish Woman*, p. 50.

"Mah-jong sets": *Hadassah Newsletter*, Dec. 1940–Jan. 1941, p. 26.

236 **In one . . . household of the 1920s:** Personal communication, Dec. 7, 1992.

"many new and beautiful": Goldstein, "More about Hanukkah," p. 16.

237 **it "always gleams":** "The House of Zion for the Ideal Chanukah Gift," *New York Post*, Dec. 2, 1942.

"Every Jewish boy and girl": Morris Freedman, "Sweets for Heterodox New York: The Story of Barton's," *Commentary*, May 1952, p. 478.

"a real live character": A. W. Binder, *Chanukah Songster* (New York, 1922), Foreword.

"very marked and singingly": Binder, *Chanukah Songster*, p. 10.

238 **"musical vision":** Binder, *Chanukah Songster*, p. 7.

"A Hanukkah Party": Emily Solis-Cohen, *Hanukkah: The Feast of Lights* (Philadelphia, 1937), pp. 333–35.

"The Jewish woman": Isaacs and Weiss Rosmarin, *What Every Jewish Woman*, p. 51.

"bright with candle lights": Betty Greenberg and Althea O. Silverman, *The Jewish Home Beautiful* (New York, 1941), p. 24.

239 **a "period for mirth":** Greenberg and Silverman, *The Jewish Home Beautiful*, pp. 52, 69–70.

"Maccabean sandwiches": Joselit, "A Set Table," p. 64.

"Menorah fruit salad": Greenberg and Silverman, *The Jewish Home Beautiful*, pp. 70, 101.

latkes: Isaacs and Weiss Rosmarin, *What Every Jewish Woman*, p. 51.

"value of latkes": Betty Greenberg, "Chanukah Ramblings and Reflections," *Outlook*, vol. 7, no. 2, Dec. 1936, p. 3.

"Just in Time": *Jewish Life*, vol. 19, no. 2, Nov.–Dec. 1951, p. 68.

"chocolate elephants and lions": Samuel H. Markowitz, *Leading a Jewish Life in the Modern World* (New York, 1958), p. 219.

"Let this be": Goldstein, "More about Hanukkah," p. 30.

"cruel month": Goldin, "Christmas-Chanukah," p. 416.

"better facilities": Sarah L. Kopelman, "President's Page," *Outlook*, vol. 20, no. 2, Dec. 1949, p. 3.

"loveliness of the day": Louis Witt, "The Jew Celebrates Christmas," *The Christian Century*, vol. 56, Dec. 6, 1939, p. 1499.

survey of holiday practices: Milton Matz, "The Meaning of the Christmas Tree to the American Jew," *Jewish Journal of Sociology*, vol. 3, no. 1, June 1961, pp. 129–37.

240 **"antidote" to Christmas:** Goldin, "Christmas-Chanukah," p. 417.

"Hanukkah is only one": Abraham Segal, "Christmas in the Public School—The Problem," *The Reconstructionist*, vol. 14, no. 16, Dec. 10, 1948, p. 22.

241 **"the Jewish Christmas":** Marshall Sklare and Joseph Greenbaum, *Jewish Identity on the Suburban Frontier*, second ed. (Chicago, 1979), p. 58.

"cultural oneness": Thomas A. Clemente, "Double or Nothing," *Commonweal*, vol. 53, no. 11, Dec. 22, 1950, p. 274. See also "Committee on Church and State," *CCAR Year Book*, vol. 59, 1949, p. 84.

"Midwinter Festival": See, for example, *20th Anniversary Pamphlet, Henry Street Settlement, 1893–1913* (New York, 1913), p. 29.

"holiday assembly": Clemente, "Double or Nothing," pp. 273–74.

Chanukah's "transfiguration": Goldin, "Christmas-Chanukah," p. 417.

"back-door means": "Chanukah," *Jewish Life*, vol. 20, no. 2, Nov.–Dec. 1952, pp. 5–6.

242 **Young Judea:** "Leader's Manual of Programs and Projects for 1931–1932/5692, Prepared by Ben M. Edidin for Young Judea," p. 23, Young Judea Collection, Hadassah National Archives, New York.

"The character of the holiday": Goldin, "Christmas-Chanukah," p. 417.

"need to compensate": Goldstein, "More about Hanukkah," p. 16.

reliance on "borrowings": "Chanukah," *Jewish Life*, pp. 5–6.

"Recently, the observance": Emma Bienenfeld, "Days of Dedication—Days of Light," *Outlook*, vol. 6, no. 2, Dec. 1935, p. 3.

243 **"It all goes to show":** Albert Gordon, *Jews in Transition* (Minneapolis, 1949), p. 117.

"holiday consciousness": Emil Lehman, "National Survey Charting Synagogue Attendance," United Synagogue of America, 1950, p. 53.

"too close proximity": Joseph Krauskopf, "A Change of Confirmation Day," *CCAR Year Book*, vol. 22, 1912, pp. 323, 328.

"has . . . been neglected": Isaacs and Weiss Rosmarin, *What Every Jewish Woman*, p. 44.

245 **"Jewish mothers who pity":** Isaacs and Weiss Rosmarin, *What Every Jewish Woman*, p. 45.

miniaturized sukkah: Samuel H. Markowitz, *Leading a Jewish Life*, pp. 182–83.

"Conscious of ourselves": Esther Jane Ruskay, *Hearth and Home Essays*, p. 32.

annual Purim Ball: See, for example, *Annual Report, Beth Israel Hospital*, 1907, p. 28.

246 "holiday of merriment": Isaacs and Weiss Rosmarin, *What Every Jewish Woman*, p. 52.

"Jewish women's special holiday": Isaacs and Weiss Rosmarin, *What Every Jewish Woman*, p. 52.

"womanly practice": Greenberg and Silverman, *The Jewish Home Beautiful*, p. 27.

"It is quite appropriate": Isaacs and Weiss Rosmarin, *What Every Jewish Woman*, p. 54.

"season and sentiment": Krauskopf, "A Change of Confirmation Day," p. 327.

"vacation habit": "The Ghetto and the Summer Resorts," *American Israelite*, Aug. 20, 1903, p. 3.

"happy holiday": Isaacs and Weiss Rosmarin, *What Every Jewish Woman*, p. 60.

247 "Holiday consciousness is on the wane": Lehman, "National Survey," p. 53.

"neither-here-nor-there attitude": "The Yom Kippur Jews," AH, Aug. 25, 1905, p. 346.

249 "new custom": "New Year Greetings: The Development of a New Custom," AH, Aug. 18, 1905, p. 325.

"tawdry and bedizened": "New Year Greetings," p. 325.

"Uniongrams": "Report of the National Committee on Uniongrams," *Proceedings, Third Biennial Meeting, National Federation of Temple Sisterhoods*, 1919, p. 56.

"same difficulty": "New Year Greetings," p. 325.

251 "The only way . . . to reach all your friends": *Jewish Times* (Baltimore), Aug. 22, 1930, p. 27.

Alfred: *Jewish Times* (Baltimore), Sept. 19, 1930, p. 77.

"we are too prone to magnify": Mrs. Caesar Misch, "Address of the National President," *Proceedings of the Council of Jewish Women, Sixth Triennial Convention*, 1911, p. 52.

252 "a sign of the degeneration": Isaacs and Weiss Rosmarin, *What Every Jewish Woman*, p. 40.

"sabbathless" behavior: Israel Harburg, "Observance of Sabbath," *CCAR Year Book*, vol. 47, 1937, p. 327.

253 "Not all Jewish working men": *American Jewish Chronicle*, vol. 1, no. 7, June 23, 1916, p. 194.

Jennie Grossman's husband: Neil Cowan and Ruth Schwartz Cowan, *Our Parents' Lives* (New York, 1989), p. 275.

Wilkes-Barre . . . synagogue: Jack Wertheimer, "The Conservative Synagogue," in Jack Wertheimer, ed., *The American Synagogue: A Sanctuary Transformed* (New York, 1987), p. 120.

"Sabbath consciousness": Isaacs and Weiss Rosmarin, *What Every Jewish Woman*, p. 34.

"habitual": Mrs. David A. Goldstein, "The Sabbath in America," *Outlook*, vol. 11, no. 4, May 1941, p. 14.

"Alas, today": Israel Levinthal, "What the Sabbath Meant to the Jew," Feb. 18, 1916, Sermons and Addresses, Israel Levinthal Collection, Ratner Center Archives, Jewish Theological Seminary of America, New York (hereafter Ratner Center Archives).

"No honest observer": Goldstein, "The Sabbath in America," p. 14.

Sabbath-attendance statistics: Lehman, "National Survey," p. 9.

"Our rabbis are . . . admitting": Hannah G. Solomon, "President's Address," *Proceedings of the Council of Jewish Women, Third Triennial Convention*, 1902, p. 11.

254 "woman's institution": Israel Levinthal, "The Synagogue and Jewish Womanhood," March 17, 1922, Sermons and Addresses, Israel Levinthal Collection, Ratner Center Archives.

"Under modern conditions": Deborah Melamed, *The Three Pillars: Thought, Practice and Worship for Jewish Women* (New York, 1927), p. 67.

"must 'educate' her husband": Samuel H. Markowitz, *Leading a Jewish Life*, p. 119.

"It requires hard thinking": Isaacs and Weiss Rosmarin, *What Every Jewish Woman*, p. 35.

"spiritual wrong": Mathilde Schechter, "A Plea for Jewish Ceremonials," a 1904 address republished in *Outlook*, vol. 17, no. 4, May 1947, p. 5.

"shopping on Shabbos": Israel Levinthal, "The Synagogue and Jewish Womanhood."

"We pledge": *Proceedings of 4th Biennial Meeting, National Federation of Temple Sisterhoods*, 1921, p. 72. See also Jenna Weissman Joselit, "The Special Sphere of the Middle-Class American Jewish Woman: The Synagogue Sisterhood, 1890–1940," in Jack Wertheimer, ed., *The American Synagogue: A Sanctuary Transformed* (New York, 1987), pp. 206–30.

255 **Sabbath-observance statistics:** Albert Gordon, "Towards a Philosophy of Conservative Judaism," *Proceedings of the Rabbinical Assembly of America*, vol. 12, 1948, p. 158.

"The principal thing": Leah Morton, *I Am a Woman—And a Jew* (New York, 1926), p. 230.

"King Canute": Simon Greenberg, "President's Message," *Proceedings of the Rabbinical Assembly of America*, vol. 6, 1939, p. 27.

"*sine qua non* of Jewish . . . loyalty": Harburg, "Observance of Sabbath," p. 330.

"the temple-going habit": *24th Annual Report, National Federation of Temple Sisterhoods*, 1937, p. 103; "Report of the President," *15th Annual Report, National Federation of Temple Sisterhoods*, 1927, p. 15.

"lost cause": Lehman, "National Survey," p. 41.

"On Sunday mornings": Edna Ferber, *A Peculiar Treasure* (New York, 1939), p. 180.

256 **the "next best" thing:** Nathan Kollin, "Religion and the Home—Discussion," *Proceedings of the Rabbinical Assembly of America*, vol. 7, 1940, p. 205.

"In the pews": Morton, *I Am a Woman*, p. 238.

families . . . as a "unit": Lehman, "National Survey," p. 9.

"too much jewelry": Morton, *I Am a Woman*, p. 238.

"Paradoxical and outrageous": Lehman, "National Survey," p. 10.

"avoidable work": Rabbi Jacob Agus, "The Revitalization of the Sabbath," *Proceedings of the Rabbinical Assembly of America*, vol. 15, 1951, p. 106.

Sabbath Institute, Norwich: "Our Branches," *Outlook*, vol. 23, no. 2, Dec. 1952, p. 20.

257 **Sabbath Institute, Miami:** "Our Branches," *Outlook*, vol. 23, no. 3, March 1953, p. 23.

258 **"know-how and know-why":** "Unroll the Scroll," *Outlook*, vol. 25, no. 3, March 1955, p. 5.

"heartwarming and gratifying": "National Sabbath Observance Effort," *Outlook*, vol. 22, no. 2, Dec. 1951, p. 5.

"Large segments": "Responsum on the Sabbath," *Proceedings of the Rabbinical Assembly of America*, vol. 14, 1950, p. 121.

"realities of modern life": "Responsum on the Sabbath," p. 120.

"positive values": "Responsum on the Sabbath," p. 132.

"Actually, the question": Meyer Kripke, "Towards a Philosophy of Conservative Judaism," *Proceedings of the Rabbinical Assembly of America*, vol. 12, 1948, p. 164.

"I have been waiting": Simon Greenberg, "The Revitalization of the Sabbath—Discussion," *Proceedings of the Rabbinical Assembly of America*, vol. 15, 1951, p. 114.

259 **"Sabbath-minded":** Harburg, "Observance of the Sabbath," p. 338.

"temporal map": Eviatar Zerubavel, *Hidden Rhythms: Schedules and Calendars in Social Life* (Chicago, 1981), p. 14.

"although the Sabbath": Glazer, "West Bronx," p. 579.

"spiritual nourishment": Israel Levinthal, "What the Sabbath Meant to the Jew."

"All week we're rushing about": Mrs. Jen S. Margolies, "Shabbat Shalom," *Outlook*, vol. 23, no. 2, Dec. 1952, p. 10.

"Let us keep": "Report of the Committee on Religion," *Proceedings of the Council of Jewish Women, Second Triennial Convention*, 1900, p. 77.
"Kindling the Sabbath lights": Markowitz, *Leading a Jewish Life*, p. 141.
"jolly welcome": Israel Levinthal, "What the Sabbath Meant to the Jew."
260 **"It seems to me":** *Proceedings of the 1950 Biennial Convention of Women's League*, p. 58.
"Mental uneasiness": "Responsum on the Sabbath," p. 116.
"brain-sufferers": Israel Levinthal, "What the Sabbath Meant to the Jew."
"quickens the spirit": "Responsum on the Sabbath," p. 116.
"Affection is a living . . . experience": Leon Lang, "Jewish Family Living and the Sabbath," *Conservative Judaism*, vol. 8, no. 4, June 1952, p. 10.
261 **"never . . . a dull Sabbath":** Isaacs and Weiss Rosmarin, *What Every Jewish Woman*, p. 38.
262 **"So start your little club":** "Foundation Stones of Judaism," *Helpful Thoughts*, vol. 1, no. 4, May 1896, p. 35.
"But . . . the real objective": Mrs. Reuben Weilerstein, "Living a Jewish Life Through Your Child," *Outlook*, vol. 1, no. 5, June 1931, p. 2.
"Let them have a party": Mrs. S. J. Winer, "Coordinating Jewish Training in Home and School," *Outlook*, vol. 3, no. 1, Sept. 1932, p. 2. See also Trude Weiss Rosmarin, ed., *The Oneg Shabbath Book* (New York, 1940).
"prospect is bright": Goldstein, "The Sabbath in America."
263 **like fine silver:** Mrs. Henry Gichner, "Speaking for the East," *Proceedings of the 1948 Biennial Convention of Women's League*, p. 2, Women's League Archives.

CHAPTER SEVEN: A LAST FAREWELL

265 **"Don't people die":** Sholom Aleichem, "Beryl Isaac and the Wonders of America," in Melech Grafstein, ed., *Sholom Aleichem Panorama* (London and Ontario, 1948), p. 173.
"sham and show": Rabbi Leo Franklin, "A Few Words about Funeral Reforms," *CCAR Year Book*, vol. 7, 1898, p. 48.
"created their own death-style": Stuart E. Rosenberg, *The Real Jewish World: A Rabbi's Second Thoughts* (New York, 1984), p. 168.
"When Death strikes": Albert Gordon, *In Times of Sorrow: A Manual for Mourners* (New York, 1949), p. 1.
266 **"The free-thinking, non-partisan funeral":** B. Z. Goldberg, "In the Course of the Day: On Funerals," *Der Tog*, Feb. 23, 1949, p. 6.
"When death occurs": "The Funeral," AH, Feb. 7, 1930, p. 492.
"annoying details": John C. Gebhart, *Funeral Costs* (New York, 1928), p. 20.
"To move people about": Robert Habenstein and William Lamers, *The History of American Funeral Directing* (Milwaukee, 1955), pp. 385 ff.
"that quality of considerateness": "The Funeral," AH, Feb. 7, 1930, p. 492.
"It is a comfort": Riverside Memorial Chapel, *Prayers* (New York, 1929), p. 24.
"American way of death": James J. Farrell, *Inventing the American Way of Death, 1830–1920* (Philadelphia, 1980).
"ritual novelties": Rosenberg, *The Real Jewish World*, p. 169.
"were unusually economical": Gebhart, *Funeral Costs*, pp. xx, 147.
268 **"religious tradition of simplicity":** Gebhart, *Funeral Costs*, p. 120.
"In the early days": Cited in Albert Gordon, *Jews in Transition* (Minneapolis, 1949), p. 142.
"the presence of flowers": Alexander Laurie, *The Flower Shop* (Chicago, 1930), p. 99. See also Chicago Florists Publication, *Funeral Flowers: Albums of Designs* (Chicago, 1934).
"funeral offerings": Laurie, *The Flower Shop*, p. 119.
"It is the essence of the modern funeral": Farrell, *Inventing the American Way of Death*, p. 161.

"In architecture": AH, Jan. 3, 1930, p. 356.

269 **"beauty softens grief":** AH, Nov. 16, 1928, p. 70.

"This building contains": Riverside Memorial Chapel, *Prayers*, p. 3.

"dignified beauty": Riverside Memorial Chapel, *Prayers*, p. 3.

270 **"last farewell":** "A Personal Message," Brooks Funeral Home, *Memorial Prayers*, (Bridgeton, N.J., n.d.), p. 2.

the Jewish funeral home: See, for example, Arthur Goren, "Traditional Institutions Transplanted: The Hevra Kadisha in Europe and America," in Moses Rischin, ed., *The Jews of North America* (Detroit, 1987), pp. 62–78.

271 **"This development":** "The Funeral," AH, Jan. 3, 1930, p. 356.

"Our modern equipment": "A Personal Message," p. 2.

"With cherished memories": AH, Dec. 7, 1928, p. 222.

"All too frequently": Gordon, *In Times of Sorrow*, p. 1.

"I cannot find": "Chaos in Burial Customs," AH, Feb. 7, 1930, p. 486.

272 **"funeral parlor rabbi":** Jacob Freedman, "The Problem of the 'Free Lance' Rabbis in America," *Proceedings of the Rabbinical Assembly of America*, vol. 5, 1938, p. 487.

"species of easygoing rabbis": Mordecai M. Kaplan Diaries, Dec. 22, 1956, p. 191, Jewish Theological Seminary of America Archives.

"Would you allow": Cited in Samuel Dresner, *The Jew in American Life* (New York, 1963), p. 33.

"simplicity and equality in funerals": Samuel Dresner, "Simplicity and Equality in Funerals," *United Synagogue Review*, vol. 14, no. 1, Spring 1961, p. 8.

"vigorous protest": Joseph Stolz, "Funeral Agenda," *CCAR Year Book*, vol. 7, 1898, p. 39.

"senseless extravagance": "Substituting Contributions for Flowers," *Second Biennial Convention, National Federation of Temple Sisterhoods*, 1917, p. 53. See also "Report of the National Committee on Scholarship," *Proceedings of the Fifth Biennial Assembly, National Federation of Temple Sisterhoods*, 1923, p. 73; *CCAR Year Book*, vol. 25, 1915, p. 132.

"display of every kind": Franklin, "A Few Words about Funeral Reforms," p. 50.

"From the Jewish custom": Mrs. J. Schwartz, "Memorial Fund," *Proceedings, Council of Jewish Women*, 1914, p. 143.

273 **"Let the women of Israel":** Schwartz, "Memorial Fund," p. 144.

"charming courtesy": Schwartz, "Memorial Fund," p. 143.

"A funeral should not be like a meeting": Goldberg, "In the Course of the Day," p. 6.

"Propriety should rule": Stolz, "Funeral Agenda," p. 41.

"sarcophagus monuments": "What Is Jewish Burial?" *United Synagogue Recorder*, vol. 2, no. 2, April 1922, p. 4.

"Deeds, not stones": Stolz, "Funeral Agenda," p. 39.

"simplicity is the outstanding feature": "What Is Jewish Burial?" p. 4.

"beautiful mortuary memorials": AH, Dec. 30, 1910, p. 271.

Solomon Rich's monument: Documents and photographs of this monument can be found in Peter H. Schweitzer's private collection of Jewish Americana.

274 **"A strange place":** David Einhorn, "Picnics among the Graves at the Jewish Cemeteries," JDF, Nov. 19, 1949, p. 3.

275 **"Most of the complaints":** Harry Gersh, "The Kauliper B. and S.B.S. of New York—Social Security Through the 'Landsmanshaften,' " *Commentary*, vol. 8, no. 5, Nov. 1949, p. 473.

"imposing, yet not gaudy or proud": "First Jewish Mausoleum Lays Cornerstone," AH, March 21, 1930, p. 691.

"Come and plan": AH, March 7, 1930, p. 607.

276 **"Far-Thinking Men and Women":** AH, March 7, 1930, p. 607. Most traditional Jews were opposed to cremation and adopted "an attitude of antagonism" toward the practice. For Reform Jews, however, the issue was open to discussion. As early as the 1890s, the Central Conference of American Rabbis debated whether

"cremation is in accord with the spirit of Judaism." Some argued that it ran counter to Jewish tradition and hence could not be sanctioned; others were far less certain. One rabbi went so far as to recommend that the issue be discussed "not by a conference of rabbis . . . but by physicians and professors in medical colleges, by conferences of scholars who understand the science of hygienics." Ultimately, the Reform movement resolved that should rabbis be invited to officiate at a cremation service, they "ought not to refuse on the plea that cremation be anti-Jewish or irreligious." See Louis Epstein, "Report of the Committee on Jewish Law," *Proceedings of the Rabbinical Assembly of America*, vol. 6, 1939, p. 156; Dr. B. Felsenthal, "On Cremation from a Jewish Standpoint," *CCAR Year Book*, vol. 2, 1891–92, pp. 53–68, esp. pp. 67–68.

"beautifully laid out": Advertisement for the Riverside Cemetery, AH, May 14, 1915, p. 44.

"Its light and comfort": Advertisement for Montefiore's Temple of Rest, AH, April 4, 1930, p. 777.

"book of views": Advertisement for Woodlawn Cemetery, AH, May 14, 1915, p. 44. See also "A Word about Woodlawn," AH, Nov. 18, 1910, p. 84.

a Jewish "Valhalla": Quoted in Goren, "Traditional Institutions Transplanted," p. 74.

A "new country": S. Druckerman, *Reverend's Hand Book and Speaker's Supplement for Various Occasions* (New York, 1923), p. 149.

"pilgrims": Jewish Ministers' Association, *The Burial of the Dead: A Handbook for Ministers* (New York, 1890), p. 12.

"separate, specialized landscape": Kenneth Ames, "Ideologies in Stone: Meanings in Victorian Gravestones," *Journal of Popular Culture*, vol. 14, no. 4, Spring 1981, p. 651.

278 "purely American": Abraham G. Duker, "Emerging Culture Patterns in American Jewish Life: The Psycho-Cultural Approach to the Study of Jewish Life in America," *Proceedings of the American Jewish Historical Society*, vol. 39, Sept. 1949–June 1950, p. 372.

"Reached by Brooklyn 'L' ": "Jewish Cemeteries," *Jewish Communal Register of New York* (New York, 1918), p. 337.

Euclid Hotel: "Yearly Calendar—Compliments of the Euclid Hotel," 1904, Peter H. Schweitzer Collection.

"We Cater Shivahs": Quoted in Samuel H. Dresner, "The Scandal of the Jewish Funeral," *The Jew in American Life* (New York, 1963), p. 26.

279 "afternoon cocktail party": Cited in Dresner, "The Scandal," p. 29.

280 "I know that people bring gifts": Correspondence of Mr. C. Weinberg and Rabbi Michael Higger, Nov. 26–Dec. 1, 1950, Committee on Jewish Law and Standards, Rabbinical Assembly Archives.

"Inasmuch as we have . . . abolished": Stolz, "Funeral Agenda," p. 45.

"Do you encourage": "Funeral Practices," p. 15, in Findings of the Committee on Ritual Survey, n.d., Rabbi Simon Greenberg Papers, RG 27, box 2, folder 16, Ratner Center Archives of the Jewish Theological Seminary, New York (hereafter Ratner Center Archives).

281 "fashionable tribulation": Cited in Karen Halttunen, *Confidence Men and Painted Women: A Study of Middle-Class Culture in America, 1830–1970* (New Haven, 1982), p. 142.

"cultural revulsion": Farrell, *Inventing the American Way of Death*, p. 180.

"The rite of *keriah*": "Committee on Jewish Law and Standards," *Proceedings of the Rabbinical Assembly of America*, vol. 23, 1959, p. 116. See also Sanders A. Tofield, "The Rite of Keriah by Means of Ribbon," n.d., typescript manuscript, Committee on Law and Standards, Rabbinical Assembly Archives.

"The mores of our day": "Committee on Jewish Law and Standards," p. 116. See also Martin Berkowitz, *Services of Consolation—With Special Guide to Mourners* (Merion, Pa., 1960), p. 3.

282 **"avoided kaddish like the whirlwind":** Goldberg, "In the Course of the Day," p. 6.
"chief duty": Franklin, "A Few Words about Funeral Reforms," p. 51.
"All day long": Maurice Samuel, "Cantor, Let's Go," *Jews on Approval* (New York, 1932), p. 174.
283 **"Once a day":** Samuel, "Cantor, Let's Go," p. 175.
"Every mourner . . . shouts": Elias Solomon, "Downtown Synagogues," Unpublished manuscript, n.d., p. 5, Elias Solomon Papers, Jewish Theological Seminary Archives.
"The influence of Catholicism": Stolz, "Funeral Agenda," pp. 35 ff.
"Author of all things": Franklin, "A Few Words about Funeral Reforms," p. 52.
"spirit of blind superstition": Franklin, "A Few Words about Funeral Reforms," p. 53.
"be made intelligble": Franklin, "A Few Words about Funeral Reforms," p. 51.
"printed in Latin letters": Samuel, "Cantor, Let's Go," p. 175.
284 **transliterated kaddish:** See, for example, Jewish Ministers Association, *The Burial of the Dead: A Handbook for Ministers* (New York, 1890); New York Board of Jewish Ministers, *The Door of Hope—A Manual of Prayers and Devotional Readings Upon Visiting the Cemetery* (New York, 1898).
"*yizkor* Jews": See "Mourning Customs in General," Report of the Committee on Responsa," *CCAR Year Book*, vol. 23, 1913, p. 179; *CCAR Year Book*, vol. 24, 1914, p. 153. See also Abraham G. Duker, "Emerging Culture Patterns," p. 366; I. Steinbaum, "A Study of the Jewishness of Twenty New York Families," *YIVO Annual*, vol. 5, 1950, pp. 247, 255.
"In a large number": Morris Silverman, "Vitalizing Public Worship," *Proceedings of the Rabbinical Assembly of America*, vol. 7, 1940, p. 160.
"The Yizkor Service": "To You Who Are Here for Yizkor," Congregation B'nai Israel, *Additional Services for Rosh Hashanah and Yom Kippur*, n.d., Peter H. Schweitzer Collection.
285 **"How many have":** Kaufmann Kohler, "Mourning Customs," Report of the Committee on Responsa, *CCAR Year Book*, vol. 33, 1913, p. 179.
286 **"Rolls of Remembrance":** See, for example, Radio City Synagogue, "Roll of Remembrance," n.d., Peter H. Schweitzer Collection.
"I reverently cherish": Temple Adath Israel of the Bronx, Yizkor Memorial Services Postcard, n.d., Peter H. Schweitzer Collection.
"Experience has shown us": "Substituting Contributions for Flowers," p. 53.
"a new source of income": AH, Dec. 8, 1939, p. 51. See also "Artistic Bronze Tablet Co.," *Morgen Zhurnal*, April 2, 1949, p. 2.
"We unveil these plates": Rabbi Simon Greenberg, "For the Unveiling of Memorial Tablets and Plates," typescript address, March 13, 1928, Rabbi Simon Greenberg Papers, RG 27, box 3, folder 3, Ratner Center Archives. See also Jenna Weissman Joselit, *New York's Jewish Jews: The Orthodox Community of the Interwar Years* (Bloomington, 1990), p. 52.
288 **"You do not need":** Advertisement for *Corresponding Date Calendar and Family Record*, Hebrew Publishing Co., n.d., Peter H. Schweitzer Collection.
"This handy volume": Reverend E. M. Myers, *The Centurial: A Jewish Calendar for One Hundred Years, 1890–1990* (New York, 1918).
"solemnizing" the occasion: "Mourning Laws and Customs," Brooks Funeral Home, *Memorial Prayers*, p. 17.
"give us the name and date": Riverside Memorial Chapel, *Prayers and Meditations* (New York, 1939), p. 5.
289 **"Suppose a death":** "To Ascertain the Date of Anniversary of Death (Jahrzeit)," Riverside Memorial Chapel, *Prayers*, p. 41.
290 **"this glass is kosher":** Label copy for the B. Manischewitz Company's Yahrzeit Lamp, n.d., Peter H. Schweitzer Collection.

"pretested bulb": Label copy for the Vogue Company's Flame Glo, n.d., Peter H. Schweitzer Collection.

291 **"Many innovations":** Abraham G. Duker, "Emerging Culture Patterns," p. 374.

"Judaism reduced to a *memento mori*": Samuel, "Cantor, Let's Go," p. 176.

"kaddish Judaism": Israel Goldstein, "The Menace of Secularism in the Synagogue," *Proceedings of the Rabbinical Assembly of America*, vol. 3, 1929, p. 99.

"emptied of one function after another": Robert Gordis, "New Vistas for Conservative Judaism," *Proceedings of the Rabbinical Assembly of America*, vol. 10, 1946, p. 71.

292 **"death sustains the life":** Tsvi Hirsch Masliansky, *Maslianski's Zikhroynes* (New York, 1924), p. 195.

PAGE — CONCLUSION

293 **"Can a minority":** Rabbi Maurice Harris, "The Dangers of Emancipation," *CCAR Year Book*, vol. 4, 1893, p. 61.

"it was so simple": Harris, "The Dangers," p. 58.

"This is the age of freedom": Harris, "The Dangers," p. 63.

294 **"Jewish at heart":** I. Steinbaum, "A Study of the Jewishness of Twenty New York Families," *YIVO Annual*, vol. 5, 1950, p. 252.

"symbol of allegiance": See, for example, Mary Douglas, "The Bog Irish," in *Natural Symbols: Explorations in Cosmology* (New York, 1973), p. 40.

"Looking at Jewish homes today": Mrs. Jacob J. Gittleman, "Fostering Religious Observance," *Outlook*, vol. 8, no. 1, Sept. 1937, p. 5.

"memory feasts": Rabbi Charles J. Freund, "Character-Building and the Home," *CCAR Year Book*, vol. 25, 1915, p. 319.

"renascence" of tradition: Leon J. Lang, "Jewish Values in Family Relationships," *Conservative Judaism*, vol. 1, no. 2, June 1945, p. 11.

"defunct heirlooms": Lang, "Jewish Values," pp. 10–11.

"bagels and lox and gefilte fish": Mrs. Anna Bear Brevis, "Judaism in the Home Enters Second Phase," *Proceedings of the Biennial Convention, National Women's League*, 1950–52, p. 82.

Photograph Credits

Center for Judaic Studies, University of Pennsylvania: 14, 69, 146, 147, 173.
Barr Forman: 83, 128.
Donna Forman: 37, 82, 138.
Jewish Historical Society of the Upper Midwest: 107, 117.
Jewish Museum: 5, 168.
Jenna Weissman Joselit: 52, 143, 155, 164, 165, 185, 188, 238.
Judy Lerner: 156.
Library of the Jewish Theological Seminary of America: 153, 167.
Nassau County Museum Reference Library: 150.
New York City Municipal Archives: 60, 206, 209, 213.
New York Public Library: 35, 38, 46, 77, 111, 141, 244, 277.
Ratner Center for the Study of Conservative Judaism, Jewish Theological Seminary of America: 119, 124.
Buddy Levine: 196.
Peter H. Schweitzer: 9, 16, 23, 25, 29, 31, 41, 66, 74, 78, 91, 95, 99, 101, 103, 104, 106, 160, 189, 191, 194, 199, 200, 205, 207, 210, 212, 215, 222, 224, 228, 229, 231, 234, 236, 240 (bottom half), 248, 250, 251, 252, 257, 261, 267, 269, 270, 274, 279, 282, 285, 287, 288, 289.
Jeffrey Shandler: 136, 240 (top half).
Paul Tobin: 97.
YIVO Institute for Jewish Research: 13, 57, 63, 67, 71, 79, 80, 179 (bottom), 226, 275.
YMHA Archives: 179 (top half).
Judy Zabar: 291.
Ziontalis: 81.

Index

ABOUT THE AUTHOR

Jenna Weissman Joselit is currently a visiting professor of American Studies at Princeton University. The author of many highly praised works of cultural history, including *A Perfect Fit: Clothes, Character, and the Promise of America*, Joselit has also curated and consulted on more than thirty exhibitions throughout the country. She lives in New York City.